Foreign Policies of India's Prime Ministers

Also by Harish Kapur

Soviet Russia and Asia 1917-27: A Study of Soviet Policy towards Turkey. Iran and Afghanistan

The Soviet Union and the Emerging Nations. A Case Study of Soviet Policy towards India

The Embattled Triangle: Moscow, Peking, New Delhi

The Awakening Giant: China's Ascension in World Politics, (also in Chinese)

China in World Politics

L'Historien et les Relations Internationales; Recueil d'etudes: En Hommage à Jacques Freymond, (edited by Harish Kapur, Saul Friedlander & André Rezler)

The End of an Isolation: China After Mao (edited) (also in Chinese)

China and the European Community: The New Connection

As China Sees the World: Perception of Chinese Scholars

Distant Neighbours: China and Europe

India's Foreign Policy 1947-1992: Shadows and Substance

Diplomacy of India: Then and Now

Diplomatic Journey: Emerging India

Taiwan in a Changing World: Search for Security

FOREIGN POLICIES OF INDIA'S PRIME MINISTERS

Harish Kapur

"I will never be a great man. There aren't many of them, and you have to stand a long way off to see their true size."

J.B. Priestley, *I have been here before*

Lancer * New Delhi * Frankfort, IL
www.lancerpublishers.com

LANCER
INTERNATIONAL

Published in the United States.

by Lancer Publishers,
a division of Lancer InterConsult, Inc.
19558 S. Harlem Ave., Suit 1,
Frankfort, IL. 60423.

Published in India.

by Lancer International
2/42 (B), Sarvapriya Vihar,
New Delhi-110016

© Harish Kapur 2009

All rights reserved. No part of this publication
may be reproduced, stored in a retrieval system or transmitted,
in any form or by any means, electronic, mechanical, photocopying,
recording or otherwise, without the prior permission of the publishers.
For additional information, contact Lancer Publishers.
Printed at Sona Printers, New Delhi.

Printed and bound in India.

ISBN: 0-9796174-8-0   978-0-9796174-8-5

Online Military Bookshop
www.lancerpublishers.com

To

Shanna with love

Contents

Preface
11

Introduction
13

Part I
THE NEHRU-GANDHI ERA

Chapter I
Jawharlal Nehru
15 August 1947—27 May 1964
23

Chapter II
Lal Bahadur Shastri
9 June 1964—11 January 1966
77

Chapter III
Indira Gandhi
24 January 1966- 24 March 1977
121

Chapter IV
Morarji Desai
27 March 1977–22 July 1979
149

Chapter V
Charan Singh
28 July 1979—14 January 1980
177

Chapter VI
Indira Gandhi
14 January 1980–31 October 1984
185

Chapter VII
Rajiv Gandhi
31 October 1984—1 December 1989
215

Part II
POST-NEHRU-GANDHI ERA

Chapter VIII
Vishwanath Pratap Singh
2 December 1989— 7 November 1990
247

Chapter IX
Chandra Shekhar
10 November 1990—21 June 1991
277

Chapter X
P. V. Narasimha Rao
21 June 1991—16 May 1996
295

Chapter XI
Atal Behari Vajpayee
16 May 1996—28 May 1996
327

Chapter XII
H.D. Deva Gowda
1 June 1996-21 April 1997
331

CONTENTS

Chapter XIII
Inder Kumar Gujral
21 April 1997—19 March 1998
347

Chapter XIV
Atal Behari Vajpayee
19 March 1998—22 May 2004
365

Chapter XV
Manmohan Singh
22 May 2004—
385

Chapter XVI
The Summing Up
405

Notes
415

Select Bibliography
432

Index
439

Preface

Many factors determine the foreign policy of nations – factors as diverse as history, geography, geopolitics, environments (national and international), ideological orientations, normative goals, etc. While the inputs emanating from these generally recognised elements cannot be ignored in any competent analysis, we have in this study, opted to focus on the mutating dimension – the personality factor and leadership in the determination of foreign policy. For long, the ones who were the formal decision makers, and who constructed and operationalised foreign policy were placed on the backburner. Political theorists have advanced the argumentation that the so-called objective factors are more relevant and powerful in all political analysis than the individual personality connected with the decision.

But, during decades of teaching international relations at the Graduate Institute of International Studies in Geneva, Switzerland this dimension often surfaced in my interactions with students and colleagues. Many of us doggedly asked the question as to how it was possible to investigate the history of World War II without taking into account such personalities as Adolf Hitler, Winston Churchill, Charles de Gaulle, Franklin Roosevelt, and Joseph Stalin; how we could examine the Indian independence movement without looking at M.K. Gandhi, Jawaharlal Nehru and Mohammed Ali Jinnah, and post-war China without Chiang Kai-shek and Mao Zedong.

Though this writer had reflected on this dimension in some of his previous writings on foreign policy, in this present study he has opted to focus mainly on this theme.

While investigating on the subject I did the obvious—of meeting with the actors for off-the-record chats, with personalities in the corridors of power, with close advisers of the personalities in question, and with a host of media representatives who closely shadowed the actors.

I would like to thank the ones I encountered in the course of this process: Vishwanath Pratap Singh, P.V. Narasimha Rao and Inder Kumar Gujral. To all of them I am indeed grateful. Unconnected with this book, I have had occasions of encountering Jawaharlal Nehru, Indira Gandhi, Morarji Desai, Chandra Shekhar, Atal Behari Vajpayee and Manmohan Singh. Also, I had the privilege of meeting some of the Foreign Secretaries, including T.N. Kaul, A.P. Venkateswaran and Lalit Mansingh, with whom I had occasions to discuss the subject. There were of course many others—including Indian and foreign Ambassadors. It would be impossible to mention all of them.

But, I would like to particularly thank Prime Minister I.K. Gujral with whom I have been linked with personal ties for many years. To him I am especially grateful, for I have had many opportunites of informally discussing with him the whole dimension of India's foreign policy. Competent as he is on the subject, my relaxed and unhibited discussions with him were very useful in understanding India's foreign policy.

I had access to US, British and Soviet documentation—the US because of the easy accessibility of Presidential and State Department papers, the British because of the strict operationalisation of the thirty year rule, and the Soviet after the disappearance of the Soviet Union when massive amount of archival documentation surfaced. The Indian archives were alas unavailable because of persistent bureaucratic obstacles, notwithstanding the applicability of a thirty year rule, and notwithstanding the official acceptance of the Freedom of the Information Act. I had to compensate for this terrible handicap through informal discussions with personalites in the know of things.

Since many of these encounters were informal, bilateral and off-the-record, I decided to simplify all the findings of these meetings by inserting them as "personal notes."

My grateful thanks also go to persons, responsible at different Indian libraries, for having assisted my assistant, Neelima Singh, for permitting her access to the documentation pertaining to the subject. In this connection I would particularly like to mention the Jawaharlal Nehru University, the Institute for Defence Studies and Analyses, the Indian Council of World Affairs, and the photo division at Soochna Bhawan.

Last but not least I must thank Neelima Singh for all the intelligent sifting she did from the forest of documentation she had at her disposal.

Finally, I must declare that all views expressed in this study are my own for which no one else is responsible.

Ravoire, Switzerland.

INTRODUCTION

The personality factor is being increasingly recognised as a crucial dimension in foreign policy making, perhaps as crucial as the established institutions. Already in the sixties, the political scientist, Joseph Frankel viewed it as "a legitimate and important topic of historical analysis"[1] in all investigations pertaining to external State behaviour. More recent studies have gone even further; they have evoked a panoply of psychological approaches to understand "the decision makers' cognitive system:" how it is formed and modified, and how it operates "so as to structure perceptions and hence determine behaviour"[2] in all sectors of political life. It is thus being increasingly argued that to understand the foreign policy of a nation, it is necessary to understand the decision maker, his background, his education, his perceptions, his biases and prejudices, etc., for they all are, in many ways, vital inputs responsible for a decision.

But, the personality factor is one thing; it is built in in all decision making since the person has the constitutional or the political responsibility in the process. Leadership, on the other hand, is another matter. For the level of the role and the quality of leadership differs from one person to the other.

While the concept of the personality factor is identifiable with all leaders, the leadership quality would depend on the personality of the person, his motivations, his determination, his ability to lead the society, and his capacity to rally people to the cause he is defending.

If Anglo-Saxon literature on decision making is increasingly veering around to the theory that the personality factor is equally important in[3] countries where institutions are "the most permanent element of politics in Western society,"[4] it is even more so in a developing country where institutions are less institutionalised, where politicians possess stupendous clout, and where individual manouvrability is at its optimal height.

So far as India is concerned there are three broad explanations that support such an argumentation. Institutions generally concerned with foreign policy are either not developed enough or assertive enough to influence the behaviour of those who are at the helm of affairs. The impact of the bureaucracy, intelligence, Parliament and so on may not be as overwhelming on the decision maker in India; it may indeed be only negligible. The leeway the decision maker possesses, the leadership he offers, the power he wields, and the influence he exercises is indeed considerable; in any event much more so than in most developed countries. Consider the first Prime Minister of India, Jawaharlal Nehru, his personal capacity of overcoming institutional hurdles was far greater than in any developed country. Admittedly this may be attributed to his charismatic personality, to the quality of his leadership, to his universally recognised savviness in international affairs, and to the newness of Indian independence when institutions were few and far between. Nehru, to risk a generalisation, was the sole decision maker in Indian diplomacy—at least during the early years of his mandate. There was indeed hardly anyone— persons or institutions— who could challenge the vast decisional authority that he had built around himself. But, the unavoidable magnification of institutional proliferation, necessitated by the requirements of good societal governance, slowly resulted, through the years, in the decline in individual leverage of Nehru's successors. No one after him was as unencumbered as he was in diplomatic activity, for institutional expansion had overtaken the political system.

However, notwithstanding this unavoidable institutional growth, no Indian Prime Minister really became as cramped institutionally in the decisional process as their counterparts in the West. The personality factor still continues to sway and underpin Indian politics. Probably, it was the emergence of coalition politics within the Indian system that maintained the survivability of the personality factor in the diplomatic sector. Interestingly, while the Prime Minister's decisional leverage was considerably curtailed in domestic politics with the onset of coalition governments, it was enhanced in the diplomatic sector. So engrossed and entwined, on the other hand, were the coalition partners in their intramural domestic manipulations, they neither had the time nor the inclination to delve in international affairs as long as the Prime Minister did not wake them up by taking warlike and dramatic decisions. At least three Prime Ministers, whe were the worst victims or sufferers of heavy coalition politics confirmed this state of affairs in their conversations with the author.[5]

The second explanation is cultural. India is still a religious and highly hierarchical society where all those who have risen to political summitry are unquestioned by those are close to them, and are generally revered by those who are at a distance. The aura and the arrogance of power has an imposing effect in most societies, but in caste ridden India, it is more impactful. This is due to a pattern of behaviour that is firmly embedded in the Hindu psyche. Admittedly, decades of corruption, moral degradation and self-centred politiking have tarnished the image of many of those involved in politics, but still not enough to shake the traditional built-in behaviour. Where would one find the phenomenon of a former Chief Minister of Bihar (Laloo Prasad Yadav), formally charged with massive corruption, and who still is revered by the people of his State, holding a responsible ministerial position in the central Indian Government? He even managed to install his own illiterate politically marginal wife as the head of the State government! And where would one find the spectacle of a former Prime Minister (Rajiv Gandhi), accused of corruption in the Bofors arms deal with Sweden, who would have certainly become the Prime Minister again had he not been assassinated. And what about Chandra Shekhar, who was the very embodiment of Gandhian simplicity in his day-to-day life, but who had openly and even proudly consorted with doubtful moneyed characters because money, in his view, was important in politics. Apparently, he never hesitated in procuring it for his political advancement. And, yet he remained nationally an esteemed figure. One of the obituaries, after his recent death, declared that "his recent death marked the end of an era," and expressed the amazing view that "he made a good prime minister, nurturing the office with simplicity and earthiness."[6] Consider also Narasimha Rao. There appears to exist a consensual reverentiality of his performance as Prime Minister. Some have gone to the extent of evaluating him as the best Prime Minister of India. A recent publication devoted to Rao is full of adulatory biographical glimpses of his life and performance.[7] And yet after his prime ministership was over, he was accused of bribery and corruption, and was sentenced by a lower court to a three years of imprisonment. While, it was overturned by a higher court, Rao devoted much of his life, after his mandate, fighting to clear his name.

The third explanation is educational. The Indian public, on the whole, does not have the necessary background to comprehend foreign affairs. And, those who possess such abilities are so minuscule in numbers that their impact can only be minimal. With the oncoming impact of electronic media, and the emergence of a large, more knowledgeble middle class, compounded with the increasing globalisation of the international system has indeed upgraded international affairs in the minds of many in India. But, foreign affairs, nonetheless, still has not become as overwhelming and as significant as in developed countries. The political shroud around foreign affairs is still considerable and it shall take quite some time before it is lifted.

If one accepts the hypothesis that the personality factor, and the quality of leadership are indeed crucial for foreign policy making, then the question we have to address ourselves to is whether there is anyone in particular who embodies such a role, and whether that role has the tendency to fluctuate from person to person.

It would seem that in a country like India it is the office of the prime minister which performs such a role. It is the Prime Minister who is the central figure in the foreign policy arena. It is he who has the responsibility of taking decisions, and it is around him that the decision making process really functions. There is no other personality that has replaced the Prime Minister. The role of the Foreign Minister has never been crucial, since India never had one who was independent, and who was politically powerful enough to leave his own imprint on foreign policy. If anything, most of the foreign ministers—unlike in many Western countries—were ineffectual, and there is no archival or mediatic record to show the contrary. So any analysis of the Indian decision making process has to centre on the Prime Minister, his personality, his interests and his role.

But, on the other hand, it must be argued that the level of the Prime Minister's influence, and the importance of his role is very much contingent on his personality, the quality of his leadership, the magnitude of his interests, and the security of his position within the political system. The Prime Minister is indeed the central figure when he is personally interested in this sector, when he has a powerful and determined personality, and when he is politically secure. The decision making process, in this case, becomes restrictive, limited to the Prime Minister's office, where most of his formal advisers cluster together, and to the Prime Minister's residence (an extra constitutional institution), where sycophants operate, where family members interact, and where much happens orally and through unwritten hints. Inversely, the personality factor becomes less important when the Prime Minister is not, or is less interested in foreign affairs, and when he is seriously hemmed in by a political situation over which he has little control.

The decision making process, in this case, becomes more diffused, and even more collective with different institutions competing to have more influence on the whole process.

The only way, then, of really understanding the role of the personality factor is to analyse the personality, the perception, the interest, and the level of political clout of successive prime ministers. This is what we have striven to do in this study.

The Growing Importance of Foreign Policy

However, notwithstanding the relative minuscality of interest in foreign affairs among Indians, in comparison to the western world, it has nonetheless continued to expand in the lives of people. Indeed, there has been a secular expansion since the independence of the country. During Nehru's time, India's foreign policy was dualistic; it was either concerned with palpable issues relating to its neighbours or it addressed itself to macro international issues around which the Indian Prime Minister constructed a broad conceptual framework. But after Nehru, the concerns slowly began to undergo a change. While Indians could not possibly ignore the divisive issues that exacerbated tensions with their neighbours, for these concerned them directly, they took a distant and passive attitude on such Nehruvian issues like non-alignment, war and peace, and mediation, that did not directly concern them even if they expanded India's prestige.

But, after Nehru things began to change. No one was interested in macro international issues—neither the Prime Ministers nor the people. Only policies pertaining to the neighbouring countries apparently held the field.

It was in early nineties of the twentieth century that India's interest in foreign affairs once again took an upturn by expanding into macro international issues. But this new interest was not of the Nehruvian variety (non-alignment, mediation, etc.) but on new issues connected with globalisation, with more palpable issues pertaining to direct foreign investment, with Indian search for international acquistions and mergers, with trade, with a search for a new type of relations with regional economic groupings emerging everywhere, with emigration, with ecological issues, etc; in sum on issues in which India had acquired a new stake in an age of globalisation. Even on issues pertaining to neighbouring countries, India's policy experienced some degree of modification. While palpable divisive issues held their ground, new issues emerged—issues pertaining to economic interaction within the framework of South Asian Regional Economic Cooperation (SAARC), international terrorism, religious fundamentalism, etc. Thus, by the turn of the century, the nature, form and content of India's foreign policy was undergoing a major innovation taking India in a direction that needed new type of personnel, a new pattern of thinking, and new forms of national international actions.

The Broad Framework

The focal point of analysis in this study is to examine the formative years of the Prime Ministers, to investigate the broad framework of foreign policy, inherited or constructed by each of them, to scrutinise the environments (national and international) in which he or she was operating, to identify the decisional process that was established in this sector, and to evaluate their role and performance in international affairs.

While the upbringing and the level of interest of each prime minister was naturally different, all of them had to unavoidably deal with foreign affairs at some stage of their prime ministership. In fact, even more and more as years went by, and as the era of globalisation had firmly set into the international system. The quality of the leadership they offered, however, differed from person to person, depending upon their personalities and their determination.

The contents of foreign policy, to risk a generalisation, is roughly composed of three parts: the routinised action, the nationally visible issues in which the country is heavily involved– issues generally pertaining to neighbouring countries, and the continuously emerging macro issues with which countries may be unavoidably faced with. Using this broad framework, we propose to evaluate the role of each of the Prime Ministers.

PART I
THE NEHRU-GANDHI ERA

Jawharlal Nehru

Chapter I

JAWHARLAL NEHRU:
15 AUGUST 1947—27 MAY 1964

Jawaharlal Nehru arrived at India's helm in 1947 as someone fully equipped in international affairs. There was really no one in the country, among the public figures, who could match him in knowledge and experience regarding the outside world. And, what is more, there was hardly anyone of consequence in the mainstream of Indian politics who diverged from this consensual estimation.

He was a combination of many diverse elements—elements that bestowed his personality with an inestimable and unique dimension among the nationalist leaders. The aura that was built around him was so prodigious that he was unanimously perceived as someone who could unravel the mysteries that shrouded international affairs. And what made his image even more sustainable was Gandhi's declaration that he considered Nehru as his mentor in foreign affairs.[8]

Formation

Jawaharlal Nehru hailed from a rich joint family. Headed by his anglicised father, Motilal Nehru, who, by the dint of his abilities, had reached the summit of the legal profession, and who had, at the same time, slowly cast his lot with the emerging nationalist movement. To Motilal, westernisation and nationalism were not contradictory terms; for a person of his stature, education and orientation it was perfectly normal—indeed desirable—to be attracted to what was generally considered superior British education and exemplary British system of governance. He was quite convinced of this appreciation, while identifying himself, at the same time, with the emerging nationalist movement, which, at the time, was appreciative of the British and what they represented in terms of ideas, governance and education. The dimension of Motilal's westernisation can be discerned by the fact that he had become mistrustful of all appeals to religious tradition, required his children to study even Sanskrit in English translation, dressed Jawaharlal in a sailor suit, encouraged the use of English nicknames for his two daughters, and decreed in 1890 that English was the only language to be spoken at home—a language his wife neither spoke or understood.

It was this imitative behaviour which pushed Motilal to expose his son to exclusive British education: to private English education at home, to an English school (Harrow) in England, to the University in Cambridge and to London's Inner Temple where Jawaharlal received his bar degree.

While the trend of sending youngsters to British universities for higher education was expanding among affluent Indian anglophiles, educational exposure to British schools was however rare—in fact very rare. For sending a young boy, at a vulnerable age, to an English school in the UK deprived him of the basics of India "during the most formative period of his life."[9] Besides, who could afford it; very few.

Nehru's complete exposure to British education thus resulted in an overwhelming anglicisation in dress, mannerism, ideas and even English accent—clearly much more than among the many of his contemporaries who also went in for higher British education.

But, Nehru nonetheless remained steadfastly close to India. His westernisation did not damper his emotional and political interest in what was happening in his country. In fact, he sympathetically supported his father's increasing involvement with the nationalist movement, even though he disagreed with his politics of moderation – a brand of politics that often resulted, in the words of one witness, in "heated arguments between father and the son at the dinner table" that were "not only full of sparkle but (were) also very penetrating."[10] The letters he continuously wrote to his father, mother, daughter and the two sisters also fill out the picture of a man deeply attached to his family. Many of them are indeed revelatory of the man, for they are often sentimental, and talk of the nitty-gritty aspects of life, far removed from the rough and tumble of politics. Concerned about his father's health, he wrote to him in October 1906 to be careful " about yourself this time for my sake—for dearest father it comes from my heart and as such, I hope you will receive it."[11] To his sister, (Vijaya Lakshmi Pandit) it was the same sentimental refrain. "I write to you," he declared in September 1934, "because you are very dear to me. There are few persons who really count in my life and you are one of them, and you have brought great comfort to me in moments of trial."[12] Equally revelatory is his correspondence with his daughter (Indira)—a correspondence that unravels the dimension of his closeness to her.[13] Consider this, written on 29th July 1934 from Almora District Jail: "I sit down to write to you on cover sheet after sheet of thin airmail paper, trying somehow to bridge the many thousand miles that separate us. I hope that my letters will carry with them, somewhere hidden between the lines, a bit of me to you, and that if you care to look for it, you will find it; just as I seek for you in your letters, behind and between the lines that you have written."[14]

Perceptions

When Nehru finally came to the helm of Indian governmental affairs in 1947 he was generally perceived as self-assured, savvy, competent, far-sighted and charismatic enough to singly focus his attention on the affairs of the world.

The whole process of this attraction and even eventual immersion in international affairs really began with his emotional involvement in the nationalist movement—an involvement that really began in England. It was a gut reaction of a young man against colonial occupation of his country, and it was men like Giuseppe Mazzini, Camillo Cavour, Giuseppe Garibaldi, embodying Italian nationalism, and the *Sinn Fein* movement— Irish resistance to British colonialism—that underpinned Nehru's initial interest in politics. Compounded later with the emergence of intellectual curiosity relating to political ideas, and with years of living and travelling in tremulous Europe, which, at the time, was the hub of ideas floating across nations of the continent, opened great possibilities for Nehru to equip himself intellectually through a long process of self-education and interaction—a process that finally unravelled itself in the publication of remarkably incisive and intelligently written reflections on historical and global developments. He fell into that very small category of highly intellectualised politicians who took time out of their engrossed and strenuous political activities to inform themselves, and to write extensively about international affairs; in sum, living in the world of ideas, a trait that accompanied him all his life. Though Nehru characterised his first voluminous publication, *Glimpses of World History*—running into 992 pages and written in the thirties of the 20th century—as "a brief and simple account of the early days of the world,"[15] it is indeed a remarkable *tour de force* for a person educated in physical sciences and formed in law. No politician—at least in India—had acquired such a monumental knowledge of what had happened in the past and presented it to the world at large. It is indeed a remarkable book that covers a brief history of practically the entire world combining, in the author's own words, an "elementary writing for the young and a discussion at times of the ideas of grown-ups."[16] Vincenc Lesny of the Oriental Institute of Czechoslovakia wrote to Nehru in 1935 to say that, after having read the book,[17] he was "specially struck by your comprehensive grasp of the main current events." Though his other main publications, *The Discovery of India* and *An Autobiography*, were focussed on India's past and his own life, they nonetheless give an interesting insight to Nehru's intellectual dimension, his emotional make up, and his growing vision of the world. All the three major publications, interestingly, were written while he was serving his different imprisonments—imprisonments that gave him time to reflect, and the leisure to write.

But, there was nothing really very original in his perception of the world. It was indeed a standard vision that mirrored his time and his space. The time was the thirties, and the space was Europe, irrevocably torn between democracy and dictatorship, and between capitalism and socialism. Like many left-wing intellectuals of his time, Nehru had committed himself to the anti-fascist cause and to socialism. While his antipathy to Hitler can partly be explained by the fact that the German Nazi leader had "pointedly declared himself in favour of British rule in India,"[18] but partly it can also be explained by Nehru's own character, for Fascism and Nazism were hardly compatible with his emotional make-up and his humanitarian and non-racial instincts. Ideologically, he began as a fabianist with "vague socialist ideas" of his college days, but soon found himself attracted to the Soviet brand of socialism and to Marxism. But all this was very confusing since his irresolute (Hamletian) character always made him question what he really believed in. He saw the different sides of the coin. He was fascinated by the Soviet experiment, but at the same, he disliked "the ruthless suppression of all contrary opinions, the wholesale regimentation, the unnecessary violence," all of which were a part of the Soviet system.[19] The philosophy of Marxism, as Nehru wrote in his autobiography, "lightened up many a dark corner of my mind" and "gave me comfort and hope,"[20] but a little later in life when he had lengthily experienced the responsibility of power, and had observed the complexity of political life, he was less sure of Marxism and the corners it had lit during the earlier years.

Basically, Nehru was an impulsive intellectual, who liked living with ideas, while playing with them. His assistant of many years, M.O. Mathai, who had observed him more closely than anyone else outside of his family had this to say of him: "Nehru's was an imitative and absorptive mind. He had infinite capacity to borrow ideas from others, and make them his own with remarkable speed. Essentially Gandhi was an original mind, while Nehru was a second rate one. He was all heart and less mind. This reflected in his books also."[21]

Constant playing with ideas was also a part of Nehru's character. There are many anecdotes to prove the point, but the one narrated by Sarvepalli Gopal, his biographer, is perhaps the most appropriate and most telling of his personality. Urgently called by Nehru to come to his office, in the midst of the Sino-Indian crisis, Gopal thought that the Chinese had attacked India. When he arrived at his office, Nehru said "I've been waiting for you. This has been worrying me the whole of last night. Tell me, do you think that Danton was a better man than Robespierre?" The surprised civil servant, who had only an elementary knowledge of the actors of the French Revolution, did some homework to answer Nehru's question. When he went to see him again to give his answer he was asked to repeat it to the Cabinet which was assembling at the time. Gopal later observed: "Nehru was not diverted by Chinese attacks or anything. The regions of the mind. Those were the most important thing to him."[22]

But Nehru not only acquired an intellectual vision; he was actively involved in meeting international personalities, in taking a position on specific issues facing the world in the thirties, in travelling to tremulous areas to manifest his solidarity with movements with which he had identified himself. His participation in the Brussels Congress of Oppressed Nations in 1927 was a major landmark in his international experience, since it was here in this consequential international event, dealing with the third world, that he met, for the first time, representatives of a number of countries of the Middle and the Far East, North Africa, South and Central America, Italy, France and Britain. Though this was certainly a significant manifestation of Nehru's interest in international affairs, there were myriad other occasions: his goodwill visit to Soviet Russia in the twenties (1927) which resulted in the publication of a series of supportive articles in the Indian newspaper, *The Hindu;* his open solidarity with Czechoslovakia against Hitlerian onslaught; his fraternisation with Republican Spain during the height of the Spanish Civil war in the thirties; and his visit to China just before World War II—all of them are emblematic of the level of interest he had acquired in international affairs, and all of them are important hallmarks of the experience he had gained. No one in the country could really match him.

Even more significant was the crucial role he played in educating the Indian public on international affairs. He held general meetings, to inform the Indians of what was happening to the world, and how it affected India. Also, he did everything to mobilise members of his own party to take positions on international affairs. Of all the mainstream leaders that India had projected onto the political scene, he was the only one who attempted to place Indian independence in global perspective, and who went on reiterating that the "freedom of India is a part of the freedom of the world... and that the problem of discrimination, racial or otherwise...is a part of the problem of racial and other discrimination prevalent in the world as a whole."[23] There is, therefore, a great deal of substance in the tribute that Mahatma Gandhi paid to him when he wrote: "Pandit Jawaharlal Nehru, Indian to the core, but he being also nationalist, has made us accustomed to look at everything in the international light instead of the parochial."[24]

Nehru also ceaselessly highlighted the fact that given India's gigantic dimension, its strategic centrality and its richness in natural resources, it will earn an important place in the international diplomatic roster. "India," he declared in one of his very first speeches after independence, "is a great country. Great in her resources, great in manpower, great in her potential in every way. I have little doubt that a free India on every plane will play a big part on the world stage, even in the narrowest plane of material power."[25] On another occasion he was even more explicit. "I hope," he declared "that while India will play a great part in all the material spheres, she will always lay stress on the spirit of humanity.... May the time come when this ancient land will attain its rightful place in the world and make its full swing to the phenomenon of world peace and the welfare of mankind."[26] These were not just words for the benefit of Indians, he genuinely believed in them.

Nehru's confidence in India's role in world affairs, thus continued to grow throughout his political career, but more particularly when he was at the helm of affairs after the independence of the country. If one were to extract his views on the subject from his myriad speeches and declarations, one would come across such expressions as "India even counts in world affairs;" "the emergence of India in world affairs is something of major consequence in world history;" "India is growing into a great power;" "India can play a big part, and perhaps an effective part, in helping to avoid war;" and "India has gone on in the scale of nations in its influence and in its prestige."[27]

What did Nehru think when he was repeatedly reiterating the Indian role in global politics? Did he have anything palpable in mind, or were they just rhetorical declarations of which Nehru had the expertise? While he may not have been thinking about anything in particular regarding what India could do internationally, his myriad declarations were clearly meant to place India in a global context.

What is Role Playing?

But, what is international role playing for a developing country? Is there a broad definition or a framework that is generally acceptable? Can one use the expression "role playing" in foreign policy as one does in domestic politics?

"Role playing," to risk a generalisation, is of two types. The first type of "role playing" requires a "larger normative system level concern in world affairs,"[28] a high level of neutrality on discordant issues dividing the bipolar world, a credible political independence, a moral authority that inspires confidence—even respect—within the international community, and a political determination to act and to initiate. With Nehru at the helm, they were all present. Sensitive as he was, he was haunted by the perspective of a global war—a war that would "bring barbarism, wiping out any semblance of civilisation."[29] He had also constructed a strategy of non-alignment, established credible political independence, manifested considerable political determination to act internationally. Also there appeared to exist a fairly large consensus within the country as well as outside that India had some moral authority—perhaps more than any other developing country—that could make it possible for it to be useful to a turbulent world.

The spreading awareness of the existence of such a moral authority can be attributed to what India embodied in terms of philosophy and religion. There were many who were fascinated by these facets. "Everywhere," wrote Nehru, "there is a feeling of respect and friendship for India, for old memories endure, and people have not forgotten that there was a time when India was the mother country to them and nourished them with rich fare from their treasure house."[30] Others—mainly non-Indians—were even more eloquent. There was Max Mueller who wrote about India's impact on the western world; there was Rene Grousset who highlighted "the indelible impress" that India had left of her culture on the rest of the world; and there was the philosopher Will Durant, who, reflecting on the impact of Indian heritage on other cultures, went even further and wrote that "Mother India is in many ways the mother of us all."[31]

If there were many philosophers and scientists who were impressed with what India embodied traditionally, there were others belonging to the academic, media and the political world who were struck by the steps India had taken to continue, nurture and even develop political democracy in the country.

In this connection, much credit should also go to Nehru, for he was the one who preached the importance of democracy within a system, and who practiced it tirelessly. Indeed, it was one of his lasting contributions to the Indian system, all the more so when one considers the fact that it was being hurriedly abandoned by third world countries in the aftermath of their independence. For many who visited India during the early years after the independence of the country, this factor was perceived as being very significant even from the global angle. "The Republic of India today," wrote a well-known correspondent, Robert Trumball, "is the largest democracy in the world in terms of population. As such she may hold the balance of the future of Asia, and perhaps most of the world."[32]

The second role is different. It is related to national interests—interests that are linked to security, to material development of the country, to the establishment of good relations with other nations, etc. All this requires either the utilisation of force or pressure by means of which a nation can modify a given situation or through which it can change the behaviour of other nations. The obvious precondition for its success is the capacity of the nation and the political determination of its leaders to do so. Both the elements are important, and must operate in unison, for in the absence of one, the other can hardly become operational. In this connection, defining foreign policy, political scientist, K.J.Holsti had argued that power was essential "to control the behaviour of others." For him it was "basically a form of communication intended to change or sustain the behaviour of those upon whom the acting government is dependent for achieving its objectives."[33] While, his stress on power was certainly appropriate, the dimension of political determination is however absent. For power and capability by themselves are not sufficient to bend others or to control the behaviour of other states, if political determination to reach the objectives of those who are at the helm of affairs is missing.

The pattern of diplomatic strategy, conceived and constructed, for one role is different from the other. To comprehend and evaluate them, it is of course important to analyse the decision making process and the Nehruvian model of foreign policy during his mandate.

THE DECISION MAKING PROCESS

While there were no institutionalised "formal mechanisms"[34] around the Prime Minister to shape the contours of foreign policy, there were nonetheless established institutions he could not ignore, political personalities he could not disregard, and advisers he could not do without. Even a well-informed and savvy personality like Nehru could hardly shoulder the responsibility of reflecting, designing and operationalising foreign policy completely on his own. It simply was not possible.

The Ministry of External Affairs (MEA) had the vocation of putting into shape the broad options taken by the political decision makers, of implementing them, and of providing the appropriate inputs needed to take initiatives and evaluate situations. Though Nehru himself was the sole architect, he could hardly do without the Ministry for a whole series of actions and initiatives.

There was also the Parliament to be reckoned with which had to be continuously kept informed of global developments, and India's response thereof. While the consensus widely favoured what Nehru had to say, there were nonetheless dissident voices that challenged him—voices that grew in numbers with the years and with the diplomatic set-backs that he began to face.

Also there was the Cabinet. Though it was composed, at the time of independence, of powerful stalwarts of equal eminence, foreign policy making was largely left to Nehru. But with time and emerging diplomatic difficulties Nehru was not spared. Voices were indeed raised, and disagreements were indeed expressed.

But in the whole decision making process, what is perhaps even more important than the institutions, are the personalities around the decision maker who are close to him, and who have either the expertise or have some say in diplomatic matters. Politically the Deputy Prime Minister, Sardar Vallabhbhai Patel, was perhaps the most important person, since he was next to Nehru in terms of hierarchy, but equally powerful in his own right. So much so that most decision makers in the Congress Party would have probably supported him for Prime Ministership at the time of independence, if Gandhi had restrained himself from openly and determinedly opting for Nehru. Gandhi's choice is one of the events that seems incomprehensible. Why Nehru? What did he see in him? Was it because he was more popular and more loved by the common man than Patel? Was it because he loved the common man? Think of his expression, in a letter to his sister in 1947, of feeling "happy at coming into close contact with great crowds again" while addressing a vast meeting.[35] Was it because he was more secular in outlook than the Sardar? Was it that he went around all over the country reaching out to people and explaining his thoughts more effectively than his Deputy Prime Minister. All this is certainly true. But, on the other hand, Patel was less impulsive, more practical and possessed a much greater capacity of governance than Nehru—characteristics that are indeed vital to effectively run an administration. In any event, from the hindsight one has acquired from the actions and policies of the two leaders, many indeed wonder if Gandhi's choice was the right one.

Though, Patel restrained himself from offering any views on macro international issues, leaving all this to Nehru, he never wavered in firmly expressing his views on what was happening nearer home. He was firm in not giving in on Kashmir, and was against referring the matter to the UN. He warned Nehru of the endangerment to Indian security with the Chinese occupation of Tibet, communicated his fears of the adverse impact that the ongoing Burmese Civil War was having on India, and recommended that India should go slow in pushing the reforms in the Rana dominated Nepal because of the increasing Chinese presence. While, one could advance the argument that all this did not have real effect on Nehru's thinking, it is undeniable that Patel's arguments and pressures did often restrain him from going too far, though there were moments of considerable tension between the two regarding Nehru's foreign policy. Their relations had apparently come to such a pass, that Patel, notwithstanding his deteriorating health, had decided to challenge Nehru's China policy in the Congress Working Committee (CWC), especially in regard to his silence over Chinese annexation of Tibet in October 1950. But, the showdown never occurred, since Patel died a month later, and with him vanished the most important restraining element to Nehru's policy towards India's neighbours. He was then free to act more comfortably and more freely;[36j] for there was none in the government, after Patel, who had the power and/or the prestige to question him on foreign affairs.

At the bureaucratic level, there was Girija Shankar Bajpai, the Secretary General of the MEA. This was the most powerful job after the Foreign Minister. Bajpai's credentials for being in the foreign ministry were the experience he had gained as India's Agent General in Washington where, as adjunct to the British Embassy, he represented and defended British interests in India. His participation in the Washington naval conference in 1921, on behalf of the British Government, must have been a great experience, for apparently he showed great intellectual and diplomatic qualities at the meeting. He was recalled at the time of the formation of the interim government, and was assigned the bureaucratic task of heading the MEA. He collected around himself in the Ministry a group of intelligent people that the Ministry badly needed. He held lively meetings with his colleagues practically every morning whenever he was in the office. The meetings, remembered one participant, "were a masterly summing of the issues of the day, livening up the proceedings with his barbed wit."[37] Though Bajpai did not favour Nehru's broad framework of foreign policy, he served India well due to the international contacts he had established, and the thoughtful and relevant answers he gave in an atmosphere that was suffused with "high morality." Bajpai had a fairly balanced approach to foreign affairs. While he warned of the dangers of exerting State power without some moral end, he stressed that "armed power, supported by adequate industrial power, constitutes the only safeguard against a threat to a country's independence."[38]

What was the level of his interaction with Nehru, it is of course difficult to say, given his close collaboration with the British Government. But, on the other hand, it is difficult to imagine that a person in that high position—holding a post that was next to the foreign minister—did not have some influence on Nehru's foreign policy. He accompanied Nehru on most of his important visits to the West, and he went by himself to Washington in 1948 where he had been sent to highlight India's anti-communist credentials, and to assure his American interlocutors of India's openness to the US. It is also interesting to note that despite his pronounced pro-Western opinions, he strongly advised Nehru to resolve the boundary question directly with China soon after it became Communist, instead of unilaterally declaring India's position. Sir Girija attempted to mobilise Sardar Patel, whom he went to see on 25 October 1950, "much in grief on Tibet-China" question.[39] He even wrote to him to express his concern at the serious problem of security that Chinese occupation of Tibet had generated for India. Sir Girija was also very active on the Kashmir issue. He had often appeared to defend India's position before the Kashmir Commission of the UN. Even after he had retired from the foreign service, and was functioning as the Governor of Maharashtra, Nehru requested him to continue representing India at the UN Kashmir Commission.[40]

N.R. Pillai, Bajpai's successor, perhaps was the second high official of the Ministry who had Nehru's ears—probably even more so than Bajpai since he was not tainted as someone close to the British, notwithstanding his high status in the Indian Civil Service. Besides, unlike Bajpai, he was not arrogant, He never really attempted to overwhelm Nehru with his views; as a civil servant, he knew his position in the Indian hierarchy. But, on the other hand, what one knows about him and his personality, it is unlikely that he did not express his views when circumstances required of him to speak up. This he did on the Hungarian question, when he recommended to Nehru that he should re-evaluate the events in Hungary "with a view to deciding our attitude in the light of the principles we are advocating"[41]—clearly an implicit criticism of Nehru's prudence in 1956. In fact, towards the end of his mandate, when he was being considered for the governorship of the World Bank, he did make himself almost indispensable to Nehru, who did not really have the time to run the External Affairs Ministry; so much so that M.O. Mathai viewed him as almost irreplaceable. The "PM," he noted "needs more and more competent assistance as years go by and I cannot... think of any person who can replace Pillai."[42]

But more important than the bureaucrats were such personalities as K.M. Panikkar, V.K. Krishna Menon, Vijaya Lakshmi Pandit and Indira Gandhi, all of whom were close to Nehru, and all of whom were known to have played some role in the decision making process.

Pannikar, a well-known historian, had been sent as the Ambassador to the two Chinas—the Guomindang and Communist China. While in Beijing he developed a reputation as being too friendly to China, so much so that Sardar Patel, in one of his communications, had strongly attacked him for his views and actions on China. "Our Ambassador," complained Patel to Nehru (7 November 1950) "has been at great pains to find an explanation or justification for Chinese policy and action. As the External Ministry remarked in one of its telegrams, there was a lack of firmness and unnecessary apology in one or two representations that he made to Chinese Government... ."[43] Harsh words indeed from someone who was not given to using such language. Some had even characterised him as "Ambassador of China."

From whatever documentation that is available, it would seem that Panikkar, in his communications with Nehru, more often than not, justified Chinese actions and advised him against taking any firm stand on Tibet. He advised, for example, the Indian Prime Minister not to protest

Chinese invasion of Tibet as that would amount to an "interference to India's efforts on behalf of China in the UN."[44] Panikkar has also been accused of having unilaterally changed a crucial word from the Indian communication to China. The note, informing the Chinese, that India had recognized Chinese "suzerainty" over Tibet was changed to "sovereignty"—undoubtedly a serious transgression by the Ambassador for which he was not even sanctioned by the Prime Minister. In order to avoid annoying the Chinese, Panikkar recommended not to raise the border issue when concluding the agreement on Tibet, and advised Nehru to transform the important Indian mission to a simple Consulate General.

Whether Panikkar was pro-Chinese or not is really not the point; what is important is that the Indian Ambassador played a crucial role in the decision making process on many issues concerning China and Tibet since most of the recommendations made by him were accepted by Nehru.

The Prime Minister's decision to appoint Panikkar as India's representative to the two Chinas (Chiang Kai-shek and Mao Zedong), to say the least, is puzzling; for given his opportunistic past of having devoted much of his political career serving the most reactionary princely States, and of having developed a notorious reputation of succumbing to whatever political situation he found himself in, he was hardly the man to be sent to a crucial country like China—a country Nehru viewed as vital for India. Besides, he was neither a diplomat nor a China specialist who had arguably counselled Nehru wrongly on Indian diplomatic initiatives or on China. Even more dismaying is that Nehru had runned down Panikkar declaring to the U.S. Ambassador that his views on China "were very different from Panikkar's"[45]—clearly a mystifying observation by a Prime Minister of his own Ambassador to the head of the US mission which had serious reservations about Panikkar; so much so that the Truman Administration had refused to accept the Ambassador's report, which reached Washington through Nehru regarding Chinese intentions in the Korean war on the ground that he was too friendly to China and therefore not credible.

Krishna Menon was the other political personality who assisted Nehru in foreign affairs. Actually, he was more important than the others; in fact even more so than Sardar Patel.

The Deputy Prime Minister, having views different from Nehru in foreign affairs, devoted much of his time to restrain him from taking, impulsive actions, and to warn him to remain vigilant on issues endangering India's national security.

Menon, on the other hand, did the reverse. He encouraged him to continue in the direction he had chosen. For, being practically on the same intellectual wave length as Nehru, he had naturally acquired greater authority and tuneful interaction than the others. Both of them were against the capitalist west, and both of them were proponents of socialism. Translating all this into foreign policy meant that India must have a balanced approach between the East and the West, though Menon was known to be, outspokenly and explicitly, more pro-Soviet than Nehru. According to the then Soviet Foreign Minister, Andrei Gromyko, "it was... plain that (Menon) was personally friendly to the Soviet Union. He would say to me heatedly 'you cannot imagine the hatred the Indian people felt and still feel to the colonialists, the British...The methods used by American capital to exploit the backward countries may be oblique, but they are just as harsh."[46] The Soviets were clearly so pleased with Menon that they authorised the KGB residency in New Delhi "to conduct active-measures operations," including financial help, to strengthen Menon's position in the hope that he would become Nehru's successor.[47]

Clearly Moscow went overboard in its optimistic evaluation of Menon, for he had neither the power nor the popularity to succeed Nehru.

The differences between Nehru and Menon were in their personalities and in their characters. Nehru was a man of conflicting ideas, of soft rhetoric and inundated with Hamletian uncertainties, while Menon, often under the influence of drugs "and a mental case with an intense persecution mania,"[48] was more rabid in his views, more scheming in his actions, and incurably intolerant in his views of others—especially the adversaries. Besides, one of his doctors revealed that he was undergoing electric shock therapy, and his condition was such "that he should be in a nursing home and not in an office where serious work is involved."[49]

But, in many ways they complimented each other, and it is therefore not surprising that Nehru invariably defended and protected him while the others were determined to dethrone him from positions of power.

If Menon's unseemly character and disastrous performance vis-à-vis India's neighbours did result in his final and irrevocable exclusion from power, he did play a useful role in myriad diplomatic tasks assigned to him by Nehru. Consider his crucial role in India joining the Commonwealth, his behind-the-scenes excellent performance during the 1954 Geneva conference, his benign intervention with the Chinese to obtain the release of US prisoners of war, and his good offices role to persuade Washington to talk to the Chinese.

Menon thus had Nehru's ears, and had, in all probability, injected numerous inputs in Nehru's decisions on foreign policy—probably much more than the others.

Vijaya Lakshmi Pandit was another personality who was involved in a great deal of interaction with Nehru on foreign policy. She had the added advantage of being the sister of the Prime Minister, and the unique distinction—unlike the other political advisers—of having experienced weighty participation in international affairs before the independence of India, and even more so after independence. She participated as head of the Indian delegation to the annual conference of the Institute of Pacific Relations in January 1945 in Hotsprings, Virginia, travelled extensively on a lecture tour of the US during the same year, and attended the UN Charter Conference in San Francisco as an Indian Observer, where she gained prominence by presenting a memorandum to the Secretary General of the Conference denouncing British imperialism. After 1947, she was sent as India's Ambassador to Moscow in 1947, to Washington in 1949, to London in 1954 and to Madrid in 1958. She also had the distinction of representing India at the UN and of being elected as the President of the UN General Assembly. Though, the inaccessibility of Indian archival material makes it difficult to pinpoint or evaluate her exact role in the Indian decision making process, it is hardly possible, with the experience she had acquired, and the blood relationship that linked the two, that she did not have myriad discussions and interactions on foreign affairs with Nehru to which no one else was as privy as she, with the possible exception of his daughter.

Indira Gandhi too merits a word on Nehru's decision making. As his daughter, who was the official hostess at his household, and who travelled practically everywhere with him, it is not difficult to imagine all the important, informal and off-the-record conversations she must have had with him—discussions about personalities, impressions about countries, evaluations of people they had met, etc. Though it may well be that substantive issues of international affairs may not have been the centre of their political interaction, Indira Gandhi's inputs regarding international leaders and international events must have been weighty since political behaviour even on major issues, more often than not, do get heavily impacted by anecdotal facts. In Nehru's case, impulsive as he tended to be, Indira Gandhi's input either reinforced his established opinions, or restrained him from taking impulsive actions. Consider the following: at a dinner, hosted by Secretary of State, Dean Acheson, for Nehru in 1949, Indira Gandhi was sitting next to some members of the State Department. And this is what Elbert G. Mathews, Chief of the State Department's South Asian Division, who was present on the occasion, had to say in his oral interview given to Truman's Presidential Museum and Library. Describing the people around him he said: "Well, unfortunately, a little late and obviously having stopped for more than one or two bourbons and branch water, John Snyder sits down about three seats from Indira. I am not sure whether he realised that Indira was there. Well, he sure as hell did'nt know who Indira was, and at that point he did'nt care, and he started talking about these foreigners who come over here and take our money away from us. And of course on the other side it was either Dean Acheson's daughter or daughter-in-law sitting next to me. We did our best to sort of shout him down. And you know, he finally stopped because he'd no interest in it, but anyway Indira Gandhi was sitting there just seething—and you know she had every right to be. Now, she did'nt like us either but that did'nt help. Well, anyway it was that which she obviously reported to father in spades and with embellishment"[50] Nehru, who had already come to the US with great reservations, this and a number of other incidents he had witnessed or had experienced during his 1949 visit must have only reinforced his anti-Americanism.

Consider another anecdotal fact. While travelling with Nehru to Bandung for the 1955 Afro-Asian conference, Nehru learned that Air India plane, in which some members of the Chinese delegation were travelling from Hong Kong to Indonesia, had exploded. Nehru immediately and impulsively reacted by drafting a strong letter of protest to and attack on Anthony Eden, the British Prime Minister holding them responsible for this terrible tragedy. However before he could give it to the air crew to be sent out to London, Indira Gandhi restrained him from doing so, on the ground that he must await for more information before he should send out such a note.

G. Parthasarathy (popularly known as GP) was another close adviser of Nehru on foreign affairs. Hailing from the media world (Deputy Editor of *The Hindu*), he was known to be discreet, shy and a man of few words. He began his diplomatic career in Nehru's secretariat, and was assigned a number of important diplomatic responsibilities (Chairman of the International Control Commission in Cambodia and Vietnam, Ambassador to Indonesia, China and the UN). While all the diplomatic assignments were important, the one to China was most crucial, given India's growing wobbly relations with China in the late fifties. The three years he spent in China resulted in the development of warm relations with Zhou Enlai and his Foreign Minister, Chen Yi, both of whom had declared that he was a friend of China—a designation the Chinese often used for the personalities they trusted.[51]

What was the nature of his interaction with Nehru, it is difficult to say since no documentation is available on the subject. Journalist Govind Talwalkar has argued in one his articles that while GP had urged Nehru for a early border settlement the former was apparently of the opinion that the Chinese had a long-term concerted design to advance their interests in South Asia.[52]

M.O. Mathai must also be mentioned among Nehru's advisers in foreign affairs. As the Prime Minister's personal assistant, who spent most of his professional time with Nehru, he did have myriad opportunities to discuss foreign affairs. Given the frankness he possessed, and the position he held, he indeed became a lightning rod in Nehru's household with considerable opportunities of interacting with him and the MEA. Though he finally ended up badly and sadly on charges of corruption, and had to resign, the years that he spent with him are indeed important in foreign affairs.[53] In any analysis of Nehruvian decision making, it is important to keep in mind the psychological fact that people who were on the same intellectual wave length, or with whom he was emotionally involved clearly were more impactful in his decision making than those who were not. One may of course argue that this is probably a universal fact applicable to all, but in the case of personalities who have the tendency of being impulsive this is more relevant than on others. And Nehru was impulsive—probably more than many of his contemporaries.

FOREIGN POLICY NEHRUVIAN MODEL

Global Component

The factors that underpinned Nehru's global thinking stemmed from two sources. The first was anti-imperialism which flowed from the long history and tradition of the Congress Party's struggle for independence. The second was his broad socialist outlook, which originated from a variety of influences. Though essentially Fabian in character, some Marxist imprints were nonetheless also discernible in his thinking–at least during the early years.

The framework Nehru designed essentially mirrored these two influences, which concretely translated themselves into four broad components. The first was rhetorical, the second was emulative, the third was mediatory, while the fourth was normative.

Rhetorical Diplomacy

The rhetorical role was embodied in India's determination to project itself internationally as a representative of subjugated countries. Having just become independent, before the others, it considered itself under a moral obligation to be a consistent and outspoken supporter of those who were still unfree. It could hardly be otherwise given Nehru's vast anti-imperialist record during his entire pre-independence political career.

India, therefore, took initiatives and openly voiced opinions against imperialism, racism and ideological discrimination. Whenever it got an opportunity to raise its voice and act on these issues it did so: against the rampancy of colonialism, against racism in South Africa, and against the exclusion of Communist China from the comity of nations. That India took this role very seriously is evident from the fact that much of its time and its diplomatic efforts, during the early years, were devoted to these aspects.

It took, for example, the Dutch intervention in Indonesia to the UN, drawing the attention of the Secretary General to the fact that "this situation endangers the maintenance of international peace," and entreating the Security Council "to take the necessary measures provided by the Charter to end the existing situation."[54] The Indian initiative, jointly with Australia, finally resulted in the adoption of a resolution by the Security Council calling on all parties to cease hostilities forthwith, and to settle their disputes by arbitration and other peaceful means. India also took the issue to the floor of the General Assembly with the argument that, though the General Assembly could not take a decision, a discussion there " could not but prove useful."[55] The climax of these events was the convening by Nehru of an international conference in Delhi on 20-23 January 1949, where the 15 countries present outlined the modalities under which the Dutch had to transfer power to the Indonesians.[56]

Consider the South African apartheid. It was another issue on which India was at the forefront, for there was no one else at the time who could effectively project the issue internationally. Indian rhetoric was used to the hilt to denounce South African racist policies against the Indians and the Blacks. At the behest of India, many initiatives were indeed taken to get denunciatory resolutions passed in the UN, to mobilise the international media, and to informally persuade the Western nations that South Africa was guilty of violating fundamental human rights. Operationally, it also did everything to advance the cause of those who were subjugated. It agreed—along with Pakistan—to hold a round table conference with South Africa. While it diluted some of its radical declarations to rally the western powers, it decided to extend to the black Africans the original 1946 Indian complaint to the UN regarding South African Indians. Though the South African Government refused to take any action on the ground that it was a domestic matter, myriad Indian initiatives at the UN did receive large coverage in the international press. This is one of the issues for which India will be remembered for its clamorous role in the early period when Africa was still under subjugation, and when India was alone among the big nations in drawing international attention to the dire plight of Indians and Blacks in South Africa. The linkage between India's efforts in this domain, and the eventual South African revolution is not negligible. On numerous occasions, Nelson Mandela, after he came to power, recalled India's support to his long struggle against apartheid. "To India must go," he declared on 26 January 1995 during his visit to the country, "much of the credit for the fact that our aspiration for freedom and justice became one of the pre-eminent concerns of the international community for close to five decades."[57]

Nehru's rhetorical diplomacy also came out in favour of China. The installation of a Communist regime in China led the Prime Minister to conclude that he had no other credible choice but to recognise the new regime, to support its entry into the UN, and to encourage its participation in international conferences. For this strategy, he reasoned, was the only way of promoting a high level of benignity in China's international behaviour, and in maintaining international peace. So Nehru used practically all international occasions to project the new Communist regime onto the international system—at the forum of the UN, at the different summit Commonwealth meetings, and during the course of the myriad diplomatic interactions with his counterparts.

Clearly, India was fairly successful in these endeavours. Its voice was generally heard and appreciated. Nehru had publicly articulated his views with such alacrity and even moderation that they were accepted by most nations, including even the colonial powers. Gamal Abdel Nasser of Egypt perceived Nehru as a good example of a person who "interpreted others to

Asia and to Africa and interpreted Asia and Africa to others." He was, in his view, "the finest example of mutual interpretation that I have seen."[58]

Emulative Role

The second component of India's role was emulative. It was the first nation to conceptualise, articulate and proclaim a non-aligned foreign policy – a policy whose basic objective was to remain detached from the bipolar rigours and restraints of the cold war.

Clearly, Nehru's broad framework of foreign policy was an attractive State model for most developing countries. It was attractive because it was based on the principles of non-involvement in the bipolar system, and because it was hinged to the goal of active, independent and even defiant participation in the affairs of the world. In sum, it was nationalistic, and thus dovetailed with the aspirations of countless countries that had become either independent or were in the process of acquiring such a status from colonial rule. That it was an attractive State foreign policy model, serving the interests of the third world countries, is evident from the fact that most of them made non-alignment as a major plank of their foreign policies. Clearly it was a stance that, on the one hand, helped them to insulate themselves from superpower pressures, and, on the other, contributed to the wide emergence of a domestic consensus among the mainstream political parties, thereby giving the newly established government a wide legitimacy within their countries.

Equally significant was Nehru's weighty role in the establishment of non-alignment as a trans-national sub-system with a broad consensual framework of its own, as distinct from the bipolar world. It had its small beginning as some sort of an international movement around Nehru, Tito and Nasser, and finally emerged as a powerful international force during the height of the cold war. Its original purpose was to mutually concert on major international issues, to jointly defy any undue pressures from the bipolar world, and demand the establishment of a new international economic order that would meet the desiderata of the poor nations.

The emergence of a non-aligned international sub-system undoubtedly was a major landmark in post-World War II international relations. And, long after Nehru's disappearance it continues to function with an expanded membership of as many as 115 States and with a shift in focus, since the 1992 Jakarta non-aligned summit, that enables it to function on global economic issues that is almost comparable to the activities of the G-8 and the

European Union. They may not have the economic power of the developed groupings, but they do have the clout of numbers; and it does matter.

Nehru's role in all this is indeed decisive. "Nehru stands," in the eyes of an observer, "above them all. It is largely through Jawaharlal Nehru's internationalism and vision that the global character and active nature of what was to become non-aligned movement were actually envisaged."[59]

Thus, the third world countries emulated both these components (foreign policy and international sub-system). Already during Nehru's mandate — most of the Africans and Asian countries, as they became independent, had adopted non-alignment as their foreign policy, and had joined what was in the process of becoming a powerful international movement. This was indeed a remarkable development, since the movement neither had the material nor the military capabilities, hitherto perceived as vital for any efficacious international achievements.

It was this game of numbers, and politics of defiance of the rich established powers that gave them the appropriate importance and forcefulness in the international system. For the first time, international relations were no more underpinned only with material power. New dimensions had indeed emerged.

Mediatory Role

The third component of Indian diplomacy at the macro level was the utilisation of good offices and mediation to manage international crises. India was able to carve a niche for itself in a series of crises in the fifties. The general approbation of India by most belligerents was the key element that made it possible to often play a central role in managing different crises.

Consider the Korean War. The disposal of 140,000 Chinese prisoners of war had become a major stumbling block to the conclusion of the conflict. Negotiations over this apparently innocuous subject, which had opened in January 1952, generated so much controversy and animosity that the UN suspended the talks on two separate occasions for a period totalling nine months. The dispute centred on the repatriation of the Chinese prisoners of war. While the UN command, led by the US, insisted that the prisoners of war should be free to decide if they wanted to return to their country, the Chinese and North Korean governments, invoking the 1949 Geneva Convention, demanded that they be released and repatriated forthwith since the hostilities had ceased The belligerents finally called upon India to use its good offices to resolve the differences. After considerable behind-the-scene diplomacy, a 17 point Indian solution was accepted by all parties concerned. This was India's first attempt at mediatory diplomacy. Not only was it successful, but it resulted in India's nomination as the Chairman of the Neutral UN Repatriation Commission—undoubtedly a major feather in India's diplomatic cap.

India's second mediatory effort, during the Nehruvian era, was at the 1954 Geneva Conference on Indo-China and Korea. The escalation of the Vietnam war, with increasing involvement of the great powers (China and the US), combined with the dramatic defeat of the French at Dien Bien Phu, finally resulted in an agreement to convene an international conference. India did play some role. For two days before the scheduled conference was to open, Nehru put forward a six-point programme that had the backing of the so-called Colombo powers (India, Pakistan, Ceylon, Burma and Indonesia) envisaging, among other things, an immediate cease fire, a French undertaking to grant independence and a big power guarantee not to interfere in the area. Since India was not invited to participate, most of the Indian efforts were initiated behind-the-scenes in the corridors of the conference. But, the measure of Indian involvement can also be discerned from the number of informal bilateral meetings that the Indian group had with the participants. Journalists noted that during the first phase of the meeting, the Indian envoy, Krishna Menon, who arrived without any invitation, met Antony Eden sixteen times, Zhou Enlai eight times, V.M. Molotov, more than twenty times, Pham Van Dong five times, Walter Bedell Smith six times, and Pierre Mendes France twice. And during the final phase of the conference, Menon, became the key person in Geneva, who interpreted each side to the other, shunting between delegations to clear up misunderstandings, and persuading each of the participants to take into account the problems of others. The formula he finally produced—based on Nehru's six points—was the basis of the joint declaration signed by all the powers, except the US, thus bringing to an end, at least provisionally, an eight year war.[60] All the participating countries paid rich tributes to India for its crucial contribution in Geneva. Zhou Enlai, in a message of 4 August 1954, highlighted Nehru's role, and Mendes France, underlining India's crucial role, characterised the Geneva conference not an eight-power conference but a nine-power conference.

India's third important mediatory role pertained to Sino-American relations. Here too it was crucial. Nehru had apparently convinced himself that the elongated Beijing-Washington stand-off, since the Chinese

Revolution, had generated too much of tensions in Asia. And the only way out of this impasse, under the circumstances, would be the initiation of some mutual gestures on the part of the two countries. Since, there were already some new signs that the two belligerents were becoming more benign politically and more open diplomatically, after the death of Stalin and the emergence of Eisenhower as the new US President, Nehru concluded that some credible mediatory initiatives should be realisable. Therefore, when Zhou Enlai declared at Bandung his willingness "to sit down and enter into negotiations" with Washington, Nehru " put considerable pressure on the President (Eisenhower) and Secretary (Dulles) to agree to the talks."[61] In fact he wrote to the US President entreating him to meet Krishna Menon who had just returned from China (May 1955), and who would, be in a position to give some useful information regarding Chinese thinking. Though John Forster Dulles did not have much confidence in Menon, and had privately characterised him as " a very adroit and unscrupulous maneuvrer...who is very close to the Soviet and Chinese viewpoint,"[62] the US authorities –including Eisenhower – finally did see him.[63] Menon was in a good position to meet the Americans, since, as a result of his visit to China (May 1955), he had succeeded in obtaining the release of four US airmen with a Chinese promise that more would follow. It is more than possible that in his "informal and private talks"[64] with the US Administration Menon passed on useful information, which, according to Eisenhower "may have served a useful purpose, at least in clarifying our minds."[65]

All these Indian efforts finally did contribute to the release of US prisoners of war in China and the formal opening of Sino-American talks at the Ambassadorial level in the summer of 1955.

Normative Role

But, the broad framework of India's diplomatic activity was not only limited to rhetoric, non-alignment and mediation. Though they did constitute the gamut of its activity, there were nonetheless other dimensions that were an integral part of the Nehruvian model of international relations. Imbued as Nehru was with high idealism, and determined as he was to project India into the mainstream of international politics, he also directed India's international activities to the normative task of strengthening the law-making diplomacy of the UN, of promoting peaceful coexistence as defined by the Chinese and the Indians in their five principles of coexistence, of broadening the applicability of human rights, and of entreating the global acceptance of disarmament.

Also countlessly he had expressed views on myriad international issues facing the international community; and had initiated diplomatic actions on a host of tense international problems like Hungary (1956), the Suez crisis (1956), military alliances, etc.

Nehru thus successfully projected India onto the mainstream of the international system. Clearly he had the knowledge, the interest and the determination to do so. And, clearly he was globally respected, and perceived as someone who possessed the hallmarks of an international figure. He was well-received and listened to everywhere, and was generally viewed as someone who had acquired an intellectual sophistication of explaining his views in a convincing and a benign manner. Jean Houdart, in an article in the French newspaper, *Le Monde,* sums him up aptly by characterising him "as one of the principal personalities on the international scene" who embodied "the rare power of this world—and whose simplicity is not effected by the exercise of power."[66]

But this broad Nehruvian global framework had its day; for with the movement of time, compounded with global mutations, much of what Nehru had originally conceived and operationalised at the macro level had either become irrelevant or had been transfigured by new third world actors; and all this happened during Nehru's lifetime when he was still at the helm of Indian affairs. Rhetorical diplomacy, focussed on anti-colonialism, had become irrelevant with the political decolonisation of the third world; non-alignment had taken a radical turn with the rampant emergence of anti-Westernism; mediation had lost its role since direct interaction between the superpowers had become a reality; and normative goals for the fulfilment of which India was in the forefront of international diplomacy, had now been slowly replaced by new actors and by new goals. For Nehru, this was a sad mutation, since all this had diminished India's cruciality in the international system.

Regional Component

If India's role in the global system was institutionalised, it never had one for the region; for Nehru neither established any framework nor fixed any real goals vis-à-vis India's neighbours. Apparently he did not give much thought to the whole question. Besides, a different frame of mind, and a different approach is needed regarding countries nearer home, and in all probability he was not as much equipped in formulating foreign policy vis-à-vis the region than vis-à-vis the world.

It is important to note that at the regional level, the foreign policy of no country is simply composed of making rhetorical international declarations or of participating in macroscopic conferences or of supporting monumental international issues. It is much more than that. It is more concrete, more palpable and more calcified with the nitty-gritty dimension of assuring the security of the nation, of searching partners and aid-givers for domestic economic development, of safeguarding the stability of the country, of striving to forge relations with friendly neighbours, and of isolating those who prove to be problematic.

In sum the foreign policy of most nations is environmental. It is directly linked with their own immediate environment. And much of their diplomatic activities is dominated, if not determined, by what is happening across their borders. Even, in this period of globalisation where global linkages do have their place and their relevance, the geopolitical dimension pertaining to one's own region can hardly be ignored; and those who do it, do so at their own peril.

India clearly was no exception. Macro-Nehruvian diplomatic approach notwithstanding, it had to look at its own backyard, its own region and its own neighbours all of whom only a few years before were an integral part of the British Empire for almost a century, and all of whom had now become independent with India as the linchpin dimension in the histories of all of them.

At the time of its independence, South Asia was in the midst of turmoil and tensions. Much of this had to do with the process of decolonisation, and the partition of the subcontinent—a process of decolonisation that was monumental, and a partition that was sanguinary with millions of people fleeing from one country to the other. The whole environment thus had become unruly and uncontrollable where the scope of any harmonious dialogue between peoples or between States had become impossible. What made things even more difficult and even more insurmountable was the important fact that the British Empire, which had been forcefully anchored into some sort of a South Asian order by the British, had disintegrated; it was replaced by a group of countries determined to enlarge their independence; and the only big country, India—almost a successor of the British Empire—had neither the clout nor the determination nor even the vision to construct something cohesive out of this process of disintegration and disorder that had seized the area.

In its relations with its South Asian neighbours, India was also seriously handicapped by its gigantic dimension. Its size, population, GDP, natural resources and military clout, were larger than that of the other six countries combined together. It accounted for 72 per cent of the total land of the area, 77 per cent of its population, and almost 90 per cent of its coal, petroleum, bauxite, iron ore, manganese, and uranium resources, not to speak of the fact that it housed all the South Asian ethnic and cultural groups that the six countries represented

Clearly, the ramifications of all these factors was the engenderment of considerable mistrust of India among the South Asian neighbours, and the emergence of visible determination to distance themselves from their big neighbour. In sum, enlarge the scope of their independence.

In the face of this unavoidable and inexorable process, there was nothing much that Nehru could do to counter this phenomenon. How could he? Having just gained independence for India, he could hardly stop the others from achieving what he had just gained for his own country. Besides, having always projected himself internationally as someone who was a determined proponent of independence for all deprived nations, Nehru could hardly take any initiatives or any action in the opposite direction, least of all towards his neighbours who had always looked up to him as the very embodiment of nationalism and progressive ideas.

Consider India's relations with its South Asian neighbours. With each of them it had problems, and with all of them it had to reckon with the important fact that they turned elsewhere to counter-balance Indian power and Indian pressures. The balance of power dimension became rampant in their diplomatic behaviour.

Pakistan

With Pakistan, on its west and east, it had a wide array of irresolute disagreements including an armed conflict in Kashmir. The partition of the sub-continent had generated so much of mutual suspicion, and so much of animosity that nothing seemed to work between the two nations. The massacres followed by massive migrations of Hindus to India and Muslims to Pakistan only compounded the frayed relations. The Indians were apparently irritated at the partition; many were certain that this would not last, while the Pakistanis, on the other hand, were fearful of their insecurity and of their very existence. Kashmir did not arrange matters. Fearful of the Hindu Maharaja's possible option to integrate Muslim Kashmir into India, instigated Pakistan to pre-empt such an action by invading the valley—an invasion that escalated into a war. From then on the two countries have fallen apart with no let up; even when some hope of reconciliation surfaces , it lasts only for a moment only to be drowned in the frayed atmosphere of mutual recrimination.

Nehru never succeeded in solving India's relations with Pakistan—neither in the battlefield nor on the negotiating table.

It would be of course an excessive exaggeration to attribute all this solely to Nehru. Though the traditionally built-in mutual suspicion between Hindus and Muslims, compounded with inter-communal massacres following the partition, must have much to do with the fractious state of relations, Nehru's indecisive policies clearly contributed to this. His decision not to continue with the war until the expulsion of Pakistani troops from Kashmir, and his option to refer the whole matter to the UN contributed to the sustained fractiousness of Indo-Pakistan relations that are with us to this day. What if he had listened to his generals and some of his colleagues to pursue the war, and what if he had heeded the unrelenting advice of some of the members of his cabinet not to go to the Security Council, Indo-Pakistan relations may well have been a different story.

To counter this state of affairs in which Pakistan was clearly in a weaker position, the leadership turned to the US on the one hand and China on the other both of whom had reservations regarding India—China clearly more than the US.

The ramifications of these Pakistani initiatives were gruesome, for it brought the raging cold war to the very doorsteps of the sub-continent—a situation that India was attempting to contain through its policy of non-alignment. In retrospect one wonders if all this did not catalyse the Soviet activation of its diplomacy—which until then was not friendly to Nehru. In sum all the three major actors (USSR, US, China), heavily involved in the cold war, were defining and developing their national interests in South Asia with Kashmir emerging as a crucial issue for all three of them.

Nepal

With Nepal, the Himalayan neighbour, the pattern of relations were not comparable to that of Pakistan, since they were neither really confrontational nor did they explode into a war. But they were nonetheless problematic. India was faced with a dilemmic situation. It had to decide how it was going to deal with a dictatorial regime run by the Ranas—a group of feudal lords who were closely connected with the Indian Hindu society and who had taken over the country by the nineteenth century. The Ranas", wrote Erika Leuchtag, a physiotherapist close to the Royal family, "who had taken over the country by the middle of the nineteenth century, had made it theirs with great slaughter." "The Rana," argued the author, "succeeds a Rana as Prime Minister, title passing from brother to brother, or from father to sons when brothers became extinct. There grew up a complex dynasty, legitimate and illegitimate that graded itself in precedence and privilege. The Prime Minister held his position until death. Only one ever resigned, having made more than thirty million pounds by investments in Indian industry."[67] Clearly Nehru was against such a system—all the more so when it came to a neighbouring strategically placed country whose past heritage was similar to India's. With the complicity of anti-Rana Nepali Congress leaders and the King (Tribhuvan), who sought asylum in India, Nehru weakened the Ranas and successfully installed the King in a position of responsibility. In many ways the changes imposed on the northern kingdom had the smatterings of a revolution. Nehru had every reason to be satisfied of having been the architect of such a political mutation. But before these measures had been effectively carried out, differences surfaced within the Indian government regarding the strategy India should pursue in the face of the Nepalese situation. While Nehru favoured the outright political downfall of the Ranas and the restoration of the King, there were others in the government, who, fearful of India's insecurity, were thinking of another solution. The principal proponent, Patel, concerned of the possible expansion of the Chinese influence in the frontier state located between China and India, argued that since "stability" must be the "paramount consideration" in such a frontier state, India should envisage an understanding with the Ranas who, Patel thought, were "in a better position to ensure stability than anyone else."[68] Patel apparently presented this argument not because he favoured the Ranas but because he was convinced that the eventual supremacy of the Nepali people could also be reached through pressures on the Ranas, while, at the same time, their staying at the helm would effectively forestall the dangers of Chinese incursions into Nepal.

As subsequent events were to show, Patel's fears were well founded. For China indeed did launch a series of concerted initiatives to get close to Nepal. And paradoxically it was the popular Nepalese Government, dependent on and close to India, that accepted the Chinese overtures— overtures that resulted in the establishment of a Chinese Consulate in

1956, followed in March 1960 by an economic agreement, by a border agreement and by the establishment of a full-fledged Chinese Embassy in Kathmandu. Thereafter, a month later, Zhou Enlai arrived in Nepal to sign a treaty of friendship. The Chinese, it would seem, according to Koirala, the Nepalese Prime Minister, attempted in vain to persuade the Himalayan Kingdom to conclude a non-aggression pact, which in effect would have nullified India's privileged position in the country.

The ongoing Nepalese process to become more and more neutral between India and China was further accelerated after the humiliating Indian defeat in the Sino-Indian War of 1962. For the Nepalese then were assailed by a doubt regarding the Indian ability to come to the defence of Nepal. Nehru sent Lal Bahadur Shastri, the Minister without Portfolio, to assure the Nepalese of India's determination to protect Nepal. But, this apparently did not have much effect since all Nepalese Governments continued their policy of intensifying Sino-Nepalese interaction.

While some, with the benefit of hindsight, fault Nehru for India's slippage in Nepal, others attribute this to the unavoidable process of South Asian independence and decolonisation that marked the region in the late forties. There was nothing much that Nehru could do against the powerful Chinese, and the determined Nepalese to gain greater independence from India. India could hardly step into the British shoes of controlling Nepal without British power and without the broad British vision of empire building. Nehru had no such vision and no such determination to shape India into a powerful state.

Myanmar (Burma)

Myanmar is the other neighbouring country with which India had to reckon with after independence. Situated on its eastern flank with a common land (1,670 km) and maritime borders (200 km), compounded with common colonial heritage, including a comparable process of nationalism, India favoured a friendly closeness to Myanmar. Seizing the occasion of Burmese independence, Nehru underlined what held the two countries together. "As in the past," he declared, "so in the future the people of India will stand shoulder to shoulder with the people of Burma, and whether we have to share good fortune or ill- fortune, we shall share it together."[69] The closeness of the two countries had resulted in the conclusion of a treaty of friendship that was expected to last "for ever" unless explicitly denounced by one of the two parties.

But, not too long after the inauguration of these tuneful years, India began to show signs of increasing concern regarding Burmese policies, or its capacity to effectively manage its own affairs. Delhi was not at all sure, if Rangoon had the capacity to exercise effective control over the activities of dissentient ethnic minorities on its side of the Indo-Burmese border. Having the same ethnic groups on the two sides of the frontier, they had concluded an agreement to jointly contain any nefarious activities.

The second issue that India encountered pertained to Indians residing in Myanmar.

They constituted almost 7.5 per cent of the population, who, according to Aung San Suu Kyi, had not only acquired "a stranglehold on the Burmese economy" but also had "set up homes with Burmese women striking at the very roots of Burmese manhood and racial purity"[70] Nehru was in a dilemmic situation. While, on the one hand, he realised that Indians in Myanmar could not possibly expect the continuation of privileged treatment, acquired under British rule, on the other hand, as the head of the Government, he could not accept "any wrong done to Indian citizens"[71] Faced with this dilemma there was nothing much he could do; the ongoing Burmese determination to deprive all foreigners of their economic privileges, was clearly directed at the Indians since they were the largest and the most powerful in the country. "Our nationals", acknowledged Lakshmi Menon, the Deputy Minister of External Affairs, "do experience a number of hardships as a result of land legislation and various other legislative enactments in Burma", but " since there is no discrimination at all there is no point in our taking up this matter with the Government of Burma."[72]

Nehru really did not solve the problem. It solved itself since the Burmese determination to deprive privileged foreigners resulted in a massive exodus to India. The worst measure that led to this exodus was the one initiated by the Ne Win Government that affected 12,000 middle rank Indians in the early sixties; so much so that it aroused deep resentment within the Indian Government. By early 1964, relations had become so frayed that it was openly admitted by the Indian MEA in its 1964-65 report that "The presence of half a million Indians in Myanmar has on occasion tended to be a disturbing factor in the friendly relations between the two countries."[73]

The Burmese political situation was also causing concern to the Indian government. There was the ongoing civil war over which the Central Government apparently had no control. The Deputy Prime Minister, Patel, was not at all sure that the Burmese "civil war was nearing its end or that the Government forces are definitely on the top of the insurgents."[74] But the matter that was even more worrisome was the Indian fear of the Chinese intervention in Myanmar. With the end of the Chinese civil war, remnants of the Guomindang troops had entered the Burmese territory with the intention of using it as a base against the Chinese Communists. Fearing that the Chinese civil war may spillover to Burmese territory, Nehru advised the Burmese Prime Minister Thakin Nu to inform the American Ambassador of this new development "as the USA is the only country that can deal with Formosa Government effectively."[75] The whole matter was furthermore discussed within the Indian Government and arms were provided to Rangoon. Nehru also mobilised the Commonwealth countries to give a loan of six million pounds. Encouraged by India, Myanmar lodged a complaint with the UN. At the initiative of India and eight other countries a resolution was tabled calling on Chinese troops to lay down their arms or to submit to internment.

But, all this did not seem to have any effect in bringing Myanmar closer to India. The radical change in the geopolitical situation in China catalysed the Burmese authorities to move closer to Beijing. They were the first non-communist country to recognise China. By the early sixties a clear trend had set in of not only expanding its relations with China, but of avoiding any difficulties with the Chinese. But, before taking such a leap in the Chinese direction, the Burmese leadership did sound Nehru, through his Ambassador, Y.D. Gundevia, in Rangoon, to ascertain if some institutionalised relations, stipulating some military relations, could not be established with India. But Nehru turned down such a proposal, leaving no choice to the Burmese except to increasingly turn to Beijing.

Nehruvian diplomacy had failed. The security dimension had become acute. And Burmese neutrality during the 1962 Sino-Indian conflict was perhaps a landmark development in Burmese policy –a development that was indicative of the direction Burmese foreign policy had taken.

Sri Lanka

Sri Lanka was the other South Asian neighbour that Nehru had to reckon with. Already before independence, he was well-aware of the troubled relations that afflicted the two countries regarding the status of overseas Indian residing on the island. When he was sent by his party in 1939 to examine this seemingly intractable issue, he had realised the tensions that subsisted between the overseas Indians and the Sinhalese. To his dismay he found the Sinhalese resentful of the ongoing migration of Indian labour and were openly discriminating against them.

After independence, Nehru was eager to seek an honourable solution to the plight of the Tamils. He was against their forcible repatriation, and had concluded an agreement in 1954 under which Indians were given the choice of either registering as Indian nationals or opting for Ceylonese nationality. But the agreement was never implemented. Fearful of the Indians deciding to opt for Ceylonese nationality, the Sri Lankan Government dragged its feet, and the Indian Government, in retaliation, refused to carry out its side of the bargain.

The Sri Lankan Government then proposed another solution. Prime Minister, Dudley Senanayake, suggested to Nehru that if he would agree to the repatriation of 300,000 Indians, he would grant citizenship to the rest of the Indians who were still stateless. It was a straightforward proposal, and It could have been a way out of an intractable situation. But, there was no real guarantee that Senanayake would have been able to keep his side of the proposal, given rampant domestic opposition to Indians residing on the island. Besides, Nehru refused to accept such a proposal characterising the offer as a "horse deal".[76]

The troubled relations were further compounded by Sri Lanka's foreign policy choices, a policy that mostly favoured the western world. Though, Prime Minister Bandarnaike injected some non-aligned balance in the country's policy, a bias in favour of the West nonetheless continued; perhaps with one exception—that of China. After having ignored the Middle Kingdom for almost eight years following independence, a new process of opening up was inaugurated with the establishment of diplomatic relations in February 1957.

But for the American pressure against the recognition of China, there was really no rational reason against the development of harmonious Colombo-Beijing relations. After Bandarnaike adopted a non-aligned stance, the task became easier. Sri Lanka had no bone of contention with the Chinese, and did not perceive any security endangerment from them. If anything, China could be potentially a protective source against any security threat emanating from India with whom there were myriad outstanding problems.

Interestingly the improvement of Sri Lankan relations with China coincided with a commencement of a decline in Sino-Indian relations, and with the inauguration of a new process of prudence and neutrality on the growing Sino-Indian tensions. In fact, Sri Lanka projected itself as a mediator—along with six other non-aligned countries—after the 1962 conflict.

A similar scenario, comparable to Pakistan, Burma and Nepal, was thus unravelling in Sri Lanka—a scenario of distancing from India and moving closer to China.

The issue was never resolved under Nehru. It has remained a bone of contention long after Nehru's disappearance.

Hostile Global Environment

But, it was not only South Asian defiance that generated Nehru's difficulties on the diplomatic front. The global international environment too was becoming unpropitious—in fact even unfriendly. The open ideological opposition of the Communist world to the Indian establishment aggravated India's difficulties. China's occupation of Tibet brought an inimical nation to the frontiers of India which had already gone on record for its serious reservations for what the Indian Government represented. The Soviet Union too had no use for Nehru's "bourgeois reactionary regime," and the Indian Communist Party had raised the flag of revolt creating some turmoil in the east and some instability in the south of the country.

In the face of this fairly generalised unfriendly environment what could Nehru do? What initiatives could he take, and what actions could he launch to make India secure? Notwithstanding his macro luminous international image as a votary of peace, coexistence and friendliness, Nehru's leverage in his own backyard was very limited and his interaction with the communist world was delusive. He neither had the power nor the determination to effectively manage the regional fires that were burning; nor the capacity to contain the Communist threats that were dangerously looming on the horizon.

NEHRU TURNS TO THE WEST

It was this overall unstable and unfriendly geopolitical situation, that pushed Nehru to take some major diplomatic initiatives—initiatives clearly directed at reinforcing ties with the UK and the Commonwealth, and even turning to the US for arms and military collaboration. While the western world too had serious reservations about Nehru's non-alignment, it maintained its normal bridges with India. Therefore, notwithstanding his repeated proclamations of non-alignment and independence as India's basic foreign policy goal, an array of discreet initiatives were taken in the direction of the UK and US—initiatives that would have brought India closer to the West. Clearly, Nehru hardly had little choice. For there was no one else to whom he could turn to for significant assistance. But, on the other hand, given his myriad reservations about the UK and the US—often voiced publicly—he could hardly ask them openly for military and economic assistance. For, it would have been the height of hypocrisy to publicly turn to the two countries which had determinedly decided to confront the Communist world. How would he have explained such an action to the Indian public which was notoriously and traditionally anti-Western? How would he have justified such a step towards his own colleagues who had to often listen to his anti-American tirades? And what about the Chinese Communists for whom he had publicly expressed his sympathy for having carried out a popular revolution in China?

In the face of all these paradoxes and contradictions, Nehru took, first of all, the decision of joining the new and modified Commonwealth. It was a landmark decision, for it tantamounted to the building of close ties with the UK, Australia and Canada—all of whom were committed anti-communist nations, but who shared with India common democratic values of governance. Besides, they were rich and could be persuaded to give economic assistance to India and other countries in distress, as was done in the case of Burma. Furthermore, while maintaining his freedom of action in foreign policy, membership of the Commonwealth gave India a psychological protection against any Communist threat. There was of course nothing in the Commonwealth rules that stipulated such a protection, but the fact that you had linked yourself to some form of institutionalised association with politically like-minded nations must have offered some form of security. Whether such a consideration was uppermost in Nehru's mind, it is of course difficult to say. In any event it was not unanimously welcomed in India. Nehru had to field considerable hostility from the Indian left wing. His political colleague, Jayaprakash Narayan, with whom he was quite close, considered that by opting for Commonwealth membership Nehru had gone back on all they had stood for over many years, and believed that Commonwealth membership would unavoidably tie India to the UK and commit it to one of the two blocs. For the Communist world this was a confirmation of where India stood on foreign affairs, notwithstanding his affirmations of independence and non-alignment. It could be argued that Nehru was driven in the Commonwealth direction for he had no other viable choice. One could validly ask the question; what if Nehru had been received with open arms by the Communist world immediately after independence. What if Stalin and Mao Zedong had made open and concerted attempts to communicate to Nehru their wish to have friendly political relations with independent India? Would he have then, in that type of a situation, excluded the Commonwealth option?

Even more significant was Nehru's discreet and secretive initiative towards the US, far away from public scrutiny. India's military attaché in Washington, sought to buy in January 1948 bombers from Washington, and "informally indicated the interest of the Government of India in long-term military collaboration between US and India."[77] Given Nehru's independent stance in international affairs and his known lack of sympathy for the US, such an action was considered by some as an initiative taken by the military attaché on his own. In fact, it was the US which was the first to suspect the origins of this action. For US officials, whom the military attaché, B.M.Kaul had met, reported that in their view the Indo-US military collaboration "envisaged in Kaul's conversation...is at the present time strictly a figment of Kaul's own vivid and friendly imagination and should not be given a serious consideration."[78]

But this was really not the case. The initiative to open up to Washington was indeed authentic, and did originate in New Delhi. Kaul had met Nehru in late December 1947 in Delhi where, in the presence of Air Vice-Marshal S. Mukerji, he was instructed to explore the possibility of buying some medium Mitchell bombers from Washington.

The Secretary General of the MEA, Girija Shankar Bajpai, reiterated similar views during his visit to the States. Arriving in Washington in April 1948—also seeking arms— he assured the State Department that "India would, under no circumstances, align itself with the Soviet Union in a war between the latter and the US."[79] Though such a declaration was not in contradiction with India's broad macro approach in foreign affairs, the assurance given to Washington significantly was coincidental to India's request for arms.

Then in April 1949 arrived an Indian military mission in Washington to seek military aid –an aid that involved some 20 to 25 "night fighters" and spare parts for military equipment of American origin.

Finally it was Nehru himself who arrived in Washington in October 1949. His reservations of the US were so well-known, that the Deputy Prime Minister, Patel, had insisted that Nehru should always speak from a written text to avoid the emergence of any serious misunderstanding.

However written texts notwithstanding, Nehru, impulsive as he was, was critical of the undiluted nature of American capitalism, and showed his irritation at the common American tendency of equating success with money. At a get-together in New York he showed his irritation at the US business man's remarks that the Indian Prime minister was present at a "hundred dollar-lunch," or on another occasion when he was reminded that the budget of General Motors was larger than that of the Government of India. At a very early stage of his mandate he convinced himself that "Americans think they can buy countries and continents."[80] But his reservations were not only regarding financial enrichment; they were also cultural. "His way of looking at the US," said B.K.Nehru, who knew him well, " was that of an upper class Englishman of the early nineteen hundreds—that they were a country of upstarts who had a lot of money. They had no manners; they had no behaviour; they had no knowledge; they had no culture. This was the prejudice that Jawaharlal came back with from Harrow."[81]

In this connection it is important to note that all US efforts to build up economic relations were stalled. Economic aid was accepted, but when it came to US investments in some important economic sectors they were rejected. The US government had sent a mission to India to work out arrangements to enable Washington to import large quantities of manganese for its steel industry. It was rejected by Nehru despite the fact that many concerned Ministries had shown an interest in the scheme. Again, Orissa Governor's (Asaf Ali, first Indian Ambassador to US) scheme to expand, with US cooperation, plans of developing iron ore and coal deposits, in the province were rejected by the Prime Minister.[82]

In an off-the-record conversation with the US Ambassador Henderson, Nehru furthermore denounced the US for its policies on Kashmir. In a secret note to the State Department on 15 August 1949, Henderson declared that Nehru "said he was tired of receiving moralistic advice from (the) US" on Kashmir.[83] Similar remarks were made at the Commonwealth Conference in London where he reportedly threatened to withdraw from Commonwealth "if United Kingdom's relations with the US would continue to be closer than those with India."[84]

Interestingly, Nehru's 1949 visit coincided with Communist victory in China— a great setback to the US, heavily involved as it had been in supporting Chiang Kai-shek for decades. Even before the Communist revolution, the CIA, in its report of July 1949, had pointed out that "India was a major Asiatic power and was alone in a position to compete with Chinese communism for hegemony in Southeast Asia," and US Secretary of State, Dean Acheson, had declared to the US President that "Mr. Nehru is today and will probably continue to be for some time the dominant political figure in Asia."[85]

Clearly, the change in China must also have been of great concern to India since it involved a considerable change in the configuration of forces not very far away from the frontiers of the subcontinent. There was thus something in common between the two countries.

But Washington, on the other hand, was aware of the fact that Nehru was not very favourably disposed towards the US, and that he had repeatedly announced India's intentions of pursuing an independent and non-aligned policy. The US, furthermore, must have been puzzled with the fact that, notwithstanding geopolitical uneasiness, Nehru had formally welcomed the change in China, and had recognised the new Beijing Government soon after his return from Washington. For the US, mired as it heavily was in the cold war with the Soviet Union, Nehru's views and actions seemed strange and contradictory. All the more so, given the fact that his government, at the same time, was seeking arms from the US, and was even evoking the question of military collaboration. While avoiding any personal and direct involvement in discussions relating to military or even food aid, during his own visit, Nehru was nonetheless anxious to have a clear idea of where he stood in American reckoning and what Washington expected of him "in the event of any further deterioration in international relations in general."[86] To the US all this must have seemed incomprehensible and even hypocritical.

The US response to all these Indian initiatives were therefore not favourable. His visit in fact had been a failure. Apparently he rubbed Americans on the wrong side. His one-on-one with the US President, Truman was a disappointment, so much so that when an eminent Indian journalist, Durga Das, suggested to President Truman in a press conference, to visit India, Truman retorted "are you sure Nehru would welcome it." [87] The US Assistant Secretary of State George Mcghee disclosed that " Nehru and Truman did'nt hit it off at all. Rumor has it that, in his first informal meeting with the President, he was offended by Truman's extended discussion of the merits of bourbon whisky."[88] With Dean Acheson, the US Secretary of State, it was even worse. His 2 1/2 hours of conversation with him was apparently a disaster. Acheson complained that Nehru had talked to him "as if we were in a public meeting". He even went to the extent of declaring that Nehru and he "were not destined to have a pleasant personal relationship.... He was one of the most difficult men with whom I had ever had to deal with.[89]

In its analysis of India, Washington did not consider it as strategically important and politically reliable enough to be counted as a credible partner. Besides, finding itself in the midst of a growing and a highly polarised cold war, it had other priorities and preoccupations than meeting India's demands—demands that were not even remotely connected with the cold war.The US therefore took a decision to impose an "informal embargo" in arms on India and Pakistan.

What aggravated Nehru's irritation even more was the marked contrast in the reception received by Pakistan's Prime Minister, Liaquat Ali Khan when he visited the States eight months later (May-June 1950). It was more cordial. For Nehru it was incomprehensible that Pakistan, hardly a country with any international weight, was given a more friendly reception than to him.

In a letter to his sister (10 May 1950), Vijaya Lakshmi Pandit, this irritation, came out very vividly. "I must say," he wrote, " that the Americans are either very naïve or singularly lacking in intelligence. They go through the identical routine whether it is Nehru or the Shah of Iran or Liaquat Ali."[90]

It cannot be excluded that after this initial setback, Nehru's traditional reservations about the US became even more pronounced. In all probability he came to the conclusion that not much could be expected from Washington. But, on the other hand, Nehru was realistic enough to realise that under the circumstances, with China looming dangerously on the horizon, and with the country's growing economic crisis, aid, assistance and protection could come only from the US. Besides, Nehru was also aware of the fact that though US was unhappy with his non-alignment, Washington had nonetheless kept its connections with India.

US changes attitude under Eisenhower

With the arrival of Dwight Eisenhower at the helm of US affairs in 1952, the US attitude changed. The new President arrived at the conclusion that

India should be cultivated, and that Washington should soften its opposition to non-alignment. The new Administration even acknowledged that in some instances neutralism could serve US security interests, in as much as it strengthened the determination of non-aligned countries to preserve their sovereign independence. In a note to Secretary Dulles, the President in fact urged that the new US Ambassador Sherman Cooper to India should "do everything possible to win the personal confidence and friendship of Nehru," and recommended that the State Department "should avoid putting chores on our Ambassador that would almost compel him to show an unsympathetic attitude towards the Premier."[91] Substantial economic assistance was given to enable New Delhi to keep its second and third five year plans afloat. Military assistance too was given. And a huge agricultural assistance programme was set up in 1959 that averaged three million tons of wheat annually. Eisenhower, personally adopted a friendlier attitude towards Nehru inviting him to the States, sending his own plane to fetch the Prime Minister from London where he was attending the Commonwealth meeting, congratulating him in his devotion to the cause of peace and disarmament, and conveying his greetings to Nehru on his 70th birthday in November 1959. "The important milestone in your career," he wrote "offers me the opportunity to felicitate you on your many accomplishments during the (time) that you have devoted to India and its people."[92] Clearly, the US attitude towards India was changing.

Politically too the US was becoming more outgoing towards India. Realising that the balance was shifting in Asia, John Foster Dulles made an offer of supporting an "Indian Monroe doctrine" in Southern Asia in 1953, and evoked in 1958 the possibility of India even taking over China's seat in the Security Council ; and in 1958 military aid was given to India.

Even more important was US pressure on Nehru to give asylum to the Dalai Lama after the abortive revolt in 1959. The Tibetan dissidents (a) sought US "intersession with the Indian Government to permit their passage to India", and (b) requested US supplies for the Tibetan resistance. The US Administration accepted both the requests.[93] Closely watching the Tibetan situation, the US administration apparently had come to the conclusion that, for safety reasons, the Dalai Lama had no other choice but to leave his kingdom. Neighbouring India, clearly, was the only country where he could seek asylum. Given the deteriorating state of Sino-Indian relations, and given the Dalai Lama's large popularity among the Indians the US administration apparently calculated that his difficulties could hardly be ignored by Nehru.

But, Nehru himself was in a predicament. What should he do? How should he handle the new situation? Not giving asylum to the Dalai Lama would unavoidably result in the Tibetan leader's disappearance (death or imprisonment)—a disappearance that would generate a massive public disapproval, which he could hardly face, given all the difficulties he was facing within the country; but, on the other hand, welcoming him would inevitably worsen India's relations with the Chinese—a situation that he apparently wanted to avoid as far as possible. Though, finally, Nehru decided to grant asylum, it was clearly a half-hearted step, since he disallowed the Dalai Lama to establish a Government in exile, and since he refused him the right to function politically. Clearly, this was one of those Nehruvian decisions which hardly satisfied anyone—neither the Dalai Lama, nor the Indian public nor even the Chinese.

The US Government apparently had much to do with Nehru's decision. In fact, according to American sources, their pressures were crucial if not decisive. The difficulties in which Nehru found himself with the Chinese, presumably pushed him, not to defy Washington too much and too openly, since in the end, he probably realised, that he would need US support in the event of any direct confrontation with the Chinese. But, it is interesting to note that, amidst all these difficulties, Nehru demanded US assistance in exchange. For, according to William Corson, US marine corps intelligence agent, who was working closely with Eisenhower, Nehru demanded American assistance to manufacture nuclear weapons. The US President, again according to American sources, was not inclined to make a direct transfer of nuclear technology, but reached a compromise with Nehru under which 400 Indian students would be received by US universities for nuclear technology.[94] They were received, and their education indeed had great impact in the development of Indian nuclear technology.

Coincidental Mutation in the International System

But, all these US overtures towards India coincided with the rapid mutation of the overall international situation—a mutation that really saved Nehru from going very far in the direction of the US. Asia was waking up. Colonialism was on the defensive. Nationalism was proliferating all over the third world. Non-alignment was expanding and fast becoming an assertive and even defiant trans-national subsystem with the close collaboration between Nehru, Nasser and Tito. Even more significant was that in the aftermath of Stalin's death in March 1953, and the introduction of slow but landmark changes in the Soviet diplomatic behaviour; Moscow turned more and more towards India. And by the time the Tibetan revolt occurred, the Soviet leaders were heavily involved with India, and were fast distancing themselves from China. In fact by 1959, it was increasingly becoming evident that Sino-Soviet relations were deteriorating and were showing signs of becoming confrontational. For Nehru this was a welcome development. For he could now not only offset gentle American pressures to join them, but use the new and friendly Soviet policy to confront the Chinese. In sum the global environment had changed considerably.

The pressures on Nehru were thus off both from the US and the Soviet Union. Nehru had now reached the leveraged diplomatic stage that he always wanted since independence. And no more did he have to focus only on the US and Great Britain. He was now able to turn the changing international situation to India's advantage by being friendly with all of them. Aid came from all the developed countries. India was now considered by all the great powers as an important country to turn to. And, India, once again, was on the wing, as it had been in early and mid-fifties when its role at the macro international level was highly appreciated.

PUBLIC OPINION AND FOREIGN POLICY

But, this process of welcome change internationally coincided with the emergence of growing indigenous discontent regarding Nehru's foreign policy.

Paradoxically his problems with his public pertained to the Communist world. Much of the difficulties within his government and with the public opinion was concerning his benign attitude towards the Communist countries. A widespread feeling appeared to be spawning in the country that not everything was fine with India's policy vis-à-vis the Communist world. Something had gone wrong.

Hungary

The first festering issue was Hungary. Nehru was not spared during the 1956 Hungarian uprising when the Soviet Army marched into Budapest to brutally suppress what was clearly a popular revolt. Hungary was the small faraway European nation, and one would have thought that the Indians would gloss over the dramatic events that had seized the country.

But, this was not the case; for Nehru received the first taste of popular resentment over foreign policy decision relating to this small battered East European country. India had abstained in the UN General Assembly on a US resolution condemning Soviet military intervention in Hungary. Worse was its decision to vote with the Soviet bloc against a five-nation resolution calling for free elections in Hungary under UN control. Though it is not clear at what level such a decision was taken, it created an uproar in the country led by the highly respected socialist leader Jayaprakash Narayan.[95] According to Mathai, there was "no action of the government in foreign affairs that provoked so much hostility in Parliament and elsewhere."[96] Important leaders, belonging to different political spectrum demanded that Krishna Menon be removed from the political scene, since he was the one who had apparently taken the decision to vote with the Communist bloc on the resolution.

However, notwithstanding the Indian stance in the UN, Nehru did remain active behind the curtains. He did attempt to take some discreet diplomatic initiatives.Though, he did not criticise the Russians publicly, a note was handed to Foreign Minister Andrei Gromyko in which India declared that: "The events in Hungary shatter the belief of millions of people who had begun to view the USSR as the defender of peace and the rights of the weakest people."[97] The Indian diplomats in Eastern Europe too were hard at work. K.P.S.Menon, the Indian Ambassador to Moscow and Budapest and Jagan Nath Khosla, Indian Minister to Prague, had meetings with Hungarian leaders in which they criticised the treatment meted out to Imre Nagy, and demanded that the UN observers and the Secretary General be invited, and that free elections be held. The Hungarian leaders were warned that if Hungary did not accept Indian proposals, the Indians would not stand by them.[98] Nehru also had a meeting with Zhou Enlai in December 1956 in which he expressed his opposition to the Soviet invasion of Hungary.[99] Though, Zhou Enlai favoured the Soviet action, this did not deter Nehru from expressing his critical views . But, all this was done discreetly. The Indian Prime Minister had the disconcerting habit of being diplomatic vis-à-vis the communist world—at least publicly.

But, pressures on India continued unabated. Nehru began to receive requests from dissident Hungarians, via his own diplomats, to intervene on their behalf. His own most senior civil servant in the Ministry of External affairs, N.R.Pillai, usually very cautious, was pushing him to reconsider India's policy on Hungary "with a view to deciding our attitude in the light of principles we have been advocating."[100] Jayaprakash Narayan had denounced Nehru's hesitations. He warned him that he would be guilty of abetting "a new imperialism more dangerous than (the) old because it masquerades as revolutionary." Even the Indian Ambassador in Washington, G.L. Mehta warned him of the serious concern in America that India was silent in Hungary but had belligerently denounced western imperialism in Egypt. If he did not follow the same principle openly, warned the Ambassador, in relation to Hungary, Nehru would weaken UN authority against aggression in Egypt.[101] His own sister, Mrs Pandit, who was, at the time, the High Commissioner in London and Ireland, wrote to Nehru that she was going to Ireland to explain the Indian stand on Hungary as she was inundated with letters of protest from there.[102]

Finally, Nehru backtracked openly. For he had so far expressed his opposition to the Russians only behind the curtain. Now, under pressure, he openly denounced the Soviet action. What he was doing behind the scenes was now abandoned since it had no effect either on the Soviets or on the Hungarian Government. Publicly he became less prudent vis-à-vis the Soviet Union. On 14 November 1956, jointly with Burma, Indonesia and Ceylon, he signed a statement that criticised the UK, French and Israeli action against Egypt, and Soviet action in Hungary. The Hungarian events were the first crisis that marked a real "check which public opinion exercised on the Government of India in the sphere of foreign affairs."[103]

As a possible retaliation to the USSR, Nehru sent friendly signals to the US where he went in December 1956 and where he lauded the US' "morally leading" role in the Middle East and Hungary. Nehru was particularly impressed by the fact that Eisenhower took a benign position on Hungary. He told Nehru that he did not want war to break out because of the events in Hungary. He realises and accepts, he declared, that Hungary will continue to remain in the socialist camp.[104]

But it was not only Indian public opinion that pushed Nehru to take a critical position; Tito, in whom he had great trust, was also an important influence in changing Nehruvian attitude towards the Russian action in Hungary.

Nehru's attitude, on the whole was rather paradoxical. He would have probably continued to publicly adopt a prudent or even a pro-Soviet attitude (as was the case in the UN), had there been no rumblings of discontent that finally pushed him to openly criticise the Russians.

Tibet

Tibet was the other issue. Within the government, the most dissident and the most concerned voice emanated from Vallabhbhai Patel, the Deputy Prime Minister who was also the Minister of the Interior. He had never claimed and showed any great interest in larger international issues. This he had left to Nehru – to construct the framework and take the initiatives; but it was different regarding what was happening in India's backyard and in its neighbourhood. And Tibet was within India's neighbourhood given its strategic proximity and given the long relations India had forged with Tibet going back a millennium. In a long letter (7 November 1950) to the Prime Minister, Patel went on record to express concern at the Chinese Communist occupation of Tibet, and drew Nehru's attention at the "new threat that has developed in the east and the north-eastern areas of India."[105] He lambasted India's Ambassador, K.M.Pannikar. for having allowed the Chinese to instil in him "a false sense of confidence in their so-called desire to settle the Tibetan problem by peaceful means."[106] And, he warned Nehru of the adverse ramifications the new geopolitical situation could have on the "pro-Mongoloid" population residing on the Indian side of the border, and on the further radicalisation of the Communist Party of India , already up in arms against the government. He strongly recommended that India should conduct "a military and intelligence appreciation of the Chinese threat to India both on the frontier and to internal security."[107] Patel even evoked the idea of India reconsidering its support to Communist China's entry to the UN.

The letter was indeed a strong statement by someone who was next to Nehru in the governmental hierarchy. But, this was not the only occasion he expressed his concern regarding the Chinese Communists. As far back as June 1949, when China was in the midst of a civil war, he had written to Nehru that "we have to strengthen our position in Sikkim as well as in Tibet. The further we keep away the Communist forces the better. Tibet has long been detached from China. I anticipate that as soon as the Communists have established themselves in the rest of China they will destroy its (Tibet's) autonomous existence." In sum, even before the conclusion of the civil war, Patel had already told Nehru that "you have to consider carefully your policy towards Tibet in such circumstances and prepare for now for that eventuality."[108]

Patel indeed had a geopolitical vision, and realised the vital importance of keeping adversaries far away from India's borders.

Patel had also expressed his views on other foreign policy issues—such as referring Kashmir to the UN, or abstaining from taking a firm stand on Pakistan, or hesitating over taking rapid action to free Goa from the Portuguese.

Undoubdtedly, Nehru was a great visionary on macro international issues, but it was Patel who was a proponent of taking firm diplomatic positions whenever India's national interest was at stake.

What about the others in the government.? Were there no other members of the Cabinet who adopted positions similar to that of Patel on Nehru's policies when it came to neighbours, particularly in the north?

There was a general reluctance on the part of Nehru's colleagues to interject on foreign affairs, for the Prime Minister was very sensitive on the subject since he had convinced himself that he alone was the expert. But, Tibet was different. It was an area with which India had myriad cultural and religious ties going back a millennium. Nehru's monopoly over foreign affairs—at least on issues proximate to India—was therefore no more completely exclusive. On one occasion in November 1950 the question of the Himalayas was raised in the Cabinet. When one member (N.V.Gadgil) raised the question of the northern areas. He was apparently snubbed by Nehru with the remark: "Don't you realise that the Himalayas are there", whereupon another member ventured to suggest (K.M.Munshi) that "Tibetans had crossed the Himalayas and invaded Kanauj"[109] thus indirectly challenging Nehru's assertion regarding the invulnerability of the Himalayas.

With increasing Chinese assertion in Tibet, and the consequent political deterioration in the area, leading to the fleeing of the Dalai Lama to India, Nehru had no leverage left on Tibet. In fact, he never had any – neither before the Chinese Communists came into power nor after they had installed themselves.

Patel certainly was farsighted in predicting the shape of things to come in the north, but he was not realistic enough to realise that India could do very little to forestall the Chinese Communist determination to occupy Tibet. The Indian armed forces, fragmented as they had become after the partition of the country, hardly had any clout to change the northern political landscape. The arms India possessed were of World War II vintage, most of which were ineffective because of the paucity of spare parts; and the only country capable of assisting India—the US—was not interested in coming to the assistance of India at the time. Odd as it may seem, since

Communist China was Washington's declared enemy, the disgruntlement with India was equally great.

The armed conflict with Pakistan furthermore had aggravated India's security concerns. If India was helpless in the face of the Chinese Communist advancement in Tibet, it was either unable or unwilling to use its superior clout to place Pakistan on the defensive. The political determination was lacking.

So India was faced with the horrendous geopolitical situation of simultaneously confronting two adversaries on two fronts—a situation that remains with India to this day.

Compounded to all this, consider the important fact that the Gandhian non-violent tradition, spawning over fifty years, had hardly prepared the leadership to face such bruising issues as wars and conflicts; for they had devoted much of their political lives peacefully throwing the British out of the country; whereas the Chinese communists were different; for they had acquired considerable experience violently battling their adversaries in the Chinese civil war. This is a consideration that can hardly be ignored in any analysis of Sino-Indian confrontations.

So Nehru had to face the geopolitical realities of the Chinese Communists sitting on the roof of the world looking down on Indian territories over which they had laid their claims. Impassed by Pakistan and humiliated by China, Nehru's diplomatic difficulties were on the increase. And the informed public was increasingly becoming aware and even irritated about the worrisome situation.

It would be of course unfair to conclude that Nehru was unaware of the geopolitical realities, and of the potential dangers the Chinese presence in Tibet represented to India. For, he had expressed in numerous messages to his subordinates in the MEA his fears of China, and had communicated his insistence on being firm in their negotiations with the Chinese on Tibet regarding the validity of the McMahon line that separated India from China.

Consider Nehru's frank and brutal remarks on 18th March, 1958 to G. Parthasarathy, on the eve of the latter's departure to China as India's Ambassador. He came straight to the point: "So GP what has the Foreign Office told you—Hindi-Chini Bhai-Bhai? (India and China are brothers). Don't you believe it. I do not trust the Chinese one bit, despite the historic agreement of 'Panchsheel'" Nehru then went on to say: "The Chinese are arrogant, devious, deceptive and thoroughly unreliable. In fact, they have chosen to be inherently anti-India. Your brief from me is, therefore,to be extremely vigilent about the totality of Chinese intentions. All your telegrams should be marked 'top secret' and marked to me alone. You should be especially careful to see that "Krishna" (Krishna Menon) did not see your telgrams. You should also be very careful in your meetings and discussions with Krishna. All three of us share a common world view, but Krishna allows his thinking and assessments to be clouded on the matter of our relations with China."[110]

But, on the other hand, it would be fair to conclude that he made a monumental error of abandoning his original strategy—agreed upon with his subordinates—of linking the Chinese acceptance of the Sino-Indian border (McMahon line) with the Indian acceptance of Tibet as a part of China in the agreement on Sino-Indian treaty on Tibet. But, he abandoned the idea of maintaining this linkage between the two issues on the recommendation of the Indian Ambassador who counselled to Nehru that the border question should not be raised at the time of the Sino-Indian negotiations on Tibet. "On reconsideration," he wrote to the Foreign Secretary on 6 September 1952, "I accept Shri Panikkar's advice that we should not make specific mention about the frontiers."

Sino-Indian War

The 1962 Sino-Indian conflict was even worse for Nehru. Things got even more out of hand. His control over the decision making was even more shaken. Informed public opinion was even more strident in its criticism. In fact, even before the actual explosion of the crisis Nehru had come under serious pressure to abandon what was considered by many as a soft policy towards China. The Prime Minister's decision to give asylum to the Dalai Lama in the aftermath of the 1959 Tibetan revolt, and the failure to sponsor a UN resolution favouring China's admission was due to an anticipated fear of a strong public reaction. Furthermore, his original idea of ceding to the Chinese on the delineation of the Sino-Indian border was scuttled by a ferocious public debate.[111]

After India's defeat in the Sino-Indian War, it was Nehru personally rather than the Government that was targeted. "For the first time in his life," wrote the Indian journalist Kuldip Nayar, "Nehru heard his countrymen say he had betrayed them. Never before had Nehru faced such a hostile Parliament; it was not in a mood to accept any compromise formula on the Aksai Chin road. Nehru's option were rapidly closing."[112] Even some of his senior Cabinet colleagues, "including Morarji Desai and Jagjivan Ram started to say that Nehru had neglected the Sino-Indian border in an effort to have good relations with China."[113] Nehru's own anguish at the reaction of Parliament is illustrated in his letter to the Defence Minister, Krishna Menon on 28 October 1962 in which he lamented: "I do not know how I shall explain to the Parliament why we have been found lacking in equipment."[114]

It is difficult to imagine that, but for the strong public reaction against the Chinese, Nehru would have allowed the Sino-Indian relations "to reach almost a vanishing point," or would have sought large-scale Western aid even after the border war.[115]

The paradox of all this was the dichotomic reaction of the informed public opinion on international affairs. Nehru's inability to face up to the Chinese on Tibet and on the Sino-Indian border thus spawned the vigilance of Indian public opinion making them more suspicious of communism and more distrustful of Nehru's diplomacy.

The crisis that India faced with Communist China made public opinion anti-Chinese, the paranoid aspects of Stalinism had generated reservations about the USSR and what it stood for, and any crisis that the Communist world faced generated either serious disappointment or firm opposition. In sum the traditional benign Indian perception of the Communist world was changing.

Consider the Sino-Soviet crisis. For many Indians, who had looked up to communism as a form of harmonious internationalism, and as a possible solution to the miseries of the world, saw the emerging Sino-Soviet dispute as a confirmation of the overpowering influence of nationalism and national interests in the behaviour of most communist states.

Non-alignment, around which Nehru had shaped India's foreign policy was indeed in tatters. And he himself was so seriously affected by this setback, that many claim that his death, couple of years later, was brought about by the humiliating Indian defeat. For Nehru, everything had crumbled, his ideas, his foreign policy, and even his image in his own country where millions had loved him for so many years.

The most disconcerting revelation about the Sino-Indian war is a CIA report recently declassified on the subject. It would seem that most leading members of the Government were of the opinion that India should avoid an armed confrontation with the Chinese as they were better organised and better equipped. The army did not favour armed confrontation; Nehru personally was of the same opinion, not to speak of Krishna Menon, who apparently declared to a full Cabinet meeting in August 1962, that India's position in Ladakh was "untenable," and that in any major border confrontation India's forward positions would be wiped out, and that the Chinese would push the Indians far beyond their 1960 claim without any serious resistance.[116]

An yet, notwithstanding this awareness of military weakness, the Indians took the decision on 18 September 1962 to evict the Chinese from areas illegally occupied by them, particularly the Dhola area at the base of the Thagla Ridge. For the Chinese, this was a welcome opportunity to massively strike at India, for which they had already prepared themselves. . .

Was the Indian decision to take military action the result of a calculation, based on some analysis, that the Chinese would not take any massive action; or was it the result of pressures emanating from the Indian public that catalysed Nehru to take the initiative?

It was probably the combination of both the factors that catalysed the Indian decision.

In hindsight, it would seem that the Indian reasoning was based on wrong information. For the Chinese were indeed prepared and determined to attack India; and the Indian public opinion was not that glaringly exigent for the war that Nehru could not resist.

In any event, it was an action that India could have avoided.

NEHRU AND NUCLEAURISATION

Nehru was the real force behind the nuclearisation of India. He realised its cruciality in the economic development of the country. And he really was the one who established its superstructure. Soon after independence an Atomic Energy Commission (AEC) was established (1948) with government ownership of uranium, thorium and other relevant material needed for nuclear development. And in the 1950s, plans were established, and resources were explored that were needed to develop a atomic energy programme. The first nuclear cooperation agreement was concluded with France in 1951. A Department of Atomic Energy, within the government, was established, in 1954 with Dr. Homi Bhabha, a leading Indian scientist as its Secretary. And in 1955 ground was broken at Trombay for the first nuclear reactor named Aspara.

Nehru had also gone on record, repeatedly and publicly, his firm opposition to its utilisation for producing nuclear weapons. The tragic experience of its utilisation for the massive destruction of Hiroshima and Nagasaki towards the end of World War II was very much in his mind, and was evoked in many of his speeches.

By the end of Nehru's mandate in 1964, India had thus developed a reasonably advanced nuclear capability.

While Nehru's opposition to nuclear weapons was legendary, one wonders if the idea of a India going nuclear in weaponry did not flair his mind after all the armed confrontations India had experienced, including the humiliating defeat in the Sino-Indian war of 1962, and after apparent signs were becoming visible of the Chinese determination to go nuclear. Even, as early as 1948, at the time of the establishment of the Atomic Energy Commission, Nehru had alluded to the issue: "We must," he declared, "develop this atomic energy quite apart from war—indeed we must develop it for the purpose of using it for peaceful purposes—Of course if we are compelled as a nation to use it for other purposes, possibly no pious sentiments of any of us will stop the nation from using it that way."[117] And if one were to compound to all this the important fact that his principal scientific adviser, Homi Bhabha, was not against such an acquisition, as it surfaced after Nehru's death, and after the Chinese had effectuated a nuclear explosion in 1965.[118]

In any event, according to the CIA report from India, dated 22 October 1964, "The Government of India (GOI) has all of the elements to produce a nuclear weapon, and it has the capability to assemble a bomb quickly."[119] Furthermore, it declared in an another report, of 6 November 1964, "that construction of a plant for plutonium metal production, which is necessary for weapons manufacture" was under way and was expected to become operational in 1966.[120]

While no hard evidence is available regarding the evolution of Nehru's thinking on the issue, there, is no doubt that Nehru personally encouraged the development of a militarily capable nuclear infrastructure. There are nonetheless some indications and some signs that the whole subject was not absent from his mind. Consider, the Indo-US discussions in 1958 on according the Dalai Lama political asylum after the abortive Tibetan revolt against the Chinese. The US pressure on India to give asylum was apparently used by Nehru, according to the American sources, to attempt to obtain nuclear weapons in exchange. While the US government declined to give such aid, it did, however, agree to facilitate a few hundred young Indian scientists for nuclear education and training in American universities.

Another anecdotal evidence appears to confirm, implicitly, some innovation in his thinking on nuclear weapons. In 1960 Kenneth Nichols, a former US army engineer, who played a significant role in the Manhattan Project, represented Westinghouse in discussions on power plant construction in India. At a meeting with Nehru and Bhabha he relates that Nehru turned to Bhabha and asked: "Can you develop an atomic bomb?" Bhabha assured him that he could, and in reply to Nehru's next question about time, he estimated that he would need about a year to do it—he concluded by saying to Bhabha: "Well, don't do it until I tell you to."[121]

Nehru's uncertainties regarding nuclear options became even more evident when the US Ambassador to India, under instructions from President John Kennedy, had offered India nuclear weapons. Nehru apparently hesitated, but did speak to very few people, including Indira Gandhi and Homi Bhabha, both of whom recommended that he should accept the American offer.[122]

EVALUATION

If one were evaluate the role of the personality factor on the three components of foreign policy–routine, visible and macro—as we have defined them in the introduction—it could be argued that while on routine and macro issues, Nehru exercised decisive control, visible issues slowly slipped out of his hands. They were no more completely under his control. This became more and more evident a few years before his disappearance from the political scene. He was held accountable, and often had to cede. Under pressure he had to introduce some changes on foreign policy issues. The aura that had surrounded Nehru for his knowledge and performance in international affairs was seriously tarnished at the fag end of his political life. For the Nehruvian failures and setbacks in foreign policy shrouded the successes he had encountered in the past on global international issues.

He can hardly escape the judgement on the issues that India faced directly.

If one were to accept K.J. Holsti's argumentation that foreign policy essentially "is the general capacity of a state to control the behaviour of others,"[123] then it is hardly possible to give full marks to Nehru.

He was impassed by fragmented and weak Pakistan, humiliated and defeated by China, questioned by the international community on Kashmir, criticised for having aggravated India's insecurities and vulnerabilities by a two front exposure (Pakistan and China), and was not spared for having lost the influence that the British had established in South Asia.

It was a sad performance and a tragic failure in areas in which he had outshone the others during much of his political career. Gone indeed were the days, when the Indian Parliament, just after Indian independence, listened to him with rapt attention all that he said about the world How history will judge him, only time will tell; but the close distance from which we are watching him, it does not seem to have been much of a performance in India's foreign policy so far as India's national interests were concerned. A top-secret evaluation of Nehru by the British High Commission in India was far from complimentary. If anything, it was frankly negative. He was assessed as someone who was "overidealistic, inexperienced in foreign affairs, and far too vain" to make any objective evaluation.[124] Louis Mountbatten made different evaluations at different times. It was almost chameleon. When he was still the Governor General of India, he compared Nehru to Sardar Patel. " Nehru," he declared, "was not a practical statesman at all. Patel's feet were on the ground, he was running the country. Nehru's head was in the clouds."[125] In 1964, on the occasion of Nehru's funeral he declared —perhaps carried away emotionally by the tragic occasion— that Nehru was "one of the greatest men the world has known;"[126] but a decade later in the seventies while making an objective evaluation of Nehru to his biographer, S. Gopal, he declared that "If Nehru had died in 1958, he would have been the greatest statesman of the 20th century."[127] All this objectively is perhaps not far from truth, even if it is a little contradictory, for if one evaluates his remarkable contribution to the development of political democracy, and secularism, both of which are still a part of the Indian system, he shall indeed be remembered; but, on the other hand, he sadly lacked Gandhi's sagacity, Mountbatten's pragmatism, Churchill's determination, and Stalin's brutality— almost all of which are indispensible for the successful pursuit of national foreign policy. In any event, with the passage of time, Indian public opinion, revisiting Nehru, at the turn of this century, perceives him differently and evaluates him harshly by ranking him as third among the Prime Ministers who contributed most to Indian's development.[128] What a downfall; what a descent in the eyes of Indian public opinion.

LAL BAHADUR SHASTRI

Chapter II

LAL BAHADUR SHASTRI
9 JUNE 1964—11 JANUARY 1966

Lal Bahadur Shastri was different from his predecessor—in fact very different, if not the opposite. He was a diminutive, self-effacing and a shy person who came from a poor lower middle class orthodox joint Hindu family, whose members earned their modest livelihood as school teachers, or as postal employees. His middle class family was archetypal of India of those years—families that had managed to painfully extricate themselves from the poverty line through some minimal education, but who nonetheless faced a precarious material existence

Formation

Shastri really had no environmental exposure to the Western world. There was nothing in his day-to-day life that contained even a smattering of occidentalisation: the attire was exclusively Hindu; the language was Hindi/Urdu, the food was vegetarian, and the family surroundings were a microcosm of orthodox Hindu India. In sum, he was the most authentic Indian among his contemporaries. There was indeed nothing in his life that resembled even remotely what Nehru embodied.

But, like most middle class families with an educational verve, Shastri did have some intellectual exposure. He apparently read an array of books written by western intellectuals, including Kant, Hegel, Marx, Engels, Harold Laski, Aldous Huxley, etc. Bertrand Russell, he claimed, was his "mentor." When in London for the first time, in his capacity as Prime Minister, he wanted to meet Russell. Prime Minister Harold Wilson volunteered to invite him. But Shastri apparently told him "No, I must go to him. He is my mentor."[129]

Shastri certainly was no Nehru in terms of ideas, but he did have the intellectual weight and motivation to write a biography of the French Scientist, Mme Curie (in Hindi).

To what extent all this intellectual baggage he acquired through reading, had any palpable influence on his political behaviour, it is indeed difficult to say. There are no indications that all this was translated to real action.

But this is not only Shastri. It happens to many of us. All that we have read is a passing phase and invariably does not have any impactful ramifications on our lives; whereas, there are others, more sensitive and more in search of ideas, whose lives get transmuted, and whose behaviour may well be linked with the intellectual bagage they have consumed.

His formal education was contextual. Against the backdrop of growing political agitation in the country, with which he identified himself as an adolescent, he was intellectually influenced by ideas pertaining to nationalism in the country and elsewhere. Carried away by Gandhi's call to young Indians to join indigenous national institutions for university education, he entered Kashi Vidyapeeth, a national institution established in February 1921 with Hindi as the medium of instruction. There, he underwent a four year course leading to the so-called Shastri degree, later recognised as equivalent to Bachelor of Arts.

His pursuit of formal education not only enlarged his data intake, as is generally the case, but resulted in impregnating him with three strands of a basic principle— the strands of secularism, nationalism and public service— all of which remained with him and influenced his political behaviour in later life.

Secularism may seem a contradiction in terms with traditional Hinduist upbringing, given the fact that most north Indian Hindu joint families had a tendency of distancing themselves from Muslims, avoiding any social contact with them, and considering them as less cultivated and as inferior in status. This was indeed a rampant phenomenon among North Indian middle class families of pre-partition India, and may have been one of the deep-rooted sociological underpinnings that may have contributed to the aggravation of communalism. Though Shastri did not appear to have any effective and regular social interaction with the Muslims, he somehow escaped this widespread jaundiced perception since he was brought up in a region where it was customary for Hindu families to actually hire *Maulvis,* learned men of Muslim faith, to teach their children the Urdu language, social etiquette and cosmopolitan culture—all of which were perceived as important, and in all of which the educated Muslims in his area of origin were considered more competent than the Hindus. This remained with

Shastri the rest of his life, for politically he made no distinction between Hindus and Muslims.

The second was nationalism to which he was exposed to in a high school in Benares (now Varanasi) and by its rampant emergence in the country. Most of Shastri's life in pre-independent India was therefore devoted to nationalism that resulted in seven imprisonment's stretching over nine years. More than anything else it was this particular strand that influenced him markedly, since the political landscape of the country, during the early Shastri years, was heavily coloured by nationalism. In fact, he left school in 1921 in response to Gandhi's call for the boycott of schools and joined the civil disobedience movement.

The third strand, public service, came to him from home, from school and from his readings of great Indian personalities; and when Shastri was not in prison or actively involved in one nationalist campaign or the other against the British, he devoted his time rendering service to his fellow-citizens. Public service, in fact, had become his chief avocation through the Servants of India Society—a society of dedicated Hindu social activists where members undertook "to lead a pure personal life" and "to work for the advancement of the people" without distinction of caste and creed.[130] Shastri began to work for the society at the age of 21, and remained a dedicated member throughout his life actually living with the deprived, with a very little allowance that he was given by the society. The measure of the Society's high moral standard can be discerned from the fact that all members were obligated to declare their assets at the time of joining, and thereafter every five years. "It was," said Shastri, "due to my life membership of the Society that I got to serve my country the most. The Society has been instrumental in inculcating in me the true meaning of the term—servants of the people."[131]

Perception

Shastri had no fixed ideological orientations. Apart from the fact that he probably convinced himself—like most educated middle class Indians of his generation, background and status—that some sort of socialism was good for the country, he had no fixed views and no clear-cut ideological or political orientations. And if he had any, there is no way of finding out since he hardly penned anything on the subject or ever made any public statements to this effect before the independence of India. Later, after independence , Shastri was, it is true, given the responsibility of proposing a resolution on "Democracy and Socialism" at the 65th session of the Indian National Congress at Bhubaneshwar in January 1964, but this is because

Nehru, the author of the resolution, was unable to do so because of his illness. However, while proposing the resolution he tempered his remarks on socialism by warning against assigning too great a responsibility to the State in the trade sector—an indication of the state of his political thinking. In any event he had always defined himself as a "Gandhian socialist" which some thought was meaningless.[132]

In fact, when he reached the political summit, he did consider that the complex non-monolithic government India had established was causing bureaucratic delays, including enormous waste and harm. It seems he favoured loosening up, and had entrusted the task to L.K.Jha, his principal secretary. *The Times of India* then ran a story in December 1965 saying that the government was contemplating liberalizing some of the less useful controls. It was probably the first time that the word "liberalization" emerged in mainstream Indian lexicon.

By temperament and by education Shastri really was a pragmatic person. At the Kashi Vidyapeeth college, the first national educational institution established in Uttar Pradesh, he learnt from his teacher, Bhagwan Das, a basic philosophy that remained with him all his life, and that determined much of his political behaviour. Das had inculcated in his students a particular philosophical methodology that he termed *samanvay wad,* or "the integration of different points of views." This in effect meant that within diverging views on a subject there was always an element of truth in each. Nothing was completely wrong and nothing was completely right, he insisted. He taught his students to say "this is also right" and not "only this is right."[133] Bhagwan Das' influence can be discerned from the fact that Shastri wrote a thesis on " The Philosophy of Dr Bhagwan Das" in 1925 for which he was awarded the so-called Shastri degree—a title that was added to his first and middle name.

In all probability, it was Bhagwan Das' influence that made him a pragmatic person—always avoiding extremist views and always rejecting "theories of everything" that united "all the laws of nature into a single statement."[134] This was indeed a major departure from most Indian intellectuals who got carried away by strictly defined theories of Marxism, which had an explanation for all actions and for all behaviour, and which was projected as a universal solvent of all of India's problems.

It was perhaps this frame of mind that equipped him to distance himself from left-wing theories of those years of which Nehru was the leading proponent. And, yet, paradoxically, if there was anyone who had inspired him—besides Gandhi—it was Nehru with whom he worked very closely throughout his life. In any event, much more than his political contemporaries, since his association with Nehru went back to the thirties.

In many ways this mirrored the dimension of the man—as someone who respected Nehru as a nationalist leader, but not what he proposed in terms of ideological commitment. He could separate these two strands—often very difficult in the lives of most people.

So Lal Bahadur, rising through the ranks to become the Prime Minister, had really no fixed perceptions of the world, no real commitment to any ideology, and no real fascination with any systemic analysis. "I never found Shastri," confirms one of his collaborators, "quoting or referring to any of the philosophers, scientists, political or social thinkers he had read (the only exception was a reference to Bertrand Russell...and Gandhiji);"[135] Furthermore, he came to power with no experience of and hardly any knowledge of foreign affairs. In fact, before heading the Government, he had only three encounters with India's foreign policy—during the 1962 Sino-Indian war when he travelled to the North-East as India's Interior Minister to investigate the state of Indian defences; in 1963 when Nehru sent him to Nepal to assure the Nepalese that India's defeat at the hands of the Chinese would not affect it's commitments to Kathmandu; and in 1964 when he was briefly assigned the task of dealing with papers, files, etc., that came "to the Prime Minister from the Ministry of External affairs" during Nehru's last illness.[136] In sum, not much of a record in foreign policy, and not much of an experience in international affairs..

So stepping into the shoes of someone like Nehru, who had spent large parts of his political life reflecting on and dealing with international affairs, must have indeed been a daunting task; for dealing with internal affairs, to which Shastri was well-exposed, was one thing, but dealing with foreign affairs was totally another matter. For its complexity was much greater since one had to deal with other peoples and react to other situations, other cultures and other forms of behaviour, all of which were alien to Shastri.

FOREIGN AFFAIRS

On becoming Prime Minister, most of his early declarations on foreign affairs were therefore a faithful repeat of what Nehru had constructed. It could have hardly been otherwise for someone who had worked closely with Nehru for so many years, before and after independence, to introduce any mutations was scarcely possible—at least so soon after his disappearance.

Shastri had other things to turn to, including his own political survival. Besides, in a pluralistic society where mutations can only be incremental during the change of guards, the new Prime Minister, having been just elected consensually, could scarcely announce any visible changes. This became clearly evident in his very first broadcast to the nation on 11 June 1964. "In the realm of foreign affairs," he therefore declared, "we shall continue to seek friendship and develop our relations with all countries irrespective of their ideology or political systems. Non-alignment will continue to be the fundamental basis of our approach to world problems in our relations with other nations. It will be our special endeavour to further strengthen our relations with neighbouring countries."[137] In sum a declaration that announced Shastri's intentions to continue what Nehru had constructed in the sector of foreign policy.

DECISION MAKING

It would not be, therefore, incorrect to suggest that Shastri felt uncomfortable, and even insecure, while dealing with foreign affairs. And, it was probably this insecurity, compounded with his general penchant—already visible in his domestic actions—for an "institutional control of power,"[138] that catalysed him to take a series of initiatives that would institutionalise the decision making process in foreign policy–initiatives that introduced the much-needed structural changes.

Nehru neither needed nor wanted them for he considered himself well-equipped in this sector, whereas Shastri did need some structured institutional backing to handle foreign affairs. But these were not the only reasons. There was also his illness that must have pushed Shastri to institutionalise foreign affairs. As a cardiac case, he was afraid that a heavy involvement in foreign affairs might unavoidably lead to much greater travelling than he should undertake—even more so for a person who had never been outside India, with the exception of a brief trip to neighbouring Nepal.

His very first major decision, therefore, was to appoint a full-time Foreign Minister in the person of Swaran Singh who had the formal responsibility of running the Foreign Ministry. Swaran Singh, was more adept in foreign affairs than Shastri, since "he was a marvellous success in the negotiations with Pakistan on the Kashmir question," and since he had "infinite patience and inexhaustible capacity for endless talk," undoubtedly an asset in diplomacy.[139] Besides, the new Foreign Minister was a political lightweight and could not, as such, challenge or stymie any policy that Shastri may have liked to pursue. During his entire political career Swaran Singh had scrupulously avoided creating any political ripples, and was known to have carried out policies designed by his political superiors. This is what Shastri needed: someone to lighten his burden and with whom he could freely interact, but who would not frustrate or stand in the way of what the Prime Minister decided.

Contrastively, this would not have been the case had Indira Gandhi been promoted to foreign ministership from Information, the ministry she was actually holding at the time. Apparently she was waiting in the wings with the hope that she might be assigned such a responsibility. For one thing, she had far greater grounding and far greater contacts in foreign affairs than Shastri; for another, as Nehru's daughter she naturally acquired a privileged position in the country which Shastri could hardly challenge. Besides, there were indications that she was disdainful of his nomination as Prime Minister. Her vision of Shastri was that of a subaltern political figure "who had run errands at Anand Bhawan and copied letters and statements of Nehru."[140] In the eyes of Indira Gandhi he had no prescience and no intellectual sophistication to give a firm direction to the country. Basically, she declared, in an interview that he just did not have a modern mind, and that he was an orthodox Hindu full of superstitons.[141]

Most Indians, embodying the Western way of life, and enthralled by Westernism have a tendency of belittling those, hailing from the lower middle class, who are subaltern, poor and intellectually unsophisticated. Probably, this pattern of behaviour influenced Indira Gandhi's perception of Shastri. So, nominating Indira Gandhi as External Affairs Minister would have virtually meant losing hold on foreign policy. And this Shastri was not prepared to do. Besides, according to those who were in the corridors of power, the two mutually disliked each other, even more so at the time when, in the immediate aftermath of Nehru's disappearance, the power game was in full swing.[142]

During his mandate, Shastri realised that being a Prime Minister was different from being a Minister, since the head of the Government has to really lead, to act and to take the responsibility of governance. Therefore, despite his proverbial politeness, openness and softness towards others, he kept the reins of power firmly in his own hands.

His second major innovation was to appoint L.K.Jha, a civil servant as his secretary who had excellent national and international credentials.

Jha had joined the Indian Civil Service in 1936, and held a number of responsibilities before joining Shastri.

Jha conceptualised and articulated forward looking policies, including the famous industral policy resolution of 1956, that made mixed economy operational, and that provided the appropriate stimulus for the country's industrial development.

As Chairman of the Economic Administrative Reforms Commision—another responsibility he held—he was responsible for changing the direction of economic policy towards controlled deregulation as a preliminary step to full liberalization.

Jha was also India's principal representative to General Agreement For Tariff and Trade (GATT) conferences, and its chairman in 1957-58.

It can, therefore, be presumed that Shastri's decision to appoint him as his Principal Private Secretary was not so much for his experience in international affairs, as for his excellent credentials with a clear bias in favour of liberalization of the economy of the country. But Jha, growing in importance within months after his designation, became a crucial adviser in most sectors, including foreign affairs.

By changing the designation from Principal Private Secretary, during Nehru's time to Secretary to the Prime Minister, Shastri gave Jha a status that was visibly equal to all other secretaries of the government thus facilitating his task of consultation and coordination with all other ministries. That the political secretariat of the Prime Minister finally did become a major power centre is evident from the fact that it had the mandate "to prepare drafts of important speeches, statements and letters"[143]– undoubtedly a crucial responsibility since drafts invariably have the tendency of carrying the imprimatur of the drafter. According to one close political observer of the Shastri period, Jha "began having a finger in every pie and came to be called super-secretary."[144] Another observer argues that "he became a major influence in the area of foreign policy."[145] While Shastri, as suggested by one of his close collaborators, may have been a determined personality "who made his decisions,"[146] the inputs offered by the political secretariat, and particularly L.K. Jha, must have been a weighty dimension in foreign policy making, for it is now generally known that most important foreign policy decisions at the time stemmed from the Prime Minister's office of which even the Foreign Minister was not privy.

In his ongoing efforts to institutionalise changes, another important initiative, though abortive, was Shastri's attempt to create a committee of secretaries that would have coordinated the activities of the MEA with other ministries concerned with foreign affairs. The decision to take such an initiative was indeed far-sighted, for Shastri must have realised, soon after becoming Prime Minister, that foreign policy was no more just diplomacy in the traditional sense but a mix of so many diverse issues, including economy, defence, health, etc., that the foreign ministry could not possibly handle everything on its own. In practice this was already the case since Indian delegations to international conferences often included representatives of other specialised ministries; but to formally institutionalise it to shape foreign policy was not acceptable to the MEA. Perceiving this as a threat to its monopolistic control, the opposition was so stupendous and so prodigious that Shastri jettisoned the whole idea—undoubtedly unfortunate– since the successful operationalisation of this proposal would have made foreign policy a collective responsibility giving it a new dimension, an added solidity, and a far greater consensus than was the case at the time.

In these ongoing attempts to institutionally restructure foreign policy, a committee was appointed, during Shastri's time whose announced mandate was to investigate the whole foreign policy system. One can only presume that such an important decision could not have been taken without Shastri's explicit approval, particularly given the fact that L.K. Jha was all over the place closely monitoring most governmental actions. N.R. Pillai, a senior diplomat, was probably the right choice for such an assignment since, though retired, he had devoted his entire career to foreign affairs. Undoubtedly this was a far-sighted decision, for the foreign ministry did need some close analysis—in an epoch where diplomacy had become increasingly important. Nehru, with all his savviness in foreign affairs, probably did not need this type of investigation, but Shastri did with all his uncertainties in international relations. It was the first major report of the kind—a report that made three major recommendations: one was the expansion of economic and publicity divisions; the second was the appointment of a high-powered SecretaryGeneral to oversee the activities of the Ministry. But, the most important was the recommendation that "determination, evaluation and variation of policy" should be made first at the expertise level and then at the ministerial level thus giving importance to an expert analysis before decisions were taken at the ministerial level.[147]

With the Pillai recommendations, the Shastri period therefore also saw the incorporation of professionals in the decisional process for a long-term planning—a sort of a think tank. After the Indian debacle in the 1962 Sino-Indian conflict, the need for competent analysis of the changing international configuration of forces from a long-term Indian perspective was viewed as important. Some advance thinking at the expert level, as suggested by the Pillai Committee, was necessary before taking any political decisions. The increasing esotericism that shrouded international affairs clearly made it necessary that the decision makers had all the facts, all the options and all the analysis in hand which only the experts could provide. The think tank had an original mandate, for it was concerned not so much with the day-to-day issues as with macro issues that India may have to face in its foreign relations.

Myriad indeed were the issues on the table that needed information, reflection, analysis and finally a response. An array of questions needed answers: what are the problems that India would have to face in the future? How should they be tackled? In what direction is the international system heading? What about the configuration of international forces? Are they changing and how would they effect Indian diplomacy? All these and many other issues needed to be identified so that India could prepare itself with appropriate responses. The already existing MEA's small Research and Planning Division, engulfed with no real mandate and no real power, was elevated to the Policy Planning and Review division headed by a Joint Secretary and comprised a Deputy Secretary and four research officers.

The Shastri Government thus introduced new institutional structures incorporating new personnel, and reformed existing ones to give the Indian foreign policy establishment a sense of modernity that could respond efficaciously to changing circumstances and situations

The measure of the importance of these innovations can be discerned from the fact that none of them were jettisoned in later years; if anything most of them became permanent fixtures of the Indian decisional process, and were continuously refined and developed by successive Prime Ministers.

CONFIGURATION OF INTERNATIONAL FORCES

At the macro-international level Shastri attempted to introduce nuanced mutations in India's commitments and policies.

The increasing signs of Indian tie-up with the Soviet Union, characterised during the Nehru period, was not to Shastri's liking. In his vision, an excessive involvement with the Soviet Union was not in India's interest. Having no ideological hang ups for or against the Soviet Union, he felt that through a nuanced approach he could inject a degree of balance and homeostatis in India's foreign policy by opening up to the US than had been the case so far. The changing superpower configuration in the mid-sixties provided this opportunity. Khruschev, the great friend of India, had been overthrown, and the new leadership was showing signs of moving away from a confrontational posture that had characterised the Khruschev era.

The new Soviet leadership was putting a damper on its anti-American rhetoric and was constructing a more benign foreign policy. Within this new broad framework it was showing signs of becoming more friendly with Pakistan while continuing to assure the Indians of its determination to maintain privileged ties with them. But the Indians were not assured. If anything they were fearful that this new benign Soviet diplomacy might repeat itself vis-à-vis even the Chinese, another major adversary of India.

One of the most palpable manifestations of creating some distance with Moscow was Shastri's hesitation to continue Indo-Soviet negotiations on a arms deal. When Y.B. Chavan, his Minister of Defence, sought clearance to negotiate with Moscow for submarines and equipment for the army and the air force, Shastri hesitated and encouraged the minister to go to the UK to explore possibilities of a naval agreement.[148] Again, when China went nuclear, Shastri decided to turn to Great Britain for some possible protection. Discreet negotiations had also been initiated with the US by Bhabha for some nuclear assistance. It is more than unlikely that such exchanges with Washington on such a sensitive subject could have been carried out without Shastri's implicit agreement.

For Shastri the mutations in Soviet policy were a presager to introducing an element of benignity in India's policy also towards the US. Already there were indications that the US was looking at India differently; for after all, many argued, that it was the US that came to India's help by providing massive amount of arms during the Sino-Indian conflict. Again it was India which was the largest recipient of US development aid which stood at 28 billion rupees in February 1965—not to speak of the considerable—in fact the largest—US allocation of agricultural commodities to India under PL 480. Again there were many in the US administration who were willing to give nuclear aid to India.

The measure of new US perception also became apparent from the interest it took in Shastri's new economic thinking of mobilising the Indian economy to improve the living standards of Indians rather than continuing to focus and invest on the discredited process of industrialisation Nehru had introduced. In a long confidential note of 17 October 1964, running into 12 pages, the US Ambassador, Chester Bowles, welcomed Shastri's "deep interest in the welfare of the common man" and went on to give his frank views on how Indian economy could be improved.[149] "In closing," he wrote, "may I emphasise again that there is no need for India to choose between rapid economic growth and social justice in a free society. On the contrary, economic expansion is most rapid in those nations which provide the greatest freedom and incentive for the individual situation. My government and my countrymen are deeply committed to India's success as a democracy. But we believe that this success can be assured only if the welfare of the everyday Indian citizen is given higher priority in your national planning."[150]

Shastri's response to one of Bowles' notes is revelatory of the close interaction he had developed with the US Ambassador. "I am writing," he wrote, "to acknowledge, with many thanks, your letter of 1st September, enclosing a note on an integrated rural programme to increase food production. Your note, if I may say so, is an able and constructive analysis of our problems."[151] Clearly, he was on the same economic wave length as the Ambassador.

Bowles' numerous initiatives to write confidential notes to the Indian Prime Minister, and hold informal talks with him indicated the adjacency he had developed with the Indian leadership.[152]

The whole process of moving closer to India was initiated by President Kennedy, and notwithstanding tensions generated by Johnson's decision to postpone Shastri's June 1965 visit to the US, Shastri understood the importance of building bridges and accepted US President's new invitation to visit him on 1st February 1966. This was not to be since he died in Tashkent in January 1966.

So some degree of substantive diplomatic change vis-à-vis the great powers was already visible during Shastri's time. And, if he had not died suddenly, and had gone to the US in February 1966, what would have been the nature of Indian diplomacy, it is indeed difficult to say. But, from all indications it would seem that India may have taken a different road. Chester Bowles was a great proponent of Indo-US friendship, and had persuaded the Johnson Administration to take a benign look at India. In a top secret letter of 16 September 1964, he had declared to McGeorge Bundy, Special Assistant to the President, that "ominous development" of the Chinese nuclear weapons can be made to serve "our political purposes in India." India, he declared in this letter, "could take a position similar to that which we took in Cuba, i.e., an ultimatum to the Chinese to remove such installations or to see them blown up by the Indian Air Force."[153] He suggested that Washington should recommend to India that it should threaten China with military intervention in 1964 if it did not remove its defense installations from Tibet. The other options that India had was to go in for its own nuclear capability or reach an understanding with the US for a nuclear umbrella similar to one provided to Japan, the Scandinavian countries and other nations.

Though Bowles had apparently discussed the whole matter with Shastri, T.T. Krishnamachari, Y.B. Chavan and Morarji Desai before writing the letter. It is not clear what was Shastri's reaction. In any event, it is most unlikely that he would have accepted US offer—if it was really an offer—for Shastri was already independently going in the nuclear direction by keeping his options open.

FOCUS ON NEIGHBOURS

But, the substance of Shastri's foreign policy was essentially directed at India's neighbours. They were the ones with whom India really had problems, and they were the ones to whom Shastri gave diplomatic priority—much more than his predecessor. Unlike Nehru, who understood and was mentally overwhelmed with macro international issues, Shastri was neither distracted nor burdened nor even interested by faraway countries and issues. They were much beyond his intellectual framework; and were not really relevant to Indian concerns in a world that had yet to become globalised. For him, foreign affairs was the palpable environmental reality that surrounded India and that needed urgent attention.

So the focal point of foreign affairs was no more those macro declarations regarding the international system, and no more those dimensional diplomatic initiatives pertaining to the world at large that had overwhelmed Nehruvian diplomacy. Shastri, of course, did make declarations that concerned the world, but that was not where his mind was.

This pattern of his thinking became evident in the very first broadcast to the nation on 11 June 1964 after he became the Prime Minister. The basic thrust was on India's neighbours. "We have", he declared, "problems with some of them which we would like to settle peacefully and amicably on an equal and honourable basis."[154]

Especially highlighted were Pakistan and China as the two countries with whom India had problems. But the measure of contrast in his evaluation of the two countries' was indeed striking. While his remarks were benign, understanding and even friendly regarding Pakistan, announcing his determination to "reverse the tide" of adversity, he was vindictive about China emphasising the harm it had done to India. "China," he declared, "has wronged us deeply and offended our Government."[155]

Clearly, Shastri's very first public utterance sums up what he had in mind, and a forewarning of the shape of things to come. In fact, a few months after the inauguration of his mandate, he dispatched his Foreign Minister to Afghanistan, Myanmar (Burma), Sri Lanka and Nepal to signal his avidity to develop relations, and to evaluate the level of positive interaction he could expect from them. At the same time, with Shastri's personal "approval and sympathy"[156] a goodwill mission, headed by Jayaprakash Narayan, went to Pakistan in September 1964 to explore what could be done to defreeze relations between India and Pakistan. Through this goodwill mission, the Indian Prime Minister made it a point to convey to President Ayub Khan of Pakistan his wish to see him come to India "at his earliest convenience."[157]

As a part of his benign perception of Pakistan, and his bullish personal opinion was the underlying conviction that India could find some way out of the Indo-Pakistan impasse. Shastri had envisaged his own solution to the Kashmir problem"[158] a solution that basically "amounted to a rationalisation of the cease fire line", plus the ceding of some territory at the "southern end of the cease fire line."[159] In fact, in a secret message to Ayub Khan, through a trusted intermediary, he conveyed his determination not to allow obstructive constitutional provisions to stand in the way of anything they would agree upon after he had successfully faced the elections. We would of course never know if Shastri would have found a solution, since he died before; but it did mirror Shastri's inner conviction and outward perception that normalisation with Pakistan was possible and desirable.

To signal his determination to continue in the South Asian direction, Shastri also chipped in himself in this new and active diplomacy of friendly neighbourliness by making a stopover in Karachi in October 1964 to meet Ayub Khan after the nonaligned conference in Cairo in 1964, by inviting Sri Lankan Prime Minister, Srimavo Bandarnaike, to Delhi in October 1964, by flying to Calcutta to personally meet the King of Bhutan in January

1965, by visiting Nepal in November 1965 and by making an official visit to Myanmar in December 1965.

Adverse Perception Of China

On the other hand Shastri was suspicious of the Chinese. With the exception of a few general formalistic declarations underlining India's desire to develop relations with Beijing, he did not do anything to reach out to his northern neighbour. If anything, he maintained a high degree of animus towards Beijing. This became particularly evident after the Chinese showed reluctance to accept the non-aligned Colombo proposal to withdraw their seven Chinese posts from Ladakh's demilitarised zone as a compromise to start Sino-Indian negotiations on the border question.

A number of factors contributed to Shastri's adverse perception of China. There was, first of all, Nehru's death. Many in India—at least the ones who were close to him—attributed his end to the 1962 humiliating setback. Arguably Nehru was deeply affected by the Chinese onslaught; for many he took all this personally and probably contributed to the shortening of his life; "He lost,"lamented his sister Vijaya Lakshmi Pandit, "the will to live," while another remarked that "Nehru really died two years before his death. He died on the day the Chinese crossed our borders."[160]

Shastri too must have been affected by Nehru's sudden death since, outside of Nehru's family, he was very close to him and to his family, so much so that during the nationalist movement of the early forties he was hiding in Nehru's Allahabad House. Shastri admired Nehru and lived in his shadow for decades—perhaps more than any of his political contemporaries. It was not so much out of obsequiousness as it was out of admiration for what he had done for the country.

He too must have been rankled by the first military setback suffered at the hands of a neighbour for whom, many were convinced, India had done a great deal internationally. Shastri, perhaps more than the others, since the Chinese threat had given" rise to a host of problems within the sphere of the Home Ministry;"[161] of which he was in-charge; and furthermore, it would seem that, during and after the reverses of the war, "was acutely conscious of the responsibilities which he carried"[162] regarding India's security. Besides it was Shastri who was deputed to go to Kathmandu to assure the Nepalese of India's continued support and protection, and who was charged to travel to North-East India to concert with the leaders of the armed forces, and of the states, to assure the panicked Assamese, and to assess the damage the

Chinese had inflicted on the region. It would be unrealistic not to factor in this dimension into Shastri's negative perception of China.

The second was the first Chinese nuclear explosion in May 1964. It must have also played a marked role in giving even a more negative turn to Shastri's perception of the Chinese. Clearly, it created a new situation—one in which India's gigantic neighbour and perceived adversary had exacerbated the level of the threat. Not only were the Chinese well-equipped in conventional weapons, but now they had succeeded in hanging the damocles sword of nuclear weapons over India.

Ostensibly, the Chinese nuclear option was directed against the two superpowers (US and USSR) with whom Beijing's problems had become dimensional. But, since the two superpowers had no difficulty of dissuading any Chinese nuclear attack—given their credible capacity of striking back at China– the most vulnerable target really was non-nuclear India which was now faced with a new type of security threat from a nation with whom it had had myriad stand-offs, including a humiliating defeat in a full-fledged war.

Shastri could hardly afford to disregard the new situation, especially when the groundswell of pressures and divisions were emerging within the country between the opponents and proponents of the nuclear option. The Jana Sangh Party (JSP) took the squabble a notch further by introducing a motion in the Lok Sabha in November 1964 calling for the manufacture of nuclear weapons. Though the JSP proposal was defeated, it nonetheless contributed in magnifying the debate, and accelerating the pressure on the Government. Even Shastri's own political party was divided, with many delegates openly voicing their support for the nuclear option at the Congress Party's annual conference in January 1965. But, the debate reached a dramatic pinnacle with the intervention of the Chairman of the Indian Atomic Energy Commission, H.J. Bhabha. He made the controversy even more intense by jumping into the fray, and by openly declaring that he favoured the nuclear option, and by formally announcing that India could make the atomic bomb, with little cost, within 18 months after the political decision. Speaking on All India Radio on 24 October 1964, Bhabha conjured up visions of massive destruction should such a bomb be used, and should there be no Indian capacity to retaliate. Ominously he declared:

"A minimum supply of nuclear weapons coupled with an adequate delivery system confers on a state the capacity to destroy more or less totally the important cities and industrial centres. There appears to be no means of totally intercepting such an attack and even if a small fraction of it gets through, entire cities and regions would be totally devastated; the only defence against such an attack appears to be a capability and threat of retaliation."[163]

The message was loud and clear. "If we do not," he warned, "go nuclear, we will be totally destroyed should the Chinese use the weapons." Emanating from a leading and respectable scientist, who had closely worked with Nehru, it did not fail to have a weighty impact on public opinion. The swing in the country for going nuclear became even more pronounced. It almost became unstoppable.

Clearly, Shastri was now under even a greater pressure. He had to do something—act or react to Chinese action and to pressing domestic demands.

Another cause for concern for the Prime Minister was the Chinese decision to activate its diplomacy—in close cooperation with Pakistan and Indonesia—to mobilise international support to convene a second Bandung like Afro-Asian conference the specific purpose of which would have been to isolate India. In conflict with USSR, US and India—China considered the mobilisation of Afro-Asians as central to its interest. For one thing—isolated as it was becoming internationally on the eve of its Cultural Revolution—it concluded that the proposed conference could be a useful forum to attack the Russians and the Americans; for another, it could be deployed as a platform against the "reactionary" Indians who were increasingly perceived as anti Chinese by Beijing.

Here too for Shastri the situation was becoming worrisome, for the successful convening of an Afro-Asian conference—increasingly swinging in the radical direction with the complicity of China, Indonesia and Pakistan —would have isolated India from the developing world. The Indian foreign policy establishment perceived this development as equally disastrous, for India had been on the crest of a pro-Indian Third World wave during Nehru's time..

Would Shastri be able to cope with such a situation, many had begun to wonder, given his minimal experience in international affairs and with negligible international contacts. Internally, he was indeed facing a host of questions from his colleagues, regarding the type of leadership he was offering—a leadership that was wobbly. Patience was indeed wearing thin in his own political circles.

In any event Shastri had to act against any such dangers to Indian interests—especially in the face of Beijng–Islamabad–Djarkarta axis, all of whom joined hands to mobilise international support to convene such a conference, and all of whom had one thing in common: their opposition to India.

The pro-Soviet lobby in the MEA also factored in the growth of Shastri's anti-Chinese perception. Many of them, holding leading positions, were openly anti-Chinese. The well-installed pro-Soviet lobby had advanced credible arguments to Shastri against the Chinese, for they fervently argued that the Chinese shift to radicalism, both domestically and internationally on the eve of the Cultural Revolution, had made them ferociously anti-Indian, almost at par to their growing anti-Sovietism and anti-Americanism. To their way of thinking, there was therefore no hope whatsoever of any understanding with the Chinese. Besides, Beijing, which had become ubiquitous all over the Himalayan frontier, had become a major security threat, given its differences with India—differences that finally exploded into a conflict from which India is still recovering. Furthermore, Beijing had become active all over in India's South Asian backyard with Pakistan as its major ally; and it was this new configuration of forces in the region that was making Pakistan more defiant, and the other South Asian countries more autonomous of India, thus rendering the Indian diplomatic task more difficult and more problematic. And, what about, argued the pro-Soviet Indian bureaucratic lobby, the Soviets who are India's ally? Would not any entente with the Chinese negatively impact on Indo-Soviet relations, especially at a time when India needed Moscow? And lastly, what about the Americans with whom Shastri was attempting to build bridges, and from whom India was expecting major food aid in the face of serious shortage that India was facing.

All these weighty considerations had spawned the perception of a threat from the north. With China having gone nuclear the perception must have become even more acute and even more palpable.

Diplomatic Initiatives

Shastri's response to the worrisome situation was multifaceted. Though he had realised the inherent cruciality of interaction with South Asian neighbours for peace in the area, the Chinese security threat must also have factored into his decision to activate Indian diplomacy in the area. He sent his foreign minister to Nepal, Afghanistan, Ceylon and Myanmar (Burma) to evaluate not only the possibilities of developing more vigorous bonds with all of them, but also to assess the degree of Chinese presence in the area. Also he invited the King of Nepal, Prime Minister of Sri Lanka and the Prime Minister of Myanmar to personally continue the ongoing task of building bridges with neighbours. And he went to Myanmar and Nepal—two countries of obvious strategic value on India's eastern and northern flanks.

Whether China was ever evoked with the Burmese leaders, during Ne Win's visit to India in February 1965, and Shastri's visit to Myanmar in December of the same year, it is of course difficult to know since the Indian archives of the period are still unavailable. Besides, Shastri was heavily involved in settling the fate of Indian residents in Myanmar, who were deprived of much of their professional activities, with the sweeping Burmese decision to nationalise the entire economic sector under the so-called "Burmese way to socialism." But so far as China was concerned, one thing was certain: Shastri must have realised the strategic importance of Myanmar; for after all it was Sardar Vallabhbhai Patel, the Deputy Prime Minister under Nehru, who had gone on record, regarding the gregarious ramifications the Burmese Civil War could have on India's security. Sardar Patel had China in mind when he was pressing Nehru to be prudent while designing India's policy towards its eastern neighbour.

The Burmese Communist Party, known for its asymmetrical linkage with its Chinese counterparts, was the pivotal force in the conflict. And its projection to power would have seriously endangered Indian security. Patel realised the geopolitical importance of keeping the existing leadership at the helm of Burmese affairs.

Was Shastri on the same wavelength so far as Myanmar was concerned, it is of course difficult to say, but as he was, like Patel, also Minister of Internal Affairs in the Nehru government it cannot be excluded that he saw a linkage between India's internal and external security especially in regard to neighbouring Burma with whom India also had a porous frontier. So, from the geo-political perspective any communist victory in Burma would have been a threatening situation for Indian security.

In any event the Chinese dimension was certainly present in Shastri's policy towards Nepal since Beijing was showing signs of becoming active in Nepal, the most important manifestation of which was Foreign Minister, Chen Yi's visit to Nepal a few weeks (March-April) before Shastri's arrival in April. In fact, the fear of China was already there during his first trip outside of India in 1962, in the aftermath of Indian defeat in the Sino-Indian conflict, when he was not the Prime Minister, and when the purpose of his visit was to assure the Nepalese of India's protection. Nepal had apparently become dubious of India's capacity to come to their rescue in the event of any Chinese pressure.

The Chinese dimension had certainly become dominant during Shastri's 1965 trip to Kathmandu. For during his stay in the Himalayan Kingdom he concluded a secret agreement—an agreement which clearly stipulated that Nepal would buy arms from India, and from Britain or US only if India was unable to meet Nepal's request. Clearly, China was kept out of any arms deal. The other important aspect of the visit was the Nepalese acceptance of the establishment of 50 Indian manned check-posts on the Nepal-Tibet border in order to keep an eye on the movement of Chinese troops from Nepal.[164]

That Nepal accepted—reluctantly—is a clear sign of the great leverage India still possessed on Nepal whereas the Chinese were nowhere in the picture at the time. They were only in the early stages of activating their policies towards the Himalayan Kingdom.

The perception of the Chinese threat, compounded with his reluctance to go militarily nuclear, emboldened the Prime Minister to come up with the strange idea of seeking protection from major nuclear powers. Notwithstanding his politics of non-alignment, Nehru, it should be recalled, had already set the precedent of turning to the West for military aid in the face of the Chinese onslaught in 1962. The question was cautiously and generally mooted with the British Prime minister, Harold Wilson, during Shastri's trip to the United Kingdom in December 1964. But, he was naturally careful in evoking the idea of nuclear protection in general terms for all the non-nuclear countries. For he realised that any attempt on his part to seek protection specifically for India could seriously compromise India's non-aligned stance to which the country was consensually committed, and to which he had publicly engaged himself. Besides, it was evident that an explosive issue such as this, would make him an open target of domestic attacks since the country was divided on the nuclear issue. Furthermore, it soon became clear that joint iron-clad guarantees from the two superpower adversaries, at the height of the cold war, was neither realistic nor credible. It was not realistic since the US army was opposed to any joint guarantees with the Russians, and since the Kremlin had rendered their support conditional to a decision within the Security Council. It was also not credible since neither of the two powers were apparently prepared to make any clear-cut declaration to this effect.

President Johnson , it is true, did go on record on 18 October 1964 to declare that "nations that do not seek nuclear weapons can be sure that if they need US support against the threat of nuclear blackmail they will have it."[165]

The operative word clearly was "if". This in effect meant that India would have to actually take the initiative of seeking such support from Washington; and this Shastri could hardly envisage since he would never have been able to carry the country with him. Such an act would have been politically suicidal given the rampant anti-Americanism that still impregnated the country. Besides, it became evident that the US did not wish to go beyond the general public declaration made by Johnson. The whole idea was therefore quickly abandoned.

How did Shastri come up with this proposition? Who spawned the idea? Where did it come from?

It would seem that the decision to evoke the idea internationally, it is now known, was never seriously discussed at the decisional level; neither the Cabinet nor the MEA, nor the Emergency Committee of the Cabinet were privy to this initiative.

Though the whole idea was master-minded in Shastri's political secretariat, Shastri must have been made aware of an Indian Army's study which argued that —in the absence of any viable and credible delivery system –it was useless to go nuclear; and India, under the circumstances should, therefore, seek some arrangement with the West for some nuclear support.

The nuclear umbrella episode goes to show that there were already signs of decisions being taken within the political secretariat, but, it also brought out the flaws of such a decision making at this early stage. The political secretariat was still very small, and did not as yet possess the appropriate infrastructure to marshal all the facts, to go through the whole process of decisional interaction, and think out all the ramifications that would unavoidably accompany such an initiative. Clearly, Shastri had made the mistake, and rapidly realised the political importance of abandoning the whole idea.

What could Shastri do?

But now that the idea of nuclear umbrella was jettisoned, Shastri had to do something else in the face of this potential threat to India's security. And this he did. He took the important initiative in April 1965 by giving Bhabha formal approval to move ahead with a peaceful nuclear explosives

(PNEs) development, the purpose of which was to reduce the time needed to develop nuclear explosives.

This was a landmark decision; for even if it was taken with the ostensible purpose of studying nuclear tests, the fact remained that the door was now opened, howsoever slight. should India ever decide to take the nuclear option in the military sector. Those who were in the know of things were quite aware of the scientific fact that "the difference between a peaceful nuclear explosive and the bomb are the tail fins."[166] Bhabha clearly knew it, and Shastri presumably was informed of the basic scientific facts.

This decision to go ahead benefited both Shastri and Bhabha. For Shastri, by giving the green light to Bhabha, managed to pacify a turbulent pro-nuclear Indian lobby favouring an explicit weapons' programme, and had, at the same time, politically neutralised the dangers of any international sanctions by declaring that the programme India was setting up was a "peaceful nuclear explosion" (PNE) programme. This was indeed ingenuous; for it was apparently the only feasible way that a weapons' programme could be pursued. India succeeded in maintaining this fiction through its first nuclear test in 1974, and right up to 1998 after its second round of nuclear testing when it finally acknowledged that its objective after all was to possess nuclear arms.

Clearly, there now was a change in India's nuclear policy. No more did Shastri continue to reaffirm Nehru's policy, but made it clear to the Indian Parliament that his Government's policy " was not rigid or static and it would change according to circumstances"[167] One could, of course, ask the question if Shastri was aware of Nehru's apparent interest in going nuclear, as we have indicated in the chapter on Nehru.

This change surfaced at diplomatic conferences. India was no more in a hurry to sign a pledge not to make a bomb while the nuclear powers unimpededly continued to increase their nuclear arsenal. When the USA and USSR, influenced by Chinese nuclear tests, sought at the UN to forge a multilateral treaty to foreclose any further nuclear proliferation, India strove to add a clause under which non-nuclear States would be able to carry out "peaceful nuclear explosions."[168] Though US firmly opposed the proposal on the grounds that no meaningful distinction could really be made between "peaceful" and "non-peaceful explosions", India continued to press the distinction. Later at the International Atomic Energy Conference (IAEA) in Tokyo the Indian delegate asked rhetorically: "How long countries capable of making a bomb would take to be able to refrain from doing so."[169]

Bhabha's gain was that he had obtained the green light to go ahead with what he wanted.[170] On 5 April 1965 he set up a nuclear explosive design group to study subterranean nuclear explosion for peaceful purposes (SNEP). In this connection he instructed one of his aides, who was undergoing training at the French national laboratory at Saclay in Paris, to scout around for useful information, especially regarding plutonium technology used for the first generation neutron initiators for weapons. By mid-1965 laboratory tests were already being conducted with large amounts of high explosives to calibrate seismographs used for nuclear test monitoring.[171]

Bhabha also turned to the Americans. It is not clear if Shastri was privy to Bhabha's initiative, which clearly were not only technical. He approached the US in March 1965 for a Plowshare device (peaceful nuclear device) and enquired from the Chairman of the American Atomic Agency (AEC) if the US "would be prepared to make a moderate amount of plutonium available for Research and Development."[172]

Interestingly enough, the US Atomic Energy Commission, according to its Chairman, John G. Palfrey, "had developed a close relationship with Bhabha"[173] personally, and a number of US officials and agencies did not reject outright Bhabha's request. In fact they had become positively interested in Indian initiatives after the Chinese nuclear explosion in October 1964. They were even willing to provide Plowshare devices (peaceful nuclear explosive), technology and even (under some conditions) nuclear weapons to India.[174] In fact, the Assistant Secretary of Defence for International Security Affairs, John McNaughton, mandated to prepare a report on "the possibilities of providing nuclear weapons under US custody," had recommended the establishment of a programme to train and equip Indian forces with nuclear weapons, and to create even a stockpile to disperse in India in times of crisis.[175] The McNaughton report made it clear that India could produce and test a nuclear device "in one or three years after the decision to do so," and could produce, "by 1970 about a dozen weapons in the 20Kt (Kiloton) range" on its own. And the only way to "preclude" India to develop an "independent national nuclear development program" was to offer US nuclear assistance to India.[176] According to the US archives, declassified recently, there was thus a great deal of debate within the Administration that was not unfavourable to India going nuclear.

In his efforts to seek American support Bhabha even attempted to politicise the issue by requesting a meeting with George Ball, US

UnderSecretary of State. He met him on 22 February 1965 in Washington and tried to impress upon him that India needed some "dramatic" peaceful achievement to offset the prestige China had gained among Afro-Asians, and declared that while India could produce a nuclear device in 18 months on its own, it could do the job even in six months should the US provide him with a blueprint."[177]

But all these discreet developments never really materialised. For one thing, senior members of US administration could not see themselves giving nuclear protection to a non-aligned India; for another, India was not interested in a unilateral guarantee from Washington, even though Chester Bowles, the US Ambassador to India, was favouring such an idea. In any event the debate within the US Administration to help India in the nuclear sector was brought to an abrupt end when the Gilpatric Committee on Nuclear Explosions recommended on 21 January 1965 to President Lyndon Johnson a disallowance of any nuclear proliferation.[178]

Multilateral Initiative Against the Chinese

Another major Shastri initiative directed against the Chinese was multilateral. At the non-aligned conference in Cairo in October 1965, he urged his fellow delegates to appeal to Beijing not to go ahead with its projected nuclear test, and proposed that a special mission be sent "to persuade China to desist from developing nuclear weapons" for "the threat to humanity from one more country having nuclear weapons at its disposal" was a serious matter—far more serious than differences between India and China.[179]

But all this fell on deaf ears. The participating countries did not wish to take sides in the Sino-Indian dispute; and Shastri's proposals to many of them tantamounted to taking a position in favour of India. Paradoxically, they were paying back Shastri in 1964 in the same coin they had done to Nehru in 1962 in the aftermath of the Sino-Indian conflict, i.e., avoiding taking any position for or against, thus remaining neutral. The Afro-Asians did what India did under Nehru and what India preached under him: neutralism.

Shastri's other proposal at Cairo calling upon all nations to renounce the use of force for the settlement of territorial or border disputes too was rejected. Though, this was a general suggestion, many participants once again perceived this as another Indian attempt directed specifically at China. Besides, there were others who did not see any merit in the proposal since border and territorial disputes were rampant all over Asia and Africa, and hardly anybody wanted to be foreclosed by such a proposal—least of all Indonesia, China's close ally at the time, which was right in the midst of a stand-off with Malaysia on the territorial question.

Though in the end, six of the nine points of the final non-aligned declaration were taken from the Indian draft, Shastri was unable to remove a general feeling among the participants that he was using the conference to advance India's national interests—very different from the image Nehru had successfully projected at the preceding non-aligned conference in Belgrade where he was one of the major icons of the non-aligned world.

Also Shastri had begun to worry about the concerted diplomatic offensive—along with Pakistan and Indonesia—to convene a second Bandung conference of African and Asian countries. Isolated as China was becoming, due to the radical turn it had taken in its internal and external policies in the mid-sixties, it strove to create a revolutionary international forum against the Americans, Russians and Indians, all of whom in the then existing Chinese perception were on the other side of the ideological and political fence.

How should India counter this move in which all the three proponents involved (China, Indonesia and Pakistan) were against India? What initiative should it take to stem the holding of such a conference—a conference that may become an anti-Indian forum? This was a worrisome situation the broad contours of which had already become visible on the occasion of the 10th anniversary of the 1955 Bandung Conference. Zhou Enlai, Pham Van Dong, Norodom Sihanouk, Zulfikar Ali Bhutto and Sukarno—all belonging to the so-called pro-Chinese Newly Emerging Forces—had stolen the show with moderates like India, Japan, Thailand, etc., completely sidelined at the main ceremonies where, according to William Hanna, a journalist, "Bung Karno's regime reserved the most clamorous accolade for the most conclusively communists Afro-Asian guests."[180] The others, more moderate, were ignored. They had the impression of watching a play as passive spectators.

At the same time Zhou Enlai, in close coordination with Bhutto (then Pakistan's Foreign Minister) and Dr Subandrio (Indonesia's Foreign Minister), had launched a major diplomatic offensive of visiting the Afro-Asian capitals to seek their support for such a conference.

In the face of this offensive, India realised that it would not get very far in stemming such an offensive, since there did appear to exist, among the Afro-Asians, a broad consensus for convening such an international gathering. The trio apparently had succeeded in persuading many African and Asians regarding the importance of such a meeting. The next best thing India could do, under the circumstances, was to neutralise any Chinese domination of the conference by manoeuvring an invitation for the Soviets on the ground that most of its territory was in Asia. It was an ingenious argument and weighty diplomatic initiative. For one thing it placed the Chinese on the defensive since any Soviet presence in the conference would have overshadowed them and thus diminish their effectiveness; for another the debate about the Soviet presence would have made many Afro-Asians prudent in openly giving their support to the Chinese. A Chinese mobilisation against the Indians was one thing, which the Afro-Asian countries could go along with, but siding with the Chinese against the Soviet Union was another matter since the latter was powerful, and with whom many of them had forged meaningful ties. Besides, an excessive, muscular and merciless Chinese rhetoric against Moscow was becoming a source of embarrassment for many Afro-Asians. Though the Chinese polemical style was generally callous against its adversaries, they had gone excessively overboard by characterising the Soviet leaders as "fascists," "reactionaries," "capitalistic," etc., openly proclaiming that the Soviet leaders were operating hand in glove with the Americans to dominate the world. The Chinese press was full of rancorous diatribes.

This did not go well with most Afro-Asian countries. The balance among them, therefore, began to shift in favour of Soviet participation in such a meeting programmed to be held in Algiers. The Indians were now reasonably sure of swinging the votes in favour of Soviet participation at Algiers non-aligned meeting, whereas the Chinese, on the other hand, were now on the defensive, and were no more sure of rallying a majority against the USSR. Uncertainty reined. Confusion was now rampant among the Afro-Asians. No one was sure of the outcome and many were indeed embarrassed at the open Chinese determination to keep the Russians out of the proposed conference. Then, suddenly and unexpectedly, a new situation developed that made things even worse for everyone, but more so for the Chinese. The host country's President, Ahmed Ben Bella, was ousted from office. A coup d'etat had taken place, to which the Chinese apparently had implicitly given their support. Total confusion now reined in Algeria.

India seized the opportunity and proposed the postponement of the conference. The Chinese—for reasons that are not very clear—now insisted on the holding of the conference as scheduled. While all this was happening another dramatic development occurred. A bomb exploded in the hall where the conference was due to be held. Many of the governments, who were already tired of Chinese pressures and Soviet counter-pressures, rallied to the Indian proposal that the conference be postponed. Over 20 African States notified Algeria that the heads of their governments would be unable to attend as they were no more sure of their safety. To further isolate the Chinese, Shastri, who, at the time, was attending the Commonwealth Conference in London, persuaded his African colleagues, attending the same meeting, that, in the face of the rapidly changing situation in Algeria, no useful purpose would really be served in holding the Algiers conference. He successfully persuaded most of them to issue a joint statement proposing its postponement.

But, the Chinese and the Indonesians nonetheless insisted that a meeting be held, not of the foreign ministers but of the 15 member Ambassadorial Committee to discuss a conditional postponement.

The Indians countered by convening a meeting of the moderates at the Indian Embassy in Algiers where the Algerian proposal to postpone the meeting until 15 November 1965 was formally agreed upon.

The meeting of the 15-member Ambassadorial Committee was never convened. The whole idea passed away into the limbo of oblivion. One of its main supporters, Sukarno, viewed as the icon of such a conference, was overthrown on 30 September 1965 by a group of junior military officers who had apparently refused to accept his close involvement with the Chinese and his confrontational politics vis-à-vis Malaya. Beijing too lost interest. On the eve of its Cultural Revolution, the country was slowly sinking into confusion, chaos, and extreme radicalism. No one, among the main leaders, had any time or the inclination to review the Chinese strategy for Algiers. Fear had gripped the nation and its leaders.

Finally, when the Conference's preparatory committee met in the third week of October 1965 to take the decision the impossible conditions that Beijing proposed sounded its death knell. Through its Foreign Minister, Chen Yi, it declared that it would participate in such a meeting only if its three demands were met. The first was that the conference agreed to condemn the US imperialist aggression over Vietnam and demanded the withdrawal of all the American troops. Second, that the invitation extended to the UN Secretary General UThant to attend the meeting be withdrawn, and third, that the Soviet Union must not be invited.

Clearly, all of these were radical demands, and the preparatory committee refused to accept any of them. In the face of such rampant opposition, supporters of China thereupon demanded another postponement. But no one, with the possible exception of Algeria, was any more interested in salvaging the conference. It was apparently dying even before its birth.

India inflicted the final blow by insisting that the Soviet Union be invited.

In the face of this major disagreement, the foreign ministers had no choice but to adjourn the conference sine die. And this is what happened. The meeting was never called again.

With the end of this episode, Sino-Indian animosity reached a high point with no hope of any return to normalisation.

Shastri had no choice but to continue in the anti-Chinese direction. In fact, for the first time during his mandate, a systematic and a coherent anti-Chinese policy showed sign of spilling over onto the overall Indian diplomatic behaviour—in the UN, in other international conferences, and in different diplomatic initiatives towards Pakistan.

Growing Alienation with Pakistan

While constructing an anti-China policy, Shastri had set his eyes on Pakistan. He continued to take a benign attitude towards Pakistan. Somehow, he convinced himself that India must seek out its sub-continental neighbour –a conviction that reposed on the idea that the two countries had a common history, a shared culture and an identical ethnicity; and there was therefore no reason why the two countries could not reach a lasting understanding. Clearly this reasoning was based on the belief that the goal of mutual understanding was more easily achievable with those with whom one had some degree of commonality. While there are no historical and credible antecedents that uphold such a persuasion, Shastri clearly was convinced of it, and was determined to move ahead—a naive thought indeed for someone who should have realised the brutal reality of the Indo-Pakistan situation. Though he was being very naïve in making such an assessment, it had at least the merit of sincerity and determination—almost a consuming passion.

It is more than possible that the underpinnings of benignity towards Pakistan may also be attributed—at least in part—to Shastri's fear of China. For nothing was more gregarious for Indian security than to find itself in a position of conflict on two fronts. Whereas for the preceding government Pakistan was the principal adversary, for Shastri it was the reverse.

But Pakistan was thinking differently. It had other plans and other objectives. Suspicious as it always had been, it was constructing a different and a more aggressive strategy towards India. The Pakistani leaders, particularly Bhutto, had somehow convinced themselves that Indian politics, under Shastri, was getting from bad to worse. The food situation was in a disastrous state and the language issue was creating serious discord between the north and the south—not to speak of a slew of people within the Congress Party who perceived Shastri as a wrong choice, thus generating some degree of leadership insecurity within the country. In sum, a wobbly situation. For Bhutto this was the time to strike. This was the time to take action against India. Amazing as this may sound, Bhutto, in fact, considered it fit to mention his thesis about India's impending disintegration to the Indian High Commissioner, G. Parthasarthy during his farewell call to him. This was indeed unprecedented that a Foreign Minister should make such remarks to the ambassador of the country concerned. But then Bhutto had the reputation of being impulsive, brutal and frank. In any event, Bhutto's assessment was received with amusement by Indian decision makers.

The second Pakistani argumentation in favour of doing something was the Indian decision to increase its military clout in the aftermath of its defeat in the Sino-Indian conflict. In the autumn of 1964, the Indian Government announced an ambitious defence programme which called for the doubling of the defence expenditure from one billion dollars in 1962 to two billion in 1969. The strength of the army was to be increased from 600,000 to 825,000, while the number of divisions was to increase from nine to twenty nine, with the air force expanding by fifteen squadrons to a total of forty. In addition, India was moving in the direction of keeping its nuclear options open—a prospect perceived as disastrous for Pakistan.

The third consideration was Shastri's Government's sudden decision to end Kashmir's special status, and to integrate it fully into the Indian Union. The state's Premier was now re-designated as Chief Minister, and the so-called title of *Sadr-e Riasat*, was replaced by the designation governor—like governors of other States who were nominated by the Central Government; and the jurisdiction of the Supreme Court was extended to Kashmir while the Kashmiri members to the Indian Parliament were no more to be nominated but elected as in other States. In sum a clear attempt to ensure Kashmir's greater integration into the Indian fold.

It remained unclear why Shastri allowed, the Home Minister, Gulzarilal Nanda, to radically change Kashmir's status since it considerably narrowed any scope of a compromise with Pakistan, and since it buttressed position of those like Bhutto who favoured a decisive confrontation with India. Clearly this was in total contradiction with Shastri's strategy of seeking out Pakistan; and the only conclusion one can draw from the decision to integrate Kashmir more fully into the Indian fold was that that he apparently did not have complete control over the decisional process.

All these developments raised serious concern among Pakistan's leaders. The expansion of India's military clout, they feared, would heavily tilt the South Asian balance of power in India's direction and the existing one to two military ratio would be drastically altered to four to one by the end of the five year defence plan. Besides, the Indian option to go nuclear—should it ever materialise—would generate even a greater military disequilibrium between the two countries—clearly an unacceptable situation for Pakistan. Furthermore, the Indian decision to integrate Kashmir fully into the Indian Union made Pakistan's goal of disengaging Kashmir from India even more difficult in the future. This had to be stopped.

Since, Shastri's India, ran the Pakistani argumentation, was no more as stable as it was during Nehru's time, it was now time to act, for it would be too late after a few years when India would have acquired a greater military clout.

With this frame of mind some of the Pakistani leaders decided that now was the time to strike at India.

Pakistan Acts

Internally in Pakistan a Kashmir cell was secretly established in early 1964 under the chairmanship of Pakistan's Foreign Secretary Aziz Ahmad, with leading members of defence, and the intelligence establishment as its regular participants, including General Mohammad Musa, Pakistan's Commander-in-Chief. It was here in these off-the-record meetings that a decision was taken in May 1965 to begin raids on Indian-held Kashmir—apparently much against the wishes of the military establishment which did not consider Pakistan ready for such action. Musa confirms this decision: "The sponsors and supporters of the raids in Kashmir had at last succeeded in persuading the President to take the plunge that led to all-out armed conflict with India.[181]

In fact much before the "plunge", Pakistani hawks, led by Bhutto, had already developed a four phased strategy, at the end of 1964: to strike at India with a 'probing' encounter in some place of Pakistan's choosing, followed by an "all-out" but disguised invasion of some 5.000 infiltrators camouflaged by the Pakistani propaganda machine, as a "revolt" by the local population. Once this has been implemented, the third phase would begin with a full-scale army assault by the Pakistan army to cut off the Indian supply routes to Kashmir, to be continued by massive and a lightening attack to capture Amritsar, about sixteen miles inside Indian territory, and as much of other Indian territory as possible, to be exchanged eventually for Kashmir when, defeated India would sue for peace.[182]

It was a daring plan—a plan that was not limited to the disputed territory of Kashmir but was to be escalated by a massive strike into the Indian territory. The risks were enormous to take on a gigantic India; clearly it was based on a miscalculation.

However, before taking such a daring action, Pakistan leaders wanted to assure themselves of some solid international support in the event of the emergence of any unexpected difficulties during the conflict.

It would seem that the Pakistan's leaders had excluded all scenarios of the necessity of seeking some support from the US. It knew that Washington would not support Pakistan's military attack against India. President Lyndon Johnson, who had succeeded Kennedy had made it known to President Ayub Khan that he was not prepared to waste anymore time and money supporting Pakistan against India.[183] Also, he made it clear to him on 15 December 1965 in his usual picturesque manner that if " Pakistan wanted close relations with us there could be no serious relationship with the Chinese communists. We could not live with that." But, at the same time, he declared "we understand certain relationships just as a wife could understand a Saturday night fling—so long as she was the wife."[184] Ayub apparently got the point which in effect was that Pakistan could have relations with China, but must not go very far.

In any event, Pakistan was no more sure if its interests coincided with that of the US; for the latter was showing signs of getting closer to New Delhi in view of the Sino-Indian stand-off. Nonetheless what remains enigmatic in the Pakistani decision is how experienced leaders like Bhutto and Ayub envisioned that they could get away with such a daring operation in the face of US opposition. Bhutto's determination is perhaps understandable, given his open animosity towards India, and given his determined ambition to reach the political summit in Pakistan; but what about Ayub Khan who had hitherto projected himself as a moderate eager to seek some amiable solution with India? Ayub, who was initially reluctant, apparently allowed himself to make the plunge because of his growing domestic unpopularity from which, he was assured by his advisers, that he could extricate himself only by doing something dramatic; and what could be more dramatic than striking at India and thus becoming "the darling and hero of the Pakistani and Kashmiri people."[185] But, there was another more credible and more objective explanation that generated Pakistani consensus to move against India. It was China. Pakistani leaders were probably certain of Chinese support to dissuade India from taking any escalated action in the event of Pakistani decision to attack India

Already by 1963 the CIA was convinced that there "was some secret understanding" between China and Pakistan[186] under which China was expected to come to Pakistan's aid in the event of an Indian attack.[187] The military understanding was probably further reinforced in 1964 and 1965 during numerous meetings between Chinese and Pakistan leaders. Zhou Enlai visited Pakistan in February 1964, in April 1965 and again in June of the same year. And Ayub had visited China in March 1965 when he held talks with Liu Xiaoqi and Zhou Enlai. It has even been suggested that the Chinese were training Pakistani infiltrators in Azad Kashmir to carry out Chinese style guerrilla warfare in Kashmir. McGeorge Bundy, Special Assistant for National Security in the US Administration, was informed to this effect.[188]

Since by 1965 China had already undertaken two nuclear explosions, and since rumours were rife that India was going in the same direction, it is difficult to exclude the hypothesis that an understanding may have been reached on Pakistan-China nuclear co-operation—even though an agreement to this effect was reached only later.

It may have been a pure coincidence, but it should be noted that it was also in 1965 (26 March) that a Sino-Pakistan Boundary Protocol was signed in Pakistan settling the boundary between China's Xinjiang province and Kashmiri territory controlled by Pakistan—an agreement that finally led to the opening of the so-called Silk Road that was used by China for sending arms to Pakistan. Sino-Pakistan relations thus were becoming more and more dense.

Indo-Pakistan Conflict

The stage was clearly now set for Pakistan to act; and the action took place on 26th January 1965 when it chose to intrude into the Rann of Kutch—an area of 7,000 square miles that is covered by water during half the year, and by desert during the other half. Pakistan chose this area because Pakistan had always considered it as a disputed area since 1947, and because it was the weakest link in India's defence chain, ignored by the Indian Army as strategically unimportant.

Pakistan scored a number of victories by launching a massive attack on four Indian posts between 24-29 April, and occupied all of them.

India was in a weak position. It could hardly retaliate. The ground on the Indian side was so soft and marshy that tanks could not be used, whereas Pakistan's lines of communication and transportation were better, shorter and easily operationable. Besides, the Indian armed forces, as Pakistan expected, did not respond efficaciously on the ground that the Rann was indefensible area, and that" it is a mistake in strategic thinking," in their view, "that every inch of the border has to be guarded equally well."[189] This is certainly a sound reasoning, but was hardly convincing for the angry Indian public which was carried away by nationalistic fervour, and was getting more and more irritated with setbacks. To be defeated by the Chinese was one thing, but to be defeated by minuscule Pakistan was unacceptable. And in the midst of all this wave of indignation sweeping the country, Shastri hesitated. Apparently, according to reports, he told his Cabinet that "he could not reconcile himself to a war between India and Pakistan."[190] He chose another tack—the tack of British mediation in the conflict, and of implicitly accepting that the Rann was a disputed area after having repeatedly declared that the territory was not disputable. This too did not go very well with the public, and many began to wonder in the opposition parties, and even in his own party, if he really had the ability of standing firm in face of international pressures. Public opinion thus was building up against Shastri.

For Pakistan leaders all these were signs of weakness. For them, it was a confirmation of their earlier perception that India was becoming unstable and was disintegrating.

Therefore right in the midst of British mediation, Ayub took the decision of publicly linking the Rann dispute with the Kashmir problem. He declared:

> The history of this part of the world will take the right course only after the people of Jammu and Kashmir have been able to exercise their inalienable right of self-determination in a free and fair manner.[191]

And finally when a cease fire agreement was signed on 30th June 1965, under which Pakistan agreed to restore the *status quo ante*, Ayub succeeded in obtaining the inclusion of a clause in the preamble that expressed the hope that the settlement over Rann would pave the way for the settlement of other outstanding disputes between the two countries.

The linkage was established, and Pakistan was delighted with the agreement. The press hailed it as the model for other disputes; the precedent for a reference to arbitration was especially welcomed as something that could be used in other disputes, including Kashmir.

However, hardly had the cease fire agreement been concluded, Pakistan activated the second and the main part of its four phase plan, i.e., to launch an offensive to "liberate" Kashmir—an offensive that began with a massive infiltration, across the cease fire line, of 5,000 armed men in civilian clothes to disrupt everything that came their way, to be followed by a revolt of the Kashmiri people, and that would finally climax into a full-scale army assault in the Chhamb area to capture the Akhnoor bridge to cut off the Indian supply lines.

This was indeed a bold well-concerted plan the purpose of which obviously was to cut off Kashmir completely from India. Clearly Pakistan was going in for maximum objectives.

In the face of this offensive Shastri changed. He became decisive and determined and instructed the army to counter-attack massively.

Pakistan's strategy thus failed miserably. Most of the infiltrators were captured, the Kashmiri revolt never materialised, and the army assault plan was neutralised by retaliatory Indian action, under Shastri's orders, to escalate the conflict by attacking Pakistan's Punjab province, by initiating a movement of troops in Rajasthan, and by carrying out an air force attack in the Chhamb area. In sum, Shastri did what Pakistan had not expected— invading Pakistan and escalating the whole conflict. The risks were great, but Shastri decided that they had to be taken. He had no other choice.

As was inevitable, international pressures then began to build up on the two countries to stop the conflict; and the Security Council came into the picture with a resolution demanding an immediate cease fire and the withdrawal of the armed personnel of the two countries back to the position held before 5 August—the date on which Pakistani infiltrators had entered Kashmir.

Shastri readily accepted the proposal within the deadline imposed by the Secretary General, but asked for additional 35 hours to effectively operationalise the cease fire. Apparently, the Indian Army wanted some more time to further damage the Pakistan forces and destroy as much of its armed forces as possible.

Ayub, on the other hand, did not care to reply within the imposed deadline. But he finally did accept the proposal, for he had no other choice. Much of the Pakistan's arms had been effectively destroyed with the war virtually over even before the ceasefire 12 days later. The Americans, whom he had approached, had declined any help, while the Chinese, on whom Ayub was really counting on, came out with what in effect turned out to be a verbal support since the threatening ultimatum that was sent out to India on 16th September 1965 to dismantle its alleged military presence on the Chinese side of the Sino-Sikkim border was never put into effect. It wasn't really a serious and credible ultimatum; besides the Chinese began to have second thoughts in the face of rumours that Washington and London would provide India with air cover in case China attacked.

Part of the explanation for Chinese restraint may also lie in the fact that the US Secretary of State, Dean Rusk, in a statement on 15 September, had warned the Chinese not to intervene, and, on the same day, the US Ambassador John M. Cabot, in his talks with the Chinese Ambassador to Poland, Wang Kuochan, had cautioned China against interfering in the conflict.[192]

The UN ceasefire resolution had not created any real mechanism for the actual implementation of the resolution. There was nothing in it regarding the action UN would take, should either of the two belligerents—or one of them—refuse to withdraw their troops and restore the *status quo ante*. On the other hand, it had also not planned what it would do to begin a process of peace should both the parties accept the UN cease fire.

Road to Tashkent

It would seem that some sort of an implicit accord had been reached between the great powers (USA, USSR and UK) that Moscow would initiate the whole diplomatic process to bring the two belligerents to the round table.

The Soviet Union thus acquired central stage in mediation between India and Pakistan—a mediation that was indeed unique in the annals of Soviet diplomacy since it had never had any such experience before. Clearly, Moscow was keen to take up the task. It had its own reasons for doing so; and in fact had already built contacts with India and Pakistan while the conflict was still continuing.

There was first of all the Chinese dimension. Moscow was becoming increasingly fearful of the prospects of Chinese involvement on the Pakistan side in the 1965 war—a prospect that was, in Soviet perception, becoming increasingly credible with the rancorous declarations emanating from Beijing during the Indo-Pakistan war. The perspective of China sweeping down into the plains of India was the horrendous scenario looming in Soviet perception. Such a dangerous situation could, in the Soviet eyes, be avoided only with the rapid ending of the Indo-Pakistan conflict. Besides, any Chinese intervention would also undermine all the Soviet diplomatic efforts of the sixties of maintaining its privileged relations with India while constructing a new pattern of benign relations with Pakistan.

The other consideration was that successful mediatory efforts would give Moscow the image of a responsible power that was different from the confrontational Khruschev era which saw the emergence of the Sino/Soviet dispute, the Cuban missile crisis, the Berlin Wall, etc. The Soviet leaders were apparently keen to bury this image; and successful mediation in the Indo-Pakistan war, in their estimation, should be beneficial to their ongoing effort to project themselves as a responsible power in the international system.

But to go through this diplomatic process, the Soviet Union needed the accord of the US—the other superpower which had multiple capacities of deciding the fate of such a mediatory effort.

The Johnson administration went along with the Soviet Union. Heavily tied up, as it was, in Vietnam, and given the deep Indian public distrust of the US, Washington was in no position to substitute itself for Moscow. Besides, the superpowers were on the same wavelength of containing China from expanding its influence in South Asia.

The road was thus open for the Soviet Union to perform its first major mediatory diplomacy. The stage was thus set for Shastri-Ayub meeting under the watchful eyes of Soviet Prime Minister Alexis Kosygin, who persuaded them to meet in Tashkent on 4th January 1966. Both India and Pakistan had no other choice but to meet; the war had been impassed, and international pressures to find a solution had become more and more insistent on the two South Asian leaders.

Shastri had a delicate role to perform. He had a tight mandate beyond which he could not go without risking his political position. On the other hand, he was also aware of the fact that diplomatic conferences can only be successful through a politics of give and take.

The overall situation for him thus was troublesome. There were a number of paradoxical caveats that he could not transgress: (a) He could not negotiate Kashmir for it was a part of India; and yet Kashmir was the basic issue that had led to the war; (b) He had declared against vacating Hajipir and Thitwal passes, the two strategic points, the Indian forces had occupied; and yet the UN ceasefire resolution clearly stipulated that the two belligerents had to withdraw to the pre-war line; (c) Shastri wanted a no-war pact between India and Pakistan at Tashkent; and yet he knew that Ayub will never sign such a pact as long as the Kashmir issue was not resolved; and (d) Shastri was determined to obtain the withdrawal of Pakistani infiltrators who started the war; and yet he knew that Pakistan would not even discuss the matter since it had formally declared that it had nothing whatsoever to do with the infiltrators.

On all these divisive issues a mutual understanding had therefore to be reached if the conference was to end successfully. At Tashkent, though the Kashmir issue was not officially discussed, Shastri did agree that the foreign ministers could "talk" about the subject. Shastri agreed to the withdrawal of Indian troops from all of the Pakistani territory, but insisted that no specific mention was to be made to Tithwal and Hajipir in the formal agreement. Shastri's no war pact was excluded, but a general affirmation was made by the two sides reaffirming "their obligation under the Charter not to have recourse to force, and to settle their disputes in a peaceful manner."[193] And finally no mention was made of the Pakistani infiltrators, but Kosygin informally informed Shastri that as Pakistan did not take any responsibility on the issue, India could do what it wants with them.

Was the Tashkent Conference really a success? Did it resolve the major issues that divided the two countries? What is the real significance of the conference and the declaration on India?

Indeed it was a success, at least in so far as it legitimised the cessation of hostilities, made the two nations agree to renew diplomatic relations, and to resolve their disagreements peacefully.

But the nub of the problems remained. The basic issues that exploded into a war remained unresolved. The Kashmir dispute remained where it had always been since the independence of the two countries, the level of suspicion between the two adversaries remained as high as ever before, and neither economic nor political nor even cultural interaction took the great leap forward. In sum nothing was really resolved except the cessation of hostilities. Problems continued to divide the two countries, and with metronomic regularity they kept surfacing with greater violence and with great rancorousness.

Many seem to argue that but for Shastri's sudden and unexpected death in Tashkent immediately after the conference, relations may have improved, issues may have been resolved and confidence may have been restored. For this is what he wanted.

It is of course difficult to assertively make such a hypothetical statement, since it was precisely during Shastri's mandate as Prime Minister that the two countries went through a brutal war. On the other hand, there were nonetheless many indications that Shastri and Ayub had befriended themselves; and that both of them had manifested their determination to seek some mutual understanding. In fact, they had agreed to build a hot line, and the Pakistani President had invited Shastri to break journey to stop in Pakistan so that they could rapidly continue their bilateral interaction to implement what they had agreed upon in the Tashkent Declaration.

Such hypothetical assertions were never operationalised since Shastri was no more there to expand relations with Pakistan.

In any event the Tashkent Declaration was well-received by practically everyone—the great powers, the media and the international community. Whatever dissident voices that did emerge were from India and Pakistan—voices that expressed doubts regarding the Declaration.

In the case of India there were some who were genuinely critical of Shastri for having given in on too much, particularly on withdrawing from Hajipir and Tithwal, while there were others in the wings who had prepared themselves to use Tashkent Declaration to strike at Shastri for their own political purpose.

In any event, it is undeniable that Shastri's performance at Tashkent was skilful, firm and realistic. He defended India's interest, and only ceded when he had to.

EVALUATION

During his mandate of 18 months as Prime Minister, Shastri will be remembered for his heavy involvement in foreign affairs. This is indeed paradoxical for this is what he feared the most, given his fragile health, and this is what led him to delegate some authority to others in the sector of diplomacy. But, this did not protect him from being consumed by the overwhelming power of foreign affairs. In fact, he died serving it. It may seem unbelievable, but undeniable it is that Shastri's performance in foreign affairs was indeed a "spectacular record for a period of one-and-a-half years;"[194] and if one were to take into account his visits to the UK, Soviet Union. Nepal, Canada, Yugoslavia, Egypt, Burma and Pakistan, compounded with a war with Pakistan and major tensions with China–all this during his brief mandate—the record is even more impressive.

But it was not only the time he devoted to foreign affairs, or reflecting on issues, travelling, holding meetings, planning, etc., that is significant; it was also the lasting contributions he made to foreign policy—contributions that his successors picked up, expanded and followed. They have become permanent fixtures to the shadows and substance of India's Foreign policy.

The first was in the decisional process. More people and more institutions were involved in generating appropriate inputs to structure foreign policy than was the case under his predecessor. Nehru was the sole decisional maker in the sector, whereas Shastri was not. Nehru arguably did not need others, Shastri did. Nehru was universally acclaimed as the architect of India's foreign policy; Shastri was not and did not have those pretensions; He therefore made efforts to consult others and give greater life to such structures as the political secretariat, the Ministry of External Affairs, the Research Department within that ministry so that he could interact with others. But of all the institutional initiatives taken in foreign policy, the one that was most crucial was the establishment of his personal political secretariat directed by a high powered civil servant whose original purpose was to keep the Prime Minister constantly informed of the leading developments within the government machinery. Instead of going to the ministries, he now had someone directly under him who was assigned this function. In sum, the original objective was to deploy the secretariat to monitor developments within the government. But, in due course it expanded itself into a powerful agency that was permanently interacting with the Prime Minister, including advising him on a wide spectrum of issues. As Shastri had never had any experience of actually running the totality of the government with all its diverse and complex tasks, he probably calculated that having some one high powered in his own personal secretariat would lighten his burden. The original purpose of appointing L.K. Jha to the post probably was to have someone keep an eye on the domestic scene, since Jha's entire career until then was directed at administrative and economic affairs, though he did have some international assignments. However, given the fact that the Prime Minister had limited experience in foreign affairs and therefore felt insecure in diplomacy, the political secretariat naturally filled in the gap, so much so that during Shastri's mandate almost all the crucial decisions were made, and declarations, speeches, etc., were prepared within the framework of the political secretariat. More often than not, the MEA was not even privy to the diplomatic moves that the Prime Minister was making.

For the first time, the Prime Minister's Secretariat became an important centre for decision making in foreign policy. The inputs provided by the secretariat began to have an important impact on foreign policy making. There was an institutional shift away from the external affairs ministry on major issues; and had Shastri been successful in his endeavour to establish a coordinating committee of secretaries, the tilt would have been even greater. Shastri's famous idea, for example, of seeking for India "a nuclear umbrella" from the major nuclear powers against any attack, originated in the Secretariat and without the knowledge of the MEA. Again when the ministry refused to apprise the US of India's shock over the alleged American utilisation of gas in the Vietnam war (April 1965), Shastri intervened in the debate to inform the lower house of the Parliament that a representation to this effect had already been made. The importance of the secretariat can be discerned from the important fact that most of his successors had expanded it into an even more powerful decision making body, with nothing equal to it in the whole decisional process. So much so that it has now become so central to most decision making that many observers of the Indian scene today consider that India has moved away from a Cabinet Government to a prime ministerial government.

Shastri's second lasting contribution pertained to the substance of Indian foreign policy. The focus on macro trans-national issues was jettisoned, and was replaced by a greater concentration on India's national interest. The mutation was significant in comparison to the Nehru era where a good segment of Indian diplomacy was centred on broad and abstract issues relating to international relations. With Shastri, it was different. Inexperienced and neophyte as he was on macro international issues, he attended to what he saw around himself: the growing threat of China, the urgency of resolving problems with neighbours, etc. Shastri's focalisation on India's national interest has also become a permanent fixture of Indian diplomacy; for all of his successors without exception followed him by addressing issues that concerned India directly and nationally.

In sum, there was the emergence of realism in Indian foreign policy. Notwithstanding the fact that Shastri was a quintessential Gandhian with profound moralistic and normative base, it was during his prime ministership that Indian policy became more pre-occupied and more concerned with what was good for the country. The "larger normative system-level concerns in world affairs" that characterised the Nehru era was abandoned.[195]

There does not appear to be any doubt that, under Shastri, "The Prime Minister's Secretariat produced more foreign policy decisions than the Ministry of External Affairs."[196]

Shastri's own personal imprint on all foreign policy decisions was also not negligible. Consider for example his role in the 1965 Indo-Pakistan War, and in the Tashkent diplomatic conference which formally ended the war. At the commencement of the conflict when Pakistani infiltration pressures were building up in Kashmir, with its capital Srinagar under serious threat, he personally advanced the idea of escalating the war by opening another front in the plains of the Punjab. He declared in a meeting with leaders of the armed forces, that " Srinagar must not be allowed to fall, and if necessary action should be taken to forestall that by our forces bringing pressure for the fall of Pakistani Punjab's capital city."

At the same time, notwithstanding Pakistani (from East Pakistan) aerial attacks on Indian military bases in West Bengal he refused permission to the chief of the Indian Air Force (IAF) to carry out retaliatory attacks on East Pakistan, on the ground, "considering world situation," it was necessary to exercise restraint and to confine the fighting on the Western sector. Clearly, Shastri was influenced in this decision by the Chinese who had begun to make belligerent statements against India. Again, at Tashkent, where he had taken a large and powerful delegation with whom he never ceased interacting, his personal imprint was overwhelming. He made it clear to everyone participating in the conference, including his own delegation, of "the outside limit he was prepared to go," and not beyond, to make a success of the conference.

Shastri thus became heavily involved in foreign affairs. In an age of increasing globalisation and network power, it is clearly impossible for any head of a Government to ignore foreign policy—least of all for a country such as dimensional India which is burdened with problems connected with the outside world. Even by limiting the scope of India's foreign policy to neighbouring countries, Shastri was submerged by international affairs, for even their ramifications were overwhelming. So Shastri had no choice; he had to face the outside world, which he did remarkably well.

Nonetheless, Shastri remains one of the neglected figures of Indian diplomacy. He never shone, for he symbolised the poor self-effacing Indian who could have been easily lost in a crowd. He was one of those—perhaps the only quintessential Gandhian—ever to have ruled India with deep roots within the country. No one else can claim such a privilege.

INDIRA GANDHI

Chapter III

INDIRA GANDHI
24 JANUARY 1966- 24 MARCH 1977

Formation

Indira Gandhi was much more equipped in foreign affairs than Lal Bahadur Shastri. As Nehru's daughter, she had the rare privilege of being constantly exposed to the outside world. At their luxurious house in Allahabad, where she lived as a child, she was surrounded by books, and by a sweep of intellectual atmosphere created by a rich grand father and politically oriented father whose sojourn in England had made him conversant with a wide array of ideas that saturated the West at the turn of the 20th century. Her own extended sojourn in the West also greatly contributed to the enhancement of her understanding of the world. Europe, at the time, was in an tumultuous state—a Europe heavily marked by the Spanish Civil War, by Nazism and Fascism, by Soviet sponsored popular front movements, and a slew of small countries of the continent living in constant fear of dictatorial dangers looming on the horizon.

It was hardly possible for Indira Gandhi to escape the impact of these events–politically conscious as she was, and living as she did in the heart of Europe as a young girl.

Much has often been made of her lack of intellectual verbosity, and the absence of any marked capacity to dovetail dimensional global issues in abstract theoretical frameworks. This may be viewed as an handicap by those pretending to be intellectuals, but they should hardly be considered as vital instruments for comprehending what was happening in the world. Abstract theoretical frameworks often have a tendency of congealing existing realities into a set and fixed positions that may not have anything to do with the complex environments one lives in.

In her letters to her father from Europe, one can discern the socialistic options she took, the strident attacks she made on the British establishment for its contribution to European fascism, and she openly declared in one her letters to Nehru that fascism "seems to be spreading like flames."[197] In another letter to her father she went even further justifying the Soviet decision to sign the Soviet-German Pact. She wonders if the responsibility for this act did not rest "heavily on those eight years of British Foreign Policy." "Munich, England and France," she asserted, "proved definitely on which side they stood. Russia's policy of collective security having failed, she retired into her pre-Litvinov isolation, and her chief preoccupation was bound to be how to keep herself out of the impending European war."[198] While this was a standard argument among European intellectuals, it took an excessive form among the Indians in Europe because it highlighted British responsibility—an imperialist nation for which they had developed a contempt due to British colonialism in India.

The ongoing educative process continued at adult age. It must have been even more impactful than the earlier years since it really entailed a direct experience in foreign affairs. Acting as the official hostess at Prime Minister Nehru's official residence she had innumerable opportunities of meeting foreign dignitaries and interacting with them. Accompanying the Prime Minister on his myriad official visits to other lands must have also given her an additional backdrop of diplomacy, of power and of international actors. None of the other Indian mainstream politicians had the privilege of such an experience. And, finally, consider the countless informal tête-à-tête she must have had with her father on world affairs and about global leaders. As they were very close to each other, Nehru's level of openness with her must have been more exalted than with anyone else.

To all these exposures should be added the circle of Indian intellectuals she encountered during the earlier periods of her life. Their impact can be as critical as those of parents and educators. At times even more so, especially at an early age when vulnerability is at its apogee. At some moments in our early lives we can be carried away by ideas and by proponents expounding them. While in London, Indira Gandhi had an exposure to a set of radicals through Krishna Menon— like Feroze Gandhi (her future husband), P.N. Haksar (her future Secretary) a student at the London School of Economics, the journalist Nikhil Chakravarty studying at Oxford, and Mohan Kumarmanglam, a product of Cambridge who later became her Cabinet Minister. All of them were proponents of Marxist thought, rampant among Indian intellectuals residing in Europe of the thirties. And, they, all of them, remained Marxist even after the independence of the country.

In India too, when she was still in the corridors of power, with her father as the central political figure, she surrounded herself by the so-called "Kitchen Cabinet" largely composed of left-wing intellectuals. While all of them were leftists, some of them were committed Marxists, including Romesh Thapar, I.K.Gujral, Nandini Sathpathy, Pitambar Pant, Dinesh Singh, C.Subramanium, etc. But, their role was different from the London crowd. For they were not involved so much in the theoretical realm of floating ideas, as in the nitty-gritty of power politics. She could hardly keep herself away from politics while living with her father, whose house and environments were essentially political. Besides, Indira Gandhi was herself a political animal, watching and even participating in politics, and holding responsible positions in the Congress Party.

Perception

However, notwithstanding this privileged knowledge of international affairs, it is difficult to suggest that Indira Gandhi had developed a structured perception of the outside world. She had not. Temperamentally she was neither attracted by long-winded theories of international relations, nor by any abstract conceptualisation of the configuration of international forces despite the fact that she had frequented Marxist circles. She did not have the mental make-up for such intellectual wanderings, nor did she really believe that theoretical underpinnings were essential for political behaviour.

From the documentary evidence available, it can be argued that, like most Indians of her class and her epoch, she considered herself as anti-imperialist socialist who was attracted by the Soviet Union as a country that embodied socialism, and ,even more so, as a victimised country targeted by the capitalist world.

Fascination with the Soviet Union continued after the war. From her trips in 1953 and 1955 (accompanying her father) she returned greatly impressed by the Soviet system. The original perception of a victimised USSR in the thirties was replaced by a new thinking of that of a powerful country representing an economic system that dovetailed with her own ideas.

There is no evidence to suggest that Indira Gandhi had any reservations with the broad foreign policy framework that Nehru had originally established—a framework of non-alignment, a balanced equidistant approach to the two superpowers, active participation in the international system, and mediation in conflictual situations.

These were the normative goals that Nehru had established and followed. Indira Gandhi had no reason to give short shrift to any of them. But, unlike her father she was a pragmatic person interested in India's backyard. The Nehruvian record of relations with neighbours had not been impressive. If anything, it was a record of failures: impassed armed conflicts with Pakistan; humiliating defeat at the hands of the Chinese, a drift away from India by Nepal, Burma and Sri Lanka.

In the face of this debilitative record, interested as she always had been with power politics, her perception of foreign affairs was focalised on the region, and on setting the record straight by making India a powerful centre of South Asian politics. The rest was all marginal during her first mandate as Prime Minister.

In any event, whatever views one may have of Indira Gandhi's perceptual journey through the years, one thing is certain: years of continuous exposure to international affairs had given her an incomparable background and knowledge of the world when she became the Prime Minister—in any event far greater mastery than anyone else among her mainstream political contemporaries. What must have made things easier was that she had personally encountered many of them who were in office, and with whom she could interact comfortably and easily when she became the Prime Minister. Indira Gandhi was one of the persons who could completely close up, but, who also had the remarkable capacity of becoming aimiable, open and interactive whenever cirsumstances required such a behaviour.

By no means was it an intellectually abstract mastery of the underlying forces that underpinned the world. What she had acquired was more than sufficient knowledge and diplomatic savoir faire that gave her what her assistant considered as an "incomparable mastery of India's foreign policy."

Character and Personality

Indira Gandhi owned a character and possessed a personality that "covered her countless complexes."[199]

While living in a joint family as a child, with myriad relatives bustling around, she led a lonely life with a father, often away either in prison or heavily involved in politics, with a sick mother often disdained as an outsider by some members of the family, and with an aunt (Vijaya Lakshmi Pandit) who considered her ugly and stupid.[200]

As a child and young woman she was overwhelmed by politics, by books, and by an intellectual father and rich grand father, but she did not acquire anything resembling intellectuality or anything connected with advanced education. All the efforts of her father to obtain an entry into Oxford failed. Clearly she was not qualified. The same was the case of her two sons who too did not excel in higher education. The one (Rajiv) finally did end up as an pilot, while the other (Sanjay) apparently drifted as a car mechanic. And yet, belonging as they did to powerful, affluent and political family, they had all the facilities and all the opportunities of going in that direction.

Indira Gandhi's intellectual insecurities must have been further aggravated by the fact that, living with her father, she must have encountered myriad situations of being out of depth with him and the intellectual circle he moved around.

Her domestic life too did not arrange matters. She married Feroze Gandhi against the wishes of her father, but rapidly alienated herself from him by taking over responsibilities of looking after Nehru. "I am," she lamented to Dorothy Norman in 1954-55 "in the midst of a domestic crisis...I have been and am deeply unhappy in my domestic life."[201] Indeed she was. Living as she did in a joint family with one son (Rajiv) interested in a quiet comfortable marital life in the secluded company of an Italian wife and two children; and the other (Sanjay), highly ambitious politically, to the gleeful contentment of his mother, but hare-brained in striking shady economic deals, vindictive against those who disagreed, and recklessly courageous to the point of having died while performing daredevil loops with a Pitts aircraft. His wife, Maneka, "utterly fearless...and the very reincarnation of a Durga astride a tiger,"[202] openly defied her mother-in-law with continuous door slamming rows, and with open announcements to all and sundry of her political ambitions.

Indira's insecurities were further exacerbated by her mother's death and the innumerable bouts of serious illnesses she herself suffered from, including tuberculosis. Her alleged sex life apparently did not arrange matters; if anything, according to one actor, rendered her even more insecure.

The compounding together of all these difficulties and problems, through the years, must have marked her personality. They were there all the time. But now that she had finally reached the political summitry as Prime Minister without her father around, there were palpable manifestations of handicaps the most important of which was that of distrust of practically every one around her. "In the first year," observed Raj Thapar, "Indira was shaky. It was then that we noticed her reluctance to trust people, particularly those in the government," and it was then that Thapar discovered that Indira Gandhi "never wanted to reveal her hand or her mind on anything,"[203] and that she began to show, in the early stages of her mandate, a lack of " trust in herself, in her capacity to function as Prime Minister."[204] M.O. Mathai, who knew her well was even less indulgent when she became the Prime Minister. "She," he forecasted, "will play a different type of politics—the politics of manouvre, manipulation and deception" with "no loyalty to anyone except to herself." "Not being," he declared, "overburdened with scruples, She can do almost anything."[205] Equally critical was Satish Gujral, a well-know artist, who though had nothing to do with her politically, had arrived at the conclusion, after having portraited her, that "behind the façade of smiling gentility was an embittered woman concealing vengeful and arrogant traits."[206]

In fact so great was her distrust of others that none of the important decisions were taken collectively. Invariably, they were her decisions taken after individual consultations. There were actually indications of her deliberate intention of sowing seeds of distrust among her advisers. She would have a meeting say of three colleagues. After the meeting she would ask one of them to stay. The next time she would do the same in regard to another person. This was her continuous practice the net result of which was that no one knew what was happening. Her insecurities also translated themselves in some form of withdrawal, and in lack of any great confidence in her capacity of expressing herself. In fact, many who knew her called her the "Dumb Doll" during the first few months of her mandate since a general impression prevailed among those who placed her in power that she could be manipulated.

The women dimension should also be factored into her personality. At the political summitry, where decisions were taken, she was invariably surrounded by men—a situation that did not fail to have some bearing on her being withdrawn, suspicious and aggressive.

In the face of all these psychological handicaps she had to do something to empower herself. Now that she had become the Prime Minister, she made a determined effort of imposing herself, and of projecting herself as a leader. Clearly this was the first thing she had to do to survive her political adversaries.

Soon after the inauguration of her mandate, Indira Gandhi changed: she spoke well publicly, exuded greater confidence, and acquired a remarkable capacity of imposing herself on others. All this was vital for efficacious governance.

But, on the other hand, with the acquisition of power some of the other characteristics of her personality were preserved; if anything they were perpetuated, and even cultivated. For they gave the image of a charismatic leader and the embodiment of power, both of which she needed to enhance her position on the Indian political scene. Furthermore, she became even more distant, even more distrustful of her political entourage and even more aloof in her decisional process.

At the political level, Indira Gandhi always maintained some degree of distance from others. Originally this stemmed from a lack of confidence and from some degree of shyness; but after she became Prime Minister it continued; and as distance is the stuff charisma is made of, she became even more aloof.

Her distrustful mode, which had been with her for years, was continued; in fact, it was exacerbated after she rose to power. What was previously viewed as a shortcoming, now became an asset to be used against political adversaries. Also her character of being very reserved and of being taciturn, of never wanting to reveal her hand or her mind on anything was now fully used in politics.

DECISION MAKING

One of the first manifestations of these features was the establishment of some degree of distance from those with whom she used to interact before coming to power. In sum her so-called "kitchen cabinet," composed of intelligent people, who had rendered her innumerable services, and who provided her with sharp argumentations, and who had crafted intelligent strategies against her political adversaries, were slowly and discreetly dropped. She did not need them anymore, since none of them had any experience of governance, or any real knowledge of the inherent responsibility of power, and since most of them, furthermore, were known for their left wing views—clearly perceived as a handicap for someone who had acceded to the summitry of power. Having the vast machinery of the government at her disposal, she had no use for them in the corridors of power. What the Prime Minister now needed was not a bunch of left wing intellectuals but a different category of people. And this is what she did.

The first category were advisers and operators for domestic affairs, who, in the word of a journalist were a "a set of fawning wheeler dealers"[207]" "Not one of them," he wrote, "had the qualities of a mediocre politician. Bansi Lal, V.C.Shukla, D.K. Barooah, Om Mehta, Yunus, S.S.Ray, D.P.Chattopadhya, Pranab Mukerkjee, not to speak of men like Yashpal and R.K. Dhawan, were all backroom boys …who were devoid of any values. These were the men who rose to the country's top positions and debased them all. So much mediocrity, so much grossness and insignificance of character would have been hard to find even in the minor courts of the Italian Renaissance."[208]

But, in India it was all over—in the corridors of power. All of them had some basic functions: carry out her instructions, protect her interests, raise money by underhand means, and neutralise those perceived to be a threat to her. In sum, most of them had very negative roles to perform.

The second category of people were in her Secretariat—a Secretariat whose role was to monitor the functioning of the government, and to advise the Prime Minister on a host of internal and external issues. L.K.Jha, who had originally established the Secretariat under Shastri, was slowly replaced by P.N. Haksar as her Principal Secretary. Haksar was a powerful, cultivated and highly respected left-leaning diplomat with an impeccable reputation. Obviously she needed someone who seemed more trustworthy, and who had the intellectual capacity of projecting an overwhelming image of Indira Gandhi's power and role. In addition, she calculated, that as a senior member of the foreign service with considerable experience in diplomacy, Haksar would lessen her dependence on the vast bureaucracy of the foreign ministry. As some, who were close to Haksar, remarked that he was "a weighty man in all senses, weighty in bulk, in intelligence, in integrity" who had "an image of a comfortable bear whose very voice could be an assurance in times of need."[209] Clearly, this is what Indira Gandhi needed, at least in the early stages of her mandate. L.K. Jha could have been a good choice too since he was the one who had established the political secretariat, but his major disqualification, in the eyes of the Prime Minister, was that he had been too close to Shastri. Haksar expanded the secretariat and made it into the most powerful decision making agency in the country thus enabling Indira Gandhi "to concentrate all the powers in her hand." The power of the secretariat can be measured from the fact that even a Deputy Secretary in the government could not be appointed without its approval. One close observer of the Indian political scene has suggested that the secretariat had virtually become a "mini government" with each officer dealing exclusively in one area with the overall responsibility of keeping an eye on the minister and the ministry concerned. In sum, the secretariat was highly politicised in the sense that for the first time in the country's post-independence history, government machinery came to be used for political purposes, if need be the Congress party's purpose.

The third category consisted of those who had some expertise in foreign affairs. The whole process of foreign policy making was handled in an informal and secretive manner with powerful and intelligent individuals serving the Prime Minister, including L.K. Jha, T.N. Kaul, P.N. Haksar, G.Parthasarathy, B.K. Nehru, D.P. Dhar and H.Y. Sharada Prasad. All these personalities were carefully selected for delicate assignments about which a very small group had any knowledge. At times, only a few high-powered members of her own secretariat were privy to these assignments. This was in sharp contrast to the advisers she had selected for domestic affairs. This different pattern of choosing advisers in domestic and foreign affairs is revealing. In domestic affairs Indira Gandhi needed advisers who would faithfully carry out her instructions and follow her political strategy, whereas in external affairs she needed people with experience, with knowledge, with some sophistication, and with whom she could interact comfortably; and the ones she had selected were no "fawning wheeler-dealers;" they did interact– the only problem was that none of them really knew what task the other had been assigned. This way of functioning may be attributed to the fact that "she never trusted any person completely or unreservedly—" even those very close to her. This was very much a part of her character, explanations for which may lie in her childhood. This tendency became much more pronounced after 1977 when she had to go through the bitter experience of being persecuted and prosecuted by the Janata Government.

Indira Gandhi's household family can hardly be ignored in any analysis of her personality and of the decisional process. She had always lived in a joint family—with her grand father in Allahabad, with her father in Delhi, and then her own household when she became the prime minister. While in some cases the phenomenon of living together may not have any ramifications on decision making, in her case they did. Her two sons, their wives, and grand children—all of them lived under one roof, where her elder son, Rajiv Gandhi, apparently kept himself aloof from the political commotion that overshadowed the house, Sanjay Gandhi, her second son, on the other hand, became an important actor in shaping political strategies. And as Indira Gandhi's power expanded, so did his. So much so that he began to occupy centre stage not only in the house but even beyond. He had a strange influence on her, even apparently some capacity of blackmailing her. In the Prime Minister's house, he received streams of petitioners every day for three minute audience, and behaved, according to the *New York Times* Correspondent "like a Tammany boss, nodding sympathetically, questioning sharply." Nobody really doubted that he was being promoted as his mother's successor.[210] Some even went to the extent of suggesting that Indira Gandhi "became a pawn in Sanjay Gandhi's hands."[211]

The fifth category of advisers were the Indian intelligence service. Having realised the importance of intelligence in foreign affairs, she divided the whole service into two, leaving the Intelligence Bureau in-charge of internal intelligence and counter-espionage, and entrusting external intelligence to the newly formed Research and Analysis Wing (RAW). Both these services, along with revenue intelligence (which was under the Finance Ministry), were brought directly under the Prime Minister's control. This was perhaps the most important innovation of which she was the architect–an innovation that gave a new dimension to the decisional process in foreign policy.

The subsuming of these categories was by no means very strict. The edge that separated foreign from domestic affairs was so thin that persons belonging to one category could move on to the other. In fact this is what occurred.

FOREIGN POLICY

Foreign policy was not a priority for Indira Gandhi when she came to power. For there were array of domestic issues that needed her urgent attention, including the consolidation of her own authority in the face of emerging dissidence within her own party. Some of her weighty colleagues, who had throned her, were now out to oust her.

There were other problems too, like a serious drought, or the fractious language issue, that required imperative scrutiny; but remaining in power obviously was primordial since there was nothing much she could do to address these issues without having an assailable charge of the country.

Indira Gandhi, therefore, applied herself earnestly to remaining in power. With a combined strategy of rhetoric, open confrontation, devious intrigue, overwhelming courage and a calculated political swing to the left she confronted them. That she finally came out victorious was indeed remarkable—remarkable in terms of risks she had to take and the courage she had to show.

But, in the process, India had to pay a price, a downside from which it has never recovered—even years after her disappearance. For Indira Gandhi had debilitated the country's democratic framework, enhanced an unsightly decisional process, developed intrigue and corruption into an art, and projected on to the Indian political scene a distasteful group of people—at least in the domestic sector. It was indeed a total departure from the ethical mode of conduct that was so dear to her father and to her immediate predecessor, Lal Bahadur Shastri, both of whom embodied a set of moral principles and political consistency to which they remained faithful to the end of their lives. Indira Gandhi, on the other hand, was a chamelonic leader who changed whenever it suited her.

But, what about the substance of foreign policy. Did Indira Gandhi establish any broad framework of action, or institute any basic principles that underpinned her actions, or architectured any road map that steered the country?

It would seem not. Neither any conceptualised framework was discernible nor any broad principles were detectable in her foreign policy actions. She neither had the time—heavily involved as she was domestically—nor the mental inclination to venture into any fixed direction.

Given her personality and character, it could be suggested that she strove to maintain an autonomy of action to defend and safeguard what she perceived to be Indian national interest. This was a ubiquitous phenomenon in all her diplomatic actions.

CONFIGURATION OF GREAT POWERS

The US Dimension

One of the first visible changes she introduced in foreign policy was to slowly jettison Shastri's objectives of building bridges to the US. It was not so much because she had any principled objection against such an initiative as the fact that they never really took off despite some discernible efforts from both sides to introduce an element of warmth in Indo-US relations. The Johnson administration showed a conspicuous tendency of exercising exacting pressures on India that none of the preceding administrations had ventured to exert.

However, notwithstanding these reservations about Washington, her first trip abroad was to the US. Apparently this seemed unavoidable and made consummate sense. India badly needed massive food aid which only the US was in a position to provide. Besides, Washington had shown some visible signs, during Shastri's mandate, of wanting to get closer to India in which Chester Bowles' role was crucial. She wanted to see personally and directly what Johnson had in mind.

The Prime Minister had indeed received a very warm welcome from Lyndon Johnson personally. Finding her irresistible, Johnson had proclaimed in his typical Texan style to all and sundry that he wanted to see to it that "no harm comes to this girl," and immediately promised 3 million tons of food and 9 million dollars of aid.[212] But, it was a promise that had to be processed through normal US channels, and it was a promise which entailed concessions from the Indian side.

On the face of it, the visit was successful, but given India's serious economic difficulties, the US Administration opted in favour of exercising leveraged pressure on the country. From all indications it would seem that Washington wanted to push India to take another course domestically and internationally. While the whole idea had originally spawned during Shastri's time it was earnestly put into operation when Indira Gandhi became Prime Minister.

To risk a generalisation it would seem that the US had manifold objectives: (a) to encourage India to move away from the heavy industry model to a more benign objective of focussing on consumerism and agricultural development; (b) to establish a greater equilibrium in foreign policy, which, in American perception, had tilted excessively in the Soviet direction; (c) to push India to adopt a neutral position on Vietnam in which Washington was heavily involved; and (d) to devalue Indian currency so that India could become more export-oriented and more integrated into the international capitalist system.

In exchange for these mutations, Washington would give a massive food aid, allocate $900 million in non-project aid, and push the World Bank to give additional project loans.

Clearly, Johnson was more ambitious in pushing India to radically change its policies than any of his predecessors. Already, during his visit to India as Vice-President, he had sensed "an intellectual affinity or an affinity of spirit" between India and the US, and had recommended to President Kennedy that this be exploited.[213] While, in his confidential report to Kennedy, he did not consider it necessary or probable to draw "India into our sphere," he favoured a deep-rooted "cementing... an India-US friendship which would endure beyond any transition of power in India"[214] But, when he became President he did show signs of taking a more ambitious interest in India—an interest that went beyond the simple maintenance of the existing status quo in Indo-US relations.

But the US strategy never materialised. It is still not clear what really happened. Opinions differ. Could it be, as alleged by Indira Gandhi, years after the events (1979), that Johnson sat over the urgent Indian appeal for immediate assistance "in order to push India to modify its policy of friendship with the Soviet Union,"?[215] Or, even more so, could it be that the Johnson sat over the Indian request for assistance particularly after Indira Gandhi's refusal to change India's friendly posture towards North Vietnam, an issue on which the US President had very firm views.? In fact, she made her views quite clear when Vice President Hubert Humphrey was in India for Shastri's funeral. When L.K.Jha emphasised, in the presence of Indira Gandhi, that it was "of utmost importance that India remain friendly with North Vietnam, otherwise there would be an erosion of Ho Chi Minh's trust in India," Humphrey declared "My God, am I to go back and say to the President that India feels closer to Vietnam than to the US."[216] Or could it be that Indira Gandhi was irritated by US pressures and was not prepared to introduce fundamental changes in India's economic and foreign policies. Howsoever valid the US argumentation may have been regarding the options India had taken, it was unlikely—given Indira Gandhi's character and personality—that she would have reneged on the fundamental politico-economic and diplomatic options India had consensually taken at the time of independence.

The bureaucracy in Washington demanded too much, and that even continued during the very first year of her mandate when she was busy consolidating her political power. Besides, it was hardly realistic to expect India to introduce fundamental changes in its economy, and turn their back to the Russians at a time when Indira Gandhi was using left-wing rhetoric to undermine the power of her adversaries.

In any event, Chester Bowles, US Ambassador to India confirmed Washington's irritation with New Delhi. "Cables from Washington," he wrote "burned with comments about 'those ungrateful Indians,' and the shipments of wheat were further delayed. Our official logic in regard to India seemed to run as follows... If India cannot support US policy, it should at least refrain from criticising it, or accept the consequences. The spirit at its worst was reflected in a remark a White House official made to me...Mrs.Gandhi, I asserted was only saying what (UN Secretary General)

U Thant and the Pope had said over and over and over again. 'But, replied the official, 'the Pope and U Thant don't need our wheat'." [217]

The only issue on which India went along with the US was on the devaluation of the Indian rupee. The pressures were indeed very great; and not only from Washington but also from the World Bank, the International Monetary Fund, and from some of her own close advisers. India badly needed US aid and Indira Gandhi knew well that she would have to cede on something; and she decided to cede on devaluation.

But on the other issues, the Indian response was a firm no. In fact, she did the opposite. Instead of moving in the direction of market-oriented policies, she tilted even more to the left and nationalised all the commercial banks; instead of establishing some distance with Moscow she maintained the traditional Indian posture of friendliness vis-à-vis the Communist world; and finally, instead of adopting a prudent policy on Vietnam she became even more openly critical of US policies there.

While all these policies were a continuation of the traditional foreign policy pattern designed by Nehru, the rhetorical re-assertion of them all was prompted by domestic factors. Indira Gandhi was really facing the prospects of loosing power. Many of those who had manoeuvred to place her in power were now out to dethrone her. For the majority of her party colleagues, she was becoming too independent, and too defiant of the existing Congress leadership. She had to be, therefore, ousted. For them, there was no other alternative, for her continuation in power would unavoidably result in their marginalisation in Indian politics.

To counter what had really become a serious threat to her power, she mobilised everything in her armour to stage the "great split" in the party. She mobilised her own instinctive courage, her dynastic name, her popularity, and a great leap to the left consensually acceptable to the country.

Indira Gandhi came out of this political battle with flying colours, seriously weakening the dissidents who were clearly slow on the uptake.

The "great split" of the Congress Party in 1969 marked a milestone in the development of Indira Gandhi's personality, and a salient turning point in Indian politics. She "had come into her own,"[218] gaining considerable confidence in herself and in her actions; so much so that she arrived at the ominous conclusion that she was the only one capable of leading the country.

But the ramifications of this psychological revolution in her personality was calamitous for the country. She centralised power in her own hands. The

Congress Party was no more a loose organisation where different ideological groups co-existed and functioned democratically. The decisional process was further narrowed with her son, Sanjay Gandhi, always there playing a crucial but underhand role on an array or issues. The Cabinet members, radically reshuffled, were reduced to sycophancy with most of them attempting to outbid each other in oleaginous behaviour. The state leaders, who had failed to support her in her battles against the "Syndicate," were ousted, and the Indian intelligence, split into two (internal and external), was brought firmly under the direct control of the Prime Minister.

The whole Indian political system had taken an oligarchic turn with Indira Gandhi as the stellar figure. In the eyes of the *New York Times* she had become "a prime minister on her own right, and not a transitional figure trading on her legacy as the daughter of Nehru".

Her hand was further strengthened by going to the polls in 1971 and returning with a landslide victory.

It was this victory that gave her the real legitimacy that she needed. Isolating and defeating the "Syndicate" was one thing, but popular electoral victory was another matter, since it was this success at the polls that gave her the confidence she needed, and pushed her to become politically even more active.

In foreign affairs she became even more powerful and even more defiant. The domestic dimension was no more there to restrain her authority and to question her diplomatic actions. None of the Prime Ministers, before and after, had acquired such a large leverage as she had. And, She used it to the hilt.

Intervention in Bangladesh

The first important manifestation of this line was the Prime Minister's successful military intervention in East Pakistan in 1971 that gave her the self-confidence and the determination she needed in foreign affairs. The massive influx of refugees into India from East Pakistan, compounded with Karachi's repressive measures against the democratically elected Mujibur Rahman in Eastern Pakistan, and plus the Pakistani air force raids on Indian military bases catalysed Indira Gandhi to intervene militarily—an intervention that resulted in the establishment of independent Bangladesh. It was a well organised military and RAW operation. However, to neutralise any adverse US or Chinese counteraction against India, Indira Gandhi concluded a treaty with USSR under which Moscow would come to

India's assistance in the event of a third party intervention. It was indeed a machiavellian act that cleared the road for Indira Gandhi to take action. Chinese and US threats came to nothing since India succeeded in rapidly defeating the Pakistan forces and obtaining their surrender.

Bangladesh's independence marked a major milestone in India's foreign policy. It was the first time since Indian independence in 1947 that India had scored a decisive military victory over Pakistan.

This in turn was followed by a diplomatic victory in 1972 in Shimla where an agreement was concluded between Indira Gandhi and her Pakistani counterpart, Bhutto, under which the latter agreed that all the bilateral issues between the two countries would be resolved bilaterally. But, what remains an inexplicable mystery is why she did not use this overwhelming Pakistani defeat to force Bhutto to agree to the legitimacy of the line that separated India's Kashmir from the Kashmiri area occupied by Pakistan. Bhutto had apparently advanced the argument that such a step would weaken his position domestically—in fact he might even be ousted from power.

But, why should Indira Gandhi be concerned with his downfall, given the fact that he was notoriously dogmatic about his anti-Indian orientations, and had in the past, as well as in the future, did everything he could to counter India.

G. Parthsarathy, one of Prime Minister's close and sober advisers, has suggested that it was P.N. Haksar who dissuaded her from taking such a step by conjuring up the amazing thesis that Pakistan would become a militarist state the way Germany had become, after World War I, because of the unequal treaties, if Bhutto went back from Shimla without any concessions from India. "Such advise," writes G. Parthsarathy "only led to Pakistan leading us up the garden path at the Shimla summit."[219]

Should this be the correct version of the events, it is indeed astounding that a machiavellianly oriented Indira Gandhi should have accepted such an historical explanation to appease Bhutto. For Pakistan was already becoming militaristic.

Ramifications of Bangladesh

The ramifications of these victories were indeed considerable.

For the first time India had emerged as South Asia's pre-eminent regional power. Though there was naturally no formal international recognition to this effect, there is no gainsaying of the fact that the international community had realised that it had to reckon with the new South Asian configuration of forces where India had become the predominant power, having reached the peak.

Indians too became conscious of their own power. Some were already conjuring up visions of India having acquired such power that no one else could intervene in the area without its consent. In sum, the establishment of some sort of a Monroe Doctrine that would keep other powers out of South Asia, just as it did in Latin America. Since then it has never left them. Even Indira Gandhi, though normally very sober and cool-headed, was apparently carried away by this new feeling of strength

The second major ramification was the emergence of bilateralism with Pakistan having reluctantly accepted the Indian proposal that the two countries will resolve all future problems bilaterally. The trend towards bilateralism became fairly well entrenched in 1970s. In fact, it underpinned India's diplomatic behaviour vis-à-vis all South Asian neighbours.

This translated itself into exercising pressures on other South Asian countries. The first was Sri Lanka where Indira Gandhi began a discreet initiative of training the island's Tamil Tigers, who were demanding enlarged autonomy of their north-eastern areas from the central government. By doing so, she was, in effect, challenging the authority of the Colombo Government. But the Sri Lankan Tamils moved away from demanding authonomy for their areas to proclaim that their goal in fact was the independence of their areas.

The radical wing of Sri.Lankan Tamils finally became problematic for everyone: for the Colombo Government which refused to accept these demands, for India, which did not favour independence, and the Tamil Nadu State Government, which supported the demand for autonomy, but now had to go along with the new claims, not to speak of the fact that all this finally resulted in the assassination of Rajiv Gandhi by Tamil Tigers.

The new firm Indian politics also translated itself in the Himalayan region resulting, first of all, in the forcible incorporation of Sikkim as the twenty-second state of the Indian Union in April 1975. Wedged in-between Nepal in the West, Tibet in the North, Bhutan in the East, and West Bengal in the South, it had its important strategic location. Given the Chinese active diplomacy in the region, with Tibet already under their control, Indira Gandhi feared that Beijing may have designs of establishing a sphere of influence in the North of which Sikkim would also be a part. While there were some South Asian and even Chinese outcries against its annexation, the Indians announced this as yet another truimph of democracy.

With the new Indian diplomacy of bilateralism, Nepal was also Indira Gandhi's target, given Kathmandu's active diplomacy of playing the India-China game, and of continuously proclaiming its intentions of distancing itself from New Delhi. Of this, the Nepalese were warned from time to time. But, when, King Birendra of Nepal, at a meeting of the Colombo Plan Consultative Committee in mid-seventies, called upon all the regional countries to benefit from Nepal's abundant reseources, and even evoked the idea of South Asian regional cooperation, along with Bangladesh's military ruler, Zia ur-Rahman, Indira Gandhi viewed this as a deviation from her politics of bilateralism characterising it as a "gag" by small South Asian countries. And when four countries (Bangladesh, Nepal, Pakistan and Sri Lanka) evoked the idea of South Asian regional cooperation, she harshly chracterised the scheme as the scheme of the "gang of four," the purpose of which, in her view, was to embarras India.

Bhutan, on the other hand, a faithful proponent of bilateralism, was given friendly signals, so much so that its politics of expelling massively people of Nepalese origin, residing in Southern Bhutan, was neglected on the ground that it was a domestic matter between Bhutan and Nepal in which India did not wish to intervene.

Another manifestation of Indira Gandhi's ongoing policy of firmness was her decision to explode a nuclear device in May 1974 against the wishes of the big powers. The decision was taken, after it became increasingly evident that Indian representations to Washington and Moscow, to obtain an assured nuclear umbrella guarantee, was unsuccessful. A clear decision was, therefore, taken not to adhere to the Nuclear Non-proliferation Treaty (NPT), on the ground that this would have virtually blocked India's option to go nuclear. What made the Indians decisively decide to keep the nuclear option open was not only because of China, but also because of Pakistan which was showing signs of going nuclear with active Chinese assistance.

The Soviet Dimension

The other ramification was the proximity that emerged in Indo-Soviet relations. Under Indira Gandhi, India moved much closer to the Soviet Union than it had ever been under her two predecessors. One of the principal hallmarks of her first mandate was the conclusion of the Indo-Soviet Treaty of Friendship—a treaty that gave India an element of protective security against any US and/or Chinese intervention while India was heavily mired in an armed conflict with Pakistan. The Russians, it would seem, gave Indira Gandhi a blank cheque. They promised to use their veto in the UN, should the issue come up at the Security Council, made it clear to all and sundry that if Pakistan or China attacked India they would respond with an airlift of military equipment. In sum, according to Kissinger, it was "the strongest endorsement yet by the Kremlin of the Indian strategy" of confronting Pakistan.[220] The Russians apparently went much beyond the operative clause of the treaty that vaguely stipulated that the two countries would mutually consult each other "in order to remove such threat and to take appropriate effective measures to ensure peace and security of their countries"[221]

Moscow seized the opportunity of this growing tuneful atmosphere of Indo-Soviet entente to establish a vast intelligence network—a network, according to the Mitrokhin archives, that had become "one of the largest in the world outside of the Soviet bloc."[222] By the seventies the KGB was everywhere. "We had," admitted Oleg Kalugnin of the Soviet intelligence service, "scores of sources throughout the Indian Government—in intelligence, counterintelligence, the Defence and Foreign Ministries, and the Police."[223] So well was the KGB established that Kalugnin recalls one occasion when Andropov, the head of the agency, personally turned down an Indian minister's offer to provide information for $50,000 on the ground that the KGB was already well supplied with material from foreign and defence Ministries.[224] The measure of Soviet intelligence penetration can be judged from the fact that funds were allegedly being provided to all sorts of sources including Indira Gandhi to whose house "suitcases full of banknotes were said to be routinely taken."[225]

It would be incorrect to conclude from these secret Soviet intelligence reports, recently published, that Indira Gandhi was pro-Soviet ideologically. She was not. In fact, she never was, even during the periods when she was, like her father, attracted by the Soviet system. The circumstances of the seventies dictated the emergence of political and diplomatic pro-Sovietism—circumstances around the Bangladesh liberation when Indira Gandhi clearly needed Soviet support to neutralise US and Chinese pressures.

Indo-US relations, on the other hand, worsened reaching their nadir when Richard Nixon, suceeding Lyndon Johnson, was in the White House. This was a turning point in Indo-US relations, for it was the first time that Washington jettisoned its hope of building India as a counterweight to Chinese communism. It had always been there at the back of US policies, during most presidencies of the past. Notwithstanding the development of close US-Pakistan relations, dictated by the cold war, India had never been completely abandoned. But under Nixon, all this changed. The mutual personal antipathy between Nixon and Indira Gandhi go back to the days when Nixon came to India in 1969 as Vice-President. Apparently, Indira Gandhi did not treat him well—at least he returned to Washington with this perception at the back of his mind.

What could be a worst humiliation for India than being informed by the White House that Nixon would consider any negative reaction by India on the new Sino-US relations as unfriendly. What conclusion should one draw from the virtual go ahead that Kissinger gave to the Chinese to intervene in the Indo-Pakistan conflict assuring them that Washington would protect them should the Russians decide to take any action to dissuade the Chinese from acting on the subcontinent. And what should one make of Kissinger's decision to use Pakistan's good offices to secretly go to Beijing on the same visit that took him to Delhi?

What should one make of the conversation transcripts of 26th May, and 5th November 1971 between Richard Nixon and Henry Kissinger—conversations that were not only offensive against Indira Gandhi but almost abusive of the Indians. Consider the following conversations. 21 MAY 1971:

Kissinger: They are the most aggressive goddam people around there.

Nixon: The Indians?

Kissinger: Yeah.

Nixon: Sure.

5 November 1971 (after a meeting with Indira Gandhi)

Nixon: We really slobbered over the old witch.

Kissinger: The Indians are bastards anyway. They are starting a war there. While she was a bitch, we got what we wanted too. She will not be able to go home and say that the US did'nt give her a warm reception and therefore in despair. She has got to go to war.

In an another conversation with Kissinger on 4 June 1971 Nixon berates his Ambassador, Kenneth Keating, for wanting to, as Kissinger puts it, "help India push the Pakistanis out."

Nixon says: "I don't want him to come in with that kind of a jackass thing with me...Keating, like every ambassador who goes there, goes over there and gets sucked in."

Kissinger then says: "Those sons-of-bitches who have never lifted a finger for us why should we get involved in the morass of East Pakistan."[226]

The Indian public, already known for its anti-Americanism, took a turn for the worse. For all these US actions were perceived as humiliation by the Indians. And, under the circumstances, Moscow was naturally perceived as a protector with whom India had to cultivate even more than it had done in the past.

Within two years of her mandate as Prime Minister, Indira Gandhi had convinced herself that the US, at least under Nixon, was firmly anti-Indian. "The US," she declared in a private conversation "was trying a pincer hold on Asia—Vietnam and Israel—India would be encircled." "It is better," she continued, "that we die than give in to constant pressure from the USA. Chester Bowles had come to see me recently, he lectured me and did not give me a chance to say what was in my mind. So I refused to speak, was cordial, wished him a pleasant trip, but kept silent—and that was that."[227] Indira Gandhi's personality and character, being what it was, also reacted firmly to snub Nixon. She was very firm in her meetings with him, and she declined Nixon's invitation for dinner, along with other Afro-Asian leaders without giving any reason—undoubtedly an unusual act in diplomatic protocol.

Indira Gandhi's anti-Americanism was further aggravated by her conviction that the CIA was actively attempting to destabilise her government—a conviction that was reinforced by fabricated Soviet intelligence reports. More than seventy reports were planted in the press condemning CIA subversion. So much so that the Prime Minister raised the whole question with Henry Kissinger, and personally wrote to Sri Lankan Prime Minister, Sirimavo Bandaranaike to warn her of CIA activities by enclosing KGB's forged CIA documents and Indian press reports which had been taken in by them.[228]

The Chinese Dimension

However, while tilting in the Soviet direction, Indira Gandhi also began to show signs of wanting to normalise relations with China. She had to do it prudently since public opinion was very anti-Chinese in the aftermath of the humiliating defeat of 1962, and since the Chinese, heavily mired in the Cultural Revolution, were not interested in diplomatic niceties of cultivating states whom they had denounced as reactionaries. India was on the top of the list of reactionaries.

Indira Gandhi moved cautiously. But she did. She sounded her advisers, held staff meetings, invited comments from people in her entourage. One of the persons to whom she asked for an opinion was K.R.Narayanan, who later become the President of India, but who at the time was working in the MEA . He was asked to make a report—which he did recommending normalisation of relations. At the meeting of senior officials, where Indira Gandhi was also present, it was decided to take the necessary steps.[229] But it was not the report that made her decide to open up to China. She had already made up her mind to go in that direction. What she wanted was the airing of the subject.

On 1 January 1969 Indira Gandhi publicly gave expression to India's desire to normalise relations. In effect this was the first public signal in which she gave some hints of no more insisting on the Chinese acceptance of the non-aligned Colombo proposal on the Sino-Indian conflict as a precondition of any normalisation. It was a virtual abandonment of what her predecessor had been insisting upon. Indira Gandhi also made it clear that she was going to ignore the Chinese media attacks on her and her government.

The first step naturally had to be the exchange of ambassadors. And since it was the Indians who had recalled their ambassador after the Sino-Indian dispute they had to take the initiative. And this is what she did in 1971, when the Indian chargé affaires in Beijing was instructed to convey the Indian wish to exchange ambassadors. She also personally wrote to Zhou Enlai to this effect in July 1971.

The Chinese response was prudent and ambiguous. In fact it was very Chinese. On the one hand they made a dramatic public gesture on 1st May 1970 of inviting Brajesh Mishra, the Indian Representative, to meet Mao at the podium, in full public view, to exchange friendly niceties on Sino-Indian relations. On the other hand when the Indians sought clarifications after this public display, the Chinese remained vague and ambiguous, limiting their answer to the effect that the Chairman's remarks were a sufficient indication of a desire for improvement of relations, but it was up to the Indians to make concrete suggestions.

In all probability it was after this clarification that Indira Gandhi took the initiative to convey the Indian wish to exchange ambassadors.

In any event the Chinese were not ready to undertake normalisation in the early 1970s. They had not made up their mind on the subject. Besides, the country was still mired in the Cultural Revolution, and it was hardly possible for anyone in the Chinese political hierarchy to take any initiative. Finally, it took them four more years to respond to India.

An Ambassador, in the person of K.R. Narayanan, was finally despatched in 1976. He arrived in Beijing at a critical moment. The decade old tumultuous Cultural Revolution had finally come to an end. The great luminaries of the Chinese Revolution (Mao Zedong, Zhou Enlai, Chu Teh) had died. Uncertainty reined everywhere, among the people and within the Chinese leadership, mired in an fractious struggle for power, and in the politico-economic system that was increasingly becoming directionless. For the Indian ambassador it was the best of time, and, at the same time, the worst of time, since he was left to his own devices, uncontrolled and unwatched, with a message from the Chinese Ministry of Foreign Affairs, to carry out his chores even before presenting his credentials.

Indira Gandhi Style of Diplomacy

Another major ramification of the Bangladesh events was the style of Indian diplomacy. It became more firm, more determined, more defiant and even more aggressive—all of which were absent under the two preceding Prime Ministers.

Indira Gandhi's forceful personality and determination had much to do with the new style. The Bangladesh victory had given her the additional confidence to include an element of defiance whenever it was required.

She defied Nixon in 1971, decisively helped the Sri Lankan Government against extreme left-wing radicals (Janatha Vimukti Permuna) in 1971, pushed Bhutto to agree to the politics of bilateralism in Indo-Pakistan relations in 1972, conveyed to Nepal and Sri Lanka in March 1972 and February 1973 respectively, during her travels there, of her determination to maintain a firm grip on South Asia to the exclusion of others.

If one were to add to all this India's nuclear explosion in May 1974, the forceful integration of Sikkim in April 1975—not to speak of the unilateral decision to discontinue receiving US food aid in January 1972, and the banning of the landing of US military flights at Indian airports in November 1972—all of them were clear signs of determination and defiance.

As a part of this style, the decisional process too continued to mutate in the diplomatic sector. It became more oligarchical than the pattern of internal decision making; for in domestic matters, despite the onset of political authoritarianism, Indira Gandhi still had to reckon with powerful mainstream and dissident voices , whereas in foreign policy there were none. Domestically, she had a free hand in foreign policy. There was no one of any authority in the mainstream of Indian politics to challenge her. If anything there appeared to exist an overall consensus. There were of course international constraints and restraints that she had to take into account when initiating foreign policy, but Indira Gandhi developed a high level of diplomatic sophistication and realism to realise the limits beyond which she could not go.

Internally, the institutions, formally concerned with foreign policy, were marginalised. Indira Gandhi's decision to conclude the Indo-Soviet treaty was handled in great secrecy. Only two senior Cabinet Ministers (Y.B.Chavan and Jagjivan Ram) were informed after the finalisation of the draft. Other Cabinet members were informed half an hour before the formal signing of the treaty, and after it had already been released to the media.[230] The Parliament's participation was even more fruitless. It was presented with a fait accompli. The same was the case regarding the nuclear test in 1974. No one in the Cabinet was informed in advance.

Indira Gandhi also decided on her own, much against the wishes of the Cabinet and her associates, to pay a visit to Western countries on October-November 1971, when war-like situation was developing between India and Pakistan..

When Nixon despatched the US 7th fleet to the Indian Ocean, India's foreign and defence ministers proposed an immediate cease fire in a Cabinet meeting; Indira Gandhi refused point-blank.

Furthermore, the whole Bangladesh affair was managed in her usual authoritarian style. Only a few political and professional advisers like P.N.Haksar, D.P.Dhar, T.N.Kaul were consulted. The institutions were bypassed—the Parliament, the Cabinet, the MEA, etc.

The decisional process was further narrowed after the Emergency was imposed in June 1975. By then, P.N. Haksar, the most weighty of her political advisers had been eased out (January 1973). D.P.Dhar was no more present at major decision making—not even in the corridors of power. While T.N. Kaul, G.Parathasarathy and P.N.Dhar had been reduced to simple executioners.

EVALUATION

Notwithstanding her great interest in international affairs, Indira Gandhi had never really designed the broad contours of her foreign policy. She neither had the time nor the intellectual dimension, nor even the mental inclination to construct a broad vision at macro level.

But, on the other hand, she recognised the vital importance of making India a crucial factor in sub-continental politics. In this she had clearly succeeded where others had failed.

Her first mandate was therefore a major landmark in India's foreign policy in so far as it had irrevocably moved away from macro issues, and in so far as it had successfully projected India as the major factor in South Asian politics.

While continuing to proclaim India's adherence to non-alignment, India clearly tilted in the Soviet direction. Anti-US sentiments, rampant in public opinion, spilled over to Government policies. The disappointing experience with Presidents Johnson and Nixon, compounded with the latter's search for an entente with China, brought Indo-US relations to a nadir point. The balance Nehru had maintained between the two superpowers, and the subtle tilt that Shastri wanted to give to Indian diplomacy in the American direction were abandoned. And the Indo-Soviet treaty brought India closer to Moscow politically and economically. But this Soviet tilt did not mirror her ideological proclivities. For she had none. It was dictated by events in South Asia and by the pragmatic need to seek protection. Indira Gandhi was not unaware of the dangers such an orientation represented to Indian independence. Her prudence in avoiding public criticism of Soviet aggressive actions in Czechoslovakia was a proof of dominant-subaltern pattern that had slipped in Indo-Soviet relations. She was unhappy with the situation but felt that she had to remain silent for the sake of Indian interest.

In all probability it was this asymmetrical situation that germinated the notion in her head that India should seek out China as a counterweight. For one thing this would balance out the level of Indian dependence on Moscow since the fear of China originally was one of the factors that spawned Indian pro-Moscow orientations. For another, some understanding with Beijing would also diminish the security threat from the north, and may indeed help in forestalling the emergence of US-China-Pakistan axis.

However, notwithstanding this easy access to international affairs, it is difficult to advance the hypothesis that Indira Gandhi developed a structured perception of the outside world. Temperamentally, she was not a person with any inclination to be attracted by long-winded theories of international relations or by any abstract analysis of the configuration of international forces. In all likelihood she did not have the mental make-up to indulge in such intellectual wanderings.

From the evidence that is available it can be argued that, like most Indians of her class and of her epoch, she considered herself as an anti-imperialist socialist who was attracted by the Soviet Union as a country that embodied socialism, and, even more, as a country victimised by the capitalist world.

Fascination with the Soviet Union continued after World War II. Accompanying her father in 1955 to that country, she returned "greatly impressed with the Soviet system."[231] But the original perception of the thirties of a victimised Soviet Union had left her, and was replaced by a land that embodied power representing an economic system that dovetailed with her ideas.

There is no evidence to suggest that Indira Gandhi had any major reservations with Nehru's original broad framework of foreign policy- –a framework of non-alignment, of a balanced approach to the two superpowers, of active participation in the international system, and of inventing mediatory efforts in international conflicts.

These were the normative goals that Nehru had constructed and followed. Indira Gandhi had no reason to give short shrift to any of them. But, unlike her father, and without belittling what Nehru had constructed, she was a practical and pragmatic person who was basically interested in India's backyard; in sum its neighbours where the Indian record had not been impressive.

In the face of this debiltative record—interested as she had always been with power politics, her perception of foreign affairs was focalised on the region, and setting the record straight by making India a powerful centre in South Asia. The rest was unimportant during her first mandate as Prime Minister.

MORARJI DESAI

Chapter IV

MORARJI DESAI
27 MARCH 1977–22 JULY 1979

The humiliating electoral defeat of Indira Gandhi in 1977, and the victory of the opposition in the general elections, created a unique political situation. For the first time, since independence there was a landmark institutional mutation. A non-congress coalition group (Janata Party), was now installed at the helm of affairs of the country with Morarji Desai as the new Prime Minister.

There was indeed boisterous public applause at this notable political change—not so much because Desai became the Prime Minister as the fact that Indira Gandhi was thrown out of power. Her tight authoritarian emergency rule, leading to massive arrests and severe political persecution, had discredited her in the eyes of the public.

Authoritarian rule, imposed by Indira Gandhi, was not India's cup of tea. It could never digest it; for it had never happened before. While it would be unfair to suggest she had an inherent penchant for a despotic system of governanance, it was, perhaps, a combination of circumstances that catalysed her to take such a drastic step—what with the Allahabad High Court's decision to declare her election illegal, what with her politically oriented son, Sanjay Gandhi, pressing her to impose an emergency rule, and what with Jayaprakash Narayan coming out of the political wilderness to mobilse the country against her actions.

It would appear that Indira Gandhi was of two minds on taking such a step,[232] but was decisively carried away by the pressures of her son whose "pawn" she had become. Strange as it may seem, it is indeed striking that a person of her calibre, independendence, known calmness, and political determination should have clamped down on the country on the advise of the others, particularly her son who hardly had a desirable reputation. Besides, though Indira Gandhi was known to be an impatiently authoritarian and intolerant person in her political dealings with the others, no one had ever thought that she was possessed with despotic proclivities in governance.

In any event, she was out, and Morarj Desai's long-held political dream of becoming the Prime Minister had at last been realised; for he had personally convinced himself years before that he was the right man for the job. In fact, after Nehru, he had openly projected himself as the most deserving candidate.

Formation and Perception

Originally Desai was a member of the Congress Party in which he had had a long and impressive record as a nationalist fighter for Indian independence. Like many other leaders he too languished in prison, and like most of them, he was a fervent follower of Gandhi, but even more so than the others, since he had embraced much of Gandhi's Hinduist idiosyncracies. But, until an advanced age he had not acquired the stature of a national leader comparable to such nationalist icons as Nehru, Patel, Azad, etc. He had remained in an ancillary position in Indian politics.

However, after independence and after some impressive work as the Chief Minister of the Bombay State, where he had shown an enormous talent of effective governance, decisive leadership and unrelenting incorruptability he was projected onto the national level where he occupied key national posts, finally reaching the status of a Deputy Prime Minister. Nehru had much to do with his ascension to the national level; notwithstanding his myriad reservations regarding Desai's orthodox and dogmatic views, the Prime Minister did see qualities in him—qualities of effective governance which others lacked. Besides, Nehru, according to his assistant Mathai, furthermore, had singled out Desai as one of the "two straightest men he had come across in India" among the then existing leadership.[233]

Morarji was a purist. He had developed a high sense of morality, and had acquired a host of inflexible convictions to which he strictly adhered to, including a urine drinking therapy that he regularly indulged in throughout his life.

His behaviour, formation, and childhood were difficult; in fact very difficult. He came from a familiy of ancestors who were tempramentally "known for their plain-speaking, somewhat hot tempers and independence."

The religious dimension too was impactful. The deeply religious atmosphere that he was surrounded with, plus his avid readings of

Ramayana, Mahabharata and Panchtantra, all of which heavily infused his sense of morality. And if one were to compound the "hard jolts" he had received as young boy of 15, including the death of his father who had thrown himself into a well, the maintenance of his family consisting of a grandmother, mother, three younger brothers, two sisters, and the little girl he had married three days after his death, it is not suprising that Morarji became "rigid, curt, abrasive, and above all, self-righteous"[234] often describing himself as the "instrument of God's will."

Desai was no socialist. He never was. Even during periods when such claims were shortcuts to leadership he had declined to project himself as such. While working closely with contemporaries like Nehru and Indira Gandhi, whose socialist orientations were loud and well known, he continued to openly proclaim that he was a pragmatist, solely guided and motivated by what he considered to be a pragmatic approach on a wide array of politico-economic problems that India was faced with. Clearly this was his strength, for there was no one in the top party leadership who had courageously and openly expressed his dissident views under preceding governments while occupying high positions. But this was also his weakness since firm moralistic principles had made him obstinate and inflexible.

DECISION MAKING

Despite his forceful and determined character, the new Janata government radically altered the political functioning of the system, diminishing the role of the personality factor in foreign affairs. For the first time since independence, the traditional institutions once again came to the forefront, gaining in authority, while the powerful Prime Minister's Secretariat, conceived by Shastri and expanded by Indira Gandhi, was converted into a small and a weak office. It was really sidelined by the new Prime Minister.

Basically, there were three reasons that contributed to this shift. The first was the new Prime Minister himself. Having had very little to do with foreign affairs during his entire political career, he had no vision of the outside world, no perception of the international configuration of forces, and no real framework to go by except for very fixed opinions—repeatedly stated—that India had never been "genuinely non-aligned" and that its foreign policy was tilted too much on one side—the Soviet side. It, therefore, in his view, needed to be rectified by the establishment of a better equilibrium through more normal relations with China, and through the development of a more open policy towards the US.

The second reason was the overall political atmosphere in the country— one that had become stifling. The political air was full of animosity and revenge. Much of the activities of the Janata Government were focussed on berating and prosecuting Indira Gandhi— now in the opposition. It was paying her back in the same coin – the coin of hate, persecution and imprisonment. Besides, the domestic political problems had become so overwhelming, after the turbulence of the emergency rule, that they required the immediate attention of the new leadership. While foreign affairs, on the other hand, were moving smoothly; there was nothing urgent and nothing critical that needed any preoccupying attention, and there was nothing looming on the horizon that endangered Indian security. All was apparently quiet at the international front so far as India was concerned.

The third reason—and perhaps the principal one—was the character of the Government. For the first time in the post-independent history of the country, a coalition government was installed at the centre of political parties of very different political spectrums who were hitherto sparring at each other, and who had only united to oust Indira Gandhi. By nature, coalition governments are disparate and indecisive, making it exceedingly difficult for the one who is heading it to exercise the same degree of authority as a one-party government. The new Prime Minister, therefore, clearly was in a bind with very little leverage. He gave a lot of ink to government communications, and spent much of his time listening to others, seeking their advice, searching for compromises, and taking into account the different views circulating among the members of his government and the political parties they represented. Therefore, notwithstanding all the long-winded statements that were made highlighting the determination of the government to introduce changes in Indian foreign policy, the broad guidelines that had been established before were continued. Morarji Desai did not really leave any imprint. There was nothing for which he would be remembered. The institutions that benefited the most from this state of affairs were the Cabinet, Ministry of External Affairs and the Parliament- -the Cabinet because its members being disparate had greater voice in decision making than before; the MEA because it was the only body which possessed the expertise in foreign affairs, including the well established appropriate infrastructure to operationalise the decisions taken; and the

Parliament, hitherto ignored, was showing signs of some degree of assertion in foreign affairs.

The worst sufferer was the intelligence service—a service that had been built into a powerful institution, and that had begun to play a crucial role in providing information unavailable from other established institutions. The Janata Government was convinced that the Research and Analysis Wing (RAW) had played a crucial role against the opposition when Indira Gandhi had clamped down the Emergency rule. It was also alleged to have been been "instrumental in transferring hordes of money abroad for Mrs. Gandhi." Morarji personally was convinced that RAW's activities were "highly immoral and highly irregular." The organisation built over the years "was litterally shattered in a few moments" —so much so that the Prime Minister was reported to have disclosed the identity of an Indian spy to the Pakistani President. The information that India had received from its man in Pakistan was indeed valuable regarding Pakistan's latest developments in Kahuta—the centre of Pakistan's nuclear activities. Furthermore, it would seem that Desai had refused to take any action against Pakistan, when Brezhnev and Carter had brought to his attention their concern regarding Pakistan's ongoing nuclear weapons programme.

The whole decision making process, thus, was considerably modified. The inputs provided by the personality factor of the preceding Prime Ministers in foreign policy making were decimated. Routine factors, along with macro issue, were passed on to the MEA, while decisions on visible issues had to be taken collectively by the Cabinet over which no personal imprint of the Prime Minister was visible. For the first time since the independence of India the whole decision making process was diffused, with the Prime Minister no longer at the centre of foreign affairs.

Besides, the greater institutionalisation of decision making, there were at least two personalities who became crucial in foreign policy making. One was the the Foreign Minister, Atal Behari Vajpayee, and the other was the Foreign Secretary, Jagat S. Mehta. While both of them were institutionally and functionally linked with foreign affairs, their inputs in actual foreign policy making were more ponderous than was the case in similar circumstances in the past. This may be attributed to the fact that there was no one else in the Prime Minister's close entourage to really advise him on international affairs; and, he did need seem interaction, given his nodding acquaintance of foreign affairs, Therefore, notwithstanding his known inflexibility and self-righteousness. he did turn to the two of them.

It was not difficult to mesh with Vajpayee, since the Foreign Minister was on the same diplomatic wavelength as the Prime Minister. Both of them were of the opinion that it was important to open up to Washington, to detach from Moscow, and to explore with Beijing. The difference between them was of style. While Desai was openly rhetorical, blanching most of his diplomatic interlocutors, Vajpayee was more restrained and more balanced. While the Indian Prime Minister was openly and enthusiastically declaring his advocacy of moving closer to China, Vajpayee,on the other hand, was more reserved. Normalisation of relations with China? Yes, he argued, but without going overboard, given the potential difficulties that were looming on the horizon between the two countries. He accepted the politics of subtly reining in on India's relations with Moscow, but was against any dramatic ruptures or declarations; and even regarding Washington—while clearly favouring friendliness—was in opposition to any excessive immoderation.

Jagat S. Mehta, too was a restraining element on Desai. While favouring the construction of a new diplomacy vis-à-vis the three major powers (US, USSR and China), he too was against any diplomatic immoderation, with the exception perhaps of India's new relations with Washington, where he was perhaps more enthused.

It is more than likely that their influence on Desai was impactful. For, notwithstanding his forthright diplomatic rhetoric, he never really went very far with the Chinese, and never really cut himself off from the Russians.

His three Ambassadors to Moscow, China and the USA must have had some voice in decision making. For I.K. Gujral in Moscow, K.R. Narayanan in Beijing and Nani Palikhavala in Washington were basically moderate and thoughtful persons who naturally must have moderated Desai from his excessive rhetoric in the course of their duties. While, Desai had the tendency of being outspoken, but strategically placed as they were, the Prime Minister could hardly have ignored them, given their comfortable position in the countries in which they were placed.

FOREIGN POLICY

In foreign affairs Morarji Desai had little experience. Though as Finance Minister in Indira Gandhi's Government, he did have occasions to deal with international financial matters and attend international conferences, he was apparently not very familiar with how the world functioned, and what were the broad configuration of forces that constituted the international system. Clearly, this was not something that fell within the broad orbit of his interests.

However, notwithstanding this handicap Desai came to power with preconceived views relating to a wide array of issues connected with foreign affairs. He was against India acquiring nuclear weapons, was outspokenly critical of RAW, and had often declared that India was not " genuinely non-aligned." In his view, the non-aligned posture had already been compromised under Nehru, and had been seriously violated by Indira Gandhi's decision to get close to the USSR, including her option to conclude a military agreement with Moscow.

Desai was not far wrong in his evaluation of India's skewed stance in foreign affairs. While much of Indian diplomacy had been dictated by a concatenation of forced circumstances, and not by any ideological motivations, there was nonetheless some scope for its re-adaptation in the new environment looming on the international horizon.

China was indeed changing. The original votaries of a harsh policy towards India had passed away; the Cultural Revolution had become defunct, and the new leadership was groping its way towards a more benign policy vis-à-vis the outside world.

The US situation too had changed. The original architect of a hard policy towards India, Richard Nixon, was no more at the helm. Even the Soviet Union, while still very friendly towards India, was looking for a global status, that was moving Soviet diplomacy away from an excessive focalisation on India. The Palestinian situation too was evolving. Some of the Arab countries were coming to the conclusion that it was more in the interest of the Arab world to seek some modus vivendi with Israel than to continue a politics of confrontation which had led them nowhere.

So in the light of the changing environment, Desai attempted to rectify the situation by sending friendly signals to China and the US—the two countries with whom relations had reached a nadir point.

But, Morarji Desai's decision to normalise relations with China was nothing new. It was a continuation of a process already inaugurated by Indira Gandhi. The difference was in their characters and in the manner in which they handled foreign affairs. While Indira Gandhi was discreet in her initiatives, secretive in her actions, and incommunicative in her views, Morarji Desai was just the opposite—open in initiatives, outgoing in actions and firm, often dogmatic, in views.

The Chinese probably saw the difference. They were more receptive to Desai's openness, and his known reservations about the Soviet Union, than Indira Gandhi's calculating diplomacy. For Desai had built a reputation of being straight- forward, frank and authentic in his views. Besides, he had apparently expressed his reservations of Nehru's policies towards China, particularly the hastiness with which he had unnecessarily generated a showdown with Beijing by issuing all sorts of belligerent statements, just before the explosion of the Sino-Indian conflict in 1962. In his estimation they were unnecessary provocations

Signals to China

The new Prime Minister's first important initiative was directed towards China. Real non-alignment, he reasoned, would become credible when India normalises relations with its northern neighbour. He carefully calibrated this process of opening up by supporting Subramanium Swamy's visit to China. Swamy was one of his party men who favoured a dialogue, and who had a good image in China for his commendatory views about the developments in the country. At the same time, Morarji Desai, during his trip to Washington, declared that "India is ready sometimes in the future to recognise the present frontier on Indo-Chinese boundary and that India would not demand the return of territory seized by China between 1957-1962."[235] His foreign minister A.B. Vajpayee was even more forthcoming; for in one of his declarations (12 December 1977) he went to the extent of arguing that the 1962 Sino-Indian conflict was "needlessly provocative," which by implication was a criticism of Nehru's impulsive and hasty actions before the explosion of the conflict. Also he made it clear on 21 July 1977 that India would respond warmly to Chinese initiatives. "If any initiatives are taken," he declared "then India would not be found wanting in making adequate response to these initiatives."[236]

These were indeed bold declarations by the new government; for no one until then—not even Indira Gandhi—had gone as far as to suggest that mistakes may also have been made by the Indian side that led to the 1962 debacle. By doing so, the Prime Minister and the Foreign Minister were sending an important signal to the Chinese, and, at the same time, making it clear to the Russians that despite their dire warnings not to proceed with any opening up to the Chinese they had indeed decided to go ahead with the process of normalisation.[237]

During the early period of Desai's mandate, the Chinese were prudent. But in early 1978 signs of diplomatic change began to surface. The Chinese were indeed moving away from their isolationalist and aggressive policies, designed during the years of the Cultural Revolution, It had done so much of harm to the Chinese status internationally that the post-Maoist leadership, under Deng Xiaoping, was rapidly signaling to the Western world its intentions to open up. While the initial Chinese benign diplomatic behaviour was directed towards the West, it did not take long to manifest itself towards India.

As is often the case with the Chinese style of functioning, any innovations in diplomatic behaviour are first aired by commentaries in the media before any corresponding manifestation is discernible in Chinese diplomacy.

For the Chinese, Indira Gandhi's defeat in the national elections was a landmark development—a development, which, according to the comments in the media, "had marked a serious setback to Moscow's expansionist schemes in the South Asia region," and, at the same time, had "declared the bankruptcy of the internal and external policies pursued by Indira Gandhi who had tailed after the Soviet Union."[238] Consider the very first commentary, after the elections, which was, to say the least, relentless: "The national elections showed the unpopularity of the internal and external policies of the Congress Party Government. With the backing and the connivance of Soviet social-imperialism, the Congress government for years pursued a policy of expansionism, thus isolating itself not only in South Asia but in the whole world. It subjected the Indian people to fascist suppression. Especially after it declared a state of emergency throughout the country in June 1975, tens of thousands of opposition members and people were arrested and detained."[239]

Finally, the Chinese requested the Romanian President, Nicolae Ceausescu, to relay Chinese willingness to improve ties with India, and to hold border talks. Undoubtedly, this is clearly a Chinese style of diplomatic behaviour, i.e., mobilising intermediaries to sound others. Desai, however, told the Romanian leader that his government would not respond to such overtures made by third parties. "If the Chinese," he declared, "were sincere let them contact us directly"[240] This is what they finally did. In February 1978 Beijing sent a trade delegation which declared that it wished to conclude a long-term trade agreement. This was followed by a goodwill mission, led by Wang Bingnan, President of the Chinese People's Association for Friendship with Foreign Countries in March of the same year. The powerful

Chinese delegation met with members of the Desai Government, including the Prime Minister on 11 March 1978.

It is important to note that in typical Desai style he delared that while his government would expand relations with China, he frankly informed his interlocutor that the "strains" that had developed in Sino-Indian relations were because of "past Chinese actions."[241]

Desai, it would seem, was personally interested in visiting China. For this would have indeed dramatically heaved Sino-Indian relations; but the Chinese were apparently prudent. For them, it was too early for a summit visit. Besides, they were not at all sure how it would go down in India, where a anti-Chinese wave was still very forceful, and where Morarji Desai's position within the coalition government was wobbly. Therefore, when he informally enquired from K.R. Narayanan, the Indian Ambassador, who was in India for consultations, regarding the prospects of such a visit, he was informed that the Foreign Minister should go first before the Chinese would envisage a summit visit.[242]

Foreign Minister, Vajpayee, was, therefore, sent to China in February 1979. Though the trip was marred by the Chinese military intervention in Vietnam, resulting in Vajpayee's decision to cut short his visit, the trip was nonetheless important. For Deng Xiaoping met him and covered all the ground pertaining to Sino-Indian relations. Having consolidated his position in the Chinese hierarchy he made it a point to convey the Chinese interest in normalising relations with its southern neighbour. Though much of what he said on the border was a repetition of what Zhou Enlai had already proposed earlier, but the stress he laid on the bilateral character of Indo-Pakistan relations was new.

Though Desai was clearly ready to open up even more to China, the Indian bureaucracy apparently did not favour such a step. The pro-Soviet lobby was powerful enough to create hurdles—hurdles he was unable to overcome, given the constraints that stemmed from the highly diversified character of his coalition Government. Besides, the Soviets were already so heavily involved in the country's affairs that the margin of diplomatic manoeuvrability was becoming severely limited. Any open defiance of Moscow would have unavoidably endangered Indian interests. If Desai did not seem to care, Vajpayee, on the other hand, did. At least he seemed to be aware of the adverse ramifiations that an excessively friendly posture towards China would generate in Moscow. While, it cannot be excluded that he had come under the influence of the pro-Soviet lobby in the ministry,

Vajpayee personally was not free from the reservations he had about going too far in the direction of China, the only major competitor of India which had become a nuclear power. In fact, it would seem, according to some sources, he initially did delay his departure, but was finally prevailed upon to go to China.[243]

There were also serious institutional and political handicaps that made it difficult for the Desai Government to take bold diplomatic initiatives in the direction of China. For one thing, too many parties, from left to right, were involved in the government's decisional process, making it virtually impossible to reach a consensus. For another, too many people were still unreconciled to the idea of reaching an understanding with the Chinese. The memories of Nehru's humiliation in 1962 were still painfully fresh among many Indians.

Reaching Out to Washington

Even more important was the Janata Government's decision to mend fences with the US. Relations between the two countries had reached a nadir under Indira Gandhi and Richard Nixon. Part of the explanation for the strained relations lay in the disagreements between the two countries, but the known personal antipathy that the one had manifested against the other is a dimension that cannot be ignored; for this must have heavily coloured the policies of the two countries. However, now that Indira Gandhi was no more in power, and Jimmy Carter was the new President, the atmosphere had changed making it possible for the two countries to open up to each other.

Desai was no great friend or admirer of the US, particularly after the writer, Seymour Hersh, alleged in his book "The Price of Power" that the Prime Minister was a paid informer of the CIA. But nonetheless Desai was conscious of the importance of building bridges with Washington. Jimmy Carter, on the other hand, was fond of India, of its deep past and its culture, but even more so of its democratic institutions that had just been restored after two dark years of authoritarianism under Indira Gandhi. In fact, he had gone to the extent of elevating India to the status of a "pre-eminent power in South Asia."

Desai's first act in the direction of Washington was the appointment of a highly visible Ambassador in the person of Nani Ardeshir Palikhavala, a lawyer who had made himself known as a proponent of human rights, and as a committed opponent to Indira Gandhi's emergency rule. His twenty two months of tenure as Ambassador opened great possibilities of improving relations with Washington. He went around the country speaking to the Americans about India. Jimmy Carter's elections as US President had greatly facilitated Palikhivala's task since the new President had welcomed the reappearance of democratic institutions after the Indian elections of 1976. Both Carter and Desai succeeded in introducing some degree of warmth between the two countries. And the two visited each other's country in 1978. According to the then US Ambassador, Robert F. Goheen, the relations between the two countries "were the best during the time of President Jimmy Carter and Prime Minister Morarji Desai under the Janata Government."[244] Much of the interaction was political, and there was really no "economic depth" in the relations between the two countries.

The visits of the two leaders to each other's country were a landmark in the expansion of Indo-American relations. Carter was well received In India in January 1978. All the mainstream political parties consensually perceived his presence in India as something important. The so-called "Delhi Declaration", concluded by Carter and Desai, was a very general declaration that avoided mentioning any specific issues. It underlines their "unwavering faith in the democratic form of Government," and their agreement that "disparities in economic strength" between nations must be bridged if the world wants "secure international peace". The two countries, according to the Declaration, also jointly undertook to work for the elimination of existing stockpile of nuclear weapons, and to arrest the proliferation of such weapons.[245]

During Desai's visit to Washington between 9-15 June 1978, Carter-Desai agreed that there had been a significant improvement in bilateral relations over the past year as a result of Carter's visit to India in January 1978, and by a comprehensive exchange of correspondence between the two leaders. Both the leaders, furthermore, agreed to continue the bilateral dialogue "through future meetings and correspondence, and through regular official-level consultations with the India-US Joint Commission."[246]

The joint communiqué, during Desai's US visit in June 1978, dealt with a wide array of global issues. The importance of the communiqué lies in the fact that the United States gave India a global power status, and treated India on an equal basis—undoubdtedly a considerable improvement from previous years.

Some difficulties nonetheless did surface between the two countries. Because of India's nuclear ambitions, the US Nuclear Regulatory

Commission was reluctant to supply enriched uranium to the US built Tarapur Reactor. But this changed under Carter. He was able to persuade the US Congress to ship uranium to India; and to avoid any further glitches on the question.

There were also differences regarding non-proliferation of nuclear weapons. Carter was pushing India to adhere to the treaty of non-proliferation, but India had refused to do so as long as the nuclear powers where not willing to abandon their nuclear arms. For India this commitment was vital before India would even examine the problem.

Problems with the Soviet Union

Even before he became Prime Minister, Desai had hardly ever displayed any particular friendliness towards the Soviet Union. He never believed in socialism, least of all the in the Soviet brand. In fact, throughout his political career he had always remained very sceptical regarding the viability of the Soviet system, and had often expressed his concern concerning the obsequiousness of the Commmunist Party of India to Moscow; therefore despite myriad Soviet invitations to visit the country he had shown no interest in going to Moscow. The Soviet leaders even sought Nehru's intervention to persuade Desai to accept the Soviet invitation, on the ground that Desai was the only minister in the Prime Minister's Cabinet who had not visited the Soviet Union. At one point when Desai, in his capacity as Finance Minister was scheduled to go to Washington for a World Bank meeting, the Soviet leaders seized the opportunity of his forthcoming travel to request the Indian Ambassador in Moscow to persuade Desai to go to Washington via Moscow. Desai refused.

"Why?" he asked the Ambassador.

"Are they going to give more aid if I visit them."

"No," the Ambassador replied.

"But since they insist, it may be diplomatic."

"As Finance Minister," retorted Desai, "I am only interested in aid not in diplomacy."[247]

Finally, Desai did go to Moscow in 1969 the specific purpose of which was to discuss Soviet aid to India.

In the face of such an attitude, the Soviet leaders naturally developed serious reservations about Desai. In fact, as early as 1955, after Khruschev and Bulganin's visit to Bombay, where he was, at the time, the Chief Minister of the State, they had characterised him as their "public enemy number 1"[248] But, after Desai became the Finance Minister in Nehru's Cabinet, they could not ignore him and did attempt, on numerous occasions, to build bridges with him; but all this was in vain since Morarji Desai never responded positively to Soviet initiatives.

The Soviet attitude therefore continued to harden—even more so after he became Prime Minister—since Desai in his usual frank and explicit style promptly announced, after he took the reins of power, a major foreign policy shift away from the country's traditional special relations with Moscow. "We won't," he declared, "have any special relations with any country" and "if the Indo-Soviet Friendship Treaty involves any want of friendship with others, then it will have to change."[249]

His serious reservations about the Soviet Union became more evident in his numerous letters to the Indian Ambassador, I.K.Gujral, where he was even less diplomatic. " I must," he wrote, "sound another note of caution in relation to the USSR. It is impossible to study them in short term because they seldom seem to be acting only in the short term. They have a long-term policy about the expansion of their ideology as well as expansion of their influence on the world at large."[250]

Morarji Desai also did not hesitate to chafe at even Gujral's prudent diplomatic behaviour vis-à-vis the Soviet leaders with whom he had succeeded to develop warm relations. While Gujral normally had the reputation of being open and friendly with his interlocutors, he may have been even more so, given Desai's outspokeness that needed at times to be counterbalanced by benign diplomatic rhetoric. In any event, Morarji Desai, took Gujral to task for making remarks that he did not approve of. "While," he wrote, "I am on this, I should like to raise one matter. By one or two persons who have returned from Moscow, I am told that you have been indicating some views on the line that the Janata Party is not going to last very long, and the present political set-up cannot be taken for granted...with your past affiliations naturally people will give credence to such statements...I would, therefore, like what exactly is your own view of the present situation in India."[251]

By early 1978, the Soviet leadership had become disturbed by the discussions that the Indian Government was having with Western countries and probably taunted Gujral about this, who in his usual benign diplomatic manner attempted to find some excuses. This pushed Desai to write to the Ambassador on 9 February 1978: "I notice in your meeting (with Kosygin) you have tried to balance our discussions with President Carter and Prime Minister James Callaghan with full faith in Indo-Soviet friendship and again emphasized that the improved relations with the US and UK would not be at the cost of our friendly relations with the USSR. I do not think we need a balance between two friendships in this manner nor need we go out of our way to modify one or the other in regard to our discussions with the other. These discussions stand on their own and even if the countries are on the look-out to see in which direction our slant is, it is not necessary for us to explain it as we do not believe in having a slant in either direction."[252]

Since the independence of India, this was the first time that an Indian Prime Minister was openly chafing at the Soviet Union. Even during Nehru's time when the Soviets ignored India during the early stages of Indian independence, Nehru was prudent in not going overboard in his criticism of Moscow. Even Shastri, who was showing signs of going in Washington's direction, was very subtle in his analysis of the Soviet Union. But, Desai, with his frank and almost brutal character, had really gone overboard.

Gujral obviously was in a difficult postion. He arrived in Moscow, during Indira Gandhi's time when Indo-Soviet relations were on the upgrade. And then found himself in the uncomfortable situation of representing India, under Desai, who was not only critical of the Soviet Union, but was eagerly developing relations with Moscow's two adversaries, Washington and Beijing.

While Gujral's continuation as Ambassador under the Janata Government, given the difficulties he had faced under Indira Gandhi, was understandable, it is indeed incomprehensible that he continued to function in this assignment when Desai was lambasting the Soviet Union and had clearly indicated his intentions of down-grading Indo-Soviet relations—an intention with which Gujral presumably disagreed.

Prime Minister Desai's decision to normalise relations with Beijing and Washington aggravated his relations with the Soviet leaders even more. When he visited Moscow in 1978 he was bluntly told by Brezhnev that "your Foreign Minister's visit to China was not received well by our own public. I do not know how your people reacted to it but our own people took it very ill."[253]

Desai continued his politics of remaining very prudent regarding the Soviet Union. He opposed Soviet attempts to offer nuclear fuel for the

Tarapore nuclear reactor, which the US had built and to which it was reluctant to give nuclear fuel any more as it had done in the past. "I do not see", wrote Desai to I.K.Gujral, "how the question of getting it from the USSR arises. We do not get any fuel from them. In fact, we are committed to obtaining enriched uranium from the USA, and no other source for Tarapore. We need not give the impression to USSR that they can fill the breach if USA fails."[254]

As a concrete indication of his reservations vis-à-vis Moscow, Morarji Desai pulled up his Cabinet Minister, H.N. Bahuguna, for having concluded a number of agreements with Moscow in the sector of oil exploration, in certain fields of geophysics, and in the Soviet supply of crude oil without having obtained clearance from the Cabinet, and without having taken into account the important fact that once foreign powers "acquire a foothold... they try to enlarge it into a bridgehead, and from a bridgehead they eventually establish themselves firmly in a manner that it becomes difficult to dislodge them."[255]

Desai also openly manifested his dissatisfaction over the Russian acceptance of the Chinese delineation of the Sino-Indian border. And, when he became Prime Minister, his government decided to press the Soviets to rectify the maps, heavily influenced by Chinese delineation. Finally, he did succeed by making a big issue out of it forcing Moscow "to do so causing them some embarrassment."[256]

However, notwithstanding Desai's claim that he had "forced" the Moscow Government to do so, the main underlying reason was that the Sino-Soviet dispute had deteriorated to such a point that Moscow had nothing much to loose by relenting on the issue.

This was further illustrated by the Soviet intransigence on Rupee-Rouble parity. The Russians sought to significantly hike the exchange rate of the Rouble, which would have resulted in India having to pay back much more for the aid received from the Soviet Union.

What made things even worse in Indo-Soviet relations were Desai's brutal and undiplomatic remarks in the face of the Soviet leaders. In one of his meetings with Kosygin, he accused Russia of interfereing in India's internal affairs. The conversation, becoming more and more unpleasant, escalated with the following irksome exchanges. To Desai's accusation that the Soviets were interfering in Indian affairs. Kosygin asked "How"?. "You support the Communist Party with funds and advise," retorted Desai. "That is not true," countered Kosygin. "Well let's appoint an impartial judge and I will prove it to him."[257]

Another incident, analogous to the one with Kosygin, occurred in the Soviet Union when Desai went to Moscow on an official visit; and this took place at the beginning of his arrival. Deviating from the normal Soviet diplomatic practice of organising travels, outside of Moscow, for visiting dignatories at the end of the visit, Desai's trip was organised before his discussions with the Soviet leaders. While reading a newspaper, the Soviet Deputy Prime Minister, who was escorting him, casually attacked the Western countries for voicing charges of Soviet interference in their domestic affairs. Thereupon, and in the presence of his Foreign Minister and Ambassador, the Indian Prime Minister blurted out that he could prove Soviet interference in Indian affairs. No other Prime Minister, neither past nor future, had ever uttered such blunt rhetoric in the presence of their Soviet counterparts. For all of them this was simply not done even if they believed in it. But, for Morarji this was utterly normal since he believed this to be true.

An embarrasing situation ensued after Desai's outburst—so much so that the Soviet leadership was no more sure of the success of Desai's visit.

Another incident, more substantive, occurred at the fag end of Desai's visit. The Prime Minister instructed his Foreign Secretary, Jagat Mehta, to shorten the Indo-Soviet draft declaration, which in his view was too long. Thereupon, the Foreign Secretary informed his Soviet counterparts, that India would not sign the declaration in its existing form. Gromyko, at this point, informed Vajpayee and Gujral of this development. Finally, the whole situation was saved by sanctioning Mehta who was sent back to India.[258]

The Foreign Secretary was sanctioned, but he had taken such action at the the instigation of the Prime Minister. But, when he realised that adverse ramifications would unavoidably follow, he was apparently persuaded by Vajpayee and Gujral not to protect him.[259]

As a result of all this, the Soviet attitude towards Desai became so negative that it was apparently prepared to destabilise his government. A US official told the Indian Ambassador in Washington that they had learnt through their "reliable sources" that the Russians were actively hatching a plot with certain "parties in India" to overthrow Morarji Desai. It is quite possible that the 1978 dissensions within the Janata Government may have been used by the Russians to encourage factions which were opposed to Desai. During Kosygin's 1979 visit to India some Cabinet Ministers, particularly George Fernandes, who was Minister-in-waiting for Kosygin may have seized the opportunity to request Kosygin to extend an invitation to Charan Singh to visit Russia. Charan Singh was Desai's Minister of Interior and his main rival.

Was all this connected with the plot to overthrow Desai, there does not appear to be any doubt. However, one thing is certain: the Soviet Government, the Soviet Party and Soviet intelligence—all of them took various actions—to mobilise everyone they could to oust Desai. That Moscow had the resources to do so, there appears to be no doubt; what made things easier for them was that the Desai Government was in a tailspin with most of his ministerial colleagues up in arms against him–including Deputy Prime Minister,Charan Singh, who played a key role in the fall of the Morarji Desai Government.

South Asia

Morarji Desai's attitude towards South Asian nations was different from those of his predecessors. He was much more soft spoken than previous governments. His was a period when India had calmest spells with almost all of them. While differences did exist with most of the neighbours, the way in which the Desai Government diplomatically addressed the issues were in marked contrast with preceding governments.

The very first statement made by the Foreign Minister on 29 June 1977 to the Lokh Sabha transmitted the intention of his government to adopt a compassionate policy towards India's South Asian neighbours. "We have recognised," he declared, "that our first priority must be to promote a relationship of cooperation and trust with our immediate neighbours. We share with them a common history, and a great deal of common culture, but we also recognise their own right to determine their separate national fulfilment. We shall be vigilant about our territorial integrity but pose no threat to their national personalities... It is with this vision that we have been directing our policies towards Pakistan, Bangladesh, Nepal, Sri Lanka and Bhutan. We can claim that in some measure the climate for such trust and cooperation with our neighbours has already shown some significant improvement. Some old suspicions and irritants have been removed; with sustained diplomacy and reciprocal response we hope we can move steadily forward."[260]

But the most striking change was in regard to Pakistan where the Prime Minister had sent his Foreign Minister on an official visit—a visit that greatly contributed in bringing down the tensions that had dominated the two countries since Bangladesh's independence. The leading Pakistani newspaper, *Dawn*, characterised the Desai period "as the golden period" of Indo-Pakistan relations.[261] For it was under the Janata Government that India "stopped flexing its muscles and behaving like a big brother towards its smaller neighbours."[262] Desai went out of his way to create a climate of peace and understanding in the region. He backed Pakistan on the Afghanistan issue, denounced Soviet interference in Afghan affairs, and supported Pakistan's bid to join the non-aligned movement. Even more important, was that Desai shared the view that Pakistan had the right to acquire sophisticated weapons for its defence. He even conceded Pakistan's right to carry out nuclear research. For the first time since independence of the sub-continent, a genuine effort was indeed made to improve relations with Pakistan. The result was the emergence of tension free, even friendly relationship between the two countries, despite the fact that Kashmir remained an unsolved issue and New Delhi continued to acquire military hardware.

Morarji was probably the first Prime Minister who developed a good rapport with his Pakistani counterpart, Zia ul-haq whom he met for the first time in August 1978 in Nairobi on the occasion of the state funeral of Jomo Kenyatta. According to Morarji's private secretary, Hasmukh Shah, the bilateral meeting went very well. Desai told Zia on this occasion that both of them "should give and take. If we act in the interests of both our countries, there would be no conflict."Furthermore", he continued, "we should act like brothers. I am your elder brother. I have nothing to take from you. But, if anything happens you will be held responsible. I am not someone who simply talks. I take action."[263]

After this first meeting, there were regular telephone conversations between the two. It has even been suggested that Morarji had reached "an agreement on Kashmir."[264] But, before it could be finalised and announced, the Janata Government fell, thus losing, according to a leading journalist, Shyam Bhatia, "a precious opportunity to reach a durable agreement with Islamabad."[265] In any event, there appears to exist consensus among Indians that the only free and fair elections, since independence, took place in Kashmir in 1977 when Desai was the Prime Minister.

While all this may be viewed as speculation, it is important to note that Desai and Zia had developed a "chemistry" which none of the previous Prime Ministers of the two countries had acquired, so much so that six years after Morarji's downfall as Prime Minister, Zia named him for the highest Pakistani honour, *Nishan-e-Pakistan*. In a letter Zia wrote to Morarji in 1986, he said: "I request you to accept this. This is the wish of the people of Pakistan."266 But before a ceremony could be held, Zia died in a mysterious air crash. Finally, Morarji Desai received the Pakistan honour at a private ceremony held in Morarji's home on 19 May 1990.

Morarji thus remains the only Indian Prime Minister to have won the *Nishan-e-Pakistan* as well as the Indian highest honour the *Bharat Ratna*.

In a tribute paid to him, after his death, *Dawn* had this to say about his role in Indo-Pakistan relations. "Altough Janata," it wrote, "had several staunch Hindu revivalists among its top leadership, Mr. Desai's tenure as Prime Minister (1977-1979) marked one of the calmest spells in India-Pakistan relations. Unlike his predecessors, he had no inclination to adopt an arrogant posture towards Pakistan, and he repeatedly said that all neighbouring countries had a right to pursue their defence policies in accordance with what they regarded to be their genuine security needs."267 No other Indian, past or future, had received such eulogistic Pakistani comments.

Attitude Towards Nuclear Developments

Desai was faced with twin problems in the nuclear sector. One was with the Americans while the other was with his own countrymen.

With the US the issues pertained to the shipment of enriched uranium for Indian atomic installations, and the other concerned nuclear tests. President Carter, in his conversations with Desai, had insisted that before any shipment of uranium to India could be envisaged to the Tarapur Atomic Power Station, India must accept the "safeguards" ensuring that the supplies would be used for peaceful purposes. At the same time Washington demanded that India must accept full international inspections of its nuclear installation. Desai refused the two conditions. On 25th April he wrote to Carter, that if he did not reverse the decision made by the US Nuclear Regulatory Commission (NRC) to block the shipments, India might consider looking for alternatives to its dependence on US import of enriched uranium. Besides, he told Carter, that this was a breach "of the 1966 agreement between the two countries," and clearly warned him that this "will free India to adopt any course it chooses to safeguard its own interest."[268] Desai also refused to cede to the US requirement that India accepts full international inspection of its nuclear installations. "As long as," he made it clear, "the basic disarmament agreement has not been concluded among the nuclear powers," India will not be a party to any such agreement.[269] Finally, Carter overruled the US Commission, and ordered that over eight tons of enriched uranium be shipped to India for use in the Tarapur Atomic Power Station.[270] Also, he sent a message to the US Congress to the effect that "to deny a sale would hurt the prospects for getting India to accept stricter nuclear safeguards and other US nonproliferation goals."[271] At the same time, to avoid the replication of such a situation in the future, Carter encouraged France to become the replacement centre for India.

Carter clearly wished to avoid any major confrontation with India, since, in his estimation, it was important that the US maintains friendly ties with the country.

What a remarkable change from his predecessor (Richard Nixon) who had distant himself from India, and who did not seem to consider that India should be an important focal point of US diplomacy. For him, China was clearly more important than India.

The other problem that Desai had in the nuclear sector was with his own country. Clearly he did not agree with the nuclear option his predecessors had taken—the option of activating India's nuclear military option. He genuinely believed that nuclear weapons embodied an evilness on which there could be no compromise. He publicly went on record to voice his firm opposition to nuclear explosions spawned by the Indian Atomic Energy Commission in 1974. And when he became Prime Minister he continued to take a principled stand against the continuation of the nuclear weapons programme. Speaking at the special session of the UN General Assembly (UNGA) on disarmament in June 1978 (9 June) he declared: "We are the only country which has pledged not to manufacture or acquire nuclear weapons even if the rest of the world did so. I solemnly reiterate that pledge before this August assembly. In fact, we have gone further and abjured nuclear explosions even for peaceful purposes.[272]

To appease the international community, it is true, India had declared that it would not acquire nuclear weapons, and would not conduct any nuclear explosions. Desai was therefore pledging what India had already done. Solemn public declaration to announce any intention of possessing nuclear weapons, however, was one thing, but continuing clandestinely with the programme was another matter. For India, behind the scenes, was continuing what had been originally decided upon by Lal Bahadur Shastri in 1965—to continue with the nuclear programme. Instructions to this effect had already been given to the Atomic Energy Commission.

The nuclear explosion conducted in 1974 could not have been carried out without all the technical research work pursued by the Indian scientists. In sum, it was in effect discreetly conducting—away from the public eye— an ongoing programme clearly financed and blessed by the Government. The scientists, in this connection, had built research reactors, plutonium separation plants, uranium fuel rod, manufacturing and reprocessing facilities, etc. And when Indira Gandhi finally decided to conduct an explosion in late 1971 or early 1972, it took the scientists another two years to be ready for the dramatic event.

Desai was confronted with this problem when he became the Prime Minister. A decision had to be taken if India was to continue with the programme, as green lighted by Shastri and Indira Gandhi, or if the whole programme had to be interrupted now that Desai was at the helm of affairs. With his absolutist views there was clearly a danger that, with him at the helm, the nuclear option would have to be terminated.

The whole question was discussed by the Joint Intelligence Committee (JIC). In December 1978, the Committee, headed by a proponent of the nuclear option, K. Subrahmanyam, declared that Pakistan had already "gone nuclear by acquiring a nuclear weapons capability with China's help." Despite Morarji's efforts to ignore this important revelation, the Cabinet's Political Affairs Committee consisting of five Cabinet Ministers had to be convened to discuss the JIC's findings. At the meeting Morarji's opposition was overruled by a vote of three to two. The Committee "approved preparation (nuclear) testing and weaponising."   However despite these directives Morarji attempted separately, and on his own, to instruct the Atomic Energy Commission to do nothing about testing without his specific permission. To isolate the pro-bomb lobby he went further by obtaining a transfer of one of the lobbyists, Raja Ramanna, Director of the Bhabha Atomic Research Centre, to New Delhi where he was named Secretary of Defence Research, Scientific Adviser to the Defence Minister and Director General of the Defence Research and Development Organisation (DRDO).

Nonetheless the scientists continued with the programme. For one thing, the formal directive of the Cabinet favoured such programme, and for another they themselves favoured such a course of action. Desai, thus, went against the tide—indeed a courageous act—even if the country was going in the other direction, and collectively considered any abandonment of the decision as against the national interest.

Intelligence Service

One of the other Desai's "betenoire" was RAW, the Indian intelligence service established by Indira Gandhi—an intelligence service geared essentially to the outside world. Desai had characterised the organization as the *praetorian guard of Indira Gandhi*, and had promised, in his usual frank and brutal manner, that he would wind it up after coming to power.

All sorts of rumours were floated, and during the heady days of the election period, all sorts of allegations were made about its so-called activities—such incredible allegations as having a torture chamber at the basement of its office where Indira Gandhi's opponents were tortured, passing on secret funds to the sister of the Shah of Iran without the Government's permission, and harassing NRIs to obtain funds for Indira Gandhi.

After he became the Prime Minister he had all the RAW files scrutinized in the hope of finding evidence of its complicity with Indira and Sanjay Gandhi. But nothing was found, and RAW was absolved of most allegations. In fact, the Home Minister, Charan Singh had the courage to send for R.N. Kao, the head of RAW, to tell him that allegations made during the elections were wrong.

But Desai's opposition to RAW continued, particularly against Kao, who had become quite close to Indira Gandhi, and who finally decided to resign. He was replaced by his Deputy, K. Sankaran Nair. But, in his determination to trim the powers of the organization he decided to re-designate the chief of RAW as Director—on par with the Director of the domestic Intelligence Bureau—instead of Secretary as it was till then. This decision to reduce the power of the chief catalysed Nair to resign.

However, after the occurrence of two intelligence events, in one of which Desai was personally involved, his attitude changed from "negative to positive."[273] The first was concerning Ayatollah Khomeini, who, having been expelled by Saddam Hussein from Iraq, was given asylum by the French Government. Based on information received from Indian Shia leaders, Desai came to the conclusion that the ongoing Islamic revolution could not be stopped. He therefore decided to establish a secret contact with Khomeini. Through his office, he sent a top secret message to the RAW agent in Paris (B. Raman) to inform him that Ashok Mehta, the Deputy

Chairman of the Planning Commission and an officer of the MEA were on their way to Paris, and to instruct him to arrange a secret meeting with Khomeini. With great difficulty Raman succeeded, through his Iranian contact, to arrange such a meeting. Desai, obviously was impressed by this RAW action, given the fact that Khomeini was against a secret meeting.

The other concerned Pakistan's clandestine programme for setting up an uranium enrichment plant at Kahuta. It was detected by RAW, and the Indian Prime Minister was briefed of this development. But Desai, in one of his unguarded moments, told Zia ul-Haq that he was aware of the fact that Pakistan was trying to develop a military nuclear capability. While on the one hand this resulted in the exposure of the RAW agent in Pakistan, on the other this indeed impressed Desai regarding the credibility of RAW.[274]

EVALUATION

Morarji Desai was really a neophyte in foreign affairs. But, his nodding interest and understanding of what was happening in international affairs did not preclude him from advancing views on India's foreign policy. He had come to the conclusion that India's proclaimed policy of non-alignment was neither authentic nor genuine; that it had veered in the Soviet direction under Nehru, and even more so under Indira Gandhi, and that such an orientation had seriously compromised India's normative goal of maintaining its independence in international affairs.

When Desai became the Prime Minister he attempted to introduce some degree of balance in India's foreign policy by seeking out China, US and even Pakistan.

While half-hearted attempts were made even before to normalise relations with the these countries, Desai's landmark public proclamations were really the first major attempt to revise India's foreign policy. For this history will remember him.

But did he suceed in effectively injecting this transmutation in India's policies? And did India really take the Morarji direction?

Though the Government had taken a number of innovative diplomatic initiatives, the success was not that decisive, and the orientation was not that effective.

A number of factors decelerated this trend. The first was the time factor. Desai's Prime Ministership lasted for too short a time to permit the opening up of new diplomatic avenues. Foreign policy needs a longer time frame to effectively operationalise diplomatic initiatives than domestic decisions since a number of external elements are involved: and they can indeed be very time consuming. The second element was the coalition character of Desai's government. This was the first time that India was confronted with this type of a political governance where the leaders were so divided and were so disparate that a power struggle had spawned as soon as the government was constituted. The time the Prime Minister devoted to different tasks of arranging political matters, and of remaining in power was indeed stupendous. One wonders how he found the time to govern such a large country. The third dimesion was the pro-Soviet elements within the country—pressure groups who were unwilling to accept the loosening up of the ties established with the Soviet Union—a country with which India had established a strategic partnership. Lastly, and perhaps most important was the Soviet Government, the Soviet party and the Soviet intelligence. Seriously concerned, as they had become, with Prime Minister Desai's anti-Soviet posture, the Soviet establishment apparently decided to mobilise everyone it could—including the Deputy Prime minister, Charan Singh, and a host of cabinet ministers to bring about the downfall of the Morarji Desai Government.

But, Morarji, it must be noted, introduced not only some diplomatic innovations in regard to the great powers that were different from his predecessors; but also generated a new benign atmosphere vis-à-vis his immediate neighbours. What is even more interesting was his dissident attitude on nuclearisation of India—an attitude which was in marked contrast with the policies adopted by Indian Prime Ministers, past and future.

CHARAN SINGH

Chapter V

CHARAN SINGH
28 JULY 1979—14 JANUARY 1980

Charan Singh ousted Morarji Desai with the active complicity of a number of cabinet ministers, and with the almost explicit support of the USSR. Desai's open anti-Soviet stance was too much for the Russians and too risky for the future of Indo-Soviet relations.

Charan Singh's life ambition was to become Prime Minister. In the eyes of a journalist who knew him well, that was all he wanted. His ambition stopped there. "It was neither," wrote Thakur, "the transformation of society, nor the elimination of exploitation nor even the well being of the people."[275]

Indian politics had indeed reached a low point when Charan Singh came to the helm. A "shameless struggle for power" and a "competition of self-promotion" had become the law of the land. While, there were of course some prime ministers who did embody moral excellence, and who were self-sacrificing, ready to serve the country, the whole political system had indeed degenerated becoming irreversibly corrupt and horrendously flawed.

Charan Singh's mandate was short—in fact very short lasting only one hundred and seventy one days. What was even worse was that during his short mandate he "sat for less than forty seconds in the Prime Minister's seat,"[276] and the Parliament never actually met during his mandate. In other words he had no time to attend to his responsibilities as Prime Minister in the Parliament.

All those who had followed his political activities, even before he became prime minister, were less than charitable about his personality, his character and his ambitions. "He was," wrote Thakur, "a man driven by an obsession. He had to become the Prime Minister, no matter what the cost or the humiliation, no matter for how long. So desperate was he to get the crown, if only to satisfy some deep craving in his heart, or just to prove his soothsayers right, that he forgot all his Gandhian principles, all about means and ends. He swallowed all his pride and prejudices, all his allergies toward Indira Gandhi and Nehru. But having achieved his goal he reverted to his old pride and principles even at the cost of losing the crown he had wangled. All that mattered was that he had won the crown, never mind if it had turned tinsel."[277]

Charan Singh had spent so much of his time as prime minister surviving and leading his small electorate, composed of about ten million jats spread over Uttar Pradesh, Harayana, Punjab and Rajasthan that he really had no time to govern effectively, least of all in foreign affairs.

And yet, during his prime ministership, turbulent things were happening in the area. On 24 December 1979, the Soviet Union occupied Afghanistan Though it had already established a firm position in the country to the exclusion of the others, this, according to the prevailing US view, was not enough for the Soviet leadership, including Brezhnev. Washington was apparently convinced that the Soviet leaders had come to the conclusion that Afghanistan was within the Soviet sphere of influence, and therefore, invoking the Brezhnev doctrine, had decided to occupy Afghanistan.

But the grand Western theory, that the Soviets sought to use Afghanistan as a strategic springboard to control oil resources of the Gulf, has been largely discredited by the post-Soviet new information that has emerged through Soviet and East European archives.[278]

A rare exception to this theory was George F. Kennan, who, shortly after the Soviet invasion, questioned the official US logic. He expressed serious doubts that the invasion threatened Western security. While acknowledging the illegality of Soviet action, he emphasized that the action reflected "defensive rather than offensive (Soviet) impulses." Since Afghanistan was a " border country of the Soviet Union," it represented, in his view a natural security concern for the Soviets.[279]

Kennan's analysis confirmed what surfaced from Soviet sources. Moscow was perfectly content to live with neutralised and non-aligned Afghanistan, and had little interest in turning the country into a communist state. If anything, Moscow was very concerned regarding the activities of some extremist Afghan elements who were undermining stability in the southern Soviet frontier.[280]

A more credible interpretation of Soviet action was its preoccupation concerning (a) extremist Afghan communist activities, (b) the Shah of Iran's efforts in the seventies to turn Afghanistan towards the West, and (c) the emergence of islamic fundamentalism in the southern countries, the most important manifestation of which was the popular islamic revolution in Iran.

The Soviets in effect were opposed to any development in the area that would disrupt the existing status quo.

In any event, as a first step, Moscow wanted to contact India. For, under the 1971 Indo-Soviet Treaty of Peace and Friendship, the Soviet Government was under an obligation to inform India, that the Red Army, at the invitation of the Afghan Government, had marched into Kabul on 24 December 1979.

Since the Soviet Government had played a crucial role in installing Charan Singh as the Prime Minister, it had presumed that he would support Soviet action.

Yuri Vorontsov, the Soviet Ambassador in India, therefore, frantically attempted to get in touch with the Indian prime minister at about midnight of Christmas eve, But in vain. Indisposed as he was with a temperature, he had passed on the instructions to his secretariat not to be disturbed. But, given the importance of the Soviet message, Vorantsov was not in a mood to oblige the sick Prime Minister. He had urgent things to discuss with Charan Singh. The Soviet Ambassador, therefore, took an alternative step. He went to the Foreign Secretary, R.D.Sathe's residence in the middle of the night and urged him to accompany him to the Prime Minister's residence.

But the foreign secretary, without mincing words, immediately denounced Soviet action—an unsual step without the ministerial approval. Sathe took this initiative on the presumption that there really was no government to speak of. Though, Charan Singh's "caretaker" government, it is true, was hardly to be found anywhere, he was nonetheless officially the prime minister.

As the Soviet Ambassador had a top urgent letter from Brezhnev to be delivered personally to Charan Singh, Sathe had no other choice but to accompany Vorontsov to the residence of the Prime Minister.

Charan Singh, in his meeting, reacted interestingly. After having carefully thought for a while, he advised the Soviet ambassador to go back and send an urgent personal message to Leonid Brezhnev[281] that this was not quite the right thing to do. He attempted to impress upon the ambassador that the Afghan people were fiercely independent people, proud of their nationalism, and that they would not take the invasion lying low. They will fight back and fight to the last.. The prime minister pointed out that myriad British attempts to do so had failed to subjugate the country.

While Charan Singh assured the Soviet ambassador that India, under the treaty, would extend public support to the Soviet occupation of Afghanistan, he had, in private. expressed serious reservations regarding Soviet action, and urged Moscow to consider withdrawal as quickly as possible before matters get too complicated. Vorontsov, according to one observer, "was quite bowled over by the earthy wisdom of the inexperienced Prime Minister."[282]

And this is what India really did at the UN, The Permanent Representative was publicly uncritical of Soviet action, and went to the extent of even censuring certain unidentified nations for arming, training and encouraging subversive elements. He even went to the extent of declaring that he had no reason to doubt Soviet assertions.

The Foreign Secretary, who had originally criticised Soviet action, had to literally eat his words. For he was railroaded to send uttely shameless instructions to the Indian permanent representative in New York— instructions that were an apology for the Soviet Union.

The Indian reaction was badly received internationally. The Western world was disappointed. Pakistan was delighted since it put India in an embarrassing position. And, the Afghans, to say the least, were angry, for India was generally known to be their defender and their protector.

Indians, it is true, found themselves in a difficult situation. Charan Singh had handled the situation well, While declaring to the Soviet ambassador that India will support Soviet Russia under the treaty, he made it quite clear to the Soviet ambassador that he certaininly was not in favour of the Soviet invasion, and advised Brezhnev through Vorontsov, to withdraw Soviet troops before it was too late.

It would seem that Charan Singh met Vorontsov again, the next day in his office with the foreign secretary. On this occasion he spoke sternly about the Soviet invasion. He particularly deplored the killing of Amin. Vorontsov listened patiently, and then declared without any sign of exuberence: "I met Mrs. Indira Gandhi before I came here and she showed understanding of the situation." Charan Singh was totally deflated and the meeting ended.[283]

What is inexplicable is why India did not follow Charan Singh's sound strategy—of publicly supporting Soviet action unenthusiatically, while privately informing all and sundry that India was against the Soviet action. This would have been the most balanced position.

But, why did India not follow this strategy, under Charan Singh. What happened? And why this change.

It would seem that Charan Singh had virtually lost all power and was busy preparing for the election campaign—a campaign in which his chances of winning were nil. It may well be that in this confused and uncertain state Moscow may have used its long Indian arm in the MEA and outside to sway the decision in its favour.

EVALUATION

Charan Singh's projection to Prime Ministership was purely accidental. He broke with the coalition Government led by Morarji Desai and sought the assistance of practically everyone to come to power. He was even less knowledgeable and less interested in foreign affairs than his predecessor. There is really no way of finding out if he had any views of his own regarding the outside world. Besides, he was a Prime Minister for too short a period (a few months), and that too of an interim government pending elections, to permit any real analysis of his own role in foreign policy formulation. The only thing known, at least to the present writer regarding his involvement on foreign affairs was his firm and highly critical attitude to Soviet intervention in Afghanistan, which occurred during his premiership. In the middle of his election campaign he returned to New Delhi to give a dressing down to the Soviet ambassador, and demanded immediate Soviet withdrawal. In all probability he took the decision to berate the Soviet Union on his own.

INDIRA GANDHI

Chapter VI

INDIRA GANDHI
14 JANUARY 1980–31 OCTOBER 1984

Indira Gandhi returned to power after a dramatic victory in the elections. "The people welcomed, her", wrote Narasimha Rao, "on her comeback trail having become disillusioned with the other party."[284] Her position became even stronger than during her first tenure. She was firmly in control of the party, of two-thirds of the Parliament and all the major states with the exception of Bengal and Tamil Nadu. Coalition politics at the Centre had disappeared, at least for the time being, with the opposition dispersed and discredited "for reasons of internal dissension and utter non-performance."[285]

India had never experienced such a flawed governance—a governance totally inept in efficaciously handling internal and external affairs. For the first time in the history of post-independent India nothing worked. And, also for the first time it had to reckon with the sad spectacle of myriad proclaimed Gandhian politicians striving to become Prime Ministers. What was even more paradoxical was the man (Jayaprakash Narayan), who was the real power behind the making of the government was one of the few who was incorruptable, honest and integral. Unfortunately, he was indeed a bad judge of persons who had apparently fallen among miscreants.

Indira Gandhi's return was indeed a remarkable comeback to power of one who was generally perceived as irretrievably lost to politics.

Once again a strong, knowledgeable and savvy Prime Minister was at India's helm. But, it was a different Prime Minister—one who had victoriously returned to power, but with a visibly changed personal disposition, and an altered frame of mind. Personal characteristics, psychologists argue, really do not change, but evolve, becoming more visible and more acute, with the movement of time. In Indira Gandhi's case they became more visible, more sharp and even more severe during her second tenure.

Indira Gandhi had always been distrustful of people in politics even before she came to power. Clearly, this was her disposition from the lonely days of her childhood— apparently a disposition that became more accentuated with time. In 1980, she became even more so, given all the traumas she had to go through— the traumas of persecution and prosecution, under the Janata Government. Her friend and biographer, Pupul Jayakar, had this to say about this aspect of her character during the second tenure: "She was once again the Prime Minister of India, but her years in the wilderness had left deep scars that were to inhibit her actions. A suspicion of people, a sense of betrayal and a lack of trust were to journey with her for the rest of her life."[286] All this made her even more determined to personally control the entire power structure she had built around herself. From distrust to authoritarianism it is only a short cut, especially for one who possessed this characteristic even before. Indira Gandhi thus became even more authoritarian, more assertive and less patient. And what is even more striking, she became less of a listener—a characteristic in which she had outshone many of her contemporaries, and had used it optimally during her first tenure. Also, she had become vengeful, determined to strike at those who had betrayed or had assailed her.

Equally important was her new religiosity. Her attraction to Hindu religion had apparently become more and more visible. While some, less charitable, have attributed this new bewitchment to the uncertainty of retaining Muslim loyalty, most perceived this as a genuine attraction to Hindu religion. During the six weeks, after her return to power, Indira Gandhi worshipped at no less than a dozen shrines from north to south and east to west. Pupul Jayakar was dismayed at Indira Gandhi's new susceptibility to "ritual and superstition." In 1971, Indira declared that she did "not even believe in God,"[287] whereas at the 1980 swearing in ceremony as Prime Minister, God "found a place in her pledge.[288]

More than all this was Indira Gandhi's increasing predilection to turn to members of her family for political support, and for a possible successor, should she disappear from the political scene. But, this had always been there, even when she was heavily tied up in politics. Family counted more than the others—at least the two sons with whom she was close.

The one who had become a focal point of her interest was her son, Sanjay Gandhi, who slowly became her closest advisor, to the exclusion of others, during the two years of her authoritarian rule, and in the early eighties when she returned to the helm. Clearly, she had high political hopes in him, and confidently perceived him as someone who was destined to play a leading role in Indian politics—even more so after he himself gained some degree of political legitimacy after his election to the Indian Parliament.

Notwithstanding the fact that many in India had serious reservations about his policies, and his sordid political behaviour, for which he had become well known in the country, Sanjay successfully established a large supportive network. He carefully developed his own infrastructure, his own constituency, and his own group of advisers, not to speak of a massive strategy that was constructed to eulogise him all over the country. "An orgy," wrote a close observer, "of building plaster pyramids in Sanjay's honour followed. From one end of the country to the other, statues of him, often hideously crafted, were put up. Plans to start Sanjay schools, hospitals and gymnasia were breezily announced. Rare was the city or town where a road or a street was not named after him. A huge and costly pictorial exhibition on his life, called 'Son of India,' was put up at Pragati Maidan, Delhi's officially run permanent exhibition ground. State-controlled radio and television worked overtime to 'perpetuate his memory.'"[289] But, there was another, more positive, analysis of Sanjay Gandhi by one who knew him personally. "With victory," wrote Jayakar, "Sanjay was to emerge as a national leader in his own right. He was no longer the arrogant, inexperienced youth of 1975. The years out of power had given depth to his understanding of people and situations...He projected himself as a pragmatist, interested only in getting things done."[290] Sanjay Gandhi thus was indeed becoming a growing force to be reckoned with. His political behaviour was no longer comparable to the earlier days of the emergency when his personality and political life was dominated by misdeeds. He apparently gave the impression of having become more serious politically, and more determined to build up a following to help him to stand politically on his own—even independently of his mother. In sum, Sanjay was projecting himself as a political personality not far removed from the summit of power.

But, before he could effectively emerge as a national leader completely in his own right, he died in a daredevil crash in his light two-seater Pitts S-2A.

For Indira Gandhi this was indeed a great personal tragedy, and, what is more, a great calamity for having been deprived of Sanjay Gandhi's political support that she had begun to count on heavily. The tragedy was all the more terrible since she had slowly begun to perceive her son as her political successor. While the country, as a whole, including many of Indira Gandhi's own political colleagues, silently looked down upon her son as a dangerous ruffian—given his gruesome political performance during the Emergency—she lionized him as someone with enormous political flair, and with ominous determination of having his say and his way. It cannot be excluded that, given Sanjay Gandhi's threatening style of operation, even Indira Gandhi personally felt intimidated—much more from her son than anyone else. But, it would seem that, during her second mandate, her fervent wish to see him reach the summitry of Indian politics preponderated her inner apprehensions. In any event, Indira-Sanjay Gandhi connivance generated a fearful apprehension among her political colleagues regarding the direction in which India was heading. She was thus isolated from her political colleagues during her second mandate. But, strangely this did not seem to bother her since she had opted for establishing a pattern of governance with Sanjay Gandhi as the leader. Clearly the survivability and the continuation of the Nehru-Gandhi dynasty in the country had become more of a crucial preoccupation than India itself.

Compounded to this terrible loss, there emerged another personal problem—the problem of Sanjay's wife, Maneka Gandhi—who became visibly ambitious of succeeding her husband. This decision to openly project herself as her husband's successor was perceived as an implicit rivalry to Indira Gandhi's own authority—a rivalry that she had comfortably accepted from her son, but was not prepared to do so from her ambitious daughter-in-law vis-à-vis whom, and vis-à-vis whose family she had serious reservations right from the beginning. For Indira Gandhi this became a major, almost a national problem that dramatically surfaced in the media. Besides the new "draft Maneka" campaign was a major threat to her post-Sanjay important goal of creating a new successor—in the person of Rajiv Gandhi—who would keep the Nehru-Gandhi dynasty going. So it was no longer a personal domestic problem to be resolved within the four walls of the family house, for it was taking a national political dimension pertaining to her national successor.

A New Strategy of Power

For her second tenure, Indira Gandhi apparently mapped out a new strategy under which with Sanjay Gandhi "by her side,"[291] she would leave internal affairs to her son, and would free herself for designing a broad strategy in domestic and foreign affairs. For one thing, this would open doors for Sanjay to further consolidate his own position nationally, and make it possible for her to build a broad strategic framework in domestic and foreign affairs. But, now with Sanjay gone, "the agenda she had prepared with such care was in shambles."[292] The succession problem once again surfaced.

Growing National Disenchantment

This terrible loss coincided with a massive emergence of domestic discontent in much of the country. Prices rose everywhere, runaway inflation was rampant; lawlessness had become a national phenomenon. "Hoodlums and lumpens, wrote an observer, "stalked the land."[293]

Assam was in massive turmoil. The Assamese—most of them Hindus—had raised the flag of revolt against the continuous and uncontrollable influx of Bangladeshi Muslims; so much so that this massive inrush threatened to reduce the Assamese to a minority in their own state. Compounded to this was the indigenous tribal people of the same North Eastern State—mainly converted to Christianity—who rose up against high-caste Assamese Hinduist domination. So you had in the State of Assam one discontent transplanted on the other.

Punjab too was in a tumultuous state. Communal violence between Hindus and Sikhs engulfed the whole State; and the Sikh majority became more and more assertive, with numerous fundamentalists announcing their determination to "purify," Sikhism, and underpinning much of their political action to become independent from India. Indira and Sanjay Gandhi had much to do with this ugly state of affairs; while the growing discontent can partly be attributed to the inherent growth of the Sikh separatist movement, the two Gandhis were directly responsible for aggravating the situation in the Punjab by supporting some of the Sikh extremists to gain political leverage against their *Akali* adversaries—clearly a pattern of manipulative politics for which the two Gandhis were the real architects.

The political situation in the State of Jammu and Kashmir too was manipulated. Already mired in internal conflict, Indira Gandhi made things worse by deciding to dethrone Farooq Abdullah, the Chief Minister of Kashmir for having supported the Morarji Desai Government. She mobilised all her men to strike at Abdullah. There was hardly a public meeting or a press conference where Indira Gandhi's sycophants did not single out the Kashmiri leader. The attacks reached a high pitch at the Congress session in Calcutta where Rajiv Gandhi declared Abdullah a traitor. Finally, he was ousted much against the wishes of B.K.Nehru, Jawaharlal's cousin, and

Governor of the state. But then B.K.Nehru was ousted for disobeying Indira Gandhi.

Clearly, Indira Gandhi was unable to manage or contain the tumultuous crises within the country. Was it that the family problems she was mired in lessened her capacity to function efficaciously? Was it that her "political world had been completely shattered by her son,"[294] making her more insecure than she had ever been before? Was it her growing religiosity, compounded with "a sense of foreboding" that "tantric trials and black magic rites" were being performed by her adversaries to destroy, in her own words, "me and my sanity?"[295] Or was all this manipulatively spawned to gain petty political advantage? The capacity, many argued, she had shown during the good years as a remarkable manipulator, had gone. Indira Gandhi, for many, who knew her well, was really an operator, an intriguer, and a conniver but not a problem solver. During all her political life she worked well when it came to political intrigues, but not when it came to solving dimensional issues at the national level. "The lady," thought one commentator who apparently knew her well, had "crossed the Rubicon from mania to megalomania. Perhaps because it is her second coming, frenzy fits her snugly. Without batting an eyelid, she indulges in palpable untruths, such as that she neither appoints nor dismisses chief ministers of states... A Prime Minister whose second nature is uttering untruths, can be a trailblazer of an ominous kind."[296]

It is more than possible that it was the combination of all these personal and domestic setbacks that may have spawned the renewal of her interest in foreign affairs. More than often this has happened to many historic figures—particularly those who, in the midst of domestic setbacks, considered that dramatic international initiatives could help them in sprucing up of their image and in the retrieval of their national power.

Such a consideration may not have been absent in Indira Gandhi's decision to make herself visible in international affairs. Besides she was good in diplomacy, and had the advantage of being one of the most well-known and visible political figures who had "outlasted all her contemporaries" internationally.[297] Furthermore, she was remarkably astute in identifying India's national interests, and in comfortably adapting herself to changing international situations.

Foreign Affairs thus had acquired an important position in her agenda soon after she became the Prime Minister in 1980.

Changing International Environment

International environments too were evolving rapidly—environments that needed new responses. Signs of globalisation, for example, had begun to emerge. Increasingly, it was becoming evident that wide array of issues facing countries were no more completely solvable within their national frameworks. A momentous growth of trans-national movement of goods, capital, manpower, technology, etc., were germinating a consequential level of inter-dependence, one of the visible ramifications of which were that the rich nations were becoming richer while the poor were becoming poorer.

The cold war was also losing much of its old intensity and belligerence with the Soviet empire on the defensive showing some signs of decline and even of disintegration. President Ronald Reagan's aggressive campaign against the so-called "empire of evil" a term he used against Moscow—had indeed succeeded, since the Soviet Union, from that point on, slowly lost the clout that it had wielded internationally, decisively shifting the focus of international balance of power in favour of Washington. The change had not occurred overnight, but the signs were visible, albeit vague, of the shape of things to come.

The non-aligned world had also lost much of its vigour, and some of its relevance in the eighties. Radicalisation was on the up-beat, and cohesiveness was fast disappearing. Fidel Castro's elevation to the chairmanship of the non-aligned world did not help matters. For he was steering the movement into some form of extremism principally geared against the US. This was not helpful.

The US, once again, returned to Pakistan—this time in a big way, the purpose of which was to finance and arm the Islamic fundamentalists who became the principal opponents of Soviet military presence in Afghanistan.

Nearer home things were not looking up either. Islamic fundamentalism had emerged as a powerful force on India's western flank (Pakistan, Afghanistan and Iran), rendering Kashmir more tumultuous and India more unstable. Sikh fundamentalism was also expanding in the Indian State of Punjab, openly supported by Pakistan; and compounding all this was the activation of Soviet-US tensions on the very borders of India, with Soviet invasion of Afghanistan, and with US decision to support Pakistan militarily, and to enlarge its own presence in the country to contain and counter Soviet expansion in the area.

On the northern and Eastern flanks of India, the situation was no better. With China safely installed on the Tibetan plateau, and with the activation of its new and benign post-Maoist policy in South-East Asia right down to Myanmar bordering India, the level of Indian insecurity had clearly increased.

A Dense Record of Diplomatic Activity

Indira Gandhi's response to the rapidly changing global and regional situation was prompt and efficacious. In fact, her diplomatic performance, during her second mandate, was a rich and dense record of volatile activity at the multilateral and bilateral levels. If the tumultuous domestic situation, compounded with personality mutations, including the tragic loss of her son, left her out of depth, this was apparently not the case with international diplomacy. For, there she was like a sponge absorbing everything with great vivacity and speed. It was indeed a great turnaround. The people and the events appeared to excite her to action; besides it permitted her to get away from the tragedies and sordidity of domestic politics.

At the multilateral level she participated as a leading actor; and what is more with great benignity. She was in Cancun in October 1981 attending the NorthSouth Summit meeting, at Melbourne in November participating in the Commonwealth Conference, in New Delhi in February 1982 attending International Ministerial Conference of 122 developing countries that she had convened, again in New Delhi, in February 1982 participating in the seventh Non-aligned Summit of which she was elected as the Chairperson, in Belgrade in June 1983 attending the UN Conference on Trade and Development (UNCTAD), and in New York in October 1983 attending the annual conference of the UN General Assembly—undoubtedly an impressive record of heavy multilateral activities in comparison to Shastri, Desai and even her own father.

Hitherto Indira Gandhi's diplomatic experience had been principally limited to a swath of issues that were crucial to India—issues that pertained to its national interest.

All this required a specific methodology pertaining to bilateral interstate relations, the most important characteristic features of which were the game of power politics, pressures on other States, a search for optimal benefits from bilateral relations, etc. She had shown an outstanding ability and brazen courage in this pattern of diplomatic behaviour during her first mandate by laying the foundations for India to become a nuclear power by conducting the first nuclear test, established beyond any doubt India's hegemonial position in South Asia by effectively weakening Pakistan by liberating Bangladesh, and decisively tilted in the Soviet direction to forestall any aggressive US action against India, while, at the same time, discreetly seeking out China to neutralise overweening Soviet influence over India. This was the architecture of the broad strategy she constructed in the seventies.

But the eighties were different. For during her second mandate she also had to additionally reckon with the new multilateral dimension of international relations in which macro global issues had emerged, and which could hardly be ignored.

Participation in multilateral conferences

Globalisation had indeed begun to emerge—the process could no more be contained; it was spreading in all directions. Non-alignment needed more adaptations to the changing global situation where the cold war was losing much of its belligerence. It needed new orientations in which Fidel Castro's adage that Moscow was the "natural ally" of the non-aligned world had to be revisited. The ongoing unalloyed armament trend, among the great powers, was becoming threatening; and the third world collaterally was sliding into unassuaged poverty with the north becoming richer and the poor poorer. Probably this is no more the case at the turn of the 21st century since some developing countries too have begun to benefit from this inexorable process; but in the eighties of the 20th century it was different. The poorer countries were the helpless victims of this asymmetrical situation.

Indira Gandhi found herself in the midst of this phenomenon, and it must be said to her credit that she came out with flying colours by playing a leading role in all these international deliberations. At the North-South International Summit in Cancun—where she met Ronald Reagan—she played the role of a moderator by persuading her fellow delegates from developing countries not to insist on Fidel Castro's participation in the conference, who was then the Chairman of the Non-aligned Summit, since this would inevitably lead Reagan to boycott the conference, and thus defeat the very purpose of the whole exercise—the clear objective of which was to attract the White House into the maelstrom of north-south dimension—a dimension which was hitherto an anathema for most Americans. To get a reluctant Ronald Reagan to attend the Mexico meeting was indeed an achievement. For his participation would certainly have been aborted if

Castro was present. Undoubtedly, it was Indira Gandhi's sagacious diplomacy that saved the conference.

At the Non-aligned Summit in New Delhi, she was unanimously proclaimed as the Chairperson gaining in authority with the developing world. With considerable dexterity she reconciled conflicting opinions, and patiently sought a consensus on contentious issues that were on the table of the Non-aligned Summit, steering the movement away from Castro's perception that the Soviet Union was a "natural ally" of the non-aligned. And at the international ministerial meeting she had herself convened, she pressed hard for the restructuring of the world economic order.

Fidel Castros', high qualities notwithstanding, was not the right person at the moment to head the non-aligned movement. Since what the non-aligned world needed at the time was gaining the confidence of the international community, which at this time was apparently not possible with Castro's repeated undiplomatic proclamations to the effect that Russia was a "natural ally" of the non-aligned world.

From the different speeches and declarations Indira Gandhi subscribed to in numerous multilateral international occasions, the essence of her thinking and strategy were directed at: (a) meeting the problems raised by the phenomenon of globalisation, (b) drawing the attention of the international community to the stark economic stagnation the world was faced with, (c) underlining the imperativeness of international cooperation to jointly restructure international relations to meet the growing north-south dichotomy, (d) conveying to the developing world her conviction that accelerated south-south cooperation in all sectors, including science and technology, was the only way of avoiding excessive dependence on the west.

New international perspectives were indeed opening up for Indira Gandhi—perspectives of becoming a major international actor on macro issues emerging globally. Given her vast experience, her dynamic personality and established international popularity— she was emerging as a crucial element to give leadership to the developing world–more than any other third world leader– but fate was to decide otherwise, for she was assassinated before she could impose herself.

Diplomacy Towards Superpowers

The second dimension of Indian diplomacy was the launching of a massive operation of friendship vis-à-vis the international system. Naturally she started with the superpowers—first of all with the US with whom she had a heavy record of troubled relations during her first mandate—a record of open disagreements and growing tensions during the Bangladesh crisis. Though some improvement occurred under her predecessor, she convinced herself that any scope for any further understanding was truly limited given the strong prejudices that dominated the US administration and the US media against her as a person. Therefore, notwithstanding the wide array of disagreements that separated the two countries, Indira Gandhi decided to focus her attention on burnishing her own image by seeking to establish a personal rapport with President Ronald Reagan. Though she did have doubts regarding his mastery of international affairs or even the level of his understanding of subjects under discussion between Indian and US delegations, she personally hit off very well with the President in Mexico and during her August 1982 visit to the US. Reagan was past master in amiability; so was she, for she had an innate capacity of reciprocating with equal friendliness whenever circumstances required such a behaviour. In sum, relations with Washington improved, even if differences remained, and even if serious reservations persisted in her innermost thinking regarding US international behaviour.

While constructing an amiable bilateral relationship with Washington, she was apprehensive of its international policies, particularly in regard to India, She somehow convinced herself that the US was never favourably disposed towards India. This may have had something to do with her traditional adversial perception, which was probably accentuated with the difficulties she encountered with Washington. During her first mandate, she had declared that "the US was trying a pincer hold on Asia—Vietnam and Israel—India would be encircled…it is better that we die than to give in to constant pressures from Wahington."[298] US presence in Pakistan during the Afghan episode did not arrange matters. If anything, it worsened her perception since Washington was heavily involved in supporting the Islamic fundamentalists who were in the forefront battling the Soviet armed forces, and in closely cooperating with the Pakistani establishment in setting up an anti-Soviet front.

The visit to Moscow in September 1982 was meant to maintain the underpinnings of formal Indian traditional balance between the two superpowers. Having been to the US she clearly had to visit Moscow even if there was really no need for it. This was the traditional diplomatic behaviour to pre-empt any misunderstanding. Clearly, this was not much of a visit since

Brezhnev, seriously ill, was unable to participate in any effective negotiations, though he went through the formal ritual of being present at all important occasions. On the whole, it was a smooth visit even though disagreements persisted on Soviet military occupation of Afghanistan. On numerous informal occasions Indira Gandhi frankly indicated her opposition to Soviet presence in Afghanistan. In one encounter with Gromyko, who had specially come to India to explain the Soviet position, she listened to him and abruptly ended the meeting by tersely telling him: "On this I cannot help you." But, Indira Gandhi clearly avoided any diplomatic action against the Soviets, since, in her estimation, the maintenance of smooth Indo-Soviet relations outweighed the dangers of Soviet military action in Afghanistan. Nonetheless, in most of her diplomatic conversations with Western leaders she did declare that India favoured a political, rather than a military solution so that conditions could be created for the early withdrawal of Soviet troops.

India's diplomatic behaviour on Afghanistan had transmuted. Under Indira Gandhi, the government had abandoned the politics of supporting the Russians in their adventurous policies in Afghanistan. While maintaining a friendly benignity towards Moscow, Indira Gandhi told the Russians that they had to leave Afghanistan; for she was genuinely fearful of the adverse consequences on South Asia.

The third aspect in this superpower framework, was China. Indira Gandhi persisted in her diplomatic actions of seeking some degree of normalisation with Beijing. This she had already begun during her first mandate, and which was continued by her successor, Morarji Desai; but now that she had returned to power she accelerated her diplomatic initiatives in the direction of China.

As during her first mandate, a number of factors motivated her decision, the most obvious being that China was very much there as a neighbour who could not be ignored indefinitely, and where, in her estimation, India "should have a foot in there."[299] Besides, China was indeed changing. The ones who had architected China's belligerent policy against India were no more on the political scene. They were all dead, (including Mao Tsedong, Zhou EnLai, Liu Xiaoqi); and the new leadership, under Deng Xiaoping, was showing signs of opening up to the outside world. Even towards India there were benign signs of seeking an understanding. In June 1980, Deng personally spelt out to an Indian journalist his views on the Sino-Indian boundary dispute. He expressed his optimism regarding the resolution of the Sino-Indian border question.. In his view the litigious issue "can be solved through peaceful negotiations," and had recommended that both "countries should make concessions"[300] Indira Gandhi also reasoned that building bridges with China may open possibilities of moving a little bit away from the state of an excessive dependence with Moscow; and may, at the same time, make China less committed to Pakistan, which had clearly become a security headache for India.

The Indian Prime Minister thus had a point in injecting some mutations in India's diplomatic behaviour. Seeking out China could result in some positive ramifications. But, she was probably over-optimistic of the results. For, while the Chinese were opening up diplomatically, they were still in a state of transition with a diplomatic focus directed towards Washington and Moscow, the two superpower capitals with whom relations had reached a nadir point, India was certainly important, but less so than the two giants. Besides, Beijing was not completely sure if India's swing away from Moscow was really credible, given its heavy dependence on Moscow, given the abundant hold the latter still exercised on the domestic Indian opinion, and, furthermore, given Indira Gandhi's obvious reluctance to make a clean break with any of the two major actors—least of all the Soviet Union. The objective constraints thus were indeed too great, even if some determination to overcome them was visible.

Indira Gandhi perhaps was also too optimistic that her friendly initiatives in the direction of Beijing would make China less committed to Pakistan militarily. This was not the case since, China continued to give military aid, including aid in the nuclear sector. But India's friendly gestures did have some effect in so far as—it is now known—that China clearly cautioned Pakistan against military action against India: the arms aid to Pakistan, the Chinese informally but repeatedly declared that the aid was meant to pre-empt any action from the Indian side, and was not to be used for offensive purposes. [301]

As with most nations, the Chinee too could not formally change their attitude with their strategic partner, Pakistan. Nations do develop fixed diplomatic positions for years, and then find themselves inextricably stuck with a position from which extrication becomes difficult.

Deng Xiaoping had realised the growing importance of India, but found it difficult to extricate China from an overloaded position vis-à-vis Pakistan, though it had become clear that Deng did not wish anymore to involve China in an anti-India posture. Furthermore he was aware of the potential economic importance of India as China's partner. And in the changing configuration of the post-cold war international system, Deng was equally aware of the fact that India was no more overly tied up with Moscow even if they still had some important deals.

In any event Indira Gandhi continued with her efforts to build bridges with China. She accelerated the ongoing process by arranging to meet her counterpart, Hua Guofeng, on the occasion of Tito's Funeral in May 1980. Reporting on the 8th of May meeting between the two leaders, the *Xinhua News Agency* wrote that the two of them exchanged views in a friendly atmosphere on further promoting relations between the two countries, and on international issues of common concern.[302] The report was very revelatory, for it mirrored, probably for the first time, the dimension of the Chinese change towards India. Another major landmark in the ongoing process of normalisation was the visit to India of the Chinese Foreign Minister in June 1981. For it was on this occasion that an institutionalised procedure was mutually agreed upon to begin a dialogue between the two countries, and to open talks on the boundary question. Another helpful meeting was Indira Gandhi's encounter with her counterpart, Zhao Ziyang, on 28 October 1981 at Cancun at the North-South Conference.

After five round of Sino-Indian talks during Indira Gandhi's mandate it became evident that their positions were far apart. Indira Gandhi was coming around to the idea that, while the negotiations at the expertise level were important to arrive at the underpinnings of "principles and criteria" that would govern the eventual boundary demarcation, the actual line would have to be resolved politically at the summit level. "I will have to," she declared to the chief Indian negotiator, "to sit down with Deng and draw it."[303] Presumably, it was this type of thinking that led her to encourage the Indian delegation "to keep the talks going, without committing to "anything specific."[304]

And parallel to the official talks, she secretly despatched, K.N.Rao of RAW in October 1981 to Beijing "with a comprehensive proposal to settle the border dispute."[305] Kao had become Indira Gandhi's key man for delicate assignments. The Chinese did receive him well, but they were still not ready to wrap up a border agreement.

The other important and more concrete development was the one-on-one meeting of G.Parthasarathy with Deng in June 1982 when GP, in his capacity as Chairman of the Indian Council of Social Science Research (ICSSR) had led a delegation of social science scholars to China. In this meeting Deng reiterated the so-called "package deal" on the border under which China would accept India's claim on the eastern sector in return for Indians doing likewise in regard to the Chinese claim on the western sector. Reacting favourably to the proposal, GP persuaded Indira Gandhi to respond favourably and speedily to the proposal. A letter was sent out to Deng on 7th July 1982 proposing that the talks be launched between permanent secretaries of the foreign ministries.[306]

However, since the resolution of the boundary issue was not around the corner, Indira Gandhi accepted the Chinese proposal that the two countries should, in the meantime, attempt to increase cultural, and other exchanges, for they would only generate the appropriate atmosphere to make the task easier to finally resolve the border issue.

It should be noted that this was the first time that India had finally accepted the package deal that was originally proposed by Zhou Enlai to Nehru before the 1962 Sino-Indian conflict, but the Indians since then had never given a positive answer to the proposal.

All these initiatives would have resulted in a major breakthrough with the Chinese if she had not been assassinated in October 1984, thus bringing to a brutal end the long process she had cultivated during her first mandate and continued during her second.

Public Relations Diplomacy

Indira Gandhi also inaugurated an unremitting diplomatic activity of travelling to many countries. She went practically everywhere: to Switzerland, Kuwait and the United Arab Emirates in May 1981; to Kenya in August 1981; to Indonesia, Fiji, Tonga, Australia and the Philippines in September-October of the same year; to Romania, Mexico and the United Kingdom in October 1981; to the United Kingdom in March 1982; to Saudi Arabia in April 1982; to Yugoslavia, Finland, Denmark, Norway and Austria in June 1983, and finally to Cyprus, Greece, France and the US in September-October 1983.

The importance of this dimension of her diplomacy can be discerned from the fact that, during the four and half years of her last mandate, she went overseas 18 times and visited three dozen countries. Consider all the preparations made, all the speeches drafted and delivered, all the diplomatic conversations undertaken during this period, while moving rapidly from one country to the other; it is undoubtedly an unbeatable record. None of the Prime Ministers, before and even after, had gone through such a vigorous diplomatic activity. It was indeed a vast diplomatic operation in which she outshone the others—in friendliness, in openness, in diplomatic niceties, and in charming offensiveness. This was in glaring contrast to the other side of her character which surfaced domestically—that of a conniver, schemer, harsh, and ruthless woman, constantly undermining some, and continuous hassling those she perceived as adversaries.

What was it that led her to indulge in such an intense diplomatic activity? Was it her "need for establishing personal contact at heads of government level and also explaining to the western media personally" of what had happened before and during the emergency.?[307] Was it the boredom and problems of Indian politics that drove her to such action in the hope of rebuilding her declining image within the country, for this is what many politicians do? Or was it a vast calculated scheme as the Non-aligned Chairperson who wanted to project herself onto the international scene as the protector of the poor against the rich? Or was it her own personal psychological difficulties and her new-born insecurities that instigated such intense diplomatic activity. Since Indira Gandhi was generally known for not doing anything without some motivated reason, it may well be that it was the combination of all these factors that accelerated her to such action.

Whatever may be the explanation, the fact of the matter is that she excelled in diplomacy like no one else—not even her own father.

South Asian Neighbours

The fourth aspect of Indira Gandhi's multi-faceted diplomacy pertained to India's South Asian neighbours. Once a part of the vast British Empire, they had become, after World War II, seven independent and sovereign States. While the architecture of Indian diplomacy was different from country to country there was a homogenous factor common to all of them— the factor of determined firmness. Unlike her predecessors (Nehru, Shastri and Desai) who had sought bilateral understanding with each of them, she constructed a forceful diplomacy, the underpinnings of which were that India was the biggest and the most empowered South Asian actor, and had to be recognised as such. Of all the Prime Ministers, she was the only one to successfully and forcefully project India as the most powerful dimension in South Asian politics. After the forceful establishment of Bangladesh, during her first mandate, most of them had accepted India's supremacy, ramifications of which were already evident during her second prime ministership.

Pakistan

With Pakistan relations were frankly hostile. Indira Gandhi decided to maintain a high level of animosity towards India's North-Western neighbour. It had partly to do with the personality of her counterpart, Zia-ul Huq, and partly had to do with the overall political situation of the region. The personal bias she had developed against Zia was based on a number of considerations. For one thing, the exceptionally good relations Zia had forged with her predecessor, Desai, may have had something to do with her reservations, since her own relations with Desai, to say the least, had become highly inimical during his mandate as the Prime Minister. Zia's forthright execution of Bhutto, his predecessor, in April 1979, characterised by many as a "judicial murder," added to her personal reservations; for while still in the opposition, she had launched a determined international campaign to save him, but all in vain. Zia had contemptuously ignored all her appeals and those of the others. For still another, Zia'a penchant for Islamic fundamentalism, compounded with the support he had extended to anti-Indira Gandhi Sikhs in the Punjab, was yet another dimension that accelerated her personal opposition to the Pakistani leader. Her personal reservations of Zia must have been aggravated by the four meetings she had with him in Zimbabwe on the occasion of its independence—meetings that led them nowhere, since Zia was apparently not very diplomatic on these occasions. He presented Indira Gandhi with an autographed coffee table publication on Pakistan that had a map which included not only the whole of Kashmir but also three former small principalities in India's Gujarat State far away from the Pakistani border. It is most unlikely—given her character—that she appreciated what was clearly a diplomatic gaffe. Zia, furthermore, took advantage of these meetings to highlight the wonderful rapport he had developed with Morarji Desai—hardly a remark to make to Indira Gandhi who was known to be his inimical adversary. The retort was not far in coming. "You do not seem," she bluntly declared, "to realise that Mr. Desai in no longer in charge of our government."[308]

The objective conditions in the region too were not very congenial for Indo-Pakistan understanding. The Soviet occupation of Afghanistan had created a problematic situation. Not only Indira Gandhi viewed this with considerable disfavour—given India's traditional friendship with Afghanistan—but expressed her fears that the overall situation in South Asia was fast becoming explosive with the US decision to retaliate Soviet occupation by supporting Moscow's Afghan opponents, and by giving massive aid to Pakistan. "The West and especially the USA," she wrote in her letter to Krishnamurti "seems determined to destablize our sub-continent. They are fully supporting Zia, not realising his precarious and unpopular position within Pakistan."[309]

Indira Gandhi had clearly convinced herself that the West was out to destroy India. This somehow remained with her during the rest of her life. This was certainly true during Nixon's time. But to argue, as she commonly did, that Carter and Reagan too were her adversaries did not correspond with the facts. Carter had gone out of his way to be friendly with India and publicly declared that democratic India was a great achievement. And Reagan, though not an Indian fan did not consider India negatively.

So where did she acquire this percetion? How did she come to the conclusion?

One would have thought that the US, if anything, was increasingly turning to India, particularly in the light of US pre-occupation with the growth of Islamic fundamentalism in the whole of north western region, particularly during the Soviet occupation of Afghanistan, when Washington was doling out money and arms to the Taliban on the ground that they were most effective in their anti-Soviet actions.

But, while doing so, the Americans had no illusions regarding the dangerousness of the Taliban to US interests, and regarding Pakistan's increasing vlunerability as a viable state. It was only because Indians were not cooperating that Washington had to turn to Pakistan

It must be noted that the post-cold war US decision makers considered India important, and perceived it as a prime target of islamic fundamentalism.

So Indira Gandhi really did not have any palpable basis for her opinion that the Americans were out to target India as a dangerous adversary.

The growing Sikh fundamentalist and independence movement, of which Indira Gandhi was becoming the main target, was supported by Zia with arms and funds. This clearly was creating a difficult situation in the Punjab.

Finally Islamic fundamentalism was showing signs of expanding in Pakistan—signs that were clearly disturbing for secular India.

Indira Gandhi's attitude towards Zia and Pakistan was, therefore, openly and firmly hostile. No effort was really spared to isolate Pakistan.

Consider Pakistan's attempts to re-enter the Commonwealth, from which it had abruptly walked out in 1972. A general consensus appeared to exist among the members that Pakistan should be allowed to re-enter its fold. The overall situation had indeed evolved, and there really was no point in keeping Pakistan out of the Commonwealth, particularly when there was a consensual agreement for its re-admission. Even the Indian Ministry of External Affairs was prepared "to go along with the consensus." But Indira Gandhi was against such an inclusion. She clearly and firmly informed the Pakistani Ambassador to India, Abdul Sattar, that if she agreed to Pakistan's request, the Commonwealth would become "yet another forum" to "rake up Kashmir" and other bilateral disputes.[310] Again when Pakistan finally accepted the long-held Indian proposal to conclude "a no war pact," Indira Gandhi skirted the proposal and came up, instead, with another proposal—the proposal to conclude a comprehensive treaty of peace and friendship.

Pakistan had apparently accepted the original Indian proposal, for it wanted to neutralise the Indian objection to arms aid it was receiving from Washington. But the whole issue was set aside by an agreement to appoint an Indo-Pakistan commission to reconcile the position of the two parties. But, it was a fruitless operation for nothing came out of this exercise.

In her hostility to the Zia Government, Indira Gandhi came out in favour of the political agitation that had emerged in Sind in the summer of 1983 for the restoration of democracy. Presumably, Indira Gandhi's support to Sind was in retaliation to Pakistan's support of Sikh agitation in the Punjab. Indira Gandhi's hostility to Pakistan was much more open than that of her three predecessors all of whom attempted to avoid any direct confrontation. But, this was not always possible since India was obliged to have military showdowns during Nehru and Shastri's time.

It is probably undeniable that the personal good relations established between Desai and Zia could have been a good basis for Indo-Pakistan entente, but this was not to be, since Indira Gandhi, to risk a generalisation, was apparently not interested in seeking out some understanding with Pakistan.

Sri Lanka

Relations with Sri Lanka too were not propitious. If anything, they took a turn for the worse during Indira Gandhi's mandate. The age-old ethnic tensions between the Sinhalese and the Tamils reached a critical point, climaxing into pressing demands for a separate Tamil Eelam; and the bloody clashes that erupted in July 1983 spawned a massive exodus of Sri Lankan Tamils into India. For the first time a widespread, across-the-border, sympathy of Indian Tamils with their Sri Lankan counterparts spawned in the southern State of Tamil Nadu, generating, also for the first time a wide chasm between the Indian and Sri Lankan Governments; so much so that Colombo appealed for military help from a group of countries (US, UK, Pakistan, China and Bangladesh) from which India was conspicuously excluded. Indira Gandhi was upset by this exclusion, and, what is more, was clearly annoyed at the list of countries to which an appeal was made, since hardly anyone of them was friendly to India. She was fearful of this new crisis looming on the South Asian horizon. With the one that had already exploded in the north-west with Soviet occupation of Afghanistan, and with retaliatory American presence in Pakistan, she was clearly becoming concerned at the superpowers' knocking at the doors of India, and was fearful that if she did not do anything, India would be marginalised in Sri Lanka. The Indian Prime Minister acted forthwith. Through her Foreign Minister, who was hastily despatched to Colombo, she warned the Sri Lankans that this "extraneous involvement" would "complicate matters for both countries,"[311] and attempted to dissuade Colombo from such action.

In the face of such a severe warning, Sri Lanka finally concluded an agreement with India to use its good offices to find a solution to the ethnic strife.

India acted. It called an all party conference to find a consensual solution. But, all this was despairingly hopeless since the chasm between the two communities was unbridgeable, the net result of which was that India got hopelessly bogged down in the crisis. It failed because it was unable to gain the confidence neither of the Colombo Government nor of the Sri Lankan Tamils. Neither of them had any faith in New Delhi.

What was even worse was that this diplomatic failure resulted even in a bigger crisis: it failed to stem growing international involvement. The Israeli Mossad, the British SAS (Special Air Service), China and Pakistan with their military equipment, the reactivation of the Anglo-Saxon defence agreement, the modernisation of the Voice of America transmitter on Sri Lankan soil—all of which India feared was now moving into the country.

Sri Lanka thus became a centre of international activities with India watching helplessly without possessing any credible power to contain such an expanding phenomenon.

It cannot be denied that Indira Gandhi was the one who generated such a situation, since she had, with the active complicity of Kao, established militarily oriented training centres for Sri Lankan Tamils. The obvious purpose of such an action was to expand Sri Lankan Tamils' capacity to demand enlarged autonomy, if not independence, of the northern areas of the island where they were living.

This was indeed a monumental error since the island's deteriorating situation had become so unstable and so vulnerable that it became even a bigger breeding ground for international manipulations and intrigues over which India had no control.

However, before Indira Gandhi could do anything she was assassinated. And, even if she had been alive, one wonders if she could have been able to control and contain the situation that was fast degenerating.

India's credibility was seriously affected. It showed beyond any doubt that even gigantic and neighbouring India had no power to manage or contain the crisis.

Bangladesh

Relations with Bangladesh were even more difficult. Liberating Eastern Pakistan from Western Pakistan was one thing, but aiding Bangladesh to develop was another matter—in fact even more problematic and even more strenuous. For one thing, the newly liberated country was poor—very poor—with hardly any resources, and with hardly any trained manpower. For another, in its ongoing ambition to become really independent and meaningfully sovereign, it began to construct a foreign policy that moved the country away from India. Besides, there were a multitude of bilateral and traditional differences that re-surfaced soon after Bangladesh's independence. Paradoxically, they had already taken a litigious form when Indira Gandhi returned to power. There was the momentous influx of Bangladeshi nationals into eastern parts of India spawning a domestic upheaval among the Assamese who were demanding their expulsion. There was the sharing of the Ganges water dispute which had taken a serious turn with the unilateral Indian construction of the Farraka barrage in 1975. And there was the Bangladesh Islamic heritage that resulted in the widespread expansion of fundamentalist tendencies resulting in the departure of the Hindus and the Chakmas tribal minority into India.

Indira Gandhi did try to introduce some degree of normality in Indo-Bangladesh relations by concluding a trade agreement (October 1980), by signing a memorandum of understanding on technical cooperation (1981), and by encouraging the convening of the Joint Economic Commission (1982). But the differences were too great, and the chasm too wide to bring the two countries close together.

The Assamese refused to accept Indira Gandhi's compromise proposal on Bangladeshis in the north-eastern state that 25 March 1971 be made the cut off date of letting the Bangladeshis stay in Assam if they came before that date. The Ganges water dispute remained as acute as ever, and the ongoing Islamic fundamentalism continued its expansion within the country.

Indira Gandhi, in sum, found herself in a paradoxical positiion. While having liberated Bangladesh successfully from western Pakistan, she did not possess the economic power to help and rescue her liberated muslim neighbours. In diplomacy, it is indeed hazardous to deploy military power to liberate a nation. For the net result of such a deteriorating situation is the influx of other international actors into the country over which you have no control. While most major nations installed themselves in Bangladesh, the most important of which was China, a mass of Bangladeshi, on the other hand, had moved all over India in search of economic security.

Nepal

The Himalayan kingdom of Nepal continued to remain problematic. Its determined ambition to loosen its special ties, forged with India in 1950, particularly in the military sector, had become a secular trend among most decision makers. That this new Nepalese political orientation was always, firmly and consensually, opposed is evident from the actions of most Indian governments. Indira Gandhi was even more reserved since Pakistan and China had activated their diplomacies even more in favour of Nepal during Indira Gandhi's prime ministership.

A short shrift was, therefore, given in 1984 when the Nepalese King repeated his proposal of Nepalese disengagement from India. Much of Indira Gandhi's diplomacy in the north was thus directed at containing Chinese and Pakistani influences, and foreclosing Nepalese attempts to make their proposals for greater independence at international forums.

Bhutan

Bhutan, the other Himalayan kingdom, also strove to become more independent from India. This was the ongoing trend that set in during the seventies and continues to this day. But, unlike Nepal, it considered that its security was closely linked with India. And, therefore, while becoming more active internationally (UN membership in 1971, Non-aligned movement in 1973, SAARC in 1985), the underpinnings of its foreign policy continued to remain pro-Indian. Facing as it did with a host of external problems—border negotiations with the Chinese, refugees in Nepal claiming to be Bhutanese, insecurity and violence by north-eastern Indian separatists residing in Bhutan—the Bhutanese leadership was aware of the fact that it needed Indian help.

Though Indira Gandhi was heavily involved in her own domestic and external problems, her attitude towards Bhutan was not unfriendly, given the fact that the Himalayan kingdom did not really have much of a leverage of distancing itself from New Delhi.

ACTIVATION OF CHANNELS OF FOREIGN POLICY

Indira Gandhi could hardly deal with foreign affairs all by herself. Like anyone heading a government, she needed institutions and people to assist her in the construction and the implementation of the architecture of foreign policy, even more so in the eighties when she became more interested in the global aspects of foreign affairs than she had been ever before. But, this time she maintained a direct hold over all of them—institutions and people. No powerful personality was allowed to interpose between her and the institutions. She was determined to avoid the repetition of her first mandate when P.N.Haksar was allowed to establish a tight grip over decisions and decision making. None of his successors ever acquired power he had established around himself.

The Prime Minister's Office, directly concerned with foreign affairs, was once again strengthened with the attribution of centralised decisional authority of the earlier years. Once again, it became a powerful channel of communication, and the centre of foreign policy making firmly controlled by the Prime Minister- even more so than during her previous mandate- –so much so that the expanded Secretariat was no longer allowed (as was the case before) to be separated by a powerful Secretary in-charge of the Secretariat. She herself was in charge; and she herself supervised the operation of the powerful institution with a weak Principal Secretary carrying out her instructions. The Secretariat, like before, was invested with considerable power and authority to monitor the activities of the entire government, to take decisions, and to see to it that they were effectively operationalised either by the Secretariat itself or by the relevant ministry concerned. The Secretariat had indeed become a powerful institution that literally ran the country. This determined attempt to centralise power in her own hands had also something to do with the humiliating treatment she had experienced at the hands of the Janata Government while in opposition. Pupul Jayakar, her biographer, had this to say of the trauma she went through: "She was once again the Prime Minister of India, but her years in the wilderness had left deep scars that were to inhibit her actions. A suspicion of people, a sense of betrayal and a lack of trust were to journey with her for the rest of her life."[312] All this made her even more distrustful and even more determined to personally control the entire power structure she had built around her Secretariat.

The RAW too was given a new lease of life. In fact, it became even more powerful with the new added responsibility to prepare regular background briefs for the Prime Minister that were no longer based only on covert information but also contained overt information collected by agents abroad and expertly analysed at the headquarters. This was the new and powerful dimension that Indira Gandhi attributed to the intelligence agency—a practice that was common among the Western countries, but not in India. Besides, the Prime Minister often used Rameshwar Nath Kao, the head of intelligence agency, to establish numerous bilateral contacts with other countries. In fact, he was brought out of retirement, and was appointed as a senior adviser to Indira Gandhi in the cabinet secretariat in 1981.

The ground rules for such "para-diplomacy" were that there was no publicity, that such probings were informal, and no notes or minutes were really kept. Indira Gandhi, during her second mandate, used Kao to inform the Reagan Administration of India's opposition to the Soviet occupation of Afghanistan. Kao used his contacts with the US intelligence service to soften the Reagan Administration's attitude towards Indira Gandhi. Similarly, Kao made a secret visit to Beijing at the behest of Indira Gandhi in 1984, and also established contacts with the Sikh opposition leaders abroad before the Prime Minister's attack on the Golden temple in Amritsar.[313]

The third channel of foreign policy formulation was her contacts with international personalities with whom she met during her trips abroad or when they came to India. After a long period of inactivity during the Janata Government, foreign affairs suddenly surfaced when Indira Gandhi came to the helm of affairs. Within days of taking over as Prime Minister an unprecedented number of foreign dignitaries visited India–President Giscard d'Estaing of France, President Zia-ur Rahman of Bangladesh,

President Sese Seke Mobutu of Zaire, Kenneth Kaunda of Zambia, Yasser Arafat the Palestinian leader, Andrei Gromyko, Soviet Foreign Minister, a special emissary of President Jimmy Carter and a senior minister from Japan. Pupul Jayakar considered that "all came to meet and assess the mind of the Prime Minister. The world leaders were aware that with Indira Gandhi as Prime Minister, a formidable new presence had appeared in one of the most critical areas of the world."[314]

The fourth channel was her close foreign policy advisers. Though she was apparently no more a great listener, as in the past, she did interact and use advisers like G. Parthasarathy (GP), T.N.Kaul, Natwar Singh, M.L.Fotedar for different missions, and for assisting her in the drafting of her major foreign policy declarations and speeches While all of them were individially used, GP became quite close to her. Like her father, she had great confidence in him and had often used him for delicate assignments during her first and second mandates.

The fifth channel was the MEA. Though it was no longer important in designing foreign policy, it was undoubtedly another crucial source of information from which she received reports regularly, and to which she turned to for most of the formal diplomatic initiatives.

Finally, there was the Prime Minister's House; it became a powerful decision making Centre. It was an extra-constitutional institution "which is not seen but heard through its oral and unwritten hints." According to one observer when Indira Gandhi came back to power in 1980 the Prime Minister's House (PMH) was in full strength, overshadowing to some extent, the PMO (Prime Minister's Office). Though the emergence of such a decision making centre has been attributed to the fact that Sanjay Gandhi, her son and a powerful political figure, lived in the house, it has continued to remain an important powerhouse under other prime ministers.

Indira Gandhi, thus, had at her disposal six channels of information all of which were used varyingly before any major decisions were taken. And, after having received the inputs from all these sources she used them to implement decisions.

Indira Gandhi's control over foreign policy, thus, was total. Whether the issues were routine, visible or macro, she herself exercised control over decision making. She was probably India's first Prime Minister who diligently absorbed a wide array of inputs by different channels and institutions before taking a decision.

EVALUATION

Indira Gandhi's second mandate was more dense in foreign affairs than her first—more dense in diplomatic actions, and even more animated in diplomatic activity. Though, there was nothing theatrical as the 1971 Indo-Soviet Treaty, or the forced partition of Pakistan, or the open defiance of President Nixon, her involvement in the eighties was indeed global. She became heavily embroiled in such trans-national issues as non-alignment, north-south dichotomy and disarmament. As there was a paucity of any decisive third world leadership for these momentous international contentious problems, she found herself being projected on to the international system. For the first time in her political career she was on the cusp of acquiring a recognised international status; and also, for the first time, by force of circumstances, she had to reflect and inject an intellectual content to these subjects—something which she had never experienced or done before. Had she not been assassinated in October 1984, she would have found a consensual and comfortable international status. If the events of the early eighties is anything to go by, then there is little doubt that she was tempted and prepared herself for this new international role.

Indira Gandhi had also successfully established a broad balance in her relations with the established international powers. The excessive dependence on Moscow, of which she herself was the architect, compounded with the Soviet military occupation of Afghanistan, had finally catalysed her to re-inject some mutations in India's relations with the ones who were powerful internationally. While, avoiding any radical refurbishment, she did establish some distance with Moscow, went out of her way to introduce a degree of normal interaction with Washington, and took some friendly steps towards Beijing. In sum, Indira Gandhi constructed a stealth diplomacy towards the three powers.

Feeling "the need for establishing personal contact at the heads of government level,"[315] Indira Gandhi initiated remarkably a vast programme of foreign visits to countries and organisations. She visited so many countries, big and small, made her presence felt in so many organisations, and contacted so many media representatives that she succeeded in putting India on the map of the world. Indeed, it was unprecedented action, which no Prime Minister, before , had carried out such a dimensional diplomatic action.

Last, but not least, was the construction of a broad framework of diplomacy vis-à-vis South Asia—a framework whose underpinnings were to conclude agreements through confidence building gestures towards small countries, and through the maintenance of a high power profile to dissuade countries from pursuing goals contrary to India's national interests. But, the most powerful objective of India's South Asian diplomacy was to keep foreign power presence/influence at bay from the region. In sum, she devised some sort of a Monroe doctrine of her own that focussed on maintaining Indian sphere of influence over South Asia. Concretely, this was "a geographic concretisation of where the national interest lay."[316]

While this was clearly Indira Gandhi's sole objective during her first mandate, it would be incorrect that this was the case during her second mandate. It certainly was a priority, and the Prime Minister was realist enough to realise that such a tight hold on South Asia could be effectively exerted only when it is backed by material power.

But, the architecture of Indira Gandhi's diplomacy went beyond the South Asian region, since she became ambitious enough to exercise influence beyond the frontiers of South Asia—an influence for which she knew that she was not materially equipped, but which she could exercise through some moral authority as she had acquired a recognised status of a global leader.

RAJIV GANDHI

Chapter VII

Rajiv Gandhi
31 October 1984—1 December 1989

Rajiv Gandhi's emergence on to the political scene was a pure accident, a sudden political emergence with the assassination of his mother, Indira Gandhi. He had limited experience in politics with no real interest in it. He had no followers, and even no ambition to become a power centre, the only person to hold the high post without ever wanting it and without ever striving for it. One would, of course, never know if this really was the case, once he was faced with the palpable prospect of power awaiting him after the death of his brother, and the assassination of his mother; for power indeed is a strange and tempting commodity which hardly anyone can resist; especially when you are aware of the fact that it is within easy reach without having to make any real effort to acquire it.

If no one from Indira Gandhi's political entourage had fixedly set their eyes on him as her successor, and if they had not made any visible effort to exhort him to become the next Prime Minister, it cannot be excluded that he would not have made any personal effort to acquire the high office.

This is probably the first example, in post-independent Indian history, of a person who reached the political summit without ever wanting it. What a contrast with the power seekers who filled the country!

To come to politics in such a mental state could be beneficial; for not having any fixed opinion render decisions more flexible and argumentation more open. But, on the other hand, impulsive as he was. Impatient as he tended to be with long written papers, and uncomfortable as he felt with long-winded oral explanations, it must have been a serious handicap to take reflective decisions.

Prior to June 1980, he led a quiet private life as a pilot in Indian Airlines. His only great ambition was to pass the examination that would enable him to fly Boeing 747s. But fate was to decide otherwise. When his brother, Sanjay Gandhi—universally considered as the heir apparent—died in a daredevil plane crash, he was pressed into his brother's political shoes, in which he functioned in a low-key capacity before being pushed into the role of Prime Minister on his mother's assassination. With hardly any experience or even, for that matter, any ambition, he found himself at the helm of affairs in 1984–much against the wishes of his own wife, and much to the surprise of many who had watched him grow. The only qualification he possessed to be projected to the high office was the name he carried and the dynasty to which he belonged. He really had no other qualifications. He was, as some have called him, "The Reluctant Prime Minister."

It is indeed a striking characteristic of the Nehrus and Gandhis. While there were numerous politicians who hardly ever envisaged a succession of someone closely related, this aspect had very much dominated the Nehru-Gandhi family. All of them thought of a political successor.

FORMATION AND PERCEPTION

No one knew what his views were on foreign affairs, for he had not written anything or said anything on the subject before coming to power that would have enabled an understanding of his views about the world, or permitted an evaluation of his perception on India's foreign policy. And yet, considering his genealogical background, and the aura of intellectuality that overwhelmed the house of his grandfather where he had lived, it is difficult to imagine that he had no views on international affairs, no perception of the international configuration of forces, and no idea where India was heading.

Given his formal education in an anglicized high school (Doon School in Dehra Dun) to which he was exposed to, and the epoch in which he was living with a stagnating socialist international world, and with captivating updated technology, it is more than possible that Rajiv Gandhi was attracted to the western world, what it stood for, and what it represented—wealth, high standard of living, political and economic liberalism, etc.

Perception, of course, is one thing, but the India he inherited was another matter—an India that was ideologically non-aligned, officially committed to socialism, and politically aligned to the Soviet Union. In sum, very different from what he had in mind.

One can, therefore, presume that, while perceptually and emotionally seduced by the West, he was politically no different from his predecessors, all of whom had accepted the broad foreign policy architecture originally constructed by Nehru.

Rajiv Gandhi, therefore, really had no leverage, and had no choice but to broadly follow the directions that had already been given, and the contours of foreign policy that had already been embeded.

One can only presume that whatever he believed in was not different from those of his predecessors, for all that he said and did subsequently as Prime Minister was to continue the broad goals that had already been established before.

However, where Rajiv Gandhi did leave some imprint, as Prime Minister, was on foreign affairs. In fact, according to K.R. Narayanan, former President of India, "foreign affairs was one of his amazing achievements," especially when one considers the important fact that he came to the high office "with hardly any knowledge of external affairs."[317]

A number of factors—personal and political— contributed to his impact on foreign policy making. The first was personal. Rajiv Gandhi showed a conspicuous interest in foreign affairs: an interest that was free of any ideological hang-ups. "He did not," according to one author, "find himself in conflict with any world power."[318] This was the field in which he felt very much at home, since he was often in the company of people who were sophisticated and westernised. Besides, he carried himself well with his counterparts, and was dazzled by the diplomatic summits, and with all the glamour that went with it. The extent of his interest is evidenced by the fact that he made as many as 48 foreign trips in four years. No Prime Minister, before or after him, made so many visits to so many countries in so short a time–an unprecedented record, which can hardly be matched even by his foreign counterparts. It looked as if India had become very much a part of the world heavily engaged in all major issues–from non-alignment to disarmament.

FOREIGN POLICY FRAMEWORK

The broad framework of Rajiv Gandhi's foreign policy—like that of his mother—was wide ranging, varying from macro issues, to concrete problems pertaining to the region. To risk a generalisation, it could be argued that the architecture of his policy, and the thrust of his diplomatic actions were directed: (a) at projecting India as one of the visible international actors, (b) at striving for a balanced relations with the main international actors, (c) at actively involving himself with the problems of the African continent, and (d) at asserting India's leveraged position in South Asia.

Projection of India

Rajiv Gandhi was practically everywhere busily participating in numerous multilateral deliberations the most crucial of which were: The Six Nation, Five Continent Summit Meeting (Argentina, Mexico, Tanzania, Sweden, Greece, India) in New Delhi (1985), the Commonwealth Summit in Nassau (1985), the Non-aligned Summit in Harare (1986), the Africa Fund Summit in New Delhi (1987), the Afro-Asian Peoples' Solidarity Organisation in New Delhi (1988), the Non-aligned Summit in Belgrade (1989), the UN General Assembly session on Disarmament (1988). In all these meetings he expressed his views on diverse international issues, made myriad proposals, and undertook various responsibilities.

But the one issue on which he was very much internationally at the forefront was disarmament. This was the issue to which he devoted a great deal of his time, personally interacting with some of his close advisers and directly involving himself in thinking out different proposals that he could submit internationally. While in almost all his international declarations, a reference was invariably made to the subject, it was at the General Assembly of the UN in June 1988 that he presented a comprehensive "Action Plan for ushering in a Nuclear Weapon Free and Non-Violent World." Gandhi's proposal provided a detailed time bound framework for general disarmament and the total elimination of nuclear weapons by 2010. The plan is so detailed that it provides with a global security system, an international verification machinery, treaties banning other weapons of mass destruction, reduction of all conventional forces "to minimum defensive levels," and concrete measures to prevent the spread to outer space of arms based on new technologies.[319]

Voicing his opposition to nuclear weapons he declared: "It is imperative that nuclear weapons be eliminated. The recently signed INF treaty [Intermediate Range Nuclear Forces Treaty December 1987] between the US and the Soviet Union is a first major step in this direction. The process must be taken to its logical conclusion by ridding the world of nuclear weapons."[320] Similar opposition was reiterated in the "Delhi Declaration,."

It declared: "Pending the elimination of nuclear weapons, India and the Soviet Union propose that an *International Convention Banning the Use or Threat of Use of Nuclear Weapons* should be concluded immediately. This would constitute a major concrete step towards complete nuclear disarmament."[321]

Clearly, this was the issue on which he apparently had firm views, and in regard to which he wanted to project himself internationally. But, on the other hand, it was unrealistic and naïve to consider that the two superpowers would accept his proposals, for they were indeed too ambitious for the late eighties. Besides, Washington and Moscow were themselves having bilateral interaction on disarmament, and did not see any point in accepting third party proposals.

The only credible explanation for internationally tabling his "Action Plan" was not so much to get his plan accepted, as Rajiv Gandhi's desire to project himself internationally as the great proponent of general and complete disarmament. Ambitious as he had become, it may have something to do with acquiring international status and visibility.

However, while Rajiv Gandhi was publicly voicing India's opposition to nuclear weapons, and was making concrete proposals for their elimination, the Indian nuclear establishment was going ahead in developing India's nuclear power in the armament sector. The Indian Government was keeping its options open to go in for nuclear weaponry should it formally decide to move in that direction. Lal Bahadur Shastri had given Bhabha, India's leading nuclear scientist, the green light to go ahead with research in the nuclear armament sector. And Morarji Desai was voted down by his colleagues when he attempted to stem the research in the nuclear sector.

No formal decision, thus, had been taken to produce nuclear weapons, but then no formal decision had been taken to stop the nuclear establishment from proceeding with research, and the designing of nuclear weapons, as long as it did not proceed with the assembly of a nuclear device. During Rajiv Gandhi's term in office an informal but authoritative study group was established in November 1985 to study the whole question of defense planning. The group, encompassing very senior representatives of the three armed services, three leading members of the nuclear establishment (A.P.J. Abdul Kalam, R. Chidambaram, Raja Ramanna), plus K. Subrahmanyam, the strategic analyst, recommended the building of a minimum deterrent force with a strict no first use policy.

While no formal decision was taken on the report, it inspired Rajiv Gandhi to take some additional measures to improve the bomb system under the code name "New Armament Breaking Ammunition and Project" (NABAP) and the correspondingly appropriate aircraft delivery system. The original plan of using the Jaguar planes was abandoned, for the bomb, as it was then designed, was too heavy, and was replaced by Mirage-27 as more appropriate and more effective for delivery purposes. Once this decision was taken, the plane was used to routinely practice loft bombing techniques for nuclear bomb delivery.[322]

A number of other decisions were taken to support the manufacture of more sophisticated lightweight fission material during Rajiv Gandhi's mandate. In 1984 while India had imported 100 kg of high purity beryllium from West Germany, enough to provide the neutran reflecting tampers for a dozen or more weapons, it also commissioned its own beryllium production plant in Mumbai, drawing on indigenous ores from Kerala. Around this time, India also acquired a vacuum hot pressing machine, suitable for forming large high-quality beryllium forgings. Work also began at the Bombay Atomic Research Centre (BARC) to lay the foundation for thermonuclear weapons development and the manufacture of boosted fission weapons. In sum, throughout his mandate, scientific establishments continued to develop and refine weapon designs and related technologies in the Laboratory and testing ground, much as they had done since the early 1960s.

Rajiv Gandhi, thus, was well aware of the existing nuclear situation—the situation of continuing nuclear weapons related activities, and of acquiring a corresponding aircraft delivery system. Furthermore, he must have been aware of the fact that evidence was indeed piling up that Pakistan was actively going nuclear. The American intelligence community, monitoring Pakistan's nuclear activity, had arrived at the conclusion in 1987 that Islamabad had enough enriched uranium to put together six nuclear devices.[323] Dr. Abdul Qadeer Khan, Director of nuclear weapon's laboratory at Kahuta had explicitly claimed, in an interview with an Indian journalist, that Pakistan had the bomb. "What the CIA has been saying," he declared, "about our possessing the bomb is correct."[324] Even the Reagan Administration was becoming suspicious of Pakistan's nuclear ambitions. During her scheduled visit to Washington in June 1989, Benazir Bhutto, the Pakistani Prime Minister, was provided with a detailed briefing by CIA Director, William H. Webster, of the extent to which Pakistan had gone nuclear, so much so that he dramatized the extent of American knowledge by arranging to show Ms Bhutto a mock up of a Pakistan nuclear bomb.[325]

How did Rajiv Gandhi react to all this evidence? Did this not affect his thinking? In the face of all this, did he not become less firm in his opposition to nuclear weapons? Publicly, he did not change his mind. There was really no need to since he was well aware that the nuclear establishment was continuously updating India's nuclear plans, and since, now that the Russians had left Afghanistan, the Reagan Administration could no longer ignore—as it had done before—the evidence of the Pakistani bomb. As the pressure on Pakistan, Gandhi calculated, would become more empathic, there was, therefore, no need to formally and officially go nuclear as that would only antagonize the US, which the Indian Prime Minister was eager to avoid.[326]

Great Powers: a Balanced Approach

The configuration of international forces were clearly mutating. Obviously Rajiv Gandhi had to take this into account while constructing his foreign policy.

USSR

The USSR was in the midst of a major transition. The Brezhnev period had passed and Mikhail Gorbachev, heading the USSR (March 1985), and belonging to a new generation of leaders, appeared determined to democratise the Soviet system, and seek an understanding with the US. But the Soviet Union, at the same time, also began to show signs of international decline. Gorbachev withdrew from Afghanistan, diminished Soviet military presence in Eastern Europe, witnessed the decline of communism in Eastern Europe, and its disappearance in East Germany with the reunification of Germany under Western leadership.

While officially continuing to maintain Moscow's privileged relations with India, it was becoming increasingly evident to the Indians that Indo-Soviet relations could not possibly continue at the same privileged level as it had for more than two decades.

However, even if privileged relations with Moscow were no longer on the cards, Rajiv Gandhi did not take any steps to distance himself from the Soviet Union. In fact, he publicly continued to proclaim that "friendship and cooperation with the Soviet Union are an integral element of our foreign policy."[327]

Furthermore, he made it a point to establish a close personal rapport with Gorbachev who he considered was "a trusted friend of India."[328] Attraction to Gorbachev, presumably, was not so much because of Indo-Soviet relations, as it was regarding disarmament. For he found in the Soviet leader a similarity of views regarding the urgency of disarming the world. The Delhi Declaration, which Gorbachev signed with Rajiv Gandhi in November 1986 in Delhi, embodied a similarity of positions on global disarmament. So much so that according to one of Rajiv Gandhi's close advisers, the Delhi declaration "reads like a summary of Indian positions on disarmament."[329]

It was indeed a remarkable statement; for the Soviets were no more striving to keep India away from Washington. If anything, they were attempting to persuade the Americans that Rajiv Gandhi was as much their friend as Moscow's.

If Rajiv Gandhi made complimentary remarks about Gorbachev, so did the latter; and that even within the four walls of bilateral Gorbachev-Bush summit meeting in Malta (2-3 December 1989). Gorbachev told President George Bush that China and India embodied the "regrouping of forces" and that India had a dynamic policy and Rajiv Gandhi "has a deliberate approach striving to establish good relations with us and you."[330]

So there was no explicit attempt on the part of Rajiv Gandhi to move away from Moscow. There was really no point in doing so, given the personal rapport the Indian Prime Minister had forged with Gorbachev, and given the similarity of views on general and complete disarmament. Besides, having weighty relations with the Soviet Union was vital since India was still very dependent on it for a wide array of issues, the most important of which was the arms aid they were still receiving from Moscow.

USA

What was diplomatically important was to forge ties with Washington—ties that had never taken off under any preceding Prime Minister—not even under Morarji Desai who had explicitly declared that India's policy of non-alignment would be genuine and credible only when it had forged ties with Washington and Beijing; and not even under Indira Gandhi who did make discreet attempts to build bridges with Washington.

Morarji Desai, notwithstanding his visible attempts to normalize relations with Washington, was not really fascinated by the US; and Indira Gandhi, notwithstanding attempts at normalization, was known to carry some degree of anti-Americanism in her political orientations.

Rajiv Gandhi had none of these reservations. With the political formation he had received, and the political orientations he had acquired, the US was the country he was attracted to.

Admittedly, there were objective differences between the two countries on a swath of issues, but the Indian Prime Minister did not consider that they should interfere in forging ties with Washington. Clearly, he was impregnated with a single-minded desire to break down barriers with Washington, especially in the mid-eighties when there were signs of nuanced mutations in Washington's attitude towards India. In the existing Reaganian global perception a benign look at India had become expedient. With Russia on the decline, with China a potential threat, and with Pakistan moving in the direction of becoming nuclear and fundamentalist, India, in the eyes of the US Administration had become an attractive diplomatic target.

It was the first time that the two heads of their respective governments succeeded in breaking down barriers. More than anyone else, among his predecessors, Rajiv Gandhi was able to maintain an even keel relations with Moscow while building ties with Washington.

Though Indira Gandhi had taken some friendly initiatives towards Reagan, it was Rajiv Gandhi's two visits to Washington (1985 and 1987) that finally resulted in the inauguration of amiable interaction, and which has growingly continued to this day.

Clearly, there were also signs of reciprocal change from the American side. The Reagan Administration was presumably well-briefed on Rajiv Gandhi: that he was ideologically closer to Washington, that he was personally pro-western in his political make up, and that he was apparently convinced that India's economic, and technological future lay with the US.

Consider Reagan's declaration on Rajiv Gandhi's Washington visit in October 1987. "I am delighted," he declared "to welcome once again Prime Minister Gandhi to the White House. The Prime Minister and I have had useful discussions on the status of US-Indian relations. We noted that in the years since our meeting in 1985 substantial progress has been made. Bilateral trade has expanded. Collaboration between our private sectors have intensified. We've enjoyed cooperation in defence production, notably the Indian light combat aircraft. The memorandum of understanding on technology has been implemented. The US is working with India to launch its satellites. The US-India Fund for Cultural Educational and Scientific cooperation has been inaugurated. And we're working together to combat terrorism."[331]

The emergence of a benign attitude towards Rajiv Gandhi can also be discerned from the fact that it was during his mandate that military cooperation was forged between the two countries. An agreement was reached in 1988 to conduct joint exercises by the naval forces of the two countries, and while Rajiv Gandhi was Prime Minister, two US defense secretaries, Casper Weinberger and Frank Carlucci, visited India, undoubtedly historic events since none had visited for over forty years. And Reagan personally cleared the supply of General Electric's 404 jet engines for the Indian LCA.

Thus for the first time since India's independence a benign bilateral relationship was developed between the two countries. And, for the first time India was able to successfully establish a balanced relations with the two super powers—undoubtedly a great feather in Rajiv Gandhi's diplomatic cap.

China

But, Rajiv Gandhi, on the other hand, was more prudent vis-à-vis the Chinese. When he became the Prime Minister he was not interested in continuing the process of normalisation of Sino-Indian relations, discreetly inaugurated by his mother. All the advice the MEA gave him to go to China--a change from the past was ignored.[332] And, all the signals, sent out by the Chinese in 1985 seeking normalisation based on a package deal on the border question, were disregarded. Though the package deal, proposed by Deng Xiaoping was in many ways a recast of the original proposals made by Zhou Enlai in 1960 and 1962, it did contain some interesting aspects which could have been pursued at the sixth round of the bilateral talks that opened in November 1985. But Rajiv Gandhi was apparently not interested in taking this up with the Chinese. He showed no interest and took no initiative.

Furthermore, a sign of his lack of interest, Rajiv Gandhi allowed himself to be persuaded by the armed forces to carry out a "forward policy" that was originally proposed to Indira Gandhi, and that–according to some reports–had been accepted by her, though it had not been operationalised.

A forward policy was re-activated of defending Tawang and of actually moving to the Sumdurung Chu Valley–a disputable area in Tawang district.

Though an observation post had been discreetly established in the summer of 1984, the real implementation of the decision was taken by Rajiv Gandhi. The moving forward of troops led to a process of a real confrontation by mid-1986 with all the tensions that goes along with it, including the Chinese decision to send troops through Sumdurung Chu Valley in the Kameng division of Arunachal Pradesh.

While the border confrontation did expose some chinks in Indian defence that were reported by the press, the brief encounter with the Chinese was indeed revealing. Indian troops—now more well-equipped, well-trained and well-adapted to altitude— were in a better position to effectively face the Chinese troops. It was no more a Chinese walk-over as in 1962. The army leadership was confident that it could continue a controlled confrontational policy with the Chinese without any major risk of a setback or of any serious escalation. But, Rajiv Gandhi finally got cold feet, and made the army move back to its original position. He became apparently fearful of the adverse ramifications of the confrontation. What if the Chinese decided to make a massive military move? What if India lost? And what if the public opinion reacted negatively to any major military initiative by the Indian armed forces? The risks were indeed too great and hazardous. Besides, a growing group of his advisers were recommending just the opposite—to open up to China now that it had inaugurated an open and outgoing diplomacy.

It was this reluctance to maintain a confrontational policy that finally made Rajiv Gandhi initiate a process of political normalisation–to which he openly referred to in his press conference of 20 January 1987.

He then took a four pronged initiative before taking a decision, if some dramatic move was called for. The first was towards his own Secretariat and the MEA to undertake an in-depth review of Sino-Indian relations and make recommendations regarding the new steps India should take. The second was to ask an ex-Indian diplomat, heading a Centre in Delhi, to convene a meeting of eminent journalists and academics to seek their views on the whole question. The third was to send P.N. Haksar on an unofficial visit to Beijing to ascertain Chinese response. And the fourth, perhaps the most important, was to raise the issue in the Cabinet.

While all the groups favoured doing something concrete, there was no consensus regarding the level at which the initiative should be taken. The Cabinet and the bureaucracy were against a summit meeting on the ground that Rajiv Gandhi would not get any mileage out of it, and, given the forthcoming elections (1989), the Chinese might may not be prepared to hold any serious negotiations. It was therefore recommended (to which the Prime Minister agreed) that at first only a high-level political contact at the ministerial level should be initiated before any summit meeting was envisaged. The group of eminent journalists and academicians were the only ones to recommend a summit meeting.

Having formally decided that the first contact should be at the ministerial level, Rajiv Gandhi assigned the task of examining the modalities of such an initiative, and of making appropriate recommendations to the Minister of Human Resource Development, P.V. Narasimha Rao, a person with considerable diplomatic experience

Finally, when Rao took up the question again, he was informed by the Cabinet Secretary that the Prime Minister had already taken the decision to have the first meeting at the summit level, and initiatives to this effect had already been taken by his advisers. Rajiv Gandhi had thus set in motion all the institutions and relevant groups before formally taking the decision: the bureaucracy, politicians and the elite. But, finally he chose to renege upon his original decision to send a minister and decided to go himself to China.

What made Rajiv Gandhi change his attitude: from opposition, to indifference and finally to a positive attitude of personally going to Beijing? Did he cede to the pressures that were building up in different Indian circles that India should come to grips with Sino-Indian impasse? Did he himself change his mind after his successful encounters with Gorbachev and Reagan? Or did the Chinese have anything to do with Rajiv Gandhi's final decision to hold a summit meeting with China? Or was it Haksar who went to China to explore with the Chinese who played a role? Or did the Chinese have anything to do with the decision that Rajiv Gandhi himself should go to China?

It was probably the confluence of all these factors that made him decide to go himself to China between 19 to 23 December 1988.

Some discussions to this effect were apparently already under way during Indira Gandhi's mandate when she had secretly sent Kao, the head of the RAW, to Beijing, but all of which had to be abandoned after her assassination.[333] For the Chinese, thus, this was apparently not new. The question had already been raised. And they were seemingly attracted to the idea of a summit meeting—a meeting they had avoided so far.[334]

For one thing the new Chinese attraction towards India was solidified by the fact that political infighting within the leadership had been finally resolved by the definite emergence of Deng Xiaoping, in the late eighties, as the new legitimate leader who had personally gone on record of seeking an understanding with India.

Heavily immersed as Deng had become in activating some political letting up of China, and of seeking a new method of economic development, the most important aspect of which was "improving socialism with capitalist method," a general trend had emerged of avoiding international confrontation. And South Asia, in the late eighties, was one of the areas in which the Chinese leader wanted to avoid any politico-military explosiveness.

In this connection it is important to note that, while continuing to arm Pakistan, the Chinese leadership clearly informed its Pakistani counterpart that Chinese arms were purely for defensive purposes, and that Pakistan should avoid taking any military initiative of its own against India.[335]

What made Rajiv Gandhi change his mind, and move on from indifference, to opposition, and finally to the decision to open up to the Chinese, and that even at the summit level. Did he cede to the pressures that were building up that India should come to grips with the China problem? Did he himself change his mind after his successful encounters with Gorbachev and Reagan? That the 1988 visit was undoubtedly a momentous one can be discerned from the fact that no Indian Prime Minister had visited China since Nehru in 1954.

The cruciality of the visit can be evaluated (a) from the composition of the delegation which consisted of four ministers plus Sonia Gandhi and myriad Indian officials, and (b) from the important decision, personally taken by the Indian Prime Minister, that no overly litigious question would be brought on the table.[336]

Rajiv Gandhi was received by practically everyone important in the Chinese leadership: President Yang Shangkun, Zhao Ziyang, General Secretary of the Communist party, and Li Peng, the Prime Minister. But the most defining moment of Rajiv Gandhi's visit was his encounter with Deng Xiaoping at the great hall of the people, where, in the presence of journalists, the following exchange took place accompanied by a long and warm handshake:

Deng: "Welcome, so welcome my young friend. Starting with your visit we will restore our relations as friends."

Deng: "So in 1954, when your grandfather, the late Prime Minister Nehru visited China, I was also one of the leaders in China. I was Vice-Premier at that time. At that time, the relations between our two countries were very good."

Rajiv: "Yes we have been through a few difficulties in between. I hope we can bring things back and get over these difficulties."

Deng: "So this is our common wish. In the considerable period of time in between there was unpleasantness at each other. Let's forget it. We should look forward."

Rajiv; "There is so much work to do in both countries.

Deng: " The genuine start of the improvement of our relations is your visit."[337]

Clearly this was a successful visit. India agreed to drop its earlier position of insisting on the fulfilment of certain preconditions before the inauguration of normalisation of relations between the two countries. It also accepted that Tibet was a part of China, and declared, in response to Chinese complaints, "that anti-China political activities by Tibetan elements are not permitted on Indian soil."[338]

Among the different agreements concluded, the one that was most important was the establishment of a Joint Working Group on the boundary question and a Joint Group on economic relations and trade and science technology.

Underlining the importance Rajiv Gandhi attached to Sino-Indian relations, he said in a speech at Qinghua University (21 December 1988): "I represent a new generation of India. I was but a boy in the heyday of Sino-Indian frienship. I was still a young man when differences were converted into conflict. I have grown in a world which has not benefited but only been disadvantaged by estrangement between India and China. I have come to office with the firm conviction that, between ourselves, we must make a new beginning. I am heartened that the Chinese leadership is more than prepared to put behind us past rancour and past prejudices."[339]

Rajiv Gandhi had thus successfully established balanced relations with the three great powers—an unprecedented diplomatic achievement, the benefits of which are apparent to this day.

ENGAGEMENT IN SOUTHERN AFRICA

India had consistently supported African independence under all Prime Ministers. But it was essentially rhetoric in most international fora.

Rajive Gandhi was the first, and perhaps the only Prime Minister, who played a palpable role in Southern Africa. It was not so much that Gandhi was an afrophile as the fact that Africa surfaced on the international agenda in the mid-eigthies. Namibia, Angola, Mozambique, Zambia, Zimbabwe, the frontline states of Southern Africa, were on the forefront of international politics, and were figuring largely at the ministerial meetings of the non-aligned countries of which Rajiv Gandhi then was the chairman.

He made himself visible on three main issues facing the region—apartheid in South Africa, the fate of the frontline states in their confrontation with white dominated South Africa, and finally the independence of Namibia. On all three issues he played a crucial role—a role no Prime Minister had ever played before.

Though all the African issues were repeatedly discussed internationally, Gandhi found himself actively involved with all of them in three different fora—in the Commonwealth on apartheid, in the Non-aligned conferences on the AFRICA FUND (Action for Resisting Invasion, Colonialism and Apartheid), and in the UN on Namibia.

South Africa

The apartheid issue emerged within the Commonwealth. Though it had been repeatedly raised, discussed and acted upon, the airing of the issue at the Commonwealth meetings was of special importance, and this for a number of reasons: the first clearly was that South Africa had old associations of which it was a member for many years. The second was that the Commonwealth had a large African component, some of which were the so-called frontline states who were bearing the brunt of South African reprisals, and which, at the same time, were heavily dependent on South Africa economically. The third was the nature of the impact that any Commonwealth decision would have on the country, nationally as well as internationally.

If the Commonwealth could agree on the imposition of economic sanctions, it would seriously hurt South Africa since Great Britain was its most important economic partner, and since London—powerful as it was— would be able to mobilise the international community to do the same.

The possible role India could play in all this was important. For one thing, it had solid credentials of being literally the first nation to have repeatedly raised the issue of apartheid at the fora of the UN in the forties and the fifties when most of Africa was still under colonial rule. For another, as an important Asian country, it could rally many Asian countries even though they were not directly concerned.

The high visibility of an issue such as this could only be beneficial for India if it could take the lead. But, on the other hand, this was not easy, since most of Africa had become independent, and India, therefore, could not expect to occupy a centre stage in international politics on this specific question as it had done earlier.

The only way that India could carve a niche for itself was by totally identifying with the plight of the Africans, with the fate of Nelson Mandela, and the future of the African National Congress (ANC). For this, it had to jettison the idea of focussing only on the Indians in Africa as it had done in the past.

This is what Rajiv Gandhi did. The main thrust of his rhetoric was to support the imposition of sanctions on South Africa, and the liberation of the Blacks. In one of his very first statements, after acceding to Prime Ministership was, therefore, on the "removal" of the South African regime, and the liberation of Nelson Mandela. In fact, he concluded one of his speeches with a tribute to Mandela. "We have," he declared " gathered here to pledge our support to Nelson Mandela, and to the hundreds of thousand of men, women and children of South Africa, who, through their suffering are upholding our collective cause. Their victory will be our victory."[340]

However, while remaining inflexible on sanctions against South Africa, Gandhi carved for himself a negotiatory role at the Nassau Commonwealth Summit in October 1985 where the issue was discussed. Since there was a division between the majority of the participants, who favoured sanctions, and Great Britain and Sri Lanka, who argued that any decision to impose sanction would only be counter-productive, Rajiv Gandhi sought a way out of the diplomatic impasse by making all the participants agree to give South Africa a period of six months to start dismantling apartheid, or else face economic sanctions. As a concession to Margaret Thatcher, Gandhi's proposal avoided the word "sanctions" and used the phrase "economic measures."

In an effort to reach a consensus on apartheid, two additional decisions were taken at Nassau. One was to appoint a committee of seven member states including India (the others were Zambia, Australia, the Bahamas, Canada, UK and Zimbabwe) with a mandate to work out the modalities of assisting a process of political dialogue with South Africa. The second was to appoint a group of eminent leaders of the Commonwealth (Eminent Persons Group-EPG) to study the whole issue of apartheid and its consequences. The group held twenty-one meetings with South African ministers. It also met Nelson Mandela three times in Pollsmoor prison. It met others —the ANC in Lusaka and the leaders of the frontline states. The report that was finally published painted a gruesome picture of apartheid. It concluded that "in its essential elements it remains very much intact."[341]

The Committee of seven member states of the Commonwealth, mandated to take decision on sanctions, met ten months after the Nassau Summit in August 1986 to examine the report submitted by the eminent leaders of the Commonwealth and to decide on the action to be taken against South Africa.

Since Margaret Thatcher still refused to accept the Nassau accord on sanctions, a number of pre-summit consultations ensued in which Rajiv Gandhi played a crucial role. He had a series of discussions with the participants, including Thatcher, in order to prevent a showdown with Britain.

The final result of all this was another compromise. It was decided that the Communiqué would list the majority opinion on action against apartheid, and Britain's opposition to any such action.[342]

A crisis was thus averted, and it would seem that India's role was crucial. At the end of the meeting, Rajiv Gandhi did what could be described as a balancing act. On the one hand, he attacked the British Government for having compromised on "basic principles and values for economic gain," and on the other, he made it a point to underline the importance of the Commonwealth, and its head, the Queen, from whom "we derive strenth from her position."[343]

Southern Africa

The mobilisation of aid for Southern Africa was the second issue in which India played a crucial role. Within the framework of the non-aligned movement, an AFRICA FUND was established to raise money for strengthing the economic and financial capability of the frontline states in Southern

Africa, which were heavily dependent on South Africa, and which had to bear the burden of military attacks and destablization activities of South Africa. Though the fund also stipulated material assistance to the South West African People's Organization (SWAPO) and the ANC, the principal objective was to put up a large part of the funding "for a multilateral programme in the area of economic and technical cooperation." In the words of Rajiv Gandhi it was "perhaps the first concrete manifestation of a united effort based on effective south-south cooperation."[344]

India's role was indeed visible since Rajiv Gandhi was appointed the Chairman of the nine nation fund committee (which included Zambia, Algeria, Argentina, Congo, Nigeria, Peru, Yugoslavia, Zimbabwe and India) whose principal responsibility was to establish the rules of procedure for its management and to prepare a plan of action.

The Indian Prime Minister took a great deal of personal interest in the work of the committee, and was able to raise 476 million dollars in cash, kind and technical assistance by 1989.

Independence of Namibia

The third important component of visible Indian interest was the independence of Namibia, which, after World War I, had become a mandate territory, and which had been administratively entrusted to South Africa by the League of Nations in December 1920. Since South Africa had refused to conclude a trusteeship agreement with the UN on the ground that the UN was not a successor to the League, a number of international initiatives had been taken to resolve the issue.

India took an active interest. Though various fora were used to voice India's interest in Namibian independence, the principal platform was the UN which had been assigned the responsibility of negotiating Namibian independence with South Africa, and of establishing the modalities by which the people of the territory would be able to determine their future.

Without going into all the details of the discussions and negotiations, for much has already been written on the subject, suffice it is to say that Rajiv Gandhi picked up the cudgels on Namibia's behalf at the UN and at the coordinated bureau of the non-aligned countries.

Rajiv Gandhi thus attempted to carve a visible role on all the three issues that centred around Southern Africa. For this he was praised by most African leaders. Interestingly, all the three issues (apartheid, frontline states and Namibia) have been resolved. South Africa has moved away from apartheid, frontline states have become independent, and Namibia has become a sovereign state.

It would be, of course, presumptuous to suggest that all these achievements were due to India's efforts. But, it cannot be denied that Rajiv Gandh's inputs in all the three issues were indeed significant, and has been recognised by third world countries.

SOUTH ASIA

South Asia remained as intractable as in the past. Like all his predecessors he did not make any substantive headway in developing relations with any of them with the possible exception of Bhutan. None of India's neighbours looked up to India. If anything, practically all of them distrusted and feared India.

Indian diplomacy failed, for it neither gained their confidence, nor did it have the determination or the capacity of forcing them to fall in line with India.

Pakistan

Rajiv Gandhi was no exception to this general rule. When he came to power relations with Pakistan were frozen. And they really never took off, notwithstanding all the bilateral talks (six meetings) he had with Zia ul-huq, the military leader and the President of Pakistan. He had convinced himself—not without reason—(a) that Zia was heavily involved in supporting Sikh fundamentalists in the Punjab through groups of Sikh extremists whom Zia had given asylum in Pakistan; (b) that he was actively working in Nepal and Sri Lanka against India; (c) that he had taken covert steps to destabilise the Indian position in Kashmir and Siachen, and (d) that, given his Islamic orientations, he was working hand in glove with Islamic fundamentalists. In sum, Rajiv Gandhi perceived Zia as a threat to India.

But, hope once again re-surfaced, after the latter's death in a plane crash in August 1988 and the emergence of Benazir Bhutto as Prime Minister. On taking office, she invited Rajiv Gandhi to extend his visit to Pakistan, after the SAARC summit meeting due to be held in Pakistan, to discuss bilateral relations.

With all these welcome political changes, Rajiv Gandhi accepted the invitation.

The visit, at the personal level, was a great success since Bhutto and Gandhi got along very well. But at the political level, it did'nt get anywhere, Apart from an agreement–that too reached during Zia's time—that the two countries would not attack each other's nuclear installation, the visit, according to Bhutto's adviser, "in the end came to nothing."[345]

Relations, thus, never took off neither during the visit nor during the myriad discussions that took place between the officials of the two countries.

Sri Lanka

The situation in Sri Lanka was no better. If anything, it was worse. At least in Pakistan the adversary was identifiable, whereas in Sri Lanka it was not, since there were numerous actors to the conflict each of which had his demand. Besides, the conflict between the adversaries was not diplomatic but deeply political and ethnic in which one (the Central Government in Colombo) wanted to maintain its territorial integrity, whereas the other (the Liberation Tigers of Tamil Ealam - LTTE) wanted a separation of the territory where Tamils were residing. What made things even more difficult for Rajiv Gandhi was that the Tamils in Sri Lanka were supported by Tamils in India, particularly in South India.

So the Indian Prime Minister was in the midst of triple problem: diplomatic with Sri Lankan Government, political with Tamils in Sri Lanka, and domestic with Tamils in Tamil Nadu.

In the eighties, the traditional and regularly explosive Sinhala-Tamil conflict once again emerged. Indira Gandhi had wanted to support the Tamils in Sri Lanka, but really was unable to go beyond extending covert support to them. Rajiv Gandhi, as her successor inherited it; and the situation indeed worsened. More than 1,00,000 Sri Lankan Tamils fled to India, and the Colombo Government, encouraged by external military aid from Pakistan and Israel began to consider that a military solution was the only viable one.

Rajiv Gandhi had no alternative but to impose a solution—a solution based on an agreement reached between the Delhi and Colombo governments on 29 July 1987. The Tamils—at least the LTTE was opposed to the agreement since (a) it clearly excluded any territorial separation from the centre, (b) it clearly stipulated the surrender of all weapons held by Tamil separatists, and (c) it undertook to hold a referendum in the eastern province before it could be merged with the northern province—a merger the Tamils were insisting upon.

India agreed to send a large peacekeeping force to implement the agreement. Nobody was happy with the agreement, neither the Sinhalese nor the Tamils. The Sinhalese were unhappy because of the proposed Indian military presence, and an important manifestation of this was an attempt on Rajiv Gandhi's life while he was inspecting a guard of honour before his departure from Sri Lanka on 30 July 1987; the Tamils because it really did not include any of their demands, and the ultimate manifestation of which was Rajiv Gandhi's assassination a couple of years later at the hands of the Tamil Tigers.

The die was cast. Rajiv Gandhi was thus faced with a terrible impasse from which there was no hope of any extrication for the Indian peacekeeping force, more than 1,200 of whom died in the operation— not to speak of the fact that the peacekeeping force found itself in direct military confrontation with the Tamil Tigers, and earned the animosity of Tamils in India.

Nepal

Relations with Nepal were equally problematic. The decades old divide between Nepal, striving for greater independence, and India, maintaining its traditional hold, was the backdrop for an ongoing bruising relationship. It surfaced again under Rajiv Gandhi, and this time even more melodramatically. Breaking away from its original agreement that India would be the sole supplier of arms, Nepal concluded an accord to buy anti-aircraft missiles from China. Though the agreement was really not important quantitatively, since India remained the main arms supplier, it was this symbolic defiance that disturbed Rajiv Gandhi. Behind-the-scene pressures were exercised to dissuade Nepal, but all in vain. The Himalayan Kingdom was apparently determined to go ahead with its ongoing policy of seeking an independent path from India. This may seem paradoxical for a country whose economic dependence on India was intense—in fact greater than normal. Often, this is what happens when you are dependent. You look elsewhere.

Rajiv Gandhi acted promptly. In fact, many even considered that he was over-reacting. Seizing the existing domestic bruisality between the pro-democracy movement and the monarchy, the Indian Prime Minister enforced a blockade against Nepal—a blockade that generated serious hardships given its heavy dependence on India. Undoubtedly, this was a major decision, but for Rajiv Gandhi Indian security was primordial that had to be safeguarded under the circumstances. Even though Rajiv Gandhi was preparing a friendly visit to China, which came through in 1988, any major Chinese incursions in the north were *sine qua non*. For the Indians had convinced themselves that the Himalayan Kingdom was within the Indian sphere of influence.

While all these differences were attributed to a clash of national interests, one wonders if mutual personal antipathy between Rajiv Gandhi and King Birendra did not contribute to the aggravation of relations between the two countries. Apparently Rajiv Gandhi was personally upset by the absence of the King of Nepal from a banquet the former had hosted during the SAARC summit in Pakistan. Again the Indian Prime Minister was annoyed with the King, when he and his wife initially were not permitted to enter a Nepalese Hindu temple, presumably on the ground that Sonia Gandhi was not a Hindu. The role of personal animosity should not of course be exaggerated in the deterioration of relations between two countries, but nor should they be ignored or underestimated while analysing State relations.

Bangladesh

Notwithstanding India's eminent contribution to the establishment of Eastern Pakistan as an independent State of Bangladesh, bilateral relation began to take a downhill course—particularly after the brutal assassination of Sheikh Mujibur Rahman. During Rajiv Gandhi's time nothing much really happened to improve bilateral relations. Differences persisted. There was the continuous tension regarding large-scale clandestine and uncontrollable Bangladesi influx into eastern regions of India, particularly Assam. The only thing the Indian leadership could think of, during Rajiv Gandhi's mandate, was to construct a wall to stem the influx. This was not much of a help since the influx continued creating tensions and generated widespread discontent in north-eastern areas of India. Even north-western India, including the capital, New Delhi, is crowded with Bangladeshis.

The problem of water sharing remained troublesome. With fifty-four common rivers flowing between the two countries, this has become a great divisive factor. Since much of the water originates in Nepal, Rajiv Gandhi accepted the Bangladeshi proposal for tripartite talks, which previous governments had always refused, but this did not really solve the problem since India had always avoided any permanent agreement on the Ganges waters, the most important of them all.

The ongoing Bangladeshi trend—like other South Asian neighbours—to diversify its foreign relations, with a particular focus on China and the US, did not help matters.

Finally, the growing Islamic fundamentalist trend in the country generated a great deal of anti-Indian feeling which the Bangladesi authorities are unable to stem—a trend that has apparently been getting worse with the years.

The Maldives

The island of Maldives was the only South Asian neighbour with whom relations improved after the prompt Indian military action to abort the coup d'etat attempt against the legitimate government. The level of Maldives dependence on India naturally increased. There were of course divergent theories regarding Rajiv Gandhi's military action. There was one in Pakistan that dismissed the theory that there was a coup d'etat attempt but was "a drama staged by the Indian intelligence agency, the Research and Analysis Wing (RAW) itself in order to gain military hold over the island." "Besides," argued the Pakistani source, "the suspicious alacrity with which the Indians had arrived on the scene—as if they had been ready and waiting to go—our intelligence pointed to the fact that the mercenaries…had omitted to cut off the island's communications thus allowing the President to contact Delhi for help."[346] This may seem rather far-fetched given Pakistan's traditional bias against India. Another source has suggested that the Maldives authorities had approached Washington for help, and it was the Reagan Administration that recommended them to turn to India.

Bhutan

Like all of India's South Asian neighbours, Bhutan too was diversifying its foreign relations by cultivating with other countries. But the Himalayan Kingdom, fearful of Chinese pressures in the north, and equally perturbed by Indian north-eastern insurgent groups, operating in the South, perceived India as the country with which it had to maintain close ties to counteract against the security problems. Rajiv Gandhi established a relationship with King Jigme Wangchuk which "was truly a special one," with both of them "being on the same wave length."[347]

The Indian Prime Minister made a state visit to Bhutan in October 1985 "which was more of a family get-together than protocol."[348] Nonetheless, there were problems in Indo-Bhutanese relations. For one thing, deviating from the 1949 Indo-Bhutanese Treaty, which stipulated some Indian control over Bhutan's foreign relations, the Bhutanese opened talks with the Chinese on the border question. Furthermore, it begun a policy of expelling Indian workers, and of implementing very specifically a Bhutanese code of conduct and living that was imposed on all residents irrespective of their own culture and customs. While, this was an expression of Bhutanese nationalism, it was resented by the minorities, including Indians.

Rajiv Gandhi's diplomatic performance in South Asia was no better that that of his predecessors. There was really no country in the region with whom relations improved. If anything, they deteriorated even more during his mandate. His attempts to mediate in the Sri Lankan conflict failed and did not help improve bilateral relations, had stagnated with Pakistan, and deteriorated with Nepal and Bangladesh. Bhutan and the Maldives were the only countries of the region with whom relations remained on an even keel; but that too because one (Bhutan) feared China, its northern neighbour, even more than India, and the other (Maldives) was saved from a coup d'etat by prompt Indian military action.

DECISION MAKING PROCESS

The decision making process, under Rajiv Gandhi, thus, was similar to the one designed by Indira Gandhi. While the different institutions, concerned with foreign policy, were generally set in motion to receive the inputs that were necessary for a decision, the real decision making process as such was limited to a very small group of advisers centred in or around the Prime Minister's Secretariat.

But Rajiv Gandhi had no confidence in the bureaucracy. Apparently he had come to the conclusion that it was an institution that dragged change, that it was incapable of seeing the larger picture, and that it was far more interested in protecting its own interest than that of the country. In sum, an institution to be distrusted and closely monitored. As a stark manifestation of his lack of confidence, no less than 25 high-powered secretaries of the government were transferred in one major single reshuffle after he came to power. But, perhaps the most important indicator of his reservation about the bureaucracy, and of his own determination to personally play a central role in foreign affairs was the discontinuation of the weekly traditional Prime Minister-Foreign Secretary meeting which had become very much a part of the Indian system under preceding Prime Ministers. The brutal manner in which he publicly and summarily dismissed his Foreign Secretary, A.P.

Venkateswaran, during the course of a press conference, demonstrated his intolerance of any one who established a central position for himself in foreign affairs. Venkatswaren was not a pliable bureaucrat, and refused to bend to political whims. He had a strong personality, and an independent way of looking at things, and who was known for openly expressing his views even if he knew that they were not acceptable. On numerous occasions and on numerous issues he had stood up to the Prime Minister's personal advisers, proposing alternative strategies, protesting about undue interference in the activities of the MEA, and often taking a firm position regarding the sidelining of the bureaucracy in foreign policy making. On some occasions he even stood up to the Prime Minister, and developed the reputation of shooting down his ideas, often in the presence of others. Gandhi's disarmament plan was one of them.

Rajiv Gandhi's determination not to share power process with the others was confirmed by his practice of constantly changing Foreign Ministers and advisers. No one was allowed, at least among his Foreign Ministers, to stay for more than a few months. During the first two years of his mandate, he had, for example, sent off forty-seven of his Ministers "to the guillotine" of which five were Foreign Ministers, and as many as seven were Ministers of State-indeed a record in the annals of the post-independent history.

To what could one attribute this tendency of constantly hiring and firing of Ministers ? Was it his dissatisfaction with the performance of the Ministers concerned? Or was it a manifestation of his own insecurity—insecurity of finding the Minister firmly installed in his Ministry, and of becoming well-versed in his vocation—more than the Prime Minister?

Whatever may have been the reason or reasons for such an unusual behaviour, one thing is undeniable: it did not go well with those within the country and outside.

Rajiv Gandhi had also operationalised an innovative decisional structure by changing the composition of his advisers closely working with him. Instead of taking on the group that already existed, he brought into the decisional fold a new circle of advisers some of whom were old Doon school chums (Arun Singh, Arun Nehru, Madhav Rao Scindia, etc.), while the others were the new emerging political and bureaucratic figures like K.C. Pant, Natwar Singh, V.P. Singh, Gopi Arora, B.G.Deshmukh, etc. The so-called "outer circle" like T.N. Kaul, G.Parthasarathy were still there, but they had lost much of their power and much of their interaction with the Prime Minister.

While the traditional institutions, concerned with foreign affairs, like the Ministry of External Affairs , the Parliament, etc, had lost some of their influence, the Cabinet Secretariat, the Prime Minister's Office and RAW, already powerful under Indira Gandhi, continued to acquire greater hold on the decisional process in foreign affairs and greater access to the Prime Minister.

Personal characteristics of the central political figure too are crucial in the decisional process. In some instances they can be decisive. Rajiv Gandhi had some paradoxical features in his personality that must have had ramifications on the decisions he took in foreign affairs. He was known to be impulsive; he had a general reputation of being impatient with long position papers and long oral advises; he had great confidence in his own capacity and knowledge in diplomacy—much more than his entourage. But, paradoxically, at the same time, Rajiv Gandhi was a team worker, and did organise collective meetings of advisers before taking a decision. In the disarmament sector in which he was personally interested, he himself worked on his computer to draft the details of his proposals, but in close coordination with a group. On China, he finally took a decision to initiate some diplomatic steps after having shown great reluctance during the early stages of his mandate. Once he opted for such a decision he sought the advice of many, including P.N. Haksar, Gopi Arora, Narasimha Rao.

The decisional process, under Rajiv Gandhi, thus was never a uniform or standard process with a fixed group of advisers, but changed from issue to issue depending on the level of his own interest in the subject in question.

EVALUATION

Rajiv Gandhi's emergence to supreme political power was accidental. He would never have reached the political summitry if his brother, Sanjay Gandhi, had not died accidently, and if his mother had not been assassinated. Though Rajiv did gain some political experience while his mother was still alive, he suddenly and dramatically emerged at the summitry, unequipped and perceptually unaware of the complexities of the international system. Many, of course, perceived this as an advantage, for it gave the person in question the much-needed adaptability and flexibility which experienced politicians do not possess. Besides, a young and physically charming personality gave Rajiv Gandhi a supplementary advantage of national and international attention. He had these assets wherever he went in the world, and he did carry himself well in the upper echelons of the international political hierarchy. Reagan was charmed by him; and Gorbachev and Mitterand were impressed by his pleasing personality, while many others, particularly in the third world, were swept off by his polite and pleasing character.

But what was his contribution to India's foreign policy? What was his real role in international affairs.? Perhaps his most outstanding achievement was that he successfully injected an equilibrium in India's relations with the two superpowers. India, under Rajiv, was no more a pro-Soviet non-aligned country, but a country which also opened up to the US without collaterally putting on hold its relations with the Soviet Union. Actually, the process of balanced equilibrium between the two powers was activated under his predecessors (Shastri, Desai and Indira Gandhi) and has been continued by his successors; but it was truly under Rajiv Gandhi that the process reached an upgraded level. It must be, of course, noted that it was not only Rajiv Gandhi's subtle diplomacy that reached this state of diplomatic equilibrium; for it was also the international environment that greatly contributed to this state of affairs. Reagan, notwithstanding a fixed American reservation about India, had begun to look upon India as a benign international actor, and the Russians under Gorbachev had no objection to India's efforts to develop meaningful relations with Washington. In fact, Gorbachev is known to have declared his accord with this new Indian diplomacy in one of his bilateral meetings with the US President.

China was the other diplomatic target. A conspicuous opening was made at the prime ministerial level with Rajiv Gandhi's historic visit to Beijing that finally resulted in intensive interaction the ramifications of which are visible today.

Disarmament was the other issue in which Rajiv Gandhi took a personal interest. As we have seen above, he spent a great deal of his time constructing concrete and wide-ranging proposals, and presenting them at the UN. They were well-received by the international community, with the exception of the US, which perceived them to be a little too ambitious for the existing configuration of forces.

The other enlarged international issue in which Rajiv Gandhi was heavily involved was the liberation of Southern Africa. He was much more active than any of his predecessors for which he was given international recognition in the third world.

In sum Rajiv Gandhi's performance at the broad international level was positive—in any event much more than any of his predecessors.

But the real challenge for Indian diplomacy is its own region—South Asia. It is here in this area that the record of Indian diplomacy should be evaluated. For most of the problems and defiances that India was faced with were in its South Asian backyard. Rajiv Gandhi's performance was no better than his predecessors. For he too was neither able to impose India's predominant power in keeping his six neighbours under India's hegemonial control or in its sphere of influence, nor was he able to construct an architecture of peaceful regional framework based on equality and collective interaction—two of the broad diplomatic options that India has in South Asia.

PART II
Post–Nehru-Gandhi Era

ViSHWANATH PRATAP SINGH

Chapter VIII

Vishwanath Pratap Singh
2 December 1989—7 November 1990

Vishwanath Pratap Singh (V.P. Singh) emerged as Prime Minister, after the 1989 general elections, but under difficult conditions, more laborious than under any other preceding Prime Minister. The overall political situation in the country was, to say the least, tumultuous, uncertain and even unstable. He had to overcome a series of hurdles before he could effectively assume power at the summit.

First of all, he had to face the unpleasant task of becoming the head of his own party, the Janata Dal, for which he had to heavily involve himself in a whole series of manipulations, manoeuvrings and compromises—all of which eventually undermined his own position within the party. Though, he finally succeeded, underhandedly, in heading the party, he always remained politically weak with adversaries awaiting in the corridors of powers, to challenge and disrupt his leadership, particularly his main rival, Chandra Shekhar. This was nothing new in Indian politics, for most Prime Ministers had to go through such a process, but V.P. Singh's accession to power was, nonetheless, more difficult, more shaky, and even more controversial than that of any his other predecessors, since he had allegedly a long record of a "sycophantic career" of serving the Gandhis, and, at the same time, a widespread notoriety of having "betrayed" and countered the last of them (Rajiv Gandhi). To be daggers drawn with his main party rival (Chandra Shekhar) was already an awkward situation, but to compound it with his defiant standoffishness with a powerful figure like Rajiv Gandhi rendered his political status even more volatile. He had, quite wrongly, convinced himself that his own resignation from the Rajiv Gandhi Government, and the difficulties the latter was facing, with the departure of other political leaders (Arun Nehru, Arif Mohammad Khan, and Vidya Charan Shukla), would plunge the Congress into a state of considerable decrepitude that would finally result in some form of unison under his leadership. That is what he was hoping, and that is what he was trying.

The other major hurdle was to reach the prime ministership with only 143 elected Janata Dal members in a Lok Sabha of 543 members, a distinctly disadvantageous situation—which was worsened by the important fact that V.P.Singh sought to establish "the first and the only government in the world which was supported by both the left and the right."[349] His government was even worse and even more unstable than the coalition government, led by Morarji Desai, since he had established his government that consisted of practically all the major parties of very diverse and divergent political orientations, with the exception of the Congress Party which remained in the opposition.

Singh, furthermore came to power with serious and tumultuous domestic problems in many states of India: in Jammu & Kashmir, where his interior minister's twenty-three year old daughter was kidnapped by militants belonging to the radical Jammu and Kashmir Front. and where a fundamentalist revolt exploded; in Punjab where 150 persons were killed in the first fifty days of Singh's governance by the rapidly expanding Sikh fundamentalists; in Assam where massive student demonstrations, demanding greater state autonomy, became the order of the day; not to speak of the dacoity in Uttar Pradesh where, according to the State Administration, over one thousand five hundred 'notorious dacoits' had been killed in 'encounters' with the police and more than nine thousand arrested.

Add to all this the Prime Minister's own inexplicable decision to go ahead with the Mandal Commission's recommendation to reserve 27 per cent of Government jobs for the "socially and educationally backward classes"—a decision that resulted in a violent rampage among students in many cities who took exception to such a decisional option, thus further adding to political instability.

The domestic situation, thus, considerably overwhelmed V.P.Singh's coalition government, including his announced plans to determinedly "usher in a silent bloodless revolution with no parallel in world history" of eradicating corruption, of arresting inflation, of establishing "a free and open governnment," of protecting minorities—clearly a tall ambitous time-consuming objectives,[350] much beyond the capacity of a feeble government and a weak leadership.

FOREIGN AFFAIRS

If one were to compound to all this the important fact that Singh's personal interest in foreign affairs was relatively limited, and that his government lasted for less than a year (eleven months), foreign policy could hardly acquire a weighty position during his mandate.

And yet it did; for he could hardly turn a blind eye to international affairs since India was faced with portentous issues that could scarcely be ignored. There was the massive Indian military presence in Sri Lanka that was leading nowhere; both the Colombo Government and the Sri Lankan Tamils had openly come out against the abortive Indian peacekeeping operation. There was nerve-racking tensions with Nepal due to the sanctions imposed by the previous government; Bangladesh was hardly on speaking terms with India, and there was this growing confrontational situation that had emerged with Pakistan; not to speak of the oncoming war in the Persian Gulf area where a large number of Indians were residing, and from where India was importing much of its energy resources; and not to speak of the pertinacious pressures from Washington to sign the Comprehensive Test Ban Treaty (CTBT) when India was already discreetly but determinedly moving in the nuclear arms direction.

Since, it is axiomatic that international issues can have major ramifications domestically, V.P.Singh could, therefore, hardly disregard what was happening in the world, especially the impact they could have on his coalition government composed of left and right wing parties with divergent orientations in international affairs. But, there were a number of saving factors that made it easy for the government to deal with foreign affairs, much more smoothly than with affairs within the country.

While the V.P. Singh Government was compelled to adopt a policy of domestic consensus that involved regular meetings with leaders of the supporting parties, he had, paradoxically, an advantage on international issues. So heavily marked was the Government in intra-party and inner party debates regarding the tumultous domestic situation that it was not inundated by domestic pressures on international affairs. For coalition governments— at least in India—have a tendency of liberating the Prime Minister from the constraints of his coalition partners who generally have a little interest in global affairs, and who are politically busy surviving domestically. There could, of course, be exceptions to this general rule on issues where coalition partners have a direct interest. But, during Singh's brief tenure there was no such issue where he had to take into account domestic susceptibiities. The Sri. Lankan affair could have generated domestic discontent, especially in Tamil Nadu, but this apparently was not the case since the Government was heavily involved in monitoring the withdrawal of Indian troops—which everyone agreed with, including the Sri Lankan Tamils. Besides, V.P.Singh actively interacted with Tamil Nadu's Chief Minister, Karunanidhi, keeping him informed of the overall situation, and requesting him to explore the possibility of solving the Sri. Lankan conflict, thus neutralising discontent and pressures from the Indian Tamils. Though, he did actively involve himself as a go-between between the Sri Lankan Government and the radical Sri Lankan Tamis, his initiatives did not lead anywhere. If any proof was needed regarding the intractability of the Sri Lankan issue, it was the Tamil Nadu Chief Minister's active intervention ; for if he—an active proponent of the Sri. Lankan Tamil cause– was unable to persuade the radical Tamils to seek a compromise with the central government in Colombo then no one else could.

The other saving factor for Singh was I.K.Gujral, his Foreign Minister that made it possible for the smooth functioning of Indian diplomacy. In addition to his excellent political credentials within the country, he was generally recognised as an experienced diplomat with considerable savviness in international affairs. Gujral's tenure as Ambassador to Moscow also stood him in good stead. Besides, the mutual confidence on which apparently reposed their relationship made things easier and smoother.

Since there was hardly anyone in Singh's entourage who could have challenged Gujral's competence and authority in diplomatic matters, things were smoother. Arun Nehru, Minister of Commerce, did have some authority and even some pretentions in dealing with some aspects of foreign affairs, but not enough to challenge Gujral. There was, of course, Devi Lal, the Deputy Prime minister, to be reckoned with, who had made some graceless remarks about Gujral in an interview, and who was going around the country recommending that 50 per cent of India's embassies should be run by people from rural areas. But, his activities were becoming so objectionable that V.P.Singh finally had to get rid of him as Deputy Prime minister. He had no other choice.

Additionally, foreign affairs also involves the heavy and time-consuming task of visiting other countries, of receiving foreign dignatories in one's own. Given Singh's brief tenure of less than a year, his 1990 diplomatic agenda was pretty heavy: visits to Maldives in June (1990), to Malaysia in July, to the USSR also in July. Add to this the visits of heads of other countries or his own foreign counterparts in Delhi with whom he had to unavoidably discuss a number of issues for which he had to unavoidably involve himself in the time-consuming task of preparing himself: Prime Minister Michel Rocard from France (January 1990), Sir Anerood Jugnauth from Mauritius (January 1990), King Jigme Singye from Bhutan (February 1990), President Daniel T. Arap Moi of Kenya (March 1990), President Maumoon Abdul Gayoom of Maldives (March 1990), President Yassar Arafat of Palestine (March 1990), Prime Minister Tashiki Kaifu from Japan (April 1990), Prime Minister K.P. Bhattarai from Nepal (June 1990), and such renowned personalities as Nelson Mandela from South Africa.

If one were to add to all these diverse diplomatic activities, the actual construction and operationalisation of a foreign policy, the V.P.Singh Government must have had its hands full even in the diplomatic sector. He had thus enough work on his diplomatic plate, and one wonders how he could have managed these external responsibilities, tied as he was with the uphill task of political survivability.

India's foreign policy can be broadly divided into two parts: while one pertained to its neighbours, the other was focussed on the world beyond.

As with all Prime Ministers, before and after, South Asia clearly was the most important diplomatic dimension. For it was in this area that key problematic issues were focussed. But none of them were really resolved by any of the Prime Ministers before V.P.Singh; India had indeed shown a singular inability of imposing any solution either by force or by a peaceful manner.

V.P.Singh had apparently decided to focus on South Asia. The area was projected as one of his principal priorities in foreign policy. And a systematic effort was made to bilaterally rein in the problems India was faced with.

What is his record ? Did he succeed ? Did he find the correct methodology, the appropriate diplomatic behaviour and the enabling environment to gain confidence of his neighbours ? What was finally the result ? In sum, did he get his foreign policy over the barrel ? Only a systematic analysis of his diplomacy with each of them can give us the answer.

SOUTH ASIA

Sri Lanka

Sri Lanka was the first foreign policy issue to which the Singh Government had to attend to. The decision to withdraw 70,000 strong

Indian Peace Keeping Force (IPKF) was not his own, since Rajiv Gandhi had already agreed to do so in the summer of 1989. Clearly, the peace keeping operation had failed. Many, in fact, had begun to compare India's military failure in the Island with that of the flawed US operations in Vietnam. But the US, as a global power, had a long experience of military action in many areas of the world. While some had failed, most were indeed successful, since the US had the infrastructure and the mind-set to handle such siituations; whereas India hardly had any; it neither had the infrastructure nor the capacity nor even the mindset for such actions, least of all V.P.Singh even more since he had no experience nor any time to bring peace to the area.

In any event, now that the IPKF had been withdrawn (March 1990), the new V.P.Singh Government was faced with more difficult task generated by the power vacuum in the island nation. The two ethnic adversaries (Tamils and Sinhalese), after a brief understanding to get the IPKF out of the country, were back on the war path with the Sinhalese insisting on territorial integrity of the island, and the Tamil Tigers exhorting for their traditional demand for an independent Eelam (independence of the northern parts).

Compounded to this was the re-emergence of insistent pressures from the tamils in Tamil Nadu on the Central Government to come to the rescue of the Sri Lankan Tamils who were apparently on the defensive in their full blown civil war with the Colombo Government.

The V.P. Singh Government was faced with this unpleasant situation, but did'nt know how to handle it, especially the aggressive bombardment on Tamil civilians. The Prime Minister evoked on 16 September 1990 the possibility of sending his Foreign Minister, I.K.Gujral to Sri Lanka "to impress on the Sri Lankan Government India's concern over the suffering of the Tamils, and to stress the need for maintaining food supplies in Jaffna and other Tamil areas." [351]

Nothing much came out of all this. The civil war continued unabated. The Tamils, after some serious setbacks in the battles against the Sinhalese, finally recuperated and showed a remarkable capacity "to hold out indefintely in their stronghold in Sri Lanka's northern Jaffna peninsula." [352]

While India was helplessly watching the deteriorating Sri Lankan situation, the others were coming in to support the Colombo Government including Pakistan, the secret services of many countries, and the US with an eye on the strategic Trinacomalee port. The Chinese too got into the act. While the conflict was blazing, Li Peng, the Chinese Prime Minister, arrived in Colombo with a 40 member delegation, and apparently agreed to give arms to the Central Government—arms that included, among other things, a dozen 130 mm artillery pieces, six jet fighter bombers, 43 armoured vehicules and three Shanghai-class patrol boats.[353]

For a country like India whose primordial diplomatic objective had always been to keep other nations out of South Asia, Sri Lanka became a sad spectacle over which it had no control—neither on the intra- Sri Lankan ethnic conflict, nor on containing the influence there of other countries and other forces. While all Prime Ministers had to reckon with this problem—even the ones who were powerful—it was hardly possible for the V.P.Singh whose Government, to say the least, was really in no position to handle the problem efficaciously.

While the process of loosing in Sri Lanka had already begun during Indira Gandhi's second mandate, it reached a pinnacle while V.P.Singh was at the helm of affairs.

There was nothing much he could do to solve what had increasingly become an intractable issue between the Sinhalese, determined to maintain the territorial integrity of the island, and the Tamil tigers fixated to the objective of achieving independence of the northern areas where they had been residing for so many years. Hardly, anyone, among the decision makers in Delhi were proponents of independence of the northern territories, for the successful ramifications of such an act could only have been determental to India's own territorial integrity, faced as it was with myriad similar clamours in the country.

The Indians thus failed on all fronts: in their failure to persuade the Sinhalese to accord large autonomy to the northern territories, and in their efforts—obviously abortive—to prevail upon the Tamils to abandon their demand for independence. Rajiv Gandhi had tried and finally, in the end, paid with his own life.

V.P.Singh had neither the stamina nor the political clout to find a diplomatic solution to an intractable issue. In fact, no one in India had. Singh had got out of a difficult situation by monitoring the withdrawal of Indian troops without finding a political solution agreeable to the Central Sri Lankan Government regarding the devolution of power to the northern territories.

Pakistan

V.P.Singh was also faced with a confrontational situation with Pakistan. All Indian Prime Ministers invariably go through this process, irrespective of their political orientations. It has indeed become a permanent headache of Indian diplomacy; it is always there and surfaces regularly. No one has really resolved the problem, neither by peaceful means nor by military action.

For the V.P.Singh Government, it was even worse. Weak as it was, and uncertain as it had become domestically right in the beginning of its mandate, the Prime Minister had initially mused aloud, in an interview with a Persian Gulf newspaper, that relations with Pakistan should develop on an even keel, and that some understanding would be reached to abstain from any race for nuclear weapons in which both the countries were already heavily involved.

But smooth relations is not what emerged in Indo-Pakistan interaction. If anything, they were stormy, turbulent and convoluted right from the beginning. It all began in Kashmir, where the Indian Minister of Interior's daughter was dramatically kidnapped by the Kashmiri opposition—an opposition that demanded the release of its supporters from Indian prison in exchange for freedom for the kidnapped young woman. This created the political hasslement, forcing the Government to cede to their demands. Clearly this was an act of weakness, but there was nothing much that V.P.Singh could do under the circumstances. Ignoring the demands of the kidnappers would have resulted in baneful domestic consequences, which Singh could hardly afford, especially at the beginning of his mandate.

Even more dramatic than this was the explosion of a violent, well-organised, apparently armed, revolt by a group of new militant Kashmiris demanding the holding of a plebiscite to decide the future of Kashmir. The new Kashmiri political outburst was an historic event; for it brought to the surface, "a new, more militant generation of leaders"[354] most of whom were under thirty years of age and most of whom were apparently free from any Hindu-Muslim communalism.

But this did not last long; for as the revolt exacerbated, becoming aggressive and massive, Kashmiris began to turn to religious symbolism and fundamentalist groupings with transnational connections not only across the border in Pakistan, but also among Kashmiri expatriates residing in distant lands, particularly Europe and the US. It was thus no more limited to the local Kashmiri population, but had taken an external dimension.

Pakistan's reaction was loud and "highly emotional"[355] which was manifested by a sympathy strike all over the country, by the calling of a momentous all-party rally supporting the new Kashmiri upheaval, followed by a series of "hard-hitting" speeches by the Prime Minister, Benazir Bhutto, in Pakistan-held Kashmir territory openly challenging V.P.Singh. "I stand here," she declared in one of her rehetorical outbursts, "Pakistan's Prime Minister, a woman, alone, unarmed and unguarded, amongst you the people of Kashmir. Would India's Prime Minister, Mr. V.P.Singh, be able to do the same thing in Srinagar in the midst of hundreds of thousand of his troops."[356]

One wonders if this new hard-headed aggressiveness towards India was not comparable to the ruggedness during the days of Benazir's father, who, when Shastri was Prime Minister had convinced himself that the moment had arrived to strike at India, which was perceived as weak and unstable. Was Benazir Bhutto not looking at V.P.Singh in the same light; in fact, there were seemingly many in the country who were thinking in such terms. In fact, one of the leading army figures, General Aslam Beg, had apparently told U.S. Commander-in-Chief General Norman Schwarzkopf to the effect that "Now we are in good shape. With the support that, Iran has promised me we will win in case of war with India." [357]

At the same time she sent Ambassador Abdul Sattar as a special envoy to Delhi to warn Prime Minister, Singh, that Indo-Pakistan relations would be adversely affected if Delhi used force against the Kashmir uprising. [358]

The Indian decision makers were getting concerned at the whole situation particularly after the Pakistan Foreign Minister, Yaqub Khan, came to Delhi for a SAARC meeting, and privately gave "a nuclear ultimatum" to Foreign Minister Gujral, and apparently did the same in his bilateral meeting with the Prime Minister.[359] Both of them confirmed this to this author in separate discussions. It seemed as if Pakistan was intentionally building up tensions, not so much to have a military showdown as to force V.P.Singh to make concessions.

South Asian developments had come to such a pass that no real or meaningful concession could be made–least of all by V.P.Singh, whose domestic status, to say the least, was feeble. So the opposite happened. Indians were firm and uncompromising. Convinced that a "war-like" situation was in the process of developing India decided to take a firm stand. More than 1,00,000 troops were moved from the Sino-Indian border to the Indo-Pakistan border. The Chinese, according to Singh, were very cooperative. They agreed to withdraw their missiles, and gave their accord not to create any tensions on the frontier.[360]

At the same time, India undertook two diplomatic initiatives. The first was towards Pakistan in July 1990, proposing talks on all outstanding issues, and suggesting a number of Confidence Building Measures (CBMs). The Indian Foreign Secretary, Muchkund Dubey, who went to Islamabad for the talks, made it clear to his counterpart that if Pakistan was prepared to cooperate with India in stabilising the Kashmir situation, India was prepared to give the Kashmiris 'anything' short of self-determination.[361] But, 'anything' short of self-determination was not acceptable to Pakistan and the latter did not take the Indian proposals seriously.

Simultaneously, India turned to the US making it clear to Washington that Pakistan must be restrained before the situation escalated into a war. And, this is what Washington did. For, convinced, as it had become, that India and Pakistan were close to a nuclear war, it took a very firm position against Pakistan, warning Islamabad "not to count on an American bailout if Pakistan got itself into a war with India," and reminding it "that if Pakistan was found to be encouraging 'terrorists' in Kashmir, it could be in trouble with the law in the US."[362]

It was probably the first time that Washington showed signs of moving away from its traditional policy of supporting Pakistan. For one thing uncertainties in Pakistan were burgeoning. The political ups and downs were becoming more fixated than before. Nobody could really predict, with any conclusiveness the shape of things to come. For another, terrorism and islamic fundamentalism were looming on the horizon, growing in force and assertiveness. The US, furthermore, had become exasperated with Pakistan going nuclear, and that to with the active support of the Chinese. Besides, there were already some indications that the US was cooling off from its traditional policy of supporting the idea of deciding the future of Kashmir through plebiscite, for the increasing emergence of islamic fundamentalism in the valley of Kashmir was a dangerous option that Washington could hardly afford to accept. Now that Gorbachev had withdrawn from Afghanistan, the US need of using Pakistan as a base for anti-Soviet activities lost much of its value.

While the US evaluation that India and Pakistan were close to a nuclear war was an exaggeration, there does not appear to be any doubt that vibrant

US intervention did play a decisive role in de-escalating the war-like situation that was developing on the sub-continent.

Thus in the case of Pakistan too, Indian diplomacy had, once again, gone into a tailspin. Direct talks had not worked. The two traditional adversaries were as far apart as before, and were as distrustful of each other as before. If anything, even more so than ever in the past, since the Kashmir upheaval of 1990 had catalysed Pakistan, especially the military, to become more aggressive and more supportive of the anti-Indian Kashmir movement. So much so that the US had apparently convinced itself that a nuclear war between the two South Asian countries was looming on the horizon.

Nepal

Another South Asian target of Singh's diplomacy was Nepal. Relations between the two countries had become problematic under all preceding Prime Ministers, but they really took a sour turn when Rajiv Gandhi was Prime Minister. Notwithstanding the fact that Nepal was under a treaty obligation not to seek arms from any other source but India, it concluded an arms aid agreement with China. It was really a symbolic act of not any great military importance, and was essentially motivated by the Himalayan Kingdom's ongoing determination to become more and more independent of India. But, Rajiv Gandhi, after some vain efforts at dissuassion, finally retaliated by clamping down a series of drastic economic sanctions—sanctions that rendered Nepal considerably destitute. Many in India perceived this as an over-reactive and disproportionate act—particularly the armed forces who feared adverse ramifications on the Gurkha component of the Indian armed forces.

V.P Singh too perceived this as an excessive act against a neighour with whom it was vital to have friendly relations. But since Nepal under King Birendra was still going through an authoritarian phase when Singh came to power in December 1989, the Indian Government took a firm action by sending a new treaty to the King on 31 March 1990 for the King to sign « in return for relieving pressure on his beleagured Government. » The terms of the treaty were so harsh that they virtually took the clock back to 31 July 1950. It was worse than the 1950 Treaty. For in effect it was an Indian ultimatum.

The crux of the treaty proposal rested on four restrictions on Nepal : 1) Nepal would not import arms or raise additional military units without Indian approval ;2) Nepal would not enter into military alliance with any other country ; 3) Indian companies would be given first preference in any economic or industrial projects ; 4) India's exclusive involvement would be ensured on the « commonly shared rivers » in Nepal. Rather than sign the treaty in the hope of saving his authoritarian panchayat regime, the King pre-empted Indian pressures by abandoning power over to the alliance of the Nepali Congress and the United left front.

It was then that V.P.Singh decided to reopen negotiations with his Nepalese counterparts in the hope of reaching an amicable agreement satisfactory to both the parties. High level negotiations were inaugurated on 20 February 1990; and an agreement was finally reached between the two Prime Ministers, V.P. Singh and K.P.Bhattarai that restored the *status quo ante* on all aspects of bilateral relations including the reopening of the 15 transit trade points that Nepal used to trade with India and beyond.[363] India, furthermore, restored the standby credit facility increasing it from Rupees 250 million to 350 million.[364]

In sum, practically everything Nepal wanted in the economic sector was agreed to.[365] But, in exchange for all these concessions, India obtained what it wanted in the security sector. The Nepalese Government agreed to put off indefinitely the purchase of the last consignment of arms that Nepal had ordered from China.[366] The joint communiqé went even further. India and Nepal agreed that "the two countries shall hold prior consultations with a view of reaching mutual agreements on such defence-related issues, which, in the view of either country, could pose a security threat."[367] Nepal also agreed to support the Indian position on Kashmir.

The security and the political aspects of the agreement were indeed a major concession by Nepal. For, they in effect tied the Himalayan Kingdom's hand on political issues—issues on which, until the agreement, Nepal had followed an independent position.

While this was a diplomatic success for the V.P.Singh Government, one wonders if succeeding Nepalese governments have faithfully followed the political agreements since a strong and almost secular tradition developed in Nepal for designing an independent foreign policy.

There were, of course, two other major issues that were left open—the issue pertaining to work permits for Indian citizens residing in Nepal, and the sharing of waters from rivers flowing from Nepal to India and to Bangladesh. But the Indian diplomatic strategy was so much focussed on obtaining concessions on political and secutiry matters that it apparently decided not to push these issues.

At the dinner hosted by V.P.Singh for his Nepalese counterpart, K.P. Bhattarai, the Indian Prime Minister summed up aptly the type of relations he would like to have with the Himalayan Kingdom. While stressing equality between the two countries, he made it clear that India was not seeking reciprocity in their relations with Nepal. This in effect meant that India will give more than it will take as long as its security is assured in the north. "We are conscious," he declared, "of the inherent asymmetries, and, therefore, do not seek reciprocity in our relationship. We only seek genuine understanding of our key concerns. India will more than reciprocate such understanding."[368]

Clearly, V.P.Singh was more successful with the Nepalese than with the Sri Lankans or with the Pakistanis. An agreement was reached under which he had forestalled—at least for the time being—Chinese military presence in the Himalayan Kingdom. Furthermore, pressures on the Nepalese monarchy had resulted in the emergence of democratic institutions.

Bangladesh

Like the other South Asian countries, Bangladesh also became a crucial factor of Indian diplomacy. For it too, since its independence in 1971, was showing signs of distancing itself from New Delhi, notwithstanding the fact that the latter's role had indeed been decisive in its liberation. All the South Asian nations—even those favourably disposed towards India—were consensually moving away from maintaining too close ties with their gigantic neighbour. Bangladesh naturally was no exception to this general rule. If anything, it was even a more striking example of a newly liberated nation striving to become independent of India. By the time V.P.Singh came to power, it had already constructed a diplomatic base of actively seeking out other major international actors, included the US and China.

Therefore, one of the first foreign visits (after Maldives) that Foreign Minister, I.K.Gujral, made was to Bangladesh in February (16-18) 1990. It was expected to be an exploratory visit, but finally became a substantive one, since practically all the vexed issues that troubled Indo-Bangladesh relations were placed on the table and candidly discussed.

Gujral's savviness in international affairs, compounded with a benign temperament and outgoing character came in very handy; for he went around in his usual affable, but serious way of resolutely assuring all and sundry—

from President H.M. Ershad to the opposition—of India's determination of forging good neighbourly ties with its eastern neighbours, while firmly defending India's national interests. "We seek," he declared at the dinner hosted by his counterpart, " your government's understanding, cooperation and reciprocity by being equally responsive to our national interests and sensitivities to enable us to pursue this policy of good neighbourliness."[369]

Undoubdtedly, the Foreign Minister's visit was a masterly stroke in public relations; for the Bangladeshi Foreign Minister, Anisul Islam Mahmud, reciprocated by declaring that "we are pleased that you are showing every sign that you mean what you say."[370]

The ramifications of his visit were indeed positive—positive in the sense that relations did move forward, and that bilateral interactions began to take an upbeat turn—including some very positive and reciprocal assurances from Bangladeshi decision makers. The Joint and Technical Commission and the Joint River Commission, hitherto inert, were revived; even the evacuee properties belonging to the Hindu refugees and vested in the hands of the Bangladeshi Government after June 1984, were to be returned to their rightful owners. In one of his very first declarations, V.P. Singh underlined the wish of his government to get closer to Bangladesh, something which had not been the case for many years. "Our Government," he declared candidly, "has made clear its earnest desire to make every effort to strengthen our bilteral ties with our neighbours to our mutual benefit and for the greater advantage of our respective peoples." [371]

Another good sign that relations were moving forward on an even keel, during V.P.Singh's mandate, was the visit in early January (5-9) 1990 of the industrial mission belonging to the Confederation of Indian Industry (CII). It concluded a memorandum of understanding with a Bangladeshi Development Bank the purpose of which was to strengthen cooperation between the two organisations.[372]

As with Nepal, Indo-Bangladeshi relations developed well during V.P.Singh's mandate. But all this did not last long. For one thing, heavily involved as he was in his domestic survival, Indo—Bangladeshi relations, revived by Gujral, could not maintain their ongoing character; there was indeed a benign neglect of the eastern neighbour. Additionally, Bangladesh, again in a process of mutation, was moving in an another direction—the direction of more Islamic fundamentalism, increasing indifference to illegal migration into India, and greater insistence on its demand for more river waters. Already during the closing years of the rule of its founder, Sheikh

Mujib Rahman, Bangladesh had changed to Islamic rhetoric in its political discourse. But, by the sixties the trend had become even more pronounced—so much so that the constitution was amended to abandon secularism and make Islam the state religion. The 27 February 1991 elections confirmed this process by the successful projection into power of the nationalist party, headed by Begum Khaleeda Zia, who was known for her Islamic tilt and her attraction to the establishment of an authoritarian government. There was also, of course, the active interest that Bangladesh had begun to show towards China—an interest heavily indicative of its determination to maintain its independence from India. The tilt towards China became obvious that within a few years after V.P.Singh, the Bangladesh army had become totally dependent on Chinese military hardware.

The growing anti-Indian trend in Bangladesh was indeed very paradoxical—in fact, very contradictory. While, on the one hand, the quantum of Bangladeshi Muslims moving to India continued to rise uncontrollably, the Bangladesh Nationalist Party and Jamaat-e-Islami openly expressed their opposition to the opening up of transportation ties with India. When on 20 September 1990 a working agreement was signed between the two countries to reopen the broad gauge rail route between Singbad in India and Rohanpur in Bangladesh for the facilitation of goods traffic to relieve the growing congestion, opposition within the country was substantial. It became almost a national outcry when a decision was taken to reopen the Bongaon-Jessore route to boost partially the trade with North-Eastern states of India on the ground that it may well be used to transport Indian troops and arms through Bangladeshi territory and jeopardise national interest.

So by the end of V.P.Singh mandate, Indo-Bangladesh relations were slowly moving back to square one.

Notwithstanding all the efforts that were made to open up to Bangladesh, India's eastern neighbour remained distrustful of India. The relations really never became normal. While this may be partially explained by the important fact that a number of issues divided the two countries, the high level of Bangladeshi distrust may also be explained by the rampant existence of Islamic fundamentalism among a number of political parties who believed that India was the embodiment of Hindu imperialism.

Bhutan

The Himalayan Kingdom of Bhutan was in the midst of tumultuousnes in V.P.Singh's time—a form of tumultuousness it had never experienced before. Though the political air was full of tensions already before, it got worse by the end of 1989. In its determination to safeguard its traditional Buddhist values and its Buddhist way of life, it had systematically evicted a massive amount of Bhutanese of Nepali Hindu descent from the southern part of the country on the ground that they were not Bhutanese citizens. It was, according to the report of the UN High Commissioner for Refugees, "one of the largest ethnic expulsions in modern history"—an ethnic expulsion that resulted in the forced departure of more than 100,000 Bhutanese to Nepal, not to speak of others who sought asylum in India.[373] Many Bhutanese of Nepalese origin, who were still residing in Bhutan, fearful of potential expulsions, staged a series of massive protest rallies all over the southern part of the country–rallies that were brutally repressed, including indiscriminate firing on demonstrators,

During all these tensions, V.P.Singh's attitude was that of careful neutrality on the ground that this was a bilateral dispute between Bhutan and Nepal. And,while it may well be that the Indian Prime Minister may have evoked all these tragic happenings with King Jigme Singye Wangchuk in his bilateral meeting with him on 1st February 1990, the official Indian stance remained very cautious.

It was, of course, a difficult situation for a Prime Minister who wanted to maintain an even keel in relations with both the Himalayan Kingdoms who were in the midst of developing bilateral relations with China, and who were showing some degree of prudence vis-a-vis their southern neighbour. While Nepal had already gone pretty far in its relations with China, Bhutan too had begun to show signs of circumspection vis-a-vis Beijing. Clearly, signs of embarking on a road of friendship had begun to appear by 1990. Thimphu representatives helped to defeat various draft resolutions, perceived to be anti-Chinese, sponsored by the UN High Commissioner for Refugees. They voted against Taiwan's membership of the UN, and formally disproved Taiwan's bid to host the 2002 Asian games. The Chinese Ambassador to India made numerous visits to Bhutan and the Bhutanese Ambassador in New Delhi made his first visit to Beijing in 2000. There had also been talks of territory exchange between the two countries. For India, under the circumstances, taking a clear-cut position in favour of one (Bhutan) or the other (Nepal) would have ill-served Indian national interests.

V.P.Singh's Government was also circumspect in its trade relations with Bhutan. The Indo-Bhutanese trade agreement, concluded on 2 March 1990, clearly stipulated that the two governments would hold consultations in the event of any problems the two countries would have regarding goods of third country origin. But, notwithstanding the fact that third country goods, including Chinese, were clandestinely entering India from Bhutan, the Singh Government chose to ignore this inflow of goods running into millions of rupees.

The V.P.Singh Government also remained publicily silent regarding the Assamese separatists organisations operating from Bhutan. The Indian argumentation was that no useful purpose would be served by pressuring Bhutan since, though it was itself against such activities, it did not have the appropriate clout to stem such activities.

The only way left for India was to cooperate with Bhutan to monitor and contain such anti-separatist activities. And, this is what it did.

Maldives

After the Indian military intervention In november 1988 to abort the coup d'etat against the Maldives Government, there was apparently no problem between the two countries. This is what V.P.Singh suggested in his different public utterances. And, yet interestingly enough, it was during his brief tenure that Indo-Maldives interaction became crowded, at least in terms of visits. The first foreign visit was that of V.P.Singh's Foreign Minister, I.K.Gujral, who went to Maldives in January 1990. Ostensibly the purpose of this visit was to participate in the Joint Indo-Maldives Commission for Economic and Technical Cooperation that had probably been programmed even before V.P.Singh came to power. The Maldives President arrived in Delhi a couple of months later. And, finally it was to this offshore island that the Indian Prime Minister made his first foreign visit as the head of the Indian Government. In fact, he made it a point to underline this fact in his speech of 22 June 1990 at a banquet hosted by the Maldives President, Maumoon Abdul Gayoom. And, as in the case of Gujral, the visit was apparently non-political, the specific purpose of which was to be present in Male on the occasion of Maldives 25th year of independence.

The public utterances were the friendly remarks that are usually made on such occasions with nothing between the lines to suggest that there was a larger political motivation. For the Indian Prime Minister this visit demonstrated "the level and the extent of our close interaction, understanding and friendship."[374]

But, since India considered Maldives to be within Indian sphere of influence, it has always been very sensitive to outside influence, particularly that of China which had become active on the island, and which was showing signs of striving to have some important presence in the country.

THE WORLD BEYOND

Configuration of International forces

The world beyond was rapidly changing. Already, during Rajiv Gandhi's mandate, innovating signs were visible with Gorbachev seeking detente with Washington.. But, during V.P.Singh's brief tenure the global international system became even more ongoing, showing some clear signs of greater change and irreversability.

While the USA was in the process of acquiring a sole superpower status, the USSR was abjuring its ideological identity, and was forfeiting much of its international power, and China was becoming less and less irascible and more and more cloutish.

The USA, having become India's largest trade partner and a major supplier of high technology, now became a source of attraction to India—perhaps more than ever before. V.P.Singh, therefore, did show some signs of further developing relations with the US. But Washington, on the other hand, was less exhuberant of V.P.Singh who had chosen, paradoxically, to stage a pro-Iraqi demonstration in front of New Delhi's Jama Masjid during the Gulf crisis, and who had "excelled even his own unenviable record of political promiscuity"[375] by announcing that he would not celebrate Holi as a "mark of solidarity with the aggrieved brethren in the Gulf." [376] Besides, the US Administration was no more sure of Singh's political longevity given the uncertainities that had overtaken India at the time. Rumours were rife that V.P.Singh's government would not last even until the end of the year. Furthermore, the US Administration had placed India on its 'watch list' for refusing to conclude a bilateral agreement to provide adequate and effective protection to US intellectual property rights. Therefore, when the Indian Prime Minister informally sounded Washington for a high level State visit he was given short shrift, and was invited to come on a working visit, which he refused.[377]

The Soviet Union, on the other hand, was more generous and more friendly, as it had always been since the mid-fifties. The Indian Prime Minister was given a warm welcome in July 1990 that was embellished by all the protocol requirements of a State visit. But, this time the Soviet leadership was less outgoing and more reserved than was usually the case with Indian

Prime Ministerial visits. Like the US, Moscow, too was not sure of V.P.Singh's political longevity. The Soviet newspaper, *Izvestia*, was in fact no more sure if he would still be the Prime Minister during Gorbachev's visit to Delhi next year. Besides, the Soviet leader was personally not happy with the Indian government's rough treatment of Rajiv Gandhi with whom he had developed a warm personal rapport. So much so that he explicitly declared to this effect to one of Singh's advisers who was visiting the country (Arun Nehru), and apparently went to the extent of postponing the Indian Foreign Minister's visit to Moscow.[378] The Soviet Government, furthermore, was not too happy with the current state of bilateral cooperation, which, in its view was rather inert and inefficient,[379] and was frankly critical of the growing trade imbalance due to a disproportionate increase in Indian exports.

However, notwithstanding the emergence of a host of difficulties, V.P. Singh did not perceive any major modification in the Soviet attitude towards India. He remained—at least publicly—quite optimistic regarding the future of Indo-Soviet relations and warmly congratulated Gorbachev for having "embarked on this noble endeavour with such courage and foresight" that it "has won for you, Mr. President, the admiration and respect of the people of India and the entire world."[380] He further assured the Soviet leader that "our world-view and our foreign policy objectives are closely akin to yours."[381]

Little did the Indian Prime Minister know the rapidity with which the Soviet Union was changing—so much so that a couple of years after his visit, when he was no more the Prime Minister of India, the Soviet Union had disappeared, Gobachev was no more heading the country and Indo-Soviet special relationship had come to an end.

I.K.Gujral was on the same wavelength as V.P. Singh regarding the Soviet Union. His analysis, more intellectual and more prescient, obviously considered maintenance of relations with Moscow was vital for Indian interests—even more so now that it was moving towards social democracy. But Gujral also forewarned that post—communist Russia might well become a serious candidate for seeking increasingly sparse aid and investments from the international market, and thus become a competitor of India. India, therefore, in his view, must « seek new pastures of significant cooperation with countries close to us »–countries and regions such as ASEAN bloc, South Korea, West Asia and Latin America.[382]

While V.P.Singh was, optimistically, speaking of the Soviet Union, it should be noted that he was also sending friendly signals in the Chinese direction. When the Indian Government decided to withdraw the 100,000 troops from the north and the north-east to face the growing tensions on the Indo-Pakistani border, the Prime Minister discussed the matter with the Chinese, who according to him, were « very cooperative », and agreed to withdraw their missiles, and accepted not to generate any tensions on the Sino-Indian border.[383]

If the Chinese were really cooperative, as suggested by Singh, this was then the first palpable manifestation of a new attitude on the border. Admittedly, Rajiv Gandhi's historic visit to Beijing had indeed uplifted Sino-Indian relations, but to permit Indian troops to withdraw was a singular Chinese indication of letting up on the border issue.

It is interesting to note that Singh made it a point, in many of his public utterances, to compare India's relations with China, and its relations with Pakistan. While in Kuala Lampur, attending the meeting of the G-15 summit, established by the non-aligned countries in September 1989, he drew a parallel between India's relations with Pakistan and China, with both of whom India had border problems and territorial disputes. While China and India, declared Singh, were sincerely exploring normalisation of relations, Pakistan was playing an underhand game.[384] In a press conference, also in Kuala Lumpur, he was even more explicit. While attacking Pakistan for having missed a good opportunity of improving relations with India, he was contrastingly well-disposed towards China. Despite the 1962 Sino-Indian war, and notwithstanding the existence of boundary dispute "we had been able to move forward positively. This is because China had adopted an attitude quite different from Pakistan, and it was not out to play an underhand game." [385] In August Singh went further. He proposed a border solution based on "logistical convenience" and "Administrative considerations." [386] This would give Aksai Chin to China in the northwest and delineate the north-eastern border along the McMohan line. It was in effect a package deal similar to the one proposed earlier by Zhou Enlai and Deng Xiaoping.

What could be the reasons that the Chinese did not seize the opportunity in August 1990 ? Was it because they too were uncertain about Singh's political longevity, and were not sure if his successors would go along with it ? Or was it that China was reluctant to open negotiations at a time when a conflict between India and Pakistan seemed inevitable ? Or was it that China did not want a settlement to come about through a Chinese acceptance of an Indian offer ? Or was it that Chinese thought that Indian public opinion was not prepared for it. ? Or was it that since the devil is more in details than in the principle, the Chinese did not wish to discuss the alignment as long as they had not reached a detailed accord on the exact alignment?

In any event, whatever may be the reasons a golden opportunity was indeed lost; for had they accepted it, this would have been a major feather in V.P.Singh's diplomacy.

V.P.Singh thus was continuing with traditional Indo-Soviet relations while showing signs of opening up in the direction of Washington and Beijing.

The Gulf Crisis

The other important foreign policy issue that V.P.Singh's Government was faced with was the Gulf crisis.

While the Indian Government's stance was cautious, Singh's personal attitude was pro-Iraqi. From the time he chose to stage a pro-Iraqi demonstration after the Friday prayers in front of New Delhi's Jama Masjid, shortly after the outbreak of the Gulf war, to his announcement, after he left power and at the penultimate day of the war, that he would not celebrate Holi "as a mark of solidarity with the aggrieved brethren in the Gulf" he had consistently took a position that favoured Iraq.[387]

I.K.Gujral and his Foreign Secretary, Muchkund Dubey's position on the Gulf crisis was even more severe. They had apparently sent a communication to all missions indicating that the crisis "was the creation of Western imperialism to control the suppy of crude oil to the world."[388]

However, their sympathies notwithstanding, the globality of the Gulf war, dictated a degree of prudence while in power. Given the geographical proximity and the strategic character of the turbulent area, where oil abounded, which India imported, the Indian Prime Minister was constrained to be discreet. The responsibility of power evidently dictated prudence. Besides, the fate of countless Indians residing in the combat zone,and needing urgent help, sobered V.P.Singh's behaviour while at the helm of affairs.

At first Government adopted a non-committal attitude officially. To avoid displeasing any one among the coalition partners, and among the belligerents involved in the crisis, it avoided taking a clear-cut position. This has been likened "to playing in the centre of the sector field and trying to score goals at both ends." But, with the escalation of the conflict, the government ambitiously decided to do what it could to mediate in the crisis. Though, the Cabinet decided to send three emissaries to Washington, Moscow and Baghdad, Gujral decided to go alone to the three capitals to ascertain the position of those directly involved and to "diffuse the situation"[389] before the whole crisis escalated into a full-scale war.

But there was nothing much he could do. His first visit was to Moscow where he was frankly told by his Soviet counterpart that there was nothing much the they could do in the face of deteriorating and confrontational situation. Moscow was indeed in a weak-kneed situation. Immersed, as it was, in a major and unprecedented political transition, it could hardly defy Washington, as it had often done in the past in the Middle East and in the Persian Gulf area; and it hardly had the power to influence Saddam Hussein.

If the Soviets were paralysed, the Americans, Gujral discovered, were in a belligerent mood. They were determined to act against Saddam Hussein. When queried by the Indian Foreign Minister, in a bilateral encounter with the US Secretary of State, if anything could be done to generate a peaceful solution, he was frankly and brutally told in the negative. Saddam Hussein, James Baker, declared "should be lucky if he could save his neck." The Secretary of State, firmly declared that Saddam had to withdraw unconditionally from Kuwait, and that the US Administration could not possibly allow energy rich areas to be destablised or taken over by potential adversaries.[390] Washinton's position was more than clear.

The Arab world was also in disarray. While the Jordanian King was eager to seek a way out of what was becoming an awkward situation, the Eygptian President, Hosni Mubarak, made it clear to the King that with Washington "breathing down his neck" there was nothing much he could do. The Arab world, he insisted, had to go along with the US.

Saddam Hussein, Gujral discovered, was even more defiant. "Let them come," he declared to Gujral, "they (Americans) will be buried in the sands of the area." [391]

So Indian diplomacy's efforts of seeking a peaceful solution came to naught. And since all the configuration of forces were moving in the direction of war, Gujral sought the second best solution for India: to make arrangements to get the Indians out of the area and persuade the UN and the US to allow Indian food supplies through the blockade for the oncoming food shortage of which the Indians and other South Asians were expected to become the principal victims. The Indian Government moblised everything it could to repatriate almost 200,000 Indians residing in the area—the Indian Red Cross, voluntary agencies, airlines, ships, etc. By no means was it an easy task, since facilities offered by the governments in the area were either non-existent or minimal. What made the task difficult was all the international restrictions the Government had to reckon with, including numerous UN sanctions and restrictions. Worst of all was the closing down of the Indian Embassy in Kuwait, where most of Indians were residing. The electricity and water supply in the Embassy was disconnected, and all the diplomats in Kuwait were informed by the local authorities that diplomatic immunity would be denied to them.

Undoubdtedly, the repatriation of almost 200,000 Indians was a remarkable feat for which, Gujral, on his return, was universally cheered by the Indian Parliament.

The Indian inability to mediate or to defuse the Gulf situation was a reflection of the measure of the dimensional change that had occured in the post-cold war international configuration of forces; also it was symptomatic of how the Indian diplomacy had been transmuted from the earlier years.

Internationally, the US had indeed become the sole global power which no one was willing or able to challenge. Gone indeed were the days when the balance of power between the US and USSR offered possibilities to other intermediary actors to act as a go-between. The international system, during V.P.Singh's time, had thus become asymmetrical with Washington as the sole power centre, and with multipolarism nowhere in sight on the international horizon.

India, furthermore, had come a long way from the Nehruvian years of non-alignment, independent foreign policy, and a real determination to act on macro international issues. By the time V.P. Singh came to power, India had become more and more involved in its own backyard, and lost much of its earlier determination, its prestige, and its interest of being useful to the international system.

THE DECISION MAKING PROCESS

V. P. Singh soon realised, after coming to power, that the inchoate coaltion government he was heading, could not possibly permit him to take any decision on major domestic issues without seeking a consensus with his coalition partners, plus the Left front and the BJP who were not in the government but supported him. The Indian Prime Minister, wrote his principal private secretary, B.G. Deshmukh, was therefore "compelled to adopt a policy of not taking major policy decisions unilaterally but through a policy of consensus."[392] He had thus adopted a system of regular meetings with leaders of the supporting parties before any major decision could be taken and announced. But, all this naturally slowed down the whole process of decision making since the coalition partners had their own views and their own interests which had to be reckoned with. The new industrial policy that the government wished to adopt, for instance, was "discussed ad nauseam not only within the government but with leftists and BJP leaders too" who were supporting the government but only from the outside.[393]

While it may well be that Singh may have also discussed some foreign policy issues with his coalition partners, decision making was smoother, since the level of interest among his coalition partners was either non-existent or was very low.

After more than a decade of centralised, controlled and highly-personalised foreign policy making under the two Gandhis, (Indira and Rajiv) India once again swung in the other direction–the direction of decentralisation, based on the inputs provided by various institutions that had originally been mandated to contribute to the formulation of India's foreign policy.

Once again the change can be attributed, as in the case of Morarji Desai's coalition government, to the lack of any great interest in foreign affairs on the part of V.P.Singh, and to the fact that he was heading a popular but inchoate coalition government "which was supported by both the Left and the Right," and which had no idea of where it wanted to go and what it wanted to do. Those who constituted the government were really a heterogeneous lot who had joined hands principally to forestall the return of Rajiv Gandhi to power.

Singh's personality also did not lend itself to playing an assertive role. Though some have characterised him as "a sycophantic careerist" and " the former courtier of the Gandhis," he was generally perceived as a mild mannered, incorruptible and highly principled person who believed in governance by consensus, and who is known to have delegated authority and respected institutions that had been established. Besides, he had no experience and no idea of foreign affairs, whose entire political career was built in the State of Uttar Pradesh until he was brought to the central government by Rajiv Gandhi.

Under such circumstances, it was hardly possible for the personality factor to operate as a key element in foreign policy making, least of all by V. P. Singh who had become totally involved in domestic matters right from the beginning–in Kashmir, in the Punjab and in Harayana.

It was therefore almost inevitable that the other institutions connected with foreign affairs would re-emerge. The Prime Minister's own Secretariat was cut down to size given the lack of any major interest in foreign affairs. While Singh, in the Cabinet, was "compelled to take major domestic policy decisions « through a process of consensus",[394] it was too hetregenous and too preoccupied in domestic matters to take any interest in foreign affairs. The Parliament was nowhere in sight as an institution to take any interest in foreign affairs, except when dramatic events were looming on the horizon, which was not the case.The MEA was apparently re-asserting itself. With the PMO's cut down to size in terms of power, and Parliament displaying minimal interest, there was really no other institution that could conduct foreign affairs.

The extent of decentralisation in foreign policy can be discerned from the manner in which some of the decisions were taken and executed regarding the Gulf crisis.

The second was India's decision to mediate in the crisis. The Cabinet decided to send three emissaries to Baghdad, Moscow and Washington to ascertain the position of those directly involved, and to mediate, if possible, before the whole crisis escalated into a full-scale war. Finally, Foreign Minister, I.K.Gujral, decided on his own to go to all the three capitals. The Prime Minister was informed of this through a phone call just before Gujral left the country. Such a major decision under Indira Gandhi or Rajiv Gandhi would have been unheard of, and would have resulted in the immediate dismissal of the Foreign Minister. It would seem that during Gujral's visit to Baghdad, Moscow and Washington, most of the decisions were taken on-the-spot without any consultations with the Prime minister. It was not so much due to the authoritarian character of the Foreign Minister as it was due to indifference of the head of the government. The Prime Minister was really not interested, and was willing to leave the whole matter to the wise discretion of the Foreign Minister in whom he apparently had complete confidence.

The third decision pertained to the sending of food and medicines to stranded Indians in Kuwait and their evacuation should it be possible. Once the decision was taken to do something, all the work of negotiating the deal with the UN and the US was left to the MEA. What is, perhaps, even more revealing is that the Foreign Minister apparently himself took the decision at the last minute to personally visit occupied Kuwait, assess the situation and evacuate as many Indians as possible.

The decision making process, thus, had changed considerably. It was decentralised, with most of the routine, visible and macro decisions taken by the MEA to which the Prime Minister invariably gave his stamp of approval.

For the first time in the history of post-independent India, the Foreign Minister and his Ministry was given enough leverage to autonomously take a wide range of foreign policy decisions, so much so that all the main aspects of Indian diplomacy were attributed to the MEA. The Foreign Minister had apparently established a firm control over foreign policy. It was he who designed the so-called Gujral Doctrine of having a even-handed approach towards all the South Asian neighbours, and it was he alone who monitored developments in the Gulf. The Prime Minister was nowhere in sight.

Given the fact that much of India's foreign policy was principally focussed on South Asia, almost all the initiatives towards the neighbours had direct ramifications on India's domestic affairs, it would be difficult to argue that the Indian Prime Minister remained completely on the sidelines. He did not and could not. Clearly, he was active, but given the absence of other institutions, his reliance—and even dependence—on the MEA was indeed very significant.

So if one were to place the Prime Minister's role in foreign affairs within the framework we have established, it could be argued that while on routine and macro international issues, the MEA had acquired a central position, but on such visible issues as South Asia, V.P.Singh did play a role but in close cooperation with the MEA and the foreign minister.

EVALUATION

V.P.Singh remains to this day a controversial personality full of paradoxes. There are indeed many different aspects of his personality that are difficult to explain. He had come to power in unusual circumstances. Notwithstanding his repeated public self-disparagement that he would be a "national disaster" as Prime Minister, and notwithstanding his constant projection as someone uninterested in power, he manouvred all he could to become the Prime Minister. In the words of a close observer, it was "an act of deceit and mendacity the like of which the Central Hall of Parliament had never seen before." [395]

Inspite of his publicly announced renunciatory postures, a broad consensus appeared to exist that he was clearly seeking power. As a close observer has argued, "within three months of saying that he would not take any post, he was the President of Janata Dal, convenor of National Front, and the leader of the front's Parliamentary party, and then the Prime Minister of India." [396]

The other revelatory aspect of his confusing paradoxical personality was his changing attitude towards people he had served politically, particularly Rajiv Gandhi, who had indeed played a decisive role in projecting him on to national politics. While many had characterised him as "sychophantic careerist" and "the former courtier of the Gandhis" (Sanjay Gandhi, Indira Gandhi and Rajiv Gandhi) he did practically everything he could to downgrade Rajiv Gandhi, to openly challenge him, and to manipulate his downfall. Singh had persuaded himself that Rajiv Gandhi was the real guilty one in the so-called Bofors arms deal.

But, there was the other side of the coin regarding his paradoxical personality. He had built an image of himself as someone who was mild mannered, incorruptable, self-effacing and a highly principled person.

Regarding his domestic performance there exist diverse and contradictory evaluations. One observer considered that V.P.Singh had left the "country torn and divided as never before",[397] while the other, more harsh, went even further and wrote that he "managed to destroy Indian society more effectively than any enemy could have dared to hope by putting Indian against Indian." [398]

A more recent evaluation, on the other hand, has made a glowing evaluation of his contribution to India. "A quarter century on," wrote Praful Bidwai, "he not only retains an untarnishished personal reputation, but more important, remains a towering political personality far more important than any former prime minister in India's history, with the exception of Indira Gandhi in the period 1977 to 1980." [399]

On the other hand, his role in foreign affairs was different—perhaps more positive. He declared to this author that his foreign policy "was completely sidetracked by the whole Mandal affair. People do not know all we did in foreign affairs."[400]

The Indian Prime Minister is not far too wrong in making such an evaluation years after his mandate. For much has indeed been written of all the difficulties he had to face and all the intramural problems he was mired in during his brief tenure of 11 months, but his role in international affairs has been completely glossed over during his prime ministership.

Given his brief tenure, compounded with his relative lack of savviness in international affairs, plus his time consuming and weighty involvement in domestic affairs, his overall record in foreign affairs is not that unimpressive. But, the *New York Times,* while evaluating his role in international affairs, considered that he moved quickly in foreign affairs in comparison to his cautiousness in domestic affairs.[401]

V.P. Singh brought back Indian troops from Sri Lanka, concluded a series of agreements with Bangladesh, ended a trade war with Nepal, and persuaded Washington to restrain Pakistan before Indo-Pakistan relations exploded into a conflict. Also, while maintaining an even keel in relations with Moscow and Washington, he did make impressive efforts to seek the Chinese out, and made courageous proposals to solve the border dispute. Also, he took an active interest in multilateral trade negotiations where his previous experience as Commerce Minister must have been useful, not to speak of the role he played in building South-South cooperation in the G-15 summit.

I.K. Gujral, his foreign minister, played a crucial role in making V.P.Singh's record in foreign affairs more dense than many other Prime Ministers.

CHANDRA SHEKHAR

Chapter IX

CHANDRA SHEKHAR
10 NOVEMBER 1990—21 JUNE 1991

Chandra Shekhar became Prime Minister on 10 November 1990. While, denouncing, his predecessor, V.P.Singh, for having stealthily come to power, he followed the same pattern to oust him. The main difference was their supporters. They were different, very different–in fact just the opposite politically. Whereas Singh had built a coalition government with the support of the right-wing *hindutva* BJP, Chandra Shekhar established himself in the seat of high power with the endorsement of Rajiv Gandhi and his left wing secular Congress party. But the new Prime Minister was as weak and as freak as his predecessor, with a caretaker government that was even more short-lived than that of V.P.Singh since it lasted only seven months. His Principal Secretary, B.G.Deshmukh, considered that his determination "to become a prime minister made him cast away his scruples and morality, for it is otherwise difficult to explain why he sought the seat of power with the explicit help of Rajiv Gandhi whom he heartily disliked if not detested"[402] For a person who had never wielded governmental position, and who had spent much of his political life, contemptuously criticising others for doing so, Chandra Shekhar's political behaviour was an attestation of his temptation to appropriate high political power at any cost. It was indeed a sad reflection on the man and his personality—even more so since he knew full well that, under the existing nature of Indian politics, he will not last for more than a few months. But that was unimportant: lasting even for a short while in the seat of summit power was apparently enough for Chandra Shekhar. The obsession for power had also overtaken him, as it had overtaken others, the only difference being that while the others had made no bones of seeking office, he had; for he had devoted much of his poitical career as a rebel contemptuously attacking others for shamelessly seeking power.

Yet, before he became actively involved in the quest of governmental power, Chandra Sekhar was one of the few idealistic radicals who preached the vital importance of socialism in India, who challenged the authority of conservative economic establishment, and who did not hesitate to openly attack those who were in the seat of power. In sum, Chandra Shekhar had built a reputation for himself as one who was a strong proponent of economic and social change. Through his magazine, *Young India*, started in the seventies of the last century, he boldly expressed his views on what was happening in India, and what was wrong with the country. So much so that Jayaprakash Narayan (JP), one of the great votaries of Indian politics, had seriously thought of him as the Prime Minister of the first coalition government. Far more enamoured by him than the old top three leaders of the new party, Morarji Desai, Jagjivan Ram and Charan Singh, he would have liked a younger man to head the new government. With his background of having rebelled against Indira Gandhi, and projected himself as the « Young Turk » Chandra Shekhar seemed a better man for the job. But JP knew that this would raise a storm, and three old men would be at his throat, and that would be the end of the Janata Party.

But, there was the other side of Chandra Shekhar's personality that was negative. He constantly delivered public homilies to the people and the Parliament on the vital importance of morality and honest norms of public life.

But, all this he suddenly dumped when he became the Prime Minister. Principles no longer mattered. And given the evident brevity of his political mandate—of which he was quite aware—he did not seem to care of what people thought of him, or his connections with shady characters. Even before acquiring power, he had, more often than not, not only admitted his dalliances with dubious characters, but even revelled in them. Media headlines regarding his dalliances with con men and shady characters did not seem to bother him. There was the infamous 'godman', Chandraswami, who had been hiding for many months to escape imprisonment, was suddenly stalking the corridors of political power "like a majestic bull in the lanes of Benares."[403] There was also the well-known international arms merchant, Adnan Kashhoggi, with whom he had met socially. And there were many others. Consider Surya Deo Singh, the "chief muscle man of Dhanbad," who, declared the British journalist David Selbourne, "was a millionaire private contractor, a notorious gang leader, trade union boss, alleged murderer and a member of the State's Legislative Assembly, rolled in one."[404] He was known to be close to Chandra Shekhar with whom he often stayed when in Patna.

Even more striking was the high level of corruption that had become rampant at the summit.

Some, who knew him well attributed this type of action to Chandra Shekhar's conviction that money was important in politics, and that he should use his political power to obtain it. To this should be added the important fact that, as his political mandate was limited, he should not bother about what others thought, and continue to act the way he thought was in his interest.

But, there was the other, more positive, side of his character. He was a no-nonsense man with "an enormous potential for governance" that he carried with him when he became Prime Minister.[405] It was indeed generally known that he had convinced himself that he deserved the prime ministership, and that he would have been able to do a better job had he lasted longer.

FOREIGN AFFAIRS

Chandra Shekar's interest in foreign affairs was marginal. Much of his active political life was devoted to domestic affairs; and much of his writings, speeches declarations, etc., were focussed on what was happening in the country, or on the normative goals that he envisioned for India. If one were to closely sift through his editorials in *Young India* the focus clearly was on domestic affairs.[406] Whatever did appear regarding the world was really marginal and dealt generally with broad issues that were the very embodiment of the traditional Indian left-wing perception of the planet—a perception heavily marked by fixed ideological beliefs.

From the very beginning Chandra Shekhar was "opposed to the precepts of the World Bank and the IMF." "Any person," he wrote "conversant with the working of these institutions could have foreseen that the policies advocated by these institutions would ruin the indigenous industry and promote the economic interests of the developed world." [407] The Indian dependence on these institutions, he stressed "have opened the flood gates of interference for foreign powers in our internal and external affairs."[408]

In line with his thinking, he had also openly come out aginst the multinationals and the developed countries "who are out to exploit the resources of the developing countries and earn huge profits." [409]

Chandra Shekhar's broad world view and his socio-political and economic ideology apparently had not outgrown the idealism of his youth. In addition to his post–independence view regarding the broad configuration of international forces based on asymmetrical balance between the rich and the poor nations. One can only presume that, belonging to the Indian Socialist party, as he did, his global perception must have been influenced by the Indian socialism—a thinking that had serious reservations regarding the totalitarian Soviet system, and expressed, at the same time, serious opposition to the capitalist system as embodied by the US. For this is the broad framework to which the Socialist party was hanging on to.

In any event, one thng is certain: Chandra Shekhar had no real experience, and probably no great interest in foreign affairs when he became Prime Minister. In fact, he admitted this in so many terms when reacting to the foreign policy pursued by his predecessor. "I don't know," he said "I can't make any comment at this stage on the policy pursued by the previous government. I have never dealt with diplomacy, nor am I an expert in international affairs."[410] Similarly, the bilateral interaction that this author had with him more or less attested to this opinion before he became Prime Minister. Notwithstanding the fact that the author had spent much of his professional life as professor of international affairs in Geneva, he made no attempt to evoke the subject.

Being in power, as he did, for only six months, compounded with the fact that he hardly had any personal interest in foreign affairs, and that his position as Prime Minister was exceedingly insecure, he could hardly devote himself to international affairs. But, on the other hand, he could hardly ignore them, having acquired the seat of the Prime Minister. In fact, one of his very major acts was in the diplomatic sector, since the fifth summit of SAARC was programmed to be held in November 1990 when he was seeking the vote of confidence for his government. The summit meeting of the seven nation states had to be postponed by a few days so that he could attend. This was Chandra Shekhar's first occasion to meet his other six counterparts; and it was his first opportunity to officially express his views on foreign affairs in Maldives where the meeting was held.

With each of his counterparts, Chandra Shekhar had bilateral meetings: King Jigme Singye Wanchuk of Bhutan, Nawaz Sharif of Pakistan, H.M.Ershad of Bangladesh, K.P. Bhattarai of Nepal, Ding Banda Wyentunga of Sri Lanka, and Gayoom of Maldives. The meetings with each of them must have been instructive to Chandra Shekhar, since he had not met any one of them before. And, given the Prime Minister's tendency to be frank and even blunt, he was probably quite outgoing with his co-members from Pakistan, Bangladesh and Sri Lanka, with whom India had bilateral differences.

At the multilateral level, Chandra Shekhar's speech was well-received. While he may not have had any time to draft it, since his accession to prime ministership had just taken place, it did contain some interesting reflections on regionalism. The speech made a major linkage between intensification of regional cooperation and national development. For he had apparently convinced himself that it was no more possible even for a big country like India to advance itself economically except through economic integration within SAARC. For him it was important to "launch SAARC on a more ambitous path of economic cooperation" through common "production of goods and services and their exchange which really means cooperation in trade, industry, energy, money and finance."[411] For Chandra Shekhar "this new method of functioning" was the "fundamental basis of regional economic cooperation all over the world. Only those regional groupings," he stressed, "have succeeded which have incorporated those areas of cooperation as an integral part of their activity and made progression in them."[412]

This leap into economic integration was something new, for hitherto India expressed little faith in the future of SAARC and in economic integration of the area of which it was not the hegemonial power. Chandra Shekhar also made a number of concrete proposals, including "ministerial consultations" in order to develop common perception "strategy on international economic and environmental issues,"[413] and the extension of regional cooperation in the field of bio-technology and the coordination of common SAARC positions for international fora.

From where did all these ideas emanate? For having devoted much of his political life to nationalistic causes, and much of his rhetoric denouncing powerful international forces for seeking domination of the poorer world, how come that on coming to power he was preaching to his counterparts the vital importance of trans-national regional cooperation? The linkage he had established between national development and regional economic development was indeed unique, for none of his predecessors had gone that far in their different declarations to the SAARC summits.

Can we presume, given the fact that he hardly had the time to draft such a declaration, as he went to Male only a couple of days after accession to power that these were the reflections of his advisers. In most liklihood this was the case, but it is impossible to envision that Chandra Shekhar would have pronounced such a speech without accepting the thoughts it represented. Besides, by making such a declaration, in his capacity as Prime Minister, he was committing the country.

The first instinctive reaction of the new Prime Minister in the sector of foreign policy was to focus on India's neighbours. For, one thing he genuinely believed in it. "I shall like to," he declared on coming to power, "confine myself to neighbours, immediate neighbours." [414] For another, he was literally on his way to Male for the SAARC summit, and could hardly think of anyone else except the neighbours.

NEIGHBOURS

Pakistan

Relations with Pakistan were as difficult as before. They never improved. Pakistan continued to support militants in Punjab and Kashmir–militants who were openly declaring their determination to disengage their areas from India. And notwithstanding the emergence of moderates like Nawaz Sharif, Pakistan was slowly slipping into some form of islamic fundamentalism over which the established leadership had no control. There was some apprehensions within the leadership regarding the fundamentalist direction that the country was taking, but there was nothing much they could do. And, notwithstanding the friendly and complimentary words evoked by the Prime Minister and his Foreign Minister regarding Nawaz Sharif, Kashmir clearly divided the two countries with no real possibility of a satisfactory solution. The Indian Foreign Minister, V.C. Shukla clearly and unequivaocally declared that "Kashmir is not negotiable" since the "ultimate status of Kashmir is a settled question as far as India is concerned."[415]

Additionally, even a more dangerous dimension was emerging. Pakistan was clearly showing signs of going nuclear in the weapons sector. Chandra Shekhar's Foreign Minister, V.C.Shukla, evoked this new development in an interview given to *Indian Express*. "At this time," he delared, "I would say that they (Pakistani leaders) are working towards a new nuclear facility," and made it clear that should it really decide to manufacture nuclear weapons, India will then "consider what to do."[416] In sum, the nuclear race was on.

Nepal

The Himalayan Kingdom, Nepal, also in the midst of political difficulties, was the only neighbouring country with whom Chandra Shekhar developed personal relations before he became the Prime Minister. He had openly associated himself with the ongoing democratic movement and its nationalist leaders. Apparently he was well-known in Nepal, and was invited by the Nepalese opposition to address one of their conventions. This he did; and, according to one of the opposition leaders (Shailaja Acharya, B.P. Koirala's niece) he made "such an impressive and inspiring speech that we made thousands of cassettes and distributed them in every village of Nepal."[417]

So, therefore, when he became the Prime Minister, and went to Nepal on 13 February 1991, he was well-received and given a warm reception—apparently much more cordial than to any other Prime Minister. But, interestingly, notwithstanding the official character of his visit, he proposed to his Nepalese counterpart that there should be no formal agenda for the talks, and that there should be no official communiqué at the end of his visit. This was undoubtedly an unprecedented diplomatic move; but this is how Chandra Shekhar was—an unusual person striving to do unusual things. But, despite his unusual proposal his informal diplomacy was well-planned and well-programmed beneath the informal exterior.

A number of agreements were reached on the key areas of water resources development and of reversing Nepal's traditional and permanent negative balance of trade.

The ongoing positive development of Indo Nepalese relations, inaugurated by V.P.Singh, was thus continued under Chandra Shekhar.

But the traditional Nepalese determination to maintain balance in relations between India and China continued to rattle the two countries even under Chandra Shekhar. While the Indians continued to insist on their « special relationship » with Nepal, a segment of nationalistically oriented Nepalese decision makers continued to harp on their « equidistant relations » between India and China. Some Nepalese observers, attempting to find a solution to this traditional debate, came forward with the concept of « equiproximity, » but this was really not very helpful, since the fundamental debate in Nepal is not so much about finding an appropriate word as about a befitting policy between the nationalists who want greater independence from India by seeking out China, and the pro-Indian segment that argues that Nepal, having myriad cultural, religious and historical ties with their southern neighbour, must remain closer to India. Chandra Shekhar's visit to Nepal did not resolve this basic dilemma.[418]

Sri Lanka

The Sri Lankan political situation continued to deteriorate. After the Indian withdrawal of the armed forces, the civil war was back in full force. The Sri Lankan Vice-Minister of Defence was assassinated on 3 March 1991 along with twenty other Sri Lankans; and in June of the same year retaliatory measures were taken by the Government that resulted in the massacre of civilian Tamils. The worst was the 5,000 troop militant Tamil attack on 9 July on Colombo's army base located on the principal road between Jaffna and the main island. Armed with the new 14.4 mm guns the militant Tamils massively attacked the base. The civil war was once again on with even greater brutality, and with greater substantiation that the well-equipped Tamils were perfectly capable of effectively conducting conventional warfare.

Now that the Indian troops had withdrawn, there was nothing much the Indian Government could do except (a) to push the South Indian Tamil Nadu Government to harass Tamil extremists in the state who were assisting their ethnic counterparts in Sri Lanka; and (b) to continue to proclaim the traditional Indian policy of supporting the territorial integrity of the island while pushing the Colombo Government to devolve regional power to Tamil-held areas in the east. That none of these policies were successfully implemented by the Chandra Shekhar Government is evident from the state of chaotic confusion that dominated the island, and that was rampant in the Southern Tamil Nadu state.

While the New Delhi Government, in keeping with its traditional non-aligned policies, was against any international involvement, there was nothing much it could do to contain it even much less under Chandra Shekhar.

In this connection, it is important to note, Foreign Minister, V.C. Shukla's confusing attitude. While he categorically declared at the parliamentary consultative committee meeting that India will not 'allow' foreign forces from interfering in the civil war, the Chandra Shekhar Government, meekly and weakly, informed the Colombo Government that it would not 'like' foreign troops to interfere on the island.

When the Indian correspondent of the *Indian Express* drew the attention of the Foreign Minister to this confusing contradiction, and invited him to state India's "real position", he received the following answer: "Whether Sri Lanka, wants to have foreign troops or not is entirely upto them. It's going to be their own decision. India is not at all in a position to say what it should have or should not have. No country for that matter is in a position to say this. It is a matter entirely with the Sri Lankan Government."[419]

Clearly the Chandra Shekhar Government was helpless. It neither had the capacity nor the inclination of taking any palpable step in Sri Lanka.

What a clear decline from Indira Gandhi's days, when, in the midst of all the rumours circulating regarding the possible presence of foreign troops on the island, she dispatched her Foreign Minister, Narashima Rao, to Colombo to clearly inform the Government that India would not allow the presence of any foreign troops; and in the face of such a warning the Sri Lankan Government did not do anything.

The other South Asian Nations

Chandra Shekhar did not initiate any innovative policies towards the other three South Asian Nations, Maldives, Bangladesh and Bhutan, There was'nt much to be initiated since the policies in any of the three states had not changed. The Indian Prime Minister had met his counterparts of all the three countries on the occasion of the SAARC summit in Maldives

With the Maldives, India had "no bilateral problem" and much of the interaction between the two countries—in the words of Chandra Shekhar—was limited to "the major projects of mutual cooperation on which there was a complete identity of views."[420]

With Bangladesh, relations were stagnating. They had apparently not moved forward since Gujral's visit. Given the Prime Minister's short-lived mandate they hardly could.

And with Bhutan India's policies continued on the lines inaugurated by the preceding Prime Minister (V.P.Singh) of maintaining firm ties with the Kingdom. In the case of the Himalayan Kingdom, the Indian Foreign Minister made it clear that New Delhi "will not allow Indian territory to be used for militant activities against the Government of friendly Bhutan."[421] Militant activities were rampant in southern Bhutan against the Government.

So, there was nothing new, significant or dramatic in Chandra Shekhar's policies towards South Asia. There hardly could be since the time frame as Prime Minister was too short, and since most of he nations were on the boil, and since the asymmetrical situation between dimensional India and the relatively small countries of South Asia had generated deep traditional distrust which no Indian Government was ever able to overcome

THE WORLD BEYOND

The world beyond was even more problematic. The ongoing configuration of international forces continued to innovate. Though the Soviet Union still had not disappeared during Chandra Shekhar's time its evanescence was looming on the horizon. But, there was'nt much the Indian Government could do regarding its existing relations since it had established weighty interaction with the Soviet Union in all sectors. It could, therefore, hardly move away from the focussed relations the two countries had forged since the mid-fifties. Clearly, it was not in India's interest that its traditional big neighbour slides into a weak position. If anything, it gave "relief assistance" to Moscow so that it could "tidy over the temporary shortages" it was faced with.[422]

With the US, a secular Indian trend had indeed emerged to get closer to Washington, when Morarji Desai was Prime Minister, and had continued under all the successive Prime Ministers, including Chandra Shekhar. In fact, relations had particularly improved after V.P.Singh, who, in great secrecy, had concluded an agreement with Washington permitting US planes to refuel on Indian territory while on their way to Iraq during the Gulf war, and admitting US warships to berth and its personnel to rest on two Indian ports in Mumbai and Goa.

Since this accord had really become operational during Chandra Shekhar's time, who had endorsed the agreement, the traditional non-aligners considered this action as a clear violation of the rules and regulations of India's foreign policy—all the more so because it was implemented by a man like Chandra Shekhar who was not known to have a soft corner for the US.

The Congress Party was one of them. It was optimistically waiting in the wings to take over the administration of the country after the coming general elections from which practically everybody was convinced that Rajiv Gandhi was going to emerge as the truimpant victor. Strange as it may seem, it was Rajiv Gandhi, one of the great architects and votaries of getting closer to the US, who was the principal mainstram critic of Chandra's Shekhar's refueling policy.

But, why did Rajiv Gandhi take this fixed anti-American position after years of diplomatic efforts to seek good relations with Wahington. What happened ? Why this change ? Was he genuinely convinced that Chandra Shekhar was effectively moving away from what was India's basic and correct policy of non-alignment? Or was it that non-alignment was still a source of great electoral attraction, and Rajiv Gandhi had calculated that independent public pronouncements to this effect would add to the certainity of his winning the elections ? Whatever may be the reasons, the fact of the matter is that Rajiv Gandhi decided to withdraw his support from the Chandra Shekhar's Government. Though he did so on the officially stated flimsy and unconvincing ground that the Indian Prime Minister had posted two security agents outside his residence, the real reason apparently was that Rajiv Gandhi had decided to accelerate the general elections on the presumed ground that he would be the victor.

It is important to note that, while supporting Chandra Shekhar from the outside, Rajiv Gandhi began to construct a foreign policy parallel to that of the government. In this connection it is important to note that Rajiv Gandhi had travelled to Moscow and Teheran where he was received as if he was the head of the Indian Government.

GULF WAR

If the Gulf War was looming on the international horizon under V.P.Singh, it blazed forth when Chandra Shekhar came to office. The war was really on with US bombardment of Iraq and with significant ground military intervention in the area.

While Chandra Shekhar did express his regrets at the outbreak of war, and did call upon the belligerents to sue for peace, there was nothing much he could do—nothing palpable. Washington, in cooperation with its European allies, was in the midst of battling with Saddam Hussein's troops.

The USSR was nowhere in sight. As it was in the process of disappearing as a Socialist state there was nothing much it could do. Gorbachev did make some diplomatic noises but it was quite clear that the USSR was on the sidelines with no impactful power.

The non-aligned world, of which Yugoslavia was the chairman at the time, was down in the dumps with no capacity to act, and no power to persuade the belligerents to sue for peace.

Chandra Shekhar openly admitted his helplessness, and loudly expressed his concern of theprospective Indian suffering "because of the dislocation of the supply of petroleum", and because of the unavoidable increase in prices.

But, what really enhanced India's inability to act was its identification with US policy in the Gulf. The Indian Government demanded Iraqi withdrawal from Kuwait, and openly gave its approval for American planes to refuel on Indian territory, and by allowing US warships to call on Indian ports and by according its personnel rest and recreation facilities in Goa and Mumbai.

Chandra Shekhar was fiercely attacked by the Congress Party which had clearly come out against Indian position.

But all this controversies resulted in the outpouring of some reflections from many respectable members of the press and the foreign policy bureaucracy that the time had come for India to re-look at the very basis of its foreign policy in the light of the changing configuration of international forces in the post-cold war era. "It is time," wrote one of the thoughtful journalist (S. Nihal Singh) "India's political leadership got away from the cliches of the past to look the present and future boldly in the face. Thus far there is little attempt to cut through stale rhetoric to debate substantive issues of foreign policy." [423]

DECISION MAKING

It is difficult to trace the decisional process during Chandra Shekhar's six months of prime ministership. The period was indeed too short, and foreign policy not too central to make it possible to objectively assess how decisions were taken. All the established institutions, dealing with foreign affairs, were in place—the MEA and the Prime Minister's Office (PMO)—on which the Prime Minister depended while designing his foreign policy. But there was an additional institution with which he had to reckon with. It was the Congress Party, since Chandra Shekhar's very existence was at stake on the support extended to him to survive as Prime Minister. The Congress Party had its own views on international affairs, and often projected itself as a rival in foreign affairs.

All these triple institutions, therefore, must have impacted on what Chandra Shekhar was planning to do in foreign affairs.

The personalities that embodied the three institutions were V.C.Shukla (Foreign Minister), Muchkund Dubey (Foreign Secretary), B.G.Deshmukh and later S.K.Mishra as the Principal Secretaries in the Prime Minister's Office, and last, but not least, Rajiv Gandhi as the leader of the Congress Party.

Shukla and Dubey presumably were the key advisers with whom Chandra Shekhar had to interact in foreign affairs. Both of them were present at the multilateral SAARC conference that Chandra Shekhar attended, immediately after his nomination as Prime Minister, and it can be presumed that the main contents of his speech and his conversations had the imprint of the Foreign Minister and Foreign Secretary. Similarly, it can be presumed that the decisions regarding the gulf war—the other major issue that he had to reckon with—had the impact of the two personalities.

B.G. Desmukh, and later S.K.Mishra were really the administrators with the designation of the Principal Secretary to the Prime Minister. They were the ones who interacted with the Prime Minister regarding their different meetings, their travels, their files and the appointment of important members of the personnel. In their daily and even hourly interaction with the Prime Minister, they had often to be called upon to express their views on issues and persons.

There was of course Rajiv Gandhi, who as potential Prime Minister, had much to say regarding the government's foreign policy. For Rajiv Gandhi, more often than not, literally initiated parallel foreign policy. During the entire phase of the Gulf war, He acted parallely to the Prime Minister in travelling to other countries (Moscow and Teheran), meeting heads of states and governments, proposing solutions and actively working for peace. This was indeed a new process to which no Prime Minister was exposed to in the past and in the future.

If Chandra Shekhar had to keep close to the foreign policy framework established by institutions and aforementioned personalities, he was apparently much freer in his discussions with his counterparts—discussions in which he was direct, frank, and often brutal as was often his wont. Chandra Shekhar's method of coming to power is comparable to that of Charan Singh. He broke with the V.P.Singh, let it fall, and himself manouvred to become the Prime Minister. Like that of Charan Singh, his government was also a caretaker government since he had only very few supporters and was able to come to power only with Rajiv Gandhi's support (who was waiting in the wings for the right moment to provoke elections).

The element of political uncertainty had become much greater than under his predecessor. No one really knew, not even the Prime Minister, how long the government would last. And, no one really knew, not even the Prime Minister, where India was heading in foreign affairs. While the world was teetering over the edge of crisis in the gulf, most of the members of the government were busy surviving politically. And Chandra Shekar himself was busy defending his Foreign Minister in the court which had disqualified him from continuing as a Member of Parliament, and of ascertaining how long Rajiv Gandhi was going to support him to continue as Prime Minister. The Indian interest in foreign affairs had declined so much that an observer observed: "we have to realise that there is little that we have to teach the world, there is, in any case, nothing the world sees us fit enough to teach it; but there are myriad things the rest of the world has to teach us."[424]

Under such circumstances, it is hardly possible for the head of the Government to take any particular interest in foreign policy, particularly if one were to take into account the fact that his concern for this sector was marginal. It is indeed paradoxical that this should apply to a person who had spent much of his political life fighting for socialist causes. The Cabinet was even less interested, since most of the members were busy playing the game of political survival. The MEA–on which Chandra Shekhar had become dependent—thus continued to play a key role in foreign policy making, as it had done under the preceding government. But it was not alone. A new dimension had indeed emerged, for the first time in Indian politics: that of foreign policy making by Rajiv Gandhi as the Prime Minister-in-waiting, much to the annoyance of the MEA.

If one were to take all the three levels (routine, visible and macro) into which the Prime Minister's role has been divided in this study to understand the decision making angle, the MEA, under Chandra Shekhar gained considerable importance. While having acquired enlarged leeway in routine and macro issues, its input on visible issues had also increased significantly.

EVALUATION

Chandra Shekhar's mandate was too short to permit any serious evaluation of his foreign policy. Besides, he was so heavily involved domestically that he hardly had the time to delve in international affairs, not to speak of the fact that his own interest in what was happening in the world was really not optimal.

There were only three major diplomatic issues he was seized with or had to reckon with: the fifth SAARC summit that he had to participate in Male (Maldives) just a few days after he became Prime Minister, his visit and discussions with his counterparts in Nepal, and the Gulf war.

The only foreign visit he undertook, after the Maldives, was to Nepal—a country he apparently knew well and which he had visited unofficially when the Himalayan Kingdom was in the throes of an embattlement for democratic rule.

Apart from his bilateral meetings with six of his SAARC counterparts nothing of any great importance happened in the multilateral fora. The full weight of his speech was an unusual linkage he had established between regional economic development and national economic development. Perhaps, more than any of his predecessors, he highlighted the importance of regional economic development on India's own economic development. This stress on regionalism and national development may be perceived as a lasting landmark in Indian diplomacy, since it was only thereafter that India began to move in that direction in South Asia and elsewhere.

The outbreak of the Gulf war was also important for Indian diplomacy; for it was this conflict that brought out elements of pro-Americanism in Indian diplomatic behaviour. Signs of such a trend were already visible under some of his predecessors, but it took strikingly a conspicuous turn under V.P.Singh who concluded a secret agreement with the Americans which permitted US planes to refuel in India while on their way to Iraq. If Singh concluded such an agreement, Chandra Shekhar operationalised it in the midst of the Gulf war.

Such a decision divided the informed public opinion. While, the Congress Party came out against this decision on the ground that this was a violation of India's traditional non-alignment, and a clear indication of pro-Americanism in India's new policies. Interestingly enough this position was taken by Rajiv Gandhi, who was, during his prime ministership, one of the main votaries of developing friendly relations with Washington.

The BJP (the second biggest party), viewed, on the other hand, Chandra Shekhar's decision as a logical step in India's foreign policy since India, at the time, was a member of the UN Security which had approved Western policy in the gulf.

In any event this created a national crisis in the country—a crisis which was partially responsible for the downfall of Chandra Skekhar in June 1991. Clearly, this was a landmark development in Indian diplomacy.

Chandra Shekhar's contribution to Indian diplomacy is nothing much to speak about, though it is undeniable that what he did was significant as it was he who really inaugurated the thoughtful linkage between regionalism and national development that was subsequently followed by his successors, and, once again, it was Chandra Shekhar who concretely injected pro-Americanism which too was followed by his successors.

But, what was completely new, which nobody else apparently followed, was his frank, rhetorical and open manner in which he carried out his diplomatic conversations. But, this was more the man than the methodology. For it was indeed a part of his character that embodied these rhetorical characteristics even in the diplomatic sector and even when he was Prime Minister. Whenever he was unavoidably seized with foreign affairs, he was unambiguously blunt and decisive. One may attribute this to his character, or to political reasons; but the fact is that he was decisive. He unambiguously condemned the Iraqi occupation of Kuwait, allowed American planes to over-fly India on their way to the Gulf, threatened Pakistan's Prime Minister, Nawaz Sharif, in his bilateral meeting with him at the SAARC conference, that he would despatch all Indian Muslims to Pakistan, should he threaten Kashmir. Also, when US Congress attacked India because of the death of 200 people on the Kashmir border, he clearly told Vice-President Quayle--who was travelling in India—that as Prime Minister of India he respected the Indian Constitution and did not care what the US thought. Chandra Shekar was also firm when the IMF Vice-President declared to him that his organisation would not give any more money to India; he told him if this was the case he was going to inform the people of India of the threats emanating from the IMF. All this was clearly rhetoric, for which Chandra Shekar was well-known.

Chandra Shekhar will probably be remembered in Indian politics, but not in foreign affairs, which remained a close book all his political life, and was opened only when he had to react in his capacity as Prime Minister.

P . V. NARASIMHA RAO

Chapter X

P. V. NARASIMHA RAO
21 JUNE 1991—16 MAY 1996

Narasimha Rao's emergence as Prime Minister was a pure accident. Nobody expected it–not even him. In fact, even before the general elections were called for, after the defeat of Chandra Shekhar's Government, Rao had decided to retire from politics. This was clearly motivated by the fact that his influence in the Congress Party had declined considerably, so much so that he was not even offered a parliamentary seat to contest the forthcoming elections, considering all the services he had rendered to the Nehru-Gandhi family during his political career. He was assigned to the limbo of oblivion with no hope anymore to return to politics. It is indeed tragic how mentally alert personalities, who have spent all their life dabbling in politics, have been contemptuously discarded as if they have never even existed. While humiliating and downsizing him, Indira Gandhi always saw to it that he was around and available. But Rajiv Gandhi simply ignored him.

Most of his belongings—essentially crates of books–had already been transferred to Warangal in Andhra Pradesh, his home state, where he had decided to retire. He had already bid goodbye to Delhi and to politics, and was on his way home when Rajiv Gandhi was assassinated. Though there were many heavy weights struggling in the wings to succeed Rajiv Gandhi, Sonia Gandhi (wife of Rajiv Gandhi) turned to Rao—a man with a long history of loyalty to the Gandhis–as a possible stop-gap arrangement until the situation cleared up within the party regarding the real successor.

But fate was to decide otherwise. He survived them all–and that even for five years—certainly a beneficial situation for the country, given the fact that the preceding two Prime Ministers (V.P.Singh and Chandra Shekhar) had very short-lived administrations—under whom foreign policy suffered from inertia. In fact, everything suffered, but foreign policy even more so since the absence of diplomatic activity puts the state into a state of oblivion, undoubdtedly a grievous sitatuation for a country which had an active foreign policy.

Rao was a self-effacing, erudite and cultivated man whose knowledge of India was phenomenal, whose command of different languages was endemic, and whose understanding of the outside world was more than substantial. Unlike practically all his predecessors and even his successors he knew foreign affairs. He did not, of course, have Nehru's vision, nor the determination of Indira Gandhi, nor even the earthly charms of Rajiv Gandhi, but he compensated for all this by his knowledge and by his flair for international politics. Some have termed him "as the cleverest Prime Minister of India" (James Manor) while the others have gone further by hailing him as "India's greatest ever Prime Minister." In any event, he was one of those few Prime Ministers who was savvy in international affairs since he had often held posts of Foreign Minister under the Gandhis' even if they did not use him optimally.

Rao had come to the helm of affairs at a difficult moment. The overall political situation did not favour him. He did not have a majority in the Parliament, and had to, therefore, function as a minority head of the Government. His prime ministership depended on others who were politically more powerful. He knew that he could be dethroned any moment. But, most important of all, he was known to be an indecisive person. Temprementally he lacked the capacity of defiance, of firm leadership and of decisiveness—all of which are really crucial instruments when one is projected onto the responsibility of power. On the day he became Prime Minister, one of his senior close acquaintances from his own region walked into his office at his residence to berate him in the presence of a well-known journalist at the lack of his decisiveness all his life, and at the vital importance of his acquiring a new mode of action now that he was the Prime Minister.[425] But all this was not much of a help, for he remained basically what he had always been—an indecisive person. But, he learnt from his journalist friend of a Chinese saying that not to decide was a decision —a formula he often repeated publicly to give it a philosphical respectecability.

While much of all this could be attributed to the fact that he submissively worked for powerful figures who did not wish him to outreach them. One of them (Indira Gandhi) kept him in the shadow, often humiliating him in the presence of others. But, there was nonetheless an inherent atmosphere of indecisiveness that surrounded his personality.

UNEASY ENVIRONMENTS

In addition to all these handicaps, Rao's term of office was heavily dominated by a swath of urgent domestic issues to which he had to devote much of his time and much of his energy. In fact he was heavily bogged down in myriad domestic crises in quick succession (Babri Masjid (Mosque), bank scam, Kashmir, Bombay blasts, sugar scandal, repeated electoral reverses, corruption scandal,etc.), most of which were nationally impactful, so much so that they threatened his political survival.

The economy too could'nt have been in a worst shape. The real catalyst was external. Though India had always lived with a deficit, this had escalated considerably, and by the time Rao took office in 1991 India was on the verge of collapsing. The economy was "running out of time."[426] In fact, it had come very close to defaulting.

The national environment thus was jeopardous. Indeed many had begun to wonder how India could maintain a normal facade in the face of all these growing challenges. And, those who knew Rao personally wondered even more if he was the right man given his known indecisiveness.

As if this was not enough for the new Prime Minister, dramatic international changes had also surfaced whose ramifications on India were unavoidable: the Soviet Union had disappeared. The lengthy period of political uncertainity that Moscow had been subjected to came to an end with Gorbachev out on a limb, and with Boris Yeltsin firmly installed at the helm of Russian affairs. The Soviet Union was no more the Soviet Union, and was no more socialistic—the political and ideological options it had take in 1917. It was one of the greatest events of the twentieth century that had just disappeared, which almost everybody had thought had a great future. The communist countries of Eastern Europe were transiting in an another political direction—the direction of their hitherto political adversaries, the US and the European Union. Equally dramatic was the dismantling of the famous Berlin wall that neatly separated the western from the Communist world.

For India these were flamboyant events. Having established overly privileged relations with Moscow, going back more than four decades, Rao could hardly ignore them, particularly given the important fact that it was still very dependent on the now defunct USSR in all sectors, particularly the arms sector where reliance was most critical And, what made things even worse was that the new emerging Russian leadership, eagerly seeking a new pattern of relations with its hitherto adversaries, had begun to show disquieting signs of conspicuous indifference towards India. Gorbachev was friendly to India, but not Yeltsin. His eyes were elsewhere. The diplomatic strategy he was constructing took him to the Western world.

India's other relations were also on the decline: the interaction with the non-aligned world had become disarrayed, the north-south negotiations had virtually stopped, and the wax and waning Indo-US relations were in a state of flux with Rao apprehensive of how Washington was going to react, now that it was virtually on the top of the world, and was busy reflecting on the post-war configuration of international forces.

Such were the uneasy environments that Rao was faced with both internally and externally.

The immediate Indian reaction in the sector of foreign affairs, paradoxical as it may seem, was to mechanically follow the broad framework established by his predecessors : maintaining an atmosphere of friendliness with Russia, China, US and the non-aligned world.

As is normally India's wont, it initially behaved as if nothing dramatic had happened. But in due course, as was unavoidable, diplomatic innovations began to surface discreetly. The great originality of Rao was the discreet changes he introduced in Indian diplomatic behaviour without anyone really feeling that India was going in a new direction. All the changes to which he subjected India to were done within the general framework of continuity.

FOREIGN POLICY INNOVATIONS

To risk a generalisation, it could be suggested that Rao introduced five changes in India's foreign policy.

The Economic Sector

The first and foremost was in the economic sector. He gave a new turn-around to India's economic policies without announcing rhetorically that it was moving in an another direction. All was being done pragmatically in close cooperation and in close coordination with his finance minister Manmohan Singh. But, he did declare that "we believe that the bulk of the government regulations and controls on economic activity have outlived their utility. They are stifling the innovations of our people. Excessive controls has also bred corruption. Indeed they are coming in the way of achieving our objectives of expanding opportuities, reducing rural-urban disparities and ensuing greater social justice."[427]

During the five years of his mandate he deregulated the economy, loosened state control autarkic system, opened up to the world economically, and encourged private economy to go forward.

In sum, he really inaugurated a process of globalisation in the Indian economy, the important dimension of which, among other things, was to seek out the International Monetary Fund and the World Bank for loans to reverse the unhealthy economic trends India was facing. But for this India had to pay a price—a high price to obtain their imprimatur. "Every money lender," argued Bahaduri and Nayyar, "has his rates and the IMF and the World Bank had theirs."[428] And the price was external intrusion into the economy—an intrusion that India hitherto had stood clear of or kept it to a controllable minimum by an extensive state monpolisation. But, with the inauguration of a new open economy that generated more trade, more foreign investments, and generally enhanced considerable international economic interaction, it was no more possible to effectively exercise nationalistic state control as it had been in the past. Open and free international economic action does generate an asymmetrical system of relations in which the one which is weak and developing—at least in the beginning—finds itself in a detrimental situation—a situation in which economic ramifications are disadvantageous, and in which political power gets diluted. This is the price Rao had to pay for inaugurating new policies.

The other side of the coin is that the disadvantageous situation may be evanescent. It may not last long. For the benefits of having opted for the politics of globalistion, and the deregulation of the economy may catalyse a new process of accelerated growth, and may generate myriad advantages that accompany globalisation.

This is what has happened to the Indian economy more than a decade after the new economic process had been introduced. India has indeed become a rapidly developing economy at the turn of this century with palpably beneficial results to the country as a whole.

But, at the time, the new process was introduced Rao's critics were more concerned and more pre-occupied with short-term disadvantages than what may happen to the country in the long run.

There were parallel political ramifications that accompanied such an economic process—a process under which globalisation generated a whole series of polical and economic pressures with which the country had to reckon with.

While the tradionalists may have condemned the process as a serious transgression of the country's political sovereignty, others may have seen in all of this the emergence of a new process of interaction that is accompanied by new opportunities and unexpected setbacks under which the decision makers are no more completely sovereign as they thought they had been in the past. But this, continues the argument, is relevant for all: the poor and the rich, and the weak and the strong, depending upon the circumstances and their negotiating capacities..

In any event these were the conflicting ramifications that India had to reckon with when Rao became the Prime Minister.

Extrication from Great Power Configurations

The second major foreign policy innovation was the attempt by Rao to extricate India from an excessive involvement with the two great powers— an involvement that had dominated Indian diplomacy under all preceding prime ministerships.

Though Yeltsin, the post-Soviet head of the state, had visited India, and was well received, Indo-Soviet relations were loosing their privileged pre-eminence that had overwhelmed Indian diplomacy for over five decades. It became quite evident, under Rao, that the Indian leadership realised that India could no more rely on Russia for its economic development, its political security, and for diplomatic support on litigious issues that concerned India directly. In sum, the main plank of Indian diplomacy of remaining close to Moscow had to be abandoned—partly because the Soviet Union had ceased to exist, and partly because of the new emerging fact that the post-Soviet leadership acquired other diplomatic interests in the aftermath of the cold war. The new Russian leadership was neither willing nor able to maintain its traditional friendship with India.

Under the new circumstances, Rao was, therefore, eager to seek out the US through friendly signals by calling off the thirteenth test of the surface-to-surface missile, Prithvi, that was scheduled to be held in early May 1994;[429] and by ceding to American pressure to abandon secret plans to conduct a nuclear test; also, in line with its attempt to turn to Washington, Rao refused Iraq's plea to the UN Security Council to partially lift economic sanctions against the country, and endorsed West Asian peace plan not acceptable to the Palestinians, not to speak of the decision to establish diplomatic relations with Israel, and open up to Taiwan.

But none of this had much of an effect on the Clinton Administration, which, like other previous administrations, persisted in the traditional US policy of considering India peripheral to its objectives. While Communist China was given focalised friendly attention, India was kept on the backburner. Rao's visit to Washington in May 1994, therefore, was not much of a success. In fact, it was a failure— a humiliating failure.

In any event this was how it was perceived by the Indian administration, by the informed public opinion, and by the media. In fact, practically everyone in the country. Consider the following editorial in the *Indian Express*—very much emblematic of Indian opinion: "The humiliating televised spectacle of the India Prime Minister· playing the role of a dignatory, waiting as President Clinton answered anxious queries on such subjects as diverse as North Korea, Ho Chi Minh, MFN status, Bosnia, Haiti and health care. Notwithstanding pious homilies about the need for the world's two largest democracies to appreciate each other better it should be painfully apparent that the White House delivered a calculated snub to Narasimha Rao. Apart from stressing that the US does not entertain India's pretentiousness, the White House took care to drive home the truth about New Delhi's insignificance in Washington. No amount of adroit media management and incredible claims that Clinton endorsed Rao's non-proliferation goal in the joint communiqué can detract from the ugly fact that Rao's journey to Washington was at best a momentous non-event and at worst an utter disaster." [430]

Was it the arrogance of power, rendered even more telling, after the truimph in the cold war? Or was it the US inability to appreciate the changing configuration of forces in South Asia in which India was becoming the crucial power? Or was the Clintonian surmise that China was the Asian country to cultivate with; or was it the growing US bridlement in the face of the escalating Indo-Pakistan armed nuclearisation in South Asia.?

Any of these explanations could be valid, or all of them in their cumulativeness justified Clintonian attitude towards India.

In any event whatever may have been the reason or reasons for US indifference to India, the fact of the matter is that disappointment with the US became fairly generalised

On the other hand, relations with China were on the upbeat. Growing evidence was becoming increasingly visible from Bejing regarding the changing Chinese perception of India. While Pakistan continued to remain a friendly option, it was loosing its South Asia exclusivity of the earlier years. While the whole Sino-Indian process of growing understanding was prudently inaugurated earlier in Indira and Rajiv Gandhi's time, real signs of acceleration became visible under Rao. One of the important, though behind-the-scene signs, were the activation of Chinese discreet diplomatic efforts to restrain Pakistan from taking any untoward action against India, whereas in the past Beijing had only rhetorically reacted to events in South Asia. Some of the Chinese personalities with whom this author had informal discussions on the subject went out of their way to highlight the changed Chinese stance.[431]

The Chinese leadership was also becoming apprehensive of the emergence of Islamic fundamentalism and terrorism in Pakistan—an on-going state of affairs which the establishment was unable to contain. There were some signs that the central Chinese leadership was getting increasingly concerned with the growth of a similar phenomenon, plus nationalism, in their own north-western province of Xinjiang. What made the Chinese particularly alarmed were the traces of interaction between the Xinjiang radicals and their Pakistani counterparts. And, compounding to all this was the independence of the four oil-rich Central Asian states where fundamentalism was taking roots, and where Islamic clamour was very much in the air.

The first visible Chinese sign towards India was the official visit of the Chinese Premier, Li Peng, to India in December 1991 (11-16 December). The significance and the importance of this event is all the more striking when one takes into account the fact that the last Chinese prime ministerial visit goes back to 1960 when Zhou En-lai arrived in Delhi in the midst of the escalating Sino-Indian tensions on the border issue.

A number of agreements were reached during the visit. The two countries agreed to reopen their consulates in Shanghai and Bombay, gave their accord to the resumption of border trade, and expressed their mutual satisfaction that peace and tranquility reined on the border. The two Prime Ministers also agreed that differences on the border question should be reduced, and gave their consent to the maintenance of continuous contact in order "to provide direction to the Joint Working Group" to reach an agreement.[432]

Apart from the ritualistic Rao declarations on peaceful coexistence, on human rights, on Chinese arms aid to Pakistan and Myanmar, Li Peng's visit was an important landmark in the ongoing development of Sino-Indian relations.

In his survey of Sino-Indian relations in Parliament, Rao underlined—to the probable satisfaction of the Chinese—the Indian position on Tibet by clearly declaring that Tibet was "an autonomous region of China," and by clearly announcing Indian determination to disallow any anti-Chinese activities by the Tibetans in India.[433]

The ongoing character of Sino-Indian relation has thus been maintained under Rao. And his own visit to China in September 1993, preceded by that of the Indian President in 1992, only further accelerated this interaction. For an important agreement was concluded—an agreement to maintain peace and tranquility on the existing line of control (LAC), to renounce the use of force to make any changes, and to mutually agree that the border issue will be resolved through negotiations.

There were of course myriad litigious issue that separated the two countries, and there was still a lack of trust between the two of them, but there were nonetheless some visible signs of new determination to get closer.

The post-cold war global situation, in which the US had projected itself as the main arbiter of international politics, may also have had something to do with the improvement of Sino-Indian relations. While India and China saw advantages in improving relations with Washington, they had also begun to experience some degree of cumbersomeness in such a relationship.

The level of unreliability in US foreign policy—already legendary—had become even more so in the post-cold war era. The self-awareness of its growing power to unilaterally determine the shape of things to come had exacerbated. And the new Clintonian diplomacy of seeking out China, while containing its expansion, and of ignoring India was perceived by both of them as something outlandish and incomprehensible. Besides, notwithstanding the formal US triumph in the cold war, there were nonetheless signs of the beginning of its slow decline.

The search for some sort of Sino-Indian understanding was thus not only dictated by an imperative desire to place their bilateral relations on a normal course, but was also influenced by the unpredictabliity of US behaviour towards the two growing Asian powers.

India, disencumbered from its Soviet bondage, and encouraged by Clintonian indifference, was tempted by the idea of seeking out Beijing. Rao, it would seem, did give that impression. Consider his speech at Beijing University on 9 September 1993. He did broach the idea of a general India-China strategy. "Now that we have," he declared: "found ways of dealing with our bilateral issues, perhaps the time has come for us to evaluate the new world order that is emerging and evolve a vision and strategy for the benefit of peoples throughout the vast continent of Asia. A general agreement on India-China strategy and approach on a series of issues could be conducive to an Asia resurgence."[434]

In Rao's diplomatic mind-set, China, thus, had become a crucial dimension in India's foreign policy—in fact much more crucial than in the eyes of any other preceding Prime Minister. With Russia down in the dumps, and with Clinton up in the arrogant clouds mafficking America's emergence as the sole superpower, China seemed a potential hope for India. Admittedly, Rao was fully aware of the potential nature of the Chinese threat against which India had to prepare itself, but given the recent smooth development of Sino-Indian relations he took an optimistic view of China with whom, in his eyes, India could reach some strategic understanding, and with whom it could jointly take an economic leap.[435] But, all this required bold strategic initiatives, for which India was not ready, given the troublesome nature of Sino-Indian relations for which India had not forgiven China, and given Rao's own legendary indecisiveness.

China was even less so. Having become a prisoner of its own relations with Pakistan—originally concieved and developed during the Maoist phase—and greatly tempted by the Clintonian friendly signals, it was not ready for India.

In sum, Narasimha Rao was personally ready, but neither was his country, nor was China.

NEW DIRECTIONS

But, Rao was also ready to move in other directions: the direction of Europe, of East Asia and Southeast Asia.

Europe

Europe was the first major continent to which Rao turned to. With the emergence a new and expanding power on the international horizon, he was probably the first Prime Minister to become aware of this major development, and with which a five year "partnership and development agreement" was concluded in December 1993 providing a market access to the "highest possible degree" to the two signatories.[436] The joint political statement, signed simultaneously fixed annual ministerial meetings, and opened the door to a broad political dialogue.

The "partnership" agreement was wide-ranging covering, commercial, economic, touristic, scientific, etc., cooperation with a clear stipulation in Article 1 of the determination of the two parties "to enhance and develop, through dialogue and partnership, the various aspects of cooperation between the Contracting Parties in order to achieve a closer and upgraded relationship."[437]

This was the first time an important agreement was concluded with the EU. For, hitherto, accords were bilateral with other European countries.

The Indian economy attempted to design a new strategy to adapt itself to the requirements of the EU. First of all, it was decided to make the[438] seven traditional Indian products exported to the EU (apparel, leather manufactures, floor coverings, tea, diamonds, cotton fabrics, and pearls, including precious and semi-precious stones) more competitive so that the already etablished markets were not lost to other countries.

To activate this strategy, Indian companies, specialising in these sectors, were encouraged to strike deals with their European counterparts to assure market accessibility. The leather industry is an interesting example. The benefits the EU had accorded to East European countries in this sector catalysed the Punjab, Harayana and Delhi (PHD) Chamber of Commerce and Industry to actively examine leather exports; and it was recommended that India should focus on one EU country that would give style, design and technology to India, and that would, at the same time, take care of India's market accessability in the EU.[439] Since Germany imported 35 per cent of India's leather exports to the EU, the whole Indian strategy in this sector was geared to "seek some trade equation" in Germany that would assist India to consolidate and expand its maket.[440] Similar adaptations were made in the garment instustry; it improved designs and cut costs by inviting designers from EU countries, and by pushing for greater mechanisation of the whole sector.

But, the Rao Government did not focus only on the traditional sectors for which the market had already been established. In its ongoing strategy of seeking markets for other goods, it also attempted to concieve a strategy for other items. In fact, the Export-Import Bank of India warned business men of the possible dangers of quota hurdles in some established sectors since Article 115 of the Rome Treaty permitted the EU countries to impose bans on imports. The report, therefore, recommended that Indian business groups must also consider exporting engineering goods, electronics and computer software in which potential export opportunities were good, and in which India had already made some decisive headway.[441]

Engineering was one of the areas in which India had indeed moved forward. To meet the challenges of the European single market, Indian planners felt that their companies were ideally suited to take on "dirty" industrial products which their European counterparts—under pressure from the ecologistes and the State—preferred to leave to others. The other target in India's strategy was the various engineering components which are expensive to make in Europe. Some Indian companies (Larsen and Toubro, Secalls India, Shivananda Steel and Mukund Iron and Steel) were already involved in this endeavour, while others (Escorts and Telco) were making automobile components for European manufacturers. A related example was the takeover of sectors that companies were intending to vacate. Suzuki motors of Japan, for example, which had spread out in India, was allowing its Indian partner, Maruti, to tap the European maket on its own for small cars.

Another dimension of this strategy was the growing Indian policy of investing in Europe. Tata invested in Portugal. The Pune based boiler and pollution control manufacturer, Thermax Ltd, planned a big push in Europe, by purchasing an undisclosed UK enterprise. The process of Indian economic presence in Europe was accelerated under Rao's mandate with a total of 161 joint ventures already operational while 84 more were in various stages of construction.[442]

This ongoing process has continued to expand after Rao. In fact, much more than what took place under him. India was no more a colonial country receiving foreign aid. Having restructured and burgeoned it economy, with considerable foreign reserves India became not only a net exporter of goods but also capital, spawning a process of industrial takeovers, mergers, etc., in the West.

To accelerate Indo-EU trade interaction a mechanism called, EU-India Parternariat was set up in late 1980s under which bi-annual meetings were organised between EU and small and medium scale enterprises. The Parternariat, for example, conducted about 4,000 pre-arranged business meetings.[443]

The overall results of all this has been that India's exports to the EU had doubled since 1992. From Rs 182 billion it had shot up to Rs 381 billion in 1998-99. But India's import from the EU too went up from Rs 200 billion to 435 billion during the same period thus generating a continuous deficit with which India will have to live with for years to come.

By far the most important programme was the EU Economic Cross Cultural programme, launched on 26 November 1996, that became the foundation of EU programmes in India.

Since the conclusion of the basic Indo-EU agreement in December 1993, Indo-EU interaction thus has come a long way. During Rao's Prime Ministership there were myriad institutionalised interactions between Delhi and Brussels. It would be indeed too long to mention even the most important ones. Suffice it to say that Brussels welcomed the economic reforms initiated by Rao and adopted a firm policy of continuously encouraging India to continue in that direction.

The India-EU foundations established under Rao thus opened a new dimension in India's foreign policy.

And, within the broad EU framework, Germany was viewed as the important component with which India should cultivate. In fact, it had always been considered as the European country worth cultivating with since the formation of the Federal Republic after World War II; but, even more so when Rao came into power who visited the country twice. (September 1991 and May 1993).

Germany was Rao's first visit abroad, as Prime Minister. It was "esssentially a goodwill visit", the main purpose of which was to inaugurate the Festival of India.

The two visits mirrored the importance that Rao attached to Germany. For one thing, having already reached the rank of India's fifth trading partner, it was potentially perceived as possessing considerable promise. Now that India was in the process of loosing its privileged partnership with the defunct Soviet Union, and was apparently not getting anywhere with the US, busily reckoning with its sole superpower status after the cold war, Germany, bilaterally, was considered as a promising hope. Furthermore, the new reunited Germany, located in the heart of Europe, with a population of 80 million was also viewed as an important political dimension in Europe, more so than any other country.

So, from all angles, the Federal Republic became India's diplomatic objective during Rao's prime ministership; even more so since Germany itself was veering around to the idea of seeking strategic partnership with a democratic India. The German Chancellor, Helmut Kohl, in fact had assured Rao, during his September 1991 visit, "that despite the new burdens imposed upon Germany by the process of its unification and developments in Europe, particularly in the Soviet Union, Germany remained fully committed on its development cooperation with India."[444]

A new dimesion had thus spawned India's foreign policy; for until then its multlateralism in international affairs was devoted to politics, whereas with the new economic upsurge it was adapting its policy to new economic multilateralism, the first manifestation of which was Europe.

South-East Asia

The whole vast area between India and China was rapidly developing and integrating itself, with which the Rao Government had to reckon with. The potential was enormous, but so was the competition from China. It is important to note that, though political competition was there, it was really the economic dimension that was becoming crucial.

The second major initiative, therefore, was towards South-East Asia. For long ignored, Rao inaugurated the so-called "look east policy" soon after he became Prime Minister. Myanmar was the first country to which India turned to. In fact it was the first centerpiece of India's policy to establish close physical and economic links with the east. Sandwiched between South and Southeast Asia, Myanmar, lying on the rim of the Bay of Bengal and on India's southeastern trade routes, is a natural land bridge linking the two regions. But the military and the dictatorial character of the regime had isolated the country. None of the established powers were willing to have anything to do with the existing government. Myanmar's increasing engagement with China, which had established an all-weather road from Kunming to Mandalay and which had upgraded its radar and its naval auxilary facilities on the Coco islands, made India apprehensive of the type of relations the military regime was forging with Beijing. Given the military character of the regime, Rao could hardly have envisaged a visit to Yangon its capital. But it was decided by the Rao government to engage the military regime which led to a low level visit of Mayanmar's vice Foreign Minister, U Baswa, in August 1992 (11-13 August).

The Burmese delegations made three points during this visit. First, it said it respected India's commitment to democracy, and hoped that India would be patient about the revival of democracy in Myanmar. Second, Myanmar acknowledged that common security and political concerns existed between the two countries. Myanmar was therefore willing to cooperate with India in taking joint action. The third point, Baswa made was that his country would be willing to increase economic and technological cooperation.[445]

Notwithstanding numerous diplomatic and political pitfalls of forging such ties, India went forward with its discreet bilateral relations. The common issues that concerned the two countries were indeed too important (drug trafficking, identical anti-rebel struggles on the two sides, etc.) to be ignored, not to speak of India's heightened concern about Chinese presence in Myanmar.

But, Rao's first visit abroad to the area was to Thailand, closest ASEAN neighbour—a country which had expressed considerable reserves of developing relations with India. The Thais took their own time to respond to this initiative, but when the Rao visit eventually took place in April 1993 it was a great success. The King received the Prime Minister and gave him an audience for about two hours, a rare gesture. Both countries agreed to expand bilateral linkages, in trade, investments, joint ventures, education, etc. In a symbolic gesture, appreciated by the Thais, was the Indian waiver of visa fees for Thai monks visiting India on pilgrimage.[446]

That the South-East Asian region thereafter was viewed as a crucial diplomatic objective is indicative from the quantum of visits Rao made to the area stretching from Singapore and Malaysia to Thailand and Vietnam. The Indian Prime Minister forged what the leaders of the area called "instant personal chemistry." Be it Singapore's Lee Kuan Yew, or Malaysia's Mathir Mohammad, there was nothing but admiration for him for the way he extricated India out of the 1991 financial crisis to eventually emerge as one of the dynamic economies of Asia and the world.

Rao's visits to the region undoubtedly helped India in breaking down barriers and generating a favourable mind-set. This was indeed important since the decades spanning after independence, India was consensually perceived as a country embodying indifference towards South-East Asia.

What is perhaps even more important than Rao's visits were the rapid development of institutionalised relations with ASEAN. Already during Rao's mandate India became ASEAN's sectorial dialogue partner in January 1992, a full dialogue partner in December 1995, and a member of its regional forum in July 1996, all of which finally resulted in the establishment of viable economic and political relations—in any event more viable than ever before.

While Rao's voluntarist determination to go forward in the area should not be under-estimated, he was also helped by a series of favourable circumstances. The first clearly was political. The disappearance of the USSR, India's privileged partner for many decades, compounded with US post-cold war nonchalance towards India, had left the country isolated from the changing international balance of power. Under the circumstances, Rao had to turn somewhere; and South-East Asia, apart from Europe, apparently was the most attractive proposition.. The second was economic. The Rao decision to globalise and marketise Indian economy also catalysed his look east policy since the whole rapidly developing and integrating area could only be a beneficial to what India was doing in the economic sector. Besides, there was the additional attraction of overseas Indians in the area—Indians who were economically powerful, and who were attracted by the new Indian experiment.

The Chinese strategy of actively going forward in the region may also have contributed to the Indian awareness of reaching out to the South-East Asians. Consider all the difficulties India would have to confront strategically, if China, already installed on its northern flank and on its eastern flank (Myanmar) was also firmly present on its South-Eastern flank. It could render India even more insecure.

The South-East Asian nations were equally willing to reciprocate to India during Rao's mandate. Having got over its earlier perception of India as a country "politically suspect, economically unimportant and at times militarily threatening", it now considered that India provided a "macroeconomic counterpoint" to China in South-East Asia.[447]

Indo-ASEAN relations thus had become an ongoing expanding phenomena. Besides, India was attractive to South-East Asian nations for its long and successful experience in political democracy. They could hardly turn to China which had no democratic experience, and they could hardly turn to the West, whose experience was that of a developed area with a different methodology and with a different cultural approach. India was the real attraction, probably the only viable political model.

The great Indian diplomatic tragedy has been in this sector. Its has hardly ever used this great asset to encourage others to turn to India. And, there is indeed much to learn given the long experience it has in political democracy. But, the Indians have got so used to their system, that they do not seem to consider it as an exportable item.

The Cambodian crisis of the early nineties provided a major opportunity for ASEAN and its member states to observe India more closely and increase interaction with it at the official and political levels. As chair of the International Commission on Cambodia, India played a crucial role in resolving the Cambodian crisis and worked with ASEAN and the West to negotiate the Paris Conference and the treaty that resulted in an international agreement on Cambodia in 1991. This paved the way for a greater UN role in facilitating Cambodia's return to the international arena and its subsequent experiments with democracy. India finally played a leading role in holding and monitoring the first ever democratic elections in the Kingdom in 1993.

Nuclearisation

The third important development pertained to the nuclear sector. Rao was indeed faced with a difficult and troublesome international environment when he became Prime Minister. The defacto strategic alliance with Moscow, that had hitherto guaranteed India's security, was in shambles. The Indo-Soviet link, for long perceived as central to Indian diplomatic behaviour, had become history. And, China, its big adversial neighbour, had gained nuclear superpower status, with implicit US acceptance, thus generating deep Indian resentment that China was taken more seriously than India. Worse were Pakistani pretensions, which had been claiming—unofficially since 1987 and officially since 1992—that it possessed all the components of a nuclear bomb, and the knowhow to assemble one. While Pakistani leaders may have been exaggerating their nuclear prowess in 1987, it was no more the case when Rao come to the helm of affairs; for there was little doubt then that they could assemble a handful of nuclear devices. The Indian resentment was all the more sharp since Pakistan had acquired nuclear weaponry with China's support. And against this horrendous environmental backdrop there stood gigantic America with which India had to reckon with—an America behaving in a paradoxical manner. While apprehensive of China as a potential adversary, it was accepting its growing international status; and while expressing alarm at Pakistan's gowing nuclearisation it was flip-flopping on how to monitor the situation—a situation where Islamic fundamentalism was hovering on the horizon.

And then there was democratic India towards which Washington was designing a policy of restraining it from going nuclear. In this connection, George Bush, President of the US, was pressing India to participate in a meeting between US, Russia, China and Pakistan to contain all armed nuclearisation of South Asia.

In sum, Rao was faced with a dilemmic situation: the US was striving to restrain India from becoming nuclear, the international community was pushing India to sign the Comprehensive Test Ban Treaty (CTBT) so that it could not conduct nuclear tests, while the Indian scientists, eager to continue India's highly secretive ongoing programme of becoming a credible nuclear power were, on the other hand, pleading for the imperativness of conducting tests to modernise India's nuclear arsenal, including miniaturising the nuclear war heads for deployment on ballistic missiles.

In the face of this almost impossible situation, Rao designed a three-fold strategy. While avoiding any head-on confrontation with the US, he devised a variety of diplomatic strategems, in close coordination with his foreign secretary, J.N.Dixit, to resist US pressures. And to foreclose any international pressures to sign the CTBT, that would have compromised India's nuclear programme, he changed India's position on the treaty by now insisting on the inclusion of treaty language that would clearly call for the eradication of all nuclear weapons within a fixed time-frame; and finally he gave, clandestinely, the green light to Indian scentists to come up with a credible programme of nuclear testing as a result of which secret preparations were undertaken to go ahead with the project. The scientists had in fact already dug up an L-shaped hole in the Pokhran desert for the event. And the Ministries of External Affairs and Finance, under instructions from Rao, had estimated the costs of US sanctions that would unavoidably follow. Even the officer in the MEA, specialising in nuclear tests, had already prepared a statement justifying India's decision.

But the unexpected, yet the inevitable happened.. Despite, the so-called Indian secrecy—not much to go by—US satellite pictures began to show the Indian preparations, followed by an article in the *New York Times* that publicily broke the story. As was expected, the US pressures to pre-empt the test became so persistent, including a direct presidential telephone call to the Prime Minister, that Rao, abandoned the whole project. Clearly, Rao had neither the courage nor the determination to defy the US. For Rao, to be sanctioned after the event was one thing; for India could absorb it; but defying the US and going ahead with the project was another matter.

It is still not clear why Rao took the nuclear option, knowing full well that Indian secrecy was porous, and Washington was sitting on India to abandon the plan. Was he hoping that he might be able to make it, US pressures notwithstanding? Or was it an election ploy that were round the corner for which he needed some dramatic action?

What is even more intriguing, and more incomprehensible was the US attitude. Knowing full well that China had gone nuclear, and Pakistan was on its way, Clinton was apparently determined to stop India from going in the same direction fully aware that Sino-Indian asymmetry would leave democratic India eternally weak vis-à-vis China—by no means in US interest.

So far as Pakistan's nuclear option was concerned, US behaved irresponsibly and shortsightedly, for cognizant as it was of what Pakistan was striving at, with Chinese support,it could have used its power to stop it from going any further. It did make a lot of noise, but really did practically nothing, considering the power it had over Pakistan.

While the Indian Government abandoned the project, the internal decision to keep everything ready for conducting a test was nonetheless maintained. Rao informed his successor, Vajpayee, in 1996 to this effect. For, he revealed, after Rao's death, that when he met him to take over the prime ministership, the latter gave him a small piece of paper in which he had written that "the bomb is ready, you can go ahead with it."[448]

Though Rao never conducted the nuclear test, there appears to exist a general consensus of opinion that it was he who had really operationalised the nuclear programme. Vajpayee, who carried out the nuclear test, declared after Rao's death, that it was Rao who was really "the father of the country's nuclear programme."[449]

Israel

The fourth important mutation was regarding the Middle East. Recognising the changing configuration of forces, with the Arab world divided, and with Israel becoming a crucial dimension in the region, Rao took the important decision of formally establishing diplomatic relations with Israel. On the face of it, this may not seem a dramatic diplomatic development, since India had recognised Israel as early as 1950, but none of the preceding Prime Ministers had the courage of taking formal initiative of actually establishing diplomatic relations. The fear of Middle

East retaliation, compounded with the pervasive feeling of oneness with the once colonially dominated down-trodden Arabs, had paralysed Indian decision—making. The original Nehruvian doctrine of solidarity with the Middle East was never cast aside, even though a sense of guilt of lengthily ignoring Israel generated some discreet contacts, the basic policy remained unchanged until Rao came to power.

There were probably a number of factors that contributed to the decision to cross the Rubicon. The first clearly was the final Indian realisation that the world was changing, and one country after the other was establishing relations with Israel, including the Soviets and the Chinese, not to speak of the Eygptians who were perhaps the most vocal adversaries of Israel. Besides, a large number of Palestinians, under the leadership of Arafat, were conducting discreet neogotiations with Yitzak Rabin, the Israeli leader that finally resulted in an agreement. Furthermore, India had begun to see material advantages of developing relations with Israel, particularly in the military sector in which the latter was developing fast.

The most immediate cause, however, was Arafat's visit to Delhi just before Indian recognition. The Palestinian leader, arriving late at night, drove to Rao's residence to urge India to play a more active role beween the Palestinians and Israelis. At this point, Rao is reported to have asked: "How exactly can we do this?" Arafat is said to have responded that India could do this by establishing diplomatic relations with Israel. He then went on to reason that since India was reasonable in its dealings with the PLO and was really a non-player in the area, it would have more leverage in persuading Israel to seek out an understanding with the Palestenians—in any event, reasoned the Palestinian leader, India would have more leverage than Eygpt and Jordan. Rao is reported to have answered: "So shall it be."[450] While all this seems anecdotal in the absence of any official record, the fact that Yasser Arafat met Rao is undeniable.

But, in addition to all this, there is a strategic dimension that should be included in the new Indian decisional process to seek out the Israelis. While the Indian State was officially secular, Indian society was not; it was heavily Hindu-oriented. All the political signs during Rao's mandate—with the raging Ayodhya temple dispute between the Hindus and Muslims—were pointing in the direction of a fairly generalised Hinduist assertion, the most important manifestation of which was the political emergence of BJP (Hinduist political party), whose concern in the sector of foreign policy, at least the ones with whom the author had informal discussions, was the Indian strategic vulnerability on its western flank, with growing Islamic fundamentalism, and on its north and its eastern flanks with firm Chinese presence. Development of relations with Israel would generate some degree of equilibrium on India's western flank. This type of thinking is apparently more generalised and may also have contributed to the growth of Indian consensuaility to seek out Israel.

The Gulf and the Middle East

The fifth big mutation pertained to the Gulf and the Middle East. Though the area was always crucial for Indian interests, it had not been accorded the real diplomatic importance it deserved. All the preceding Prime Ministers, either involved in their political survival, or with their South Asian neighbours, or feverishly engaged with the central balance of power, did not have the time or the interest in designing a coherent policy towards the Gulf and the Middle East.

But the situation had evolved in the nineties. The first Gulf crisis had ended, Saddam Hussein, India's most privileged partner, was weakened considerably, and India had opened the first diplomatic window in the direction of Israel.

Under the circumstances, compounded with India's growing connection with the region, Rao became more active towards the area. For one thing, the growing energy needs were becoming more pressing, and there was no alternative source the country could turn to.

The Importance of the area can be discerned from the fact that most of what India spends there is for importing energy. Ninety per cent of what is spent in the United Arab Emirates is on energy resources, and as much as ninety-eight percent is spent in Saudi Arabia. If one were to add to this the large amount of remittances that India receives from more than half a million Indian workers there, the importance of the area becomes even more evident. Finally, saddled to all this, the new on-going globalisation of Indian economy for which it needs more capital and more markets, the region acquires much greater cruciality than every before.

India, thus, inaugurated the politics of economic diplomacy towards the oil monarchies in the nineies. The third meeting of the Indo-Saudi Joint Commission, held in Delhi in November 1991, was the inception point in this new process. It gave the necessary impetus. On the occasion of this landmark meeting, as many as fifty projects were proposed by the Saudis—projects concerning engineering, plastic, food processing and steel sectors.[451] From their side, the Indians proposed a list of 12 major projects for which they recommended that Saudi Arabia should set aside Rs 2 billion and 500 million.[452]

From this point onwards, the Indian wooing process was activated. Visiting the United Arab Emirates at about the same time as the Saudi visit to India, the Indian Commerce Minister invited them to invest in India.[453] Much more significant, of course, was the state visit to India of the Emirates' President in April 1992. On this occasion three agreements were concluded that abolished double taxation on income and capital, that laid the financial basis for the construction of a modern hospital in India, and that stipulated that the Indo-UAE Commission should meet twice instead of once a year to take stock of expanding bilateral economic transactions.[454]

The Indian Prime Minister himself visited Muscat in June 1993 to discuss joint ventures, including hydrocarbon projects and fertilizer plants in Oman. And even before this visit India signed a memorandum of understanding in March 1993 for a submarine oil pipeline.

By far the most conspicuous prime ministerial visit was to Iran in September 1993—first summit visit to Iran since the islamic revolution, and a vist that was characterised by the Iranian leader, Hashemi Rafsanjani, as " a turning point in bilateral relations."[455]

A major manifestation of this turning point was the Iranian invitation to India to attend the Teheran Conference on Afghanistan in October 1996— an invitation that was extended in spite of Pakistan's strong objection. Pakistan carried out the threat of non-participation, and in 2001, after the "9/11" terrorist attack persuaded the US to sideline India from all consultations on Afghanistan.

Iran was also crucial for India's growing energy demands. Among the many option to import natural gas, the Indo-Iranian overland pipeline option figured as the most effective and economical to address to India's long term demands. But it had to be abandoned, during Rao's time because the pipeline would have to traverse Pakistan territory—an option India refused to accept for fear of the pipeline's disruption in case of a military conflict with Pakistan.[456]

Rao's performance on global issues was thus dramatic. It outshone the diplomatic actions of other Prime Ministers that prceceded him. Palpably it was a solid record.

SOUTH ASIA

But what about his performance in South Asia? Is it as impressive? Did he go far? No, it was not. It was neither outstanding, nor more remarkable, nor even original than the performance of others. There were no major breakthroughs, no remarkable understandings, and no real diminution of tensions and disagreements with none of India's South Asian neighbours.

Pakistan

Rao met his Pakistani counterpart, Nawaz Sharif, seven times, including two hotline interactions, signed a few relatively unimportant confidence building measures (including advance notifications on military exercises), sustained a bilateral dialogue at all levels, and made some meek negotiatory advances on mutual withdrawal of troops from Siachin, and on the demarcation of the Sir Creek boundary.

But, the two countries were as far apart as ever before; in fact even more so since Pakistan was heavily and more actively engaged with Kashmiri and Punjabi dissidents, and was confronted with the ongoing, almost uncontainable expansion of Islamic fundamentalists within the country, the ramifications of which manifested themselves in the increased camouflaged Pakistani activities, and growing terrorist blasts in India.

Rao too was heavily constrained in seeking any diplomatic agreements, by the clamorous emergence of Hindu nationalism, the most dramatic manifestation of which was the destruction of the 16th century mosque in Ayodhya in December 1992, and the resurgence of Hindu-Muslim riots. Though a fervent secularist himself, he could see the dangerous emergence, on the Indian horizon, of Hindu nationalism over which he had no control.

Diplomatically Pakistan was a closed book for Rao, as it had been with all the preceding Prime Ministers.

Sri Lanka,

With Sri Lanka it was even more problematic. It could hardly be otherwise, given the assassination of Rajiv Gandhi perpetrated by the Sri Lankan Tamil extremists. The tragic event was too recent to be obliterated from the memory of the Indian public opinion; even more so since Narashima Rao had come to power to take Gandhi's place, who, everyone thought was going to be the next Prime Minister.

Rao, therefore, could hardly do anything. All the discussions his government had with the Sri Lankan Foreign Minister, Harold Hearth, who came to India in July 1991, was a reiteration of India's policy designed by the preceding Prime Ministers: (a) that the 1987 agreement must continue to remain the viable framework for Indo-Sri Lankan relations; (b) that India must continue, in accordance with the agreement, proclaim its policy of maintaining the territorial integrity of the island while devolving regional powers to the north-eastern regions where Tamils were residing; (c) that appropriate conditions must be created for the two hundred thousand Sri Lankan Tamil refugees, residing in refugee camps in India, to return to their areas on the island, and (d) that the expanding terrorist violence must be contained.

But, the Indian Prime Minister was really in no position to implement this policy, as he no more had any hold on the developments on the island.

Furthermore, the original Indian objective of keeping other powers out of the island was hardly implementable since India neither had any power nor any determination to do so. All sorts of external influences were freely operating in Sri Lanka, with India helplessly watching the events.

Bangladesh

Relations with Bangladesh were no better. They were as stagnant and as disoriented as with other countries of the region. Rao, like the others, did not make any major breakthrough, notwithstanding his bilateral interactions with his counterpart, Begum Khalida Zia, though an agreement had been concluded regarding the distribution of common water resources.

It was not so much the palpable differences that distanced the two countries as an inherent fairly generalised Bangladeshi distrust of their powerful Hindu neighbour—undoubtedly a paradoxical state of affairs since the Bangladeshis were also attracted to India by the commonality of their traditional cultures, including art, history, etc. But, even more so the attraction can be attributed to the innumerable economic opportunities India offered—opportunities that resulted in a significant migration of Bangladeshis to India. This was a principal source of irritation between the two of them. But, there was nothing much they could do, for it was a movement by the population in search of a job.

The migration of Chakma refugees from the Chittagong tracts also generated difficulties for the Dhaka government. The exit to India was perpetrated by the massacres they had been subjected to. Rao's government refused to register them after the Logang massacre of April 1992 (11 April) thus denying them refugeee status.

Rao's bilateral diplomatic performance vis-à-vis South Asian neighbours, thus, was no better than that of his predecessors. It was not so much the absence of any attempt to seek an understanding as the persistent fact of a deep traditional distrust that most of them had of India. The differences were indeed so insurmountable and the underpinnings of distrust so dimensional that nothing seemed possible. It all seemed hopeless. None of the Indian Prime Ministers had found any opening that would have rallied them in the direction of India.

The only hope left was in some form of multilateralism that may push the nations of the subcontinent to dilute some of their bilateral difficulties with India. SAARC was perceived as a possible answer. Rao was one of those who was bullishly looking at the new phenomenon of regional cooperation in other regions, and who perceived SAARC as a possible good and viable addition for South Asia. In any event, he favoured such a process and encouraged its solidification and expansion during his mandate. Consider his speech at SAARC's seventh summit in Dhaka on 10 April 1993 where he called upon other members to "evolve meaningful policy approaches to deal with world-wide trends in regional cooperation, economic groupings and trading blocs" in other regions of the world.[457] Also, he suggested that SAARC should not be "limited to the executive political sphere" but expanded into other sectors like cooperation between presiding officers of the parliaments, in spheres of academy and culture, in science and technology and between academic and the journalistic world.[458] The successful conclusion of the South Asia Preferential Trade Arrangement in April 1993 was the first landmark event in this direction.

DECISION MAKING

Decision making was problematic for Rao: for given his legendary indecisiveness, for whom not taking a decision was a decision, compounded with the continuous uncertainity of his political future as Prime Minister made the task difficult. But this was the case more with domestic affairs since Rao was leading a minority government, and since he was heavily involved in surviving politically by conducting highly controversial acts of manipulations, including bribing members of Parliament to gain their support,

Foreign affairs was, however, different. It was less problematic. The country consensually favoured a serious diplomatic restructuring in the aftermath of Soviet disappearance—India's principal ally for decades. But it should be noted that this was more relevant pertaining to planetary affairs than India's immediate South Asian neighbours—a neighbourhood in regard to whom the Indian public opinion was more fixated, more aggresively opinion oriented, and more prone to percieve them as issues that were equivalent to domestic affairs. The Indian Prime Minister, therefore, was free to apply his diplomatic skills to open up to the world at large, while he had to restrain himself from taking any important action regarding the neighbours.

It is interesting to note that all this resulted in the decentralisation of the decision making process, than its centralisation in the Prime Minister Office, as was often the case wth preceding Prime Ministers. The whole restructuring of foreign policy required the expertise of diverse institutions and the inputs of a number of different people. Foreign policy was thus more balanced than ever before in all the three aspects of foreign policy (routine, macro and visible) with a better symbiosis with all the institutions concerned with foreign policy.

However, notwithstanding this institutionalisation of foreign policy, were there not some individual personalities to whom he turned to, and interacted with on foreign affairs? It is difficult to imagine that decisions could have been confined to Rao alone. For one thing, he was not the type who could monopolise in the matter. For another, having rendered power legitimation to institutions concerned with foreign policy, he could hardly ignore the inputs they offered. Besides, the new directional orientations he was giving to Indian diplomacy Rao really needed appropriate specialised expertise; for diplomacy does not only consist of a broad architectural framework, but requires the detailed data needed for its justification and its legitimation. Rao knew it and tried to make full use of it,

The first most visible personality was his Finance Minister, Manmohan Singh. Though he was not formally dealing wih foreign affairs, but given the increasing globalisation and marketisation of the indian economy, of which he was the real architect, under Rao's direction, he was very much in the decisional picture regarding the economic dimension of international affairs. Rao knew that Manmohan Singh enjoyed the confidence of global financiers—a confidence he knew was vital to sussessfuly implement what his government wanted to undetake in economic reforms. But, before accepting

Rao's invitation, Singh sought formal assurance from the Prime Minister for sustained political support for unpalatable economic measures that he may have to take to effectively turn-around the stagnating and highly regulated Indian economy. Reaching a consensus on the contours of a broad framework is one thing, but effectively operationalising it through a series of palpable policies is another matter since that involved a host of unpopular risks.

Manmohan Singh naturally wanted to assure himself that he would have prime ministerial support. This he did, but, suave politician as he was, Rao made it clear that he may find it necessary to renege when political imperatives required such a step, as was the case with the subsidies.

However, when it came to foreign policy issues, in which economic dimension was important, Manmohan Singh was very much in the decisional picture. Rao had to take into account his views and actions. Consider Manmohan's trip to Japan in the beginning of the mandate, where he went urgently, with Rao's approval, to seek Japanese economic help, and from where he returned empty handed. The Tokyo Government showed no interest; so much so that he was not even received by the Prime Minister.

The urgent and desperate decision to sell Indian gold to extricate Indian economy from foreign exchange bankruptcy was the other matter in which Singh was heavily involved. The UK Government agreed to buy it, but only on the condition that the gold would have to be physically transported to England—an indication of the little trust the British authorities had on India.

All this was in the early stages of Rao's mandate: later when India was in the midst of economic reforms Singh's role became even more crucial in decision making pertaining to international economic affairs.

The other personalities worth noting were his foreign ministers. He had three of them successively. Madhav Singh Solanki was the first, for a year. He was succeeded by Rao himself, also for year, who then appointed Dinesh Singh as his successor for two years only to be succeeded, after his death, by Pranab Mukherjee for the remaining period of the mandate.

Since Rao's experience in Indian diplomacy as Indira and Rajiv Gandhi's Foreign Minister was considerable, and given the fact that he knew, the diplomatic direction he wished to take, his interaction with his Foreign Ministers was limited to the designing of the strategy and appropriate preparations that had to be made to achieve innovative diplomatic goals. This was certainly important, but not comparable to the foreign policy architecture that Rao designed personally.

From what we know of his Foreign Secretary, J.N. Dixit, was more important than his foreign ministers. For one thing, he was known to be a suave diplomat possessing considerable prestige. It is known that his inputs in the decisional process were more valuable and more important than his foreign ministers.

Rao, it should be noted, went beyond his administrative and government entourage while taking decisions. He always claimed that he was the "Prime Minister of consensus"[459] seeking the support and advice from different personalities. For one thing, his minority government made it imperitive that he took into account the opinion of others; for another it was a part of his personality to do so. In this connection,one of the personalities to be singled out was the well-known journalist, Nikhil Chakravarty, who was known to interact with him.[460] There were others: L.K.Advani, Vajpayee, with whom he often discussed his general plans, and, then there was I.K.Gujral with whom he discussed specific issues of foreign policy.

Of all the Prime ministers India had, he was one of the few who was less secretive, less authoritarian and more open in his decision making process.

However, his openess notwithstanding, Rao maintained a firm hold on the three aspects of foreign policy that we are discussing in this study: routine, macro and visible.

EVALUATION

Rao rose to the summit of political leadership purely by accident. Had Rajiv Gandhi not been assassinated, he would have disappeared in the limbo of oblivion in his home state, Andhra Pradesh, where he was in the process of returning to retire from politics. He was called back to take-over the high office. But, only for a brief time since he was consensually perceived as a stop-gap solution pending the emergence of a real leader from the aspirants whe were struggling in the corridors of power to take-over Rajiv Gandhi's place.

So, if accident had projected him to the position of summit power, his intelligent manouvrability kept him in power for as long as six years, much more than the other prime ministers with the exception of Jawaharlal Nehru and Indira Gandhi.

The other characteristic worth mentioning is that Rao rose from the ranks. Slowly, steadily and incrementally he emerged to national politics where he served in different positions, including foreign ministership under Indira and Rajiv Gandhi.

Rao furthermore was a highly cultivated person whose knowledge of India was prodigious, and whose awareness of the outside world was indeed exceptional. He read ceaselessly, absorbed mulitple languages comfortably, wrote continuously, and met regularly myriad global leaders during his mandate as Foreign Minister; in sum, altogether an exceptional person in Indian politics.

Lastly was his personality that showed all the characterics of scepticism and indecisiveness—characteristics just the opposite of firm leadership—and yet the record he has left, and the actions he has taken are indications of firm and lasting leadership.

History will certainly remember him for all he did for India. First of all he inaugurated the process of turning around the Indian economy from a stagnating and a highly regulated system to one that was global, open and market-oriented. This was indeed a revolution, since all the benefits we are witnessing today began under his prime ministership. Even if his Finance Minister was the architect of all the details conceived and all the policies planned, who can deny Rao's original determination to proceed in that direction, for Singh could have hardly done anything without Rao's basic decision to reform India economically.

In the sector of foreign affairs too, Rao took a new direction—a direction unprecedented in the annals of India's foreign policy; a direction that took India away from an excessive involvement with Pakistan and China. While these two neighbours are certainly important for India, there is a big wide world in which India must establish itself. Through forging relations with South-East Asia, with the European Union, and seriously undertaking the nuclear direction—both for peaceful purposes as well in the armed sector—he had taken a new diplomatic direction. It is important to mention that notwithstanding Rao's growing domestic problems, including leading a minority government, and a host of corruption and bribery charges, Rao took India in a new direction both domestically and diplomatically. That he has been evaluated by many " as the best Prime minister" of India is not off the mark. In fact, he was and will be remembered as such. But he ended badly—in fact tragically—given all he had done. "Rao was good," concluded one of his close observer, "till his machine worked, but when it collapsed he was certainly a pathetic sight, dragged from court to court in utter ignominy. For a Prime Minister to lose elections and power is no big deal; even Winston Churchill had suffered a defeat at the height of his achievements. The real tragedy of Rao's political career was the way it ended: he was denied even a ticket by the party he had ruled for five years. Here was a great lesson for those who believe that morality has no place in politics."[461]

ATAL BEHARI VAJPAYEE

Chapter XI

ATAL BEHARI VAJPAYEE
16 MAY 1996—28 MAY 1996

Atal Behari Vajpayee's first mandate as the Prime Minister was too short (13 days) to permit any real evaluation of foreign policy making during his reign. Much of the analysis regarding his formation, perception and foreign policy is made in Chapter XV when he was Prime Minister for more than six years. Suffice it to stay here that as the leader of the shaky coalition government, headed by his party, BJP, he was heavily involved in the nitty- gritty politics of survival. And, this left hardly any time to open larger windows to the outside world, to leave a mark, to test his ideas, to operationalise his vision of India, and to ascertain the place it must occupy in the community of nations.

As indicated in the previous chapter, Narasimha Rao revealed to Vajpayee that preparations to undertake a nuclear test had not been abandoned, notwithstanding his formal retreat under US pressure. "You can go ahead if you like" he told Vajpayee.

Vajpayee decided to take such a step. But, notwithstanding his determination, and even his instructions to the nuclear establishment to go ahead, his government, with a mandate of only thirteen days, could not possibly take such an initiative. Besides, to hide it from the US security authorities, who were closely watching India, needed considerable time to organise the whole action clandestinely.

But his brief stint in the high office indeed left a deep impact on the people—essentially a foretaste of what was to come later when he became Prime Minister for a much longer period. Vajpayee's party had finally put its stamp on power. Everybody who counted in politics became aware that he had the mettle of a Prime Minister, and that he would come back. "Like Milton's Lucifer," wrote one observer, "Mr. Atal Behari Vajpayee has been magnificent in his fall. The man who is being hailed as the once and the future Prime Minister seems to have wooed and won the hearts of the nation, thereby perhaps irreversibly altering the future course of the ongoing epic of Indian democracy."[462]

H.D. DEVA GOWDA

Chapter XII

H.D. DEVA GOWDA
1 JUNE 1996-21 APRIL 1997

The game of prime ministerial musical chairs continued. Atal Behari Vajpayee went and H. D. Deve Gowda surfaced on to the national scene. The heavy weights in the National Front could not decide as to who should be the Prime Minister. There were indeed numerous aspirants. Finally, the coalition partners of the National Front, which had won the elections, and which had unanimously favoured V.P.Singh as their nominee; but as he did not wish to be nominated, , so much so that he physically disappeared in order to avoid any undue pressures—amazing indeed on his part since he had done everything to become prime minister earlier. Power was something he was apparently no more interested, at least at the moment. Jyoti Basu, the Communist leader was the second choice. He was interested, but his party vetoed his nomination. So when at the instigation of Jyoti Basu, H.D. Deve Gowda, the almost unknown regional leader's name surfaced, many were indeed surprised, not excluding Deve Gowda himself, who had spent practically all his political life in Karnataka.

All these were signs of the growing poverty of the Indian system, not so much for having nominated a regional leader, as for their inability to arrive at a consensus to project a viable national leader for prime ministership.

The record of his engrossment in national politics was so minuscule, and the chances of his political survival so uncertain that Indian politics once again entered into a transitional mode bringing in its train all the uncertainities that accompany such a situation. The saving factor, of course, was the enabling governmental environment which had its own rythm and its own functionality that maintained the stability of the the system.

In foreign affairs, Deve Gowda was a total nyophyte. He had no background and no idea of the rapidly changing international configuration of international forces that were determining the international system. In fact, he did not have any idea of the broad architecture of India's foreign policy, how it was designed, what specifically were Indian interests abroad that needed to be safeguarded. But, Deve Gowda was not an exception. Many of the preceding prime ministers fell into the same category of not having any experience or knowledge of international affairs.

Once again India was faced with the spectacle that the architecture of India's foreign policy was constructed elsewhere: by I.K.Gujral,` whose nomination as Foreign Minister had been decided by the coalition partners over which Deve Gowda had no control.

From all indications it would seem that the new Prime Minister had accepted that India's foreign policy would be left in the hands of the Foreign Minister.

POST-COLD WAR CONFIGURATIONS

India had already reconciled itself to the changing global situation in which communism had effectively disappeared from Russia, and by which India was no more preceived as a privileged strategic partner. Boris Yeltsin, the new Russian leader was already looking in the direction of the West, particularly the US. But, he was finally persuaded that, with decades of privileged partnership, it was not in Russia's interest to completely ignore India. Much was indeed at stake. Indians too had the same state of mind.

The Indo-Russian interaction thus acquired a mechanical aspect. Deve Gowda went to Russia, and Yeltsin came to India. The excessive Indian dependence on Russian arms did result in an agreement in December 1994 regarding arms supply upto the year 2000; and joint efforts were made to maintain the trade level of the preceding years with the hope that it would continue to increase.

The new Russian Ambassador, Albert S. Chernyshew, who had been Deputy Minister of External Affairs before he was sent to India, was really not optimistic about the future of Indo-Russian relations. He particularly complained that the "Indian businessmen no longer consider Russia to be dependable and friendly country." [463]

Differences were also emerging in other sectors, the most important of which was the CTBT. While the Russians were orienting themselves in the direction of pushing India to accede to the treaty, the Indian mind-set was clearly moving in the opposite direction—in the direction of not acceding to the treaty. For the Indians this was a clear sign that the Russians were rallying with the West to stem India from going in the nuclear arms sector.

But all this did not sound convincing to the Indians. At the state level they had convinced themselves that while relations would continue to expand, they would hardly ever acquire the privileged interaction they had with Moscow during the Soviet period. Of this they are were convinced at the decision making level.

In any event, notwithstanding Indian pessimism, the Russian Ambassador optimistically highlighted many sectors in which there was a great hope and great scope of political cooperations. It was one of those optimistic statements that Ambassadors have a tendency of making. "We can," he declared, "continue in combating terrorism in the world. Both Moscow and New Delhi must endeavour towards bringing the warring sides in Afghanistan to the negotiating table. There is a need for a joint approach in our relations with countries in South-East Asia. In fact, Russia is very keen in developing triangular relations with New Delhi and Beijing. The same triangular relations can also be developed with individual Central Asian Republics."[464]

Attempts at reaching out to US

With the US, Indian relations did not take the great leap forward. They continued to improve, but at an incremental pace with corporate America coming out in the forefront as a major pressure group to push the American political establishment to avoid creating any economic hurdles against India, particularly the Dan Burton amendment that strove to cap US development aid. Big companies like Hughes, Amoco and McDonnell Douglas wrote to scores of Congressmen in order to further generate American business interest in the face of increasing globalisation and marketisation of the Indian economy. Some like Boeing made references to the upcoming contracts. In its letter to Congressmen, the Seattle-based Boeing company spoke of how India had just bought six 747-400s at a cost of $900 million that was going to sustain 9,000 US jobs. Also it mentioned the possibility of a further sale of twenty-three medium haul Boeing 777s.

Though the US Ambassador, Frank Wisner, showed some scepticism and some concern at some political upheavals with three governments in power in quick succession lasting three weeks, the US business world, carried away by ongoing economic reforms, were looking at India optimistically. It was probably the first time, since the independence of the country, that the US business world was pushing the US political establishment to take a more bullish attitude towards the economic direction that India was taking.

Political difficulties, on the other hand, had persisted between the two countries. India was clearly moving against the CTBT, which, in its perception, was directed against the country since it had specifically decided to continue with its nuclear programme in the armament sector.

Without going into all the details of the treaty, it can be stated that India had linked its accession to a world-wide elimination of nuclear weapons within a specific time frame. By linking the accession to such a treaty with a firm period for world-wide elimination of nuclear weapons by the nuclear powers, India knew that it could go ahead with its own nuclear programme knowing full well that abolition of nuclear weapons was realisticalily not possible.

The US administration's ambition to mediate in Indo-Pakistan disputes also generated difficulties with Washington, since the Indian leaders had taken a firm position against any external interference.

However, notwithstanding political difficulties, Indo-US relations were on the upswing. Though Indo-American economic relations had not developed conspicously in terms of trade, the bullish attitude displayed by US interest groups did contribute to this development, and did help the US political establishment not to be too harsh on the Indians. Hillary Clinton's trip to India, along with her daughter, was an indication of this attitude. "I am," she declared, "very impressed by my trip to India. My daughter and I were overwhelmed by the history and richness of the culture, and the way in which the Indian people have maintained a democray, bringing together citizens of different religions and ethnic and cultural backgrounds." For those who were still not aware of this fact, she noted that India "is the largest democracy in the entire world. So for me, visiting the largest democracy with such a rich and deep history was a personal pleasure." [465]

Sino-Indian Relations

Sino-Indian relations also developed on an even keel during Deve Gowda's time. But the boundary issue continued to lay dormant. It was still impassed. No serious discussions took place on the subject ; and the two parties really made no effort to go forward, though this was the only boundary issue that remained unresolved, as China had already concluded such agreements with Russia, Kazakhstan and Tadjikstan. Given the political uncertainities that surrounded the Deve Gowda's government, the Chinese leadership had probably concluded that this was no time to engage in any serious negotiations. They had probably estimated that the Prime Minister did not have a viable mandate for any such talks. Besides, he had a short mandate of ten months. The whole Chinese strategy appeared to be focussed essentially on non-political issues in the hope that they would generate the appropriate bullish atmosphere for more outstanding political issues.

But there were nonetheless some interesting developments in the military sector between China and Pakistan.. Though China continued to transfer M-11 missiles to Pakistan as an effective deterrent against India's ongoing Prithvi missile programme, it was made clear to the Pakistani leadership that Chinese aid was purely for defensive purposes.[466] The new Chinese stance was a part of a new strategy to go forward with its normalisation process with India, excluding the boundary question for which it wished to await a more appropriate moment when a more stable and lasting government would be on board in India. The one that was installed clearly was not in Chinese eyes..

So in addition to the unavoidable military aid to Pakistan, the principal Chinese focus in South Asia was on the expansion of non-political issues. Bilateral trade was one of them. It reached the high figure of $462 million between January-June 1996, a 15 per cent increase over the 1995 figure. It included Chinese imports of Indian products worth $ 308 million registering a whopping increase of 83.3 per cent over that of 1995 during the same period. "India has been," declared Liang Wentoo, Deputy Director of the division of foreign trade and economic cooperation ministry (MOFTE) "our number-one trading partner in South Asia for two years... and the products of the two giants among developing countries are extremely complementary" [467] with China principally focussing on importing Indian raw material.

The most dramatic development of course was the state visit by Jiang Zemin, the Chinese President. It was the first Chinese presidential visit. It was generally agreed that the purpose of the visit was to expand confidence building and create a congenial atmosphere between the two countries. In this the two countries were successful since four agreements were concluded (confidence building measures, maintenance of Indian consulate in Hong Kong after the Chinese take-over of the island in June 1996, curbing drug trafficking, expanding maritime transport) the most important of which was the accord on confidence building measures. The two countries took an historic step by committing themselves against launching any military attacks on each other, and against any crossing of the line of actual control (LAC). It was also agreed that the two countries would reduce or limit their respective military forces within the mutually agreed geographical zones along the line of actual control.[468] This was an important step, the purpose of which obviously was to decrease any remaining tensions on the border.

But the Sino-Indian talks were difficult during Jiang Zemin's visit—in fact very difficult. In his negotiations with the Chinese Foreign Minister, I.K. Gujral did attempt to persuade the Chinese to accept that Sikkim was a part of India. In his discussions with his counterpart he declared that since India had accepted that Tibet was a part of China, he invited the Chinese Foreign Minister to accept Sikkim as a part of India. But the Chinese declined to do so. While accepting that Sikkim was no longer an issue, and that China accepted the existing "status quo" he declined to make any formal explicit declaration that Sikkim was a part of India.[469] He even suggested that the whole matter be referred to the expert group, which the Indians refused. The issue of military aid to Pakistan was also raised. While the Chinese did not deny giving assistance in the missile and conventional sector, the Chinese Foreign Minister refused to accept the fairly generalised accusation that it was involved in any assistance in the nuclear sector.[470]

In any event, Sino-Indian atmospherics remained congenial, notwithstanding the sharp exchanges between the two foreign ministers on Sikkim. And, as a palpable gesture to improve relations, Deve Gowda and I.K.Gujral decided to go to the airport to see the Chinese President off—an unprecedented protocol gesture since the reception accorded to the visiting dignatories normally took place at the presidential palace.

Increasing involvement in South-East Asia

The "look east" policy, inaugurated by Narasimha Rao, was continued even more actively under Deve Gowda . While the politics of bilateralism with the nations of the region was continued, the new and real focus was on the institutionalization of multilateralism with the region. This can principally be attributed to the fact that India was inducted as a full dialogue partner with ASEAN in December 1995, and in the Asian Reginal Forum (ARF) in July 1996, a body that was designed as a security institution to fill in the vaccum arising from the fact that no all-embracing security framework existed in South-East Asia.

But, India wanted to go further in this process of expanding its Asian partnership by attempting to become a member of the Asia-Pacific Forum

(APEC) and the ASIA-Europe Meetings (ASEM). But this was not possible since there was some opposition , particularly emanating from China and the US, both of whom were important members of these organizations.

While's China's reservations were understandable since it perceived India as a competitor to the advancement of Chinese interests, Washington's opposition did not make any sense. India, on the other hand, did not consider the US as competitor. If anything, it favoured its presence to counteract the growing Chinese presence and influence in the region. Once again, all this highlighted the Clintonian diplomacy of underestimating India, and the importance China had acquired in Washington.

In any event, India's full partnership intereaction with ASEAN has resulted in an average 30 per cent increase in trade since 1990 and rose to 60 per cent by 1994. Compare this with India's relations with other partners. India 's exports grew by 40 per cent to ASEAN whereas its exports with the US grew by 28 per cent, with Japan by 18 per cent, and with the EU by 24 per cent. And India's imports from ASEAN stood at 23 per cent as against 15 per cent from US and 13 per cent from the EU.

South-East Asia, for long ignored by the Nehru-Gandhi era, thus became a crucial factor in Indian diplomacy.

Comprehensive Test Ban Treaty (CTBT)

The CTBT became a crucial issue in India's foreign policy . it had been specifically directed against India to contain its nuclear ambitions, it had acquired a national dimension within the country. Practically everyone was against it, and was generally percieved in the country as an concerted attempt to invade India's sovereignty. The Indian opposition had spread out even among those who did not comprehend the convoluted terms of the treaty. The author cannot think of any macro issue on which mobilisation was so widespread. Deve Gowda's Government had no difficulty of refusing it, notithstanding mounting international pressures, including that of the US President Clinton who had personally written to Deve Gowda imploring him to sign it in the existing form.

The Indian Government was against it. On numerous occasions, the Indian Foreign Minister had publicly declared that India went by "our own perception, and by our own security interest" and could not, therefore, accede to the treaty. The first commitment, he asserted, was to safeguard the country's interest, and there could be no compromise whatsoever. Whatever the reaction to this, he made it clear, that "we will face it."[471]

The Indian Government's opposition to CTBT can be attributed to the important fact that the decision makers had internally decided to go nuclear, and any accession to CTBT would stop the country from proceeding in that direction. The formal India argument against the treaty related to Indian insistence that the existing nuclear powers must agree to a precise time frame for abandoning their own nuclear status, for otherwise the treaty was clearly discriminatory in favour of those who were nuclear powers.

In this connection it is important to note that Deve Gowda played a crucial role in mobilising the opposition to the treaty.

Not long after coming to power, realising the authority he constitutionally had as Prime Minister, and compounded with the heigthened image the Foreign Minister had acquired through his popular diplomatic activities, he apparently decided to personally come forward on popular issues.

While continuing to maintain his oleaginous behaviour vis-a-vis his Foreign Minister, to whom he always addressed as "Sir" Deve Gowda began to show signs of taking greater interest in CTBT.

Apprarently India was not completely unanimous on CTBT. There were some—a minority no doubt— who were for accession, including the Foreign Secretary and some leading members of the Ministry of External Affairs.

In close coordination with his secretary, , the Prime Minister opened a discreet process of exploration and consultation as to what should be India's attitude. This led him to, first of all, seek the opinion of the Secretaries of Energy and Technology, the members of the Indian Atomic Energy Commission, and a host of personalities from the civilian sector. Also, he invited the Indian representative in Geneva, involved in the negotiations internationally, to come to India for consultations. She was, at his recommendation, sent to meet the leading members of the Atomic Energy Commission who gave her a six page report opposing the treaty. The Prime Minister then took a formal decision to refuse any adherence to CTBT—a decision that then became the official position of the Government.

SOUTH ASIA

Nothing of any great significance really took place with most countries of the region—nothing dramatic and out of the ordinary. Benazir Bhutto wrote to the Prime Minister Gowda feliciting him on assuming office on 3 June 1996, and her willingness to hold bilateral talks "aimed at the settlement of core issue of Jammu and Kashmir and other outstanding matters." Gujral answered the next day (4 June) declaring that India was willing to discuss "everything" with Pakistan.[473] A bilateral process was inaugurated under Benazir's successor, Nawaz Sharif, including the resumption of Foreign Secretary-level talks in March 1997, but all this led to nowhere. The levels of distrust and differences were so great that nothing seemed possible.

With Sri Lanka, New Delhi followed the same policy constructed by the Narasimha Rao Government in the aftermath of Rajiv Gandhi's assassination by the radical Tamil Tigers: of seeking out the Colombo Government, and maintaining the ban on Tamil radicals. It was really not possible to pursue any new policy so soon after the assassination. "India will give," declared the Foreign Minister, "all help to the legitimate government of Sri Lanka," which in effect meant that Deve Gowda did not wish to have anything to do with the radical Tigers.[474]

With Nepal the Mahakali River Basin Agreement, signed earlier in February 1996 was still hanging fire since it had not been ratified by the Nepalese Parliament. Besides, serious imbalance in India-Nepalese trade continued to increase, growing at the rate of over 30 percent in favour of India.

So far as Bhutan was concerned India maintained good relations by continuing to abstain from any interference in Bhutan-Nepalese refugee dispute on the ground that it was an internal matter between the two countries. Gujral further improved relations by his official visit to Thimpu on 10 August 1996.

Though a treaty was finally concluded with Bangladesh on the sharing of water resources everything remained disputatious—the original treaty of friendship and cooperation was not renewed, the illegal immigration problem continued to expand, the right to transit facilities through Bangladesh to northeastern India was never accorded, trade never improved, the problem of Chakma refugees in India was never resolved, and Bangladesh distrust of India remained as high as ever.

Bliateral relations with almost none of the South Asian neighbours thus ever took off. Basically they remained as they were before : distrustful and stagnant.

SAARC

The ongoing attempt to accelerate the increasing multilateral interaction among the members of SAARC was continued. But some in India expressed their regret that the process was not fast enough, and was too fragile to become a leading trade bloc in the global system.One of the votaries of such thinking was no less a person than P.A.Sangma, the Speaker of the *Lok Sabha*, who recommended on 8 August 1996 the growing need for intensive action among the people of the region to generate some degree of balance in trade since India was excessively dominant member in trade of 30 billion Rupees of which 3 billion 5 hundred million accounted for imports to India—really a minuscule amount for India.

Gujral was of the same opinion, and attempted to rectify the growing imbalance in India's favour by proposing the so-called « Gujral Doctrine » under which India would no more insist on reciprocal equality of exchanges—in sum proposing unrestricted imports to India from SAARC partners without any reciprocity.

Institutionalisation of the whole idea was by no means enough, given the fact that India's developed and dominant economy had the distinct advantage over the others. It needed a segment of statesmanship on the part of India to effectly operationalise the idea. However, in addition to this idea, Gujral evoked another innovation—that of bringing Myanmar and Afghanistan into SAARC's fold. Undoubdtedly this was a major proposal, since this would have taken SAARC beyond what was generally believed to be South Asia .

DECISION MAKING PROCESS

The decision making on foreign affairs was relatively smooth. Deve Gowda had taken the option of leaving the Foreign Minister and his ministry the responsibility of taking decisions. Apparently he had no other choice since his knowledge of what was happening in the world was rudimentary; besides the coalition partners had attributed this assignment to Gujral whose competence was universally known in the country—at least among those who possessed the expertise.

So the decisional process was relatively straigthforward confined to the Foreign Minister, his Foreign Secretary and the leading personalities of the ministry. But it did not take too long for the Prime Minister to realise that he was the real boss even in the diplomatic sector since his stamp of approval was required before anything could be implemented. This it would seem became a source of action in his political behaviour ; for he was apparently becoming uncomfortable at the fact that Gujral was getting all the public laurels for his diplomatic actions, whereas he was sidelined in the media. "What is this Gujral doctrine and what is this CTBT" he queried his press officer for it had become a source of national and international attraction.[475]

From different sources, it would seem he attempted to discreetly put himself in the forefront in the diplomatic sector.Decisive as he was he began to show palpable signs of projecting himself on international issues. The whole decisional process on CTBT, as we have seen, was taken over by him to decide on whether India should accede to the proposed international treaty. Similarly when the bureaucrats, in a meeting with the Prime Minister, were creating obstacles against accepting the water treaty with Bangladesh, he tilted the balance in favour of the treaty because the Bangladeshi Prime Minister Hasina was a friend of India, he was cautious vis-a-vis the visiting Chinese delegation, led by Jiang Zemin,because they were friends of Pakistan, and had greatly contributed to its nuclearisation, he decisively gave his approval to buy nuclear reactors to maintain India's nuclear option, and, to take another example, he backed anti-Taliban Afghans because the Taliban were fundamentalists.

The Prime Minister was a straightforward person who needed clear and simple answers before he would opt for a decision. And decisive as he was temperamentally, decisions were quick under his mandate. He was not one of these indecisive characters who had to, lengthily and hesitatingly reflect on the Shakespearean axiom of « to be or not to be. »

Having been apparently briefed by his predecessor, Narashima Rao, regarding the advanced preparatory state in nuclear testing, he orally raised the issue with his Foreign Minister, in the presence of his Principal Secretary, . "What do you think Sir," he queried "of conducting a nuclear test?" Though, seemingly a query, the purpose of which may have been to involve the Foreign Minister by pushing him to express an opinion, it apparently made the rounds within the bureaucracy that the Prime Minister was considering a nuclear test.[476] On the other hand, it may well also have been an indirect demonstration of his growing interest in foreign affairs.

Also, he was reported to have requested his Principal Secretary to sound the United States for going to the States.[477] But it was too late, as the end of his mandate was round the corner. But, he did nonetheless conduct a major diplomatic act towards the end of his mandate: he went to the Davos International Forum in Switzerland where he spoke about India to the great interest of the international audience.

So, if one were to apply the triple formula of routine, visible and macro decisions to Gowda's diplomacy, his role, notwithstanding his growing interest, remained essentially marginal in all these sectors.

EVALUATION

The "poor farmer," as he called himself, with a world vision, according to one of his close advisers, that did not go beyond the state of Karnataka, was the first real regional leader, who found himself at the national summit holding the post of the Prime Minister. From all that we know of him he never actively strove for the post, he just got it with no knowledge or experience in national or international affairs, though there are doubtful but nonetheless persistent theories that V.P.Singh may have animated this idea in his head.

It must be stated that it was a unique experience—never occurred before and never repeated after. It was probably one of those accidents that do happen in politics.

The first visible great phenomenon that accompanied his prime ministership was simplicity. He just abandoned much of the glamour that went with such a responsibility—the glamour of a life style, of security and of power. In fact, India never had such an un-glamourous Prime Minister either before or afterwards.

By no means is this a criticism of Deve Gowda. If anything, it is a compliment to him for having downgraded the post that had increasingly become glamourous, powerful and highly lifestylish.

The other characteristic that accompanied Deve Gowda was his decisiveness. By nature, he was one of those who took decisions decisively and promptly once he had been convincingly explained that it was in the national interest of the country. But, the prompt nature of his decisiveness could also be explained by the fact that he was not heavily involved in the rigours of Indian political intrigues that invariably chipped away any firm action.

The third element was the decisional process. Since the broad framework of any political action had to carry the imprimatur of the dominant coalition partners of the Deve Gowda Government, the Prime

Minister decided to leave the decisional process, regarding foreign affairs, in the hands of the Foreign Minister and his Ministry. The Prime Minister, of course, had the last word, for he had to affix his stamp of approval before any operationalisation of the decision. Consider the sharing of water resources with Bangladesh. The Prime Minister apparently was not interested in the fine and complicated points of the treaty, and the long-winded discussions he had with the Foreign Minister, and the drafters did not apparently convince him regarding the validity of the treaty. Only when the simple fact was advanced in the discussion that the Bangladesh Prime Minister was a friend of India did he approve the treaty.[478] Again, when the discussions were held regarding Deve Gowda's visits to Kashmir and the North-Eastern region—both with foreign policy implications—he decided to go to the areas after he was told that none of the Prime Ministers had gone to these territories; again, when informed that acceding to the CTBT would virtually result in the Indian abandonment of its option of going nuclear, he announced his firm opposition to the treaty.

What about foreign affairs? Were there any substantive innovations introduced during his mandate? Not acceding to the CTBT was of course a major diplomatic option, but there was nothing else of any great importance except a rigorous acceleration of partnership with ASEAN, and a rigorous development of SAARC the most important manifestation of which was the "Gujral Doctrine" that abandoned the politics of reciprocity with SAARC members.

Though Deve Gowda abandoned the responsibility of running foreign policy to Gujral and his Ministry, it is interesting to note that, towards the end of his mandate, he began to show conspicuous signs of taking a personal interest in diplomacy. From those who were in know of things, and who were close to him, the glamour of running foreign affairs by Gujral and the publicity that went with it was apparently too much for him, while he remained in the shadow. Signs of displaying interest in foreign affairs therefore had emerged.

In addition to boldly and publicly taking a decision not to accede to CTBT—undoubtedly a popular act—he informally evoked with his Principal Secretary the possibility of going to the US, and suggested that it be raised with the Americans. But, before it could be done, he was out of power.

Going to Davos to attend the international forum, and speaking to a select group of international leaders was probably his last dramatic act in foreign affairs.

It is hardly likely that history will remember him for his performance in international affairs. In fact, one wonders if history will remember him at all in national or international affairs; for his prime ministership was indeed a brief episode in the history of his country during which nothing much of any great importance really happened.

INDER KUMAR GUJRAL

Chapter XIII

INDER KUMAR GUJRAL
21 APRIL 1997—19 MARCH 1998

I.K.Gujral was the next Prime Minister. After Gowda's dethronement, elections would have been the best solution—given the confusion that had set in the country—but no one wanted them, least of all the governing United Front group whose popularity had declined so much that its return to power after the election would have been almost impossible. This the leaders of the coalition partners were well aware of.

So the process of shadow boxing among the heavy weights within the front once again unfolded itself with some of its leaders unashamedly manoeuvring, bargaining and intriguing for the high office. Finally the impassed situation resulted in the emergence of Gujral as the consensus candidate—a candidate who was projected unexpectedly to the highest job in the country. Now it was Gujral's turn to run a confused, distraught and unfocussed government.

Since he was a compromise candidate with no power—not even the power to appoint his own cabinet ministers—the domestic decisional process became more defused, more opaque and even more disjointed. No one knew where the real power resided, and no one had any idea of the nature and the quality of the inputs that went into the decisional process. It was all very confusing. Many did decry the continuous drift of India into a political morass, but those who were at the helm of affairs were too busy, setting up once again the revolving-door-prime ministership arrangement, to hear the admonitory voices.

But unlike his predecessor, Gujral was there on the Indian national scene, even though he was marginally operating at the periphery, and even though he had no real political underpinnings in national politics.

The process of his political visibility spawned accidently with his circumstantial meetings with the Nehru family (Nehru and Indira Gandhi)—meetings that occurred due to his brother, Satish Gujral, who was portraiting Jawaharlal Nehru and Indira Gandhi for which he needed I.K.Gujral's presence as a go-between because of his handicap of deafness.

It was these personal and non-political encounters with the Nehru family, particularly Indira Gandhi, that opened great windows of opportunities of entering politics, first at a lower muncipal level, but finally as one of the close advisers of Indira Gandhi.

To all this should be added his exposure to public life by his family (mother and father) dedicated to politics, to social and to charitable work. The political atmosphere was there as a part of the Gujral household in Jhelum, where he came from, and where he found himself constantly inculcated with ideas floating in his societal environment.

FORMATIVE YEARS

Gujral's formation in international affairs spawned with his association with the Communist Party of India—a party politically controlled and ideologically dominated by Moscow. It had, in the process, acquired a dictated vision of the international system—a vision that gave the party militants a fixed mind-set of looking at countries and events beyond their national frontiers. The author vividly remembers in the mid-forties Gujral's bilateral exposure to him in Lahore of what was happening in Eastern Europe, and what were the broad issues that were underpinning the Greek Civil War.

This dictated vision thus was very much there, and generated an interest in the world, that remained with Gujral all his life—even after he left the Communist Party.

Gujral's Ambassadorship in Moscow gave him an added dimension in international affairs, opening myriad opportunities of watching the world. His Moscow Diary to which the author had free access showed a remarkable understanding that Gujral developed of foreign affairs.

Gujral was also foreign policy adviser and spokesman of the Janata Party, and was assigned the task of drafting the foreign policy manifesto of the party.

If one were to add to all this the important fact that he officiated as Foreign Minister to Prime Ministers V.P.Singh and H.D.Deve Gowda, his knowledge and experience in foreign policy was indeed remarkable—in fact almost unique in the annals of Indian diplomacy. Where would one find, in the panorama of Indian politics, a Prime minister so savvy and so experienced as I.K.Gujral in international affairs.

There was of course Jawaharlal Nehru, the architect of India's foreign policy, who had a broad vision of International affairs, and who constructed normative goals highlighting broad underpinnings of foreign policy, including non-alignment, independence and peaceful coexistence. There was Indira Gandhi, whose savviness of international affairs though restricted, had acquired machiavellian technique of identifying national interests, and working towads their fufillment.

Though Gujral never got upto Nehru and Indira Gandhi's nose in international affairs, his international background was sound and his knowledge was vast.

PERCEPTIONS

Perceptions over time evolve. With greater knowledge and with the changing environment, the world may not look the same as it did before. This happens to all of us in our daily lives, but even more so it happens to men in politics where continuous innovations require constant adaptations.

With Gujral, perceptual change must have been striking. The ups and downs in Moscow, compounded with the growing distortion of the Soviet system had resulted in his alienation from the communist world. And, if one were to add to all this his association with power in the mainstream of Indian politics, his perceptions of the international system must have innovated radically. Furthermore, his ambassadorship in Moscow, combined with the eventual collapse of the Soviet system when he became the foreign minister of V.P.Singh and H.D. Deve Gowda must have generated the realisation in him that while the Soviet Union had been India's privileged partner for decades, it could no more be pivotal to India's foreign policy.

On the other hand, the US, in Gujral's estimation, had become important in India's policies. "To sum up," he declared to the Council of Foreign Relations in New York, "I believe that there exists today, an objective basis on which Indo-US relations can enter a qualitative new phase in the years to come. The revitalised, reinvigorated and strengthened relationship will be moulded, I believe, by three distinctive realities,"[479] the most important of which is "the commonalities that we share—democracy, an open society, rule of law, pluralism and the diginity of the individual."[480]

Changing China too had acquired a positive perception in Gujral's thinking—what with its new process of modernisation, and its movement away from the original Maoist pattern of socialism.

While perceptually the traditional Nehruvian concepts of non-alignment and Bandung type solidarity were still important, in Gujral's thinking the rapid evolution of the international system rendered them less relevant.

On the other hand, Gujral's economic thinking had evolved radically. While in the earlier socialist days his perception of economic development was closely linked with a nation, he slowly moved to the classical economic thinking that the maximisation of economic development was linked with optimal international economic interaction, and with regional economic integration. Gujral increasingly began to re-orient his thinking on revitalising the economic dimension of India's foreign policy since it had "assumed the greatest importance in India's foreign policy."[481]

CONSTRUCTION OF FOREIGN POLICY

Configuration of International Forces

What about his policies in international affairs? Was there an architecture or the contours of one that he developed in foreign policy? Was he one of those who went along with the movement of events reacting to what was emerging, or actively striving towards fixed goals?

Gujral recognised the changing configuration of international forces, and realised the vital necessity of adapting India's foreign policy to the rapidly innovating international environment. While this was already effectuated under preceding Prime Ministers, he was even more convinced that this ongoing process will continue. "It fell to my lot," he declared in his book, *Continuity and Change: India's Foreign Policy*, "to orient our foreign policy during the period of bewilderingly rapid changes wherein one kind of world was ushered out and another kind was ushered in."[482]

The Prime Minister, while maintaining relations with the Russian Federation, with which concrete agreements were concluded by Deve Gowda's Government in the military and nuclear sectors, realised that India could no more maintain privileged interaction with Moscow as it had during the Soviet period. This, in his view had come to an end; and India would have to design a new foreign policy in which the new Russia would no more be a privileged partner.

But, post-Soviet Russia, on the other hand, could not be placed completely on the backburner. For it was there—very much there—gigantic as ever, even though fragmented in size and weakened in clout. Decades of privileged relations with Communist Russia, had indeed established a whole series of relations in military and economic affairs which could not be brutally jettisoned. Who would provide the Indian armed forces all the spare parts that they would need for much of the Soviet weaponry? And who would buy massive amount of Indian consumer goods—not of great quality- for which a market had been established in Russia? So relations had to be maintained even if they were declining.

Relations with Washington, on the other hand, had become important since it had become India's biggest trade partner, and its leading investor. Now that India had globalised and marketised its economy, it had become all the more imperitive that India should forge ties with the most dimensional market economy that existed in the international system—all the more so since China was equally turning to the US.

US enchantment with Pakistan, furthermore, was loosing much of its original lustre—what with the growing instability of the country, and with the growing emergence of Islamic fundamentalism. US monitorisation of Pakistan was of course necessary to contain the expansion of fractious forces, but the country was no more perceived as vital to US interests as it had been during the earlier years.

India, on the other hand, was becoming an important object of US diplomacy—what with its increasing globalisation and marketisation, its potentially gigantic market, and its stable democratic institutions; so much so that the US Congress had passed a resolution on 9 June 1997 urging President Clinton "to cooperate with Gujral in building US-Indian relations,"[483] an unprecedented recommendation that finally resulted in the Indian Prime Minister's trip to Washington. Relations between the two countries then began to move forward with Clinton openly appreciating the "Gujral Doctrine," and with US economic interests conspicuously turning to India. Even, on Kashmir, the US no more appeared to be favouring any innovation to the existing status quo in which, to say the least, India was in a favourable position. The fear of any expansion of Islamic fundamentalism was clearly becoming a dominant concern of US policy makers. Even, notwithstanding Clinton's dramatic trip to China, where he was received with considerable friendliness, powerful American undercurrents favouring India began to surface in Washington to discreetly project India as a possible counterbalance to emerging China. This was probably the first time in US history that India was perceived as a possible attractive factor in Washington's diplomatic thinking—a marked change indeed, given the fact that hitherto India was looked down upon as a poor relation that needed economic help.

With China nothing much happened during Gujral's prime ministership, though it was Gujral as Foreign Minister of V.P.Singh and Deve Gowda who had taken a series of active steps that normalised Sino-Indian relations. Since India had accepted the Chinese argumentation that the two countries should put in place confidence building measures, and should accord priority to non-disputatious issues before dealing with controversial and divisive border issue, the relations were indeed moving forward, particularly in the economic sector where the relations appeared to be promising.

While an even keel interaction was developing, the border issue remained as deadlocked as before, and the Sino-Indian Working Group was not showing any signs of moving forward.

There appeared to exist a fixed Indian opinion that the Chinese were not in any great hurry to really resolve the border issue.

Nuclearisation of India

The maintenence of the nuclear option continued to remain India's policy. There was consensus on the subject among all Prime Ministers, with the exception of Morarji Desai, who attempted to abandon this option, during his mandate, but was firmly overruled by his ministerial colleagues,

Gujral defended the maintenance of this option by refusing to adhere to the CTBT—an adherence that would have prevented India to continue in this direction. In fact, the CTBT had already become a major foreign policy issue when he was Deve Gowda's foreign minister, and continued to remain so under his prime ministership.

The determination not to adhere to the treaty indeed became a massive issue in the Indian public domain; so much so, that it is unlikely that Gujral could have signed the treaty even if the nuclear powers had accepted the fixed Indian time frame that they abandon their nuclear weapons. It had indeed become an expression of nationalism which no one could ignore—least of all a Prime Minister.

· Gujral, therefore, notwithstanding international pressures, continued to refuse to do so. Even when he was on an official visit to the US, he made it amply clear, both publicily and privately, that India would not sign the treaty, as it would jeopardise India's security. In his speech to the Council on Foreign Relations on 23 September 1997 he frankly declared that "we do not wish to be a nuclear weapon state, but in the present circumstances to keep our nuclear option is unavoidable."[484]

The refusal to adhere to the treaty was one thing; but operationalising the nuclear option by actually conducting the test was another matter, since Gujral knew that any attempt on his part to do so would bring him in direct conflict with the US—a situation he wished to avoid, given his political weakness within the country, and given his fear of loosing his prime ministership.

On the other hand, it was evident that conducting a nuclear test would have strengthened his political position, and may have even helped him to maintain the power. But, in any event, neither Deve Gowda nor I.K.Gujral—faced as they were with this dilemma—were prepared to take any risk. The fear of the US imposing sanctions was indeed very palpable, and the adverse ramifications of such a step were perceived as probably horrendous to India in the long run.

But, there could have been another explanation. Though India was very near the stage of conducting a test, the Indian scientists needed some more time, from the point when political decision was taken, to do so. Besides, given the weakness of the government, it would have become impossible to continue to make all the technical preparations while hiding them from the US which had become actively vigilant in India, and which had indeed established a vast, but discreet, network to keep track of Indian actions and Indian activities in the nuclear sector.

SOUTH ASIA

What about India's backyard, its South Asian neighbours? What did Gujral do? How did he act? Did he make an extra effort, and did he really succeed where others had not?

Bilateral Relations

His single most contribution was gaining confidence of his neighbours who had always been suspicious of India in the past. "I fondly remember," wrote Hasina, Bangladesh's Prime minister, to Gujral on 31 January 1999, "all you have done for the development of bilateral relations." But Hasina was not the only one who remembered Gujral's suave, open and friendly bilateral diplomacy in South Asia; there were indeed many others.[485]

Gujral's broad strategy in the area can be roughly divided into three components: (a) the activation of bilateral interaction with neighbours to resolve the fractious issues; (b) the proclamation of the Gujral Doctrine based on non-reciprocity and security, and (c) the acceleration of economic cooperation and integration within the SAARC framework.

Bilateral interaction with South Asian neighbours was his first major inititiative: his first diplomatic move was towards Bhutan where the Foreign Secretary was sent to make a on- the -spot study regarding the north-eastern rebels infiltration into India from the Himalayan Kingdom where they were based and from where they were operating. With Bangladesh, the river water development system was extended through the thirty-year river water treaty, and an agreement was reached for the return of Chakma refugees from the north-eastern parts of India to Bangladesh; and the first interstate transport linkage system was established between Nepal and Bangladesh with the opening of the 61 mile Indian trade route between the two countries. With regard to Sri Lanka the Indian policy of maintaining the territorial integrity of the island was maintained.

But, the most dynamic bilateral interaction was with Pakistan with whom efforts were made to seek some understanding, and arrive at some modus vivendi. Gujral was the first Prime Minister to begin a series of bilateral interactions—a process that was inaugurated at the first summit level meeting in Male in May 1997 between him and his counterpart, Nawaz Sharif, and a process that continues to this day.

First of all the two Prime Ministers reinstated the hotline that was originally established in 1989 by Prime Ministers Benazir Bhutto and Rajiv Gandhi but which was hardly used. Gujral and Nawaz Shariff spoke on the hotline on the eve of revived Foreign Secretary level talks in June 1997 to reaffirm their commitment to the dialogue process. They also used the hotline during the period of particularly severe skirmishes and heavy artillery fire along the Line of Control in Kashmir in October 1997.

The activation of the process of bilateral interaction at the summit level by Gujral and Shariff—both Punjabis—was due to the fact that the two Prime Ministers had developed good bilateral rapport—a rapport underpinned by mutual confidence and trust. Both of them were inclined to seek out solutions, and both of them had arrived at the conclusion that barriers ought to be broken down, and an amiable atmosphere ought to be created between the two countries.

While both of them were on the same wavelength, and notwithstanding the personal goodwill he showed vis-à-vis his counterpart, Nawaz Sharif was more at a disadvantageous position than Gujral; for he represented a weaker and more vulnerable country with clearcut objective of changing the status quo in Jammu and Kashmir—a political restraint or a political obligation that made it difficult for him to freely discuss the non-political sectors.

When Nawaz Sharif, in one of his bilateral interaction, offered to sell electricity to India, Gujral immediately accepted the offer. This could have been a good starting point of expanding non-political interaction. But, this was shot down by the Pakistani Foreign Minister and the Foreign Secretary on the ground that pending the resolution of "other issues", Pakistan could not possibly strike non-political deals. This clearly meant that the Kashmir issue had to be resolved before the two countries could go forward in dealing with non-political issues. Therefore, anything non-political that was discussed (relaxation of visas, tourism, exchange of scholars, etc) invariably faced this political hurdle.

But, nonetheless it was Gujral-Shariff regular bilateral interactions that resulted in the institutionalised establishment of a bureaucratic Indo-Pakistan committee that was mandated to discuss anything under the sun, a level of interaction that continued under his successors. Gujral thus was the real inaugurator of institutionalised Indo-Pakistan interaction.

Gujral Doctrine

The so-called "Gujral Doctrine" was the other foreign policy contribution by Gujral. Originally coined by one of his first advisers, Bhabani Sen Gupta, it was basically a South Asian foreign policy construction, architecturally based on the broad idea (a) of seeking out friendly cordial relations, first of all, with neighbours like Bangladesh, Bhutan, Maldives, Nepal and Sri Lanka with whom India would not insist on any reciprocity in its bilateral relations with each of them, (b) of proposing that no South Asian country should allow its territory to be used against the other country of the region, (c) of prohibiting any interference in the internal affairs of any South Asian country, (d) of respecting "each other's territorial integrity and soverignty, and (e) of "settling their disputes through peaceful bilateral negotiations."

Conceptually the Gujral doctrine was a broad construction of a South Asian framework of India's foreign policy. Nehru, of course, was the first Prime Minister to reflect on a host of transnational constructions to rally the third world, the most important of which were the five principles of peaceful coexistence. All constructions of such a nature are simple. Nehru's too was simple and straigthforward. But the real originality in Gujral's proposal was the fact that one of the proposals embodied in his doctrine was the concessions that India, the largest of them all, would have to make without asking for anything in return. Gujral thus was the first Prime Minister who made an analogous construction of a South Asian framework that would bring most of the South Asian countries together.

If India were to sit together with Nepal, Bhutan, Sri Lanka, Bangladesh and Maldives in order to see to it that the five principles are accepted, it would be a good basis for establishing a lasting South Asian cooperation.

Because of the pecularity of Indo-Pakistan relations, Pakistan was kept out by Gujral, but, at some stage, it too, in his thinking, would have to be brought into the picture if a sound and a generalised basis had to be established in South Asia.

Bilateral Economic Cooperation

The third component was the acceleration of economic cooperation and economic integration of South Asia within the framework of SAARC. With India's increasing globalisation and marketisation, practically all the decision makers—including Gujral—have become firm proponents of accelerating economic cooperation. For one thing it is based on the broad conviction that economies of these countries are more complementary than competitive, and there is therefore a potentiality of greater economic interaction. For another, increased economic interaction would eventually result in the emergence of keenness of member states to resolve their political differences. The ultimate objective in the mind of Gujral was to eventually establish a real, viable, interactive SAARC. In fact, he appears to have gone further by favouring the expansion of SAARC through the inclusion of additional members like Afghanistan and Myanmar. On numerous occasions the Indian Prime Minister underlined the fact that revitalisation of the economic dimension of India's foreign policy had indeed "assumed the greatest importance in India's foreign policy."

Gujral had, furthermore, evoked that SAARC must not become only a customs union with the dismantlement of tariffs and non-tariff barriers, but must eventually transform itself into a South Asian Economic Community. In his declaration of 12 May 1997 at the ninth SAARC summit he proposed that the Commerce Ministers and the SAARC Committee on Economic

Cooperation should be entrusted with the task of "deciding on modalities for realising this goal."[486]

"The Ninth Summit here in Male, " Gujral concluded, "can become a landmark in our journey into the future by deciding on a holistic vision for our region for the year 2020, and in directing that the stages and the strategies for it be elaborated. 2020 has become a symbolic as well as a specific destination, representing both perfect vision and a target year. Let us too, spell out such a vision to inspire and guide us, aware that what we achieve transforms not only our region, but in good measure, changes the world as well."[487]

By the time Gujral became the Prime Minister, India, thus, had come a long way towards South Asian cooperation. From the initial hesitation to any such cooperation, when SAARC was established to proposing the establishment of a South Asian Economic Community was indeed a major landmark in Indian diplomacy.

It is, of course true, that any construction of a viable economic community between dimensional India and small South Asian neighbours would be problematic given the asymmetrical situation. The variability in size and resources among members can thwart the success of such an experiment. India, therefore, would have to make a great number of concessions—more than the Gujral doctrine– for its real accomplishment. Would it have the capacity and the willingness to do so remains a difficult and problematic issue.

Relations with other Asian Countries

In its ongoing efforts to expand its economic interaction with with other Asian countries Gujral's foreign policy attempted to institutionalise its relations with other multilateral bodies. First of all it was directed at ASEAN. After having acquired "full dialogue partnership" with ASEAN in 1996 when Gujral was Foreign Minister under Deve Gowda, an ASEAN-India Joint Cooperation Committee was established in November 1996 to specially focus on building relations between ASEAN and India. In fact, it has become the core of ASEAN-India dialogue mechanisms.

India also became a founding member of the Indian Ocean Rim Association for Regional Cooperation (IOR-ARC) which had originally seven members (Australia, India, Kenya, Mauritius, Oman, Singapore and South Africa) but which had expanded considerably. The Charter provides for a Council of Ministers and Committee of Senior Officials– assisted by a

Business forum and an academic group—whose purpose would be to steer and coordinate the activities of the organisation.

In his attempt to go even further, Gujral proposed that India be accepted as a member of the larger Asia-Pacific Forum (APEC) and the Asia Europe Meeting (ASEM)—two large Asian bodies of which a number of non-Asean countries were also members. But this did not go through since neither the US nor China were prepared to accept Indian membership.

DECISION MAKING

The Indian decision making process, during Gujral's time, relied heavily on the leading elements of Indian bureaucracy on foreign affairs. Though there were certainly others, Salman Haidar and Muchkund Dubey, were the two Foreign Secretaries on whom he relied a great deal when taking decisions on foreign affairs. Because of his own savviness and experience in international affairs, he was not really constrained by his coalition partners of his own government. This may be explained by a number of factors: the first was the real absence of any controversial diplomatic issue, during his mandate, that could have divided the country, and thus restrained the Prime Minister from taking any decision. There was not any. What did exist—like CTBT—were the ones in which his views corresponded with those of the Indian public opinion.

In Gujral's estimation, furthermore, the coalition character of his government made it, if anything, easier for decision making in foreign affairs to operate smoothly and rapidly. Since there was nothing dramatic in Indian diplomacy that divided the country, members of his government had the tendency to focus on internal matters, leaving the decision making and the operationalisation of foreign policy in the hands of the Foreign Minister.

To make decision making smooth in foreign affairs, Gujral adopted the policy of informally discussing foreign affairs with the members of the opposition to seek a consensus on international affairs. He also adopted the politics of nominating opposition leaders to be members of the Indian delegations that were sent abroad to participate in international conferences.

The decisional process in foreign policy making, under Gujral, was thus neither conflictual nor too centralised. He used all the inputs that emanated from different institutions before taking decisions, with the PMO and MEA working in good harmony.

The three aspects of India's foreign policy—routine, visible and macro—remained in his hands. He delegated authority, and largely invited comments but the final voice was his own. He was the real decision maker in foreign policy.

EVALUATION

I.K.Gujral was one of the few Prime Ministers who had acquired an interest in international affairs during his early years. Long before entering the mainstream of national politics, after the independence of the country, he kept himself abreast with the world beyond the borders of India. To do this in a provincial town like Lahore, during his university years, was a great achievement.

While some may attribute this awakening to a natural intellectual interest he may have had in the world at large, the more credible reason was his close association with the Communist Party of India; for it was the only political party which had gleaned an international commitment and an international orientation—an orientation that was inspired by its complete domination by the Communist Party of the Soviet Union; especially in a town like non-industrial Lahore where the party was essentially composed of middle class intellectuals with a global mind-set. Nationalism, directed against the British was of course there, but so was the Soviet Union with its international environment, and with its exigent requirement of total communist fidelity to the Soviet Union.

Living in Lahore as a young adoloscent, the author vividly remembers Gujral's explanations regarding the communisation of Eastern Europe, and particularly the Greek Civil War that was slowly expanding itself into an anchor issue in early post-war Europe.

Even after Gujral had parted company with the Communists in the early fifties of the twentieth century, he apparently not only continued his interest in global developments, but found himself practically involved in international affairs as Indian Ambassador to Moscow, as the foreign policy spokesman of, Janata Dal, his political party, and as Foreign Minister of Prime Ministers V.P. Singh and H.D. Deve Gowda.

Diplomacy is not only knowledge: it has much to do with savviness, style, openness, negotiatory intrigues, and with a remarkable capacity of locating national interests, including a flexibility of readily discarding old sibboleths for new ones. Gujral had all of it, so much so that he emerged as the fulcrum of India's foreign policy. Even those who wrote harsh words regarding his performance as Prime Minister recognised him as someone possessing an image of "suave, sophisticated and principled politician" in international affairs.[488]

If one were to take his entire diplomatic mandate, including foreign ministership of V.P.Singh and H.D.Deve Gowda, are there any acts, initiatives, policies for which history will sit up and recognise him?

Gujral was indeed faced with the changed global setting, after the end of the cold war, to which he had to adapt Indian diplomacy. The Soviet Union, India's privileged partner, had collapsed, and the US emerged as the sole major power in international affairs as trusting no one, and arrogantly projecting its new status; and then there was new post-Maoist China emerging on the international horizon, fully determined to become impactful. Gujral had the heavy responsibility of adapting Indian diplomacy to the new international environment.

Compounded to this dramatic development was the growing Indian economic power, universally recognised as the new emerging phenomenon of the international system—a phenomenon for which India had to wear a new garb, and had to adopt a new type of political behaviour.

The third major international environment that Gujral had to reckon with was the phenomenon of regional integration at the global level. Nationalism—at least at the economic level—was being replaced by more trade, more transnational investment, and greater international consensuality; it was no more possible to develop within the confines of national borders.

And nearer home, the Prime Minister was faced with expanding terrorism, growing Islamic fundamentalism, and increasing distrust of dimensional India.

Gujral naturally did not have the time to face all this, bogged down as he was with the anxieties of political survival. Besides, all these environmental developments had showed signs of already emerging before his time, but consolidated themselves into palpable realities when he took office. So, much of his diplomacy was an adaptive continuation of policies already designed--policies of resisting international pressures to sign the Comprehensive Test Ban Treaty, of maintaining the momentum of economic liberalisation, of seeking better understanding with the US, of promoting relations with China, of developing greater integration with new regional groupings, and of attending various international conferences (G-15 meeting in Harare, UN General Assembly in New York, Commonwealth meeting in London, etc.)

But Gujral's most conspicuous contribution—for which he will be remembered—is the bridges he built with India's South Asian neighbours, assuring them of India's goodwill, and seeking to resolve some of the intractable problems that separated India from them. The personal rapport that he had been able to forge with his South Asian counterparts, compounded with his efforts to improve bilateral relations through the « Gujral Doctrine," and intensified economic interaction, did create a congenial South Asian diplomatic atmosphere for the first time in Indian South Asian diplomacy for which he should be remembered by history.

ATAL BEHARI VAJPAYEE

Chapter XIV
ATAL BEHARI VAJPAYEE
19 MARCH 1998—22 MAY 2004

Atal Bihari Vajpayee returned to power. The game of musical chairs and the revolving-door-prime minister-arrangements had gone on for too long behind close doors by power-hungry politicians. The people had to be consulted through elections. And, the result was indeed dramatic. The Bharatiya Janata Party (BJP) became the largest party in the Parliament, but not large enough to form a government of its own. Coalition politics continued, and Vajpayee became the Prime minister only by heading a 14 party National Democratic Alliance (NDA), and that even after lengthy and difficult negotiations with some of the coalition partners.

But it was a different type of coalition government—a government that had at its helm the single largest party of the Lokh Sabha; whereas four of the five previous Prime Ministers represented relatively small groups that generated considerable byzantinism, manipulation, intrigue, uncertainity, and brevity of governments. By the fact that Vajpayee had the largest political party in the Lokh Sabha he lasted for more than six years as Prime Minister even though he too was heading a coalition government.[489]

FORMATIVE YEARS

Atal Behari Vajpayee's life is essentially political. Hailing from a middle class family in Gwalior (Madhya Pradesh) with a father professionally involved in education, there were already, during his early years, a vast panorama of landmark signs of his interest in politics– an interest he diligently pursued from his adolescent years.

Graduating in political science from Kanpur, embroiling himself in the student movement as one the leaders, and courting arrest during Mahatma Gandhi's 1942 quit India movement at the age of sixteen are three early benchmarks in his political life.

Interestingly all these stages of political development were also evident in the lives of most middle class Hindus of his generation, belonging to a similar social background in north India. But what distinguished Vajpayee from many of his contemporaries of that epoch was that he had an additiional dimension in his political armour—the dimension of an Arya Samajist who was a member of a highly organised well-disciplined Hindu movement like the *Rashtriya Swayamsevak Sangh* (RSS). Vajpayee became a full time worker of the RSS in 1947 at the age of 21.

In other words, at a very young age he linked his mainstream political nationalism with militant Hinduism, considering the one indelibly connected with the other.

Vajpayee's whole political life—centring around patriotism and Hinduist ideas—was thus based on the unshakeable conviction that India was basically a Hindu country. While avoiding any lurch into Hindu fundamentalism, the epicentre of his political discourse and belief always was that India's past and present were decisively influenced by Hinduism, by Hindu tradition, and by a Hindu way of life, all of which must be respected and nurtured. In sum, *Hindutva* (hindu way of life), as defined by Girilal Jain, one of the ruminative journalists, as "self renewal and self assertion by Hindus "became Vajpayee's article of faith.[490]

What is remarkable about Vajpayee is his consistency and courage in holding on to these ideas despite the fact that they had sidelined him from the mainstream of Indian politics, and had alienated him from intellectual influences rampant in the country—influences that stemmed essentially from the left. It is indeed very much to his credit that with considerable effort and hard work, spanning more than four decades, he has been able to elevate his ideas from marginal status to the centre of Indian politics, which have eventually pitchforked him into the highest job in the country: that of Prime Minister of India.

What a remarkable journey: from marginality to centrality in politics, and from the position of a sidelined, isolated and alienated politician to the status of one of the prinicpal content providers for the country.

This is a major milestone in contemporary India since it has given the country a direction that is comparable in importance—though perhaps not in intellectual content—to Nehru's original ideological orientations in the aftermath of Indian independence. The monopoly of socialistic ideas had indeed been shattered.

This remarkable projection onto the centre stage of Indian politics can be attributed to four factors: the first is that Vajpayee's effective emergence on the political landscape coninceded with the growing realisation among the Hindus that the Nehruvian brand of secularism, with its objective of giving maximum protection to the minorities, had taken place at the cost of the majority of the population, by weakening its clout, and by depriving it of the wider leverage it was naturally entitled to in Indian politics. It was as if the majority of the country's population had been cold-shouldered by the Government—at least that was how the situation was perceived by many in the country. "During 40 years of the rule of the Congress," lamented Vajpayee, "the policies and the programmes adopted by it in the name of secularism have, rightly or wrongly, left an impression in the mind of the Hindus that they are not being treated well."[491]

This rather generalised new mind-set generated a major situation in the country the ramifications of which are still being felt. Indeed they have become consequential since Vajpayee reached the political summit in the country.

Vajpayee's emergence also coincided with a major intellectual development. Numerous intellectuals rallied to the cause of the BJP. Intellectualism was no longer dominated by the leftists or the Nehruites as it had been since independence. The BJP had brought within its fold a wide array of academicians, media representatives, thinkers, etc., giving it a solid ideological ethos which it did not have before. What had earlier been within the party was too opinionated, too miltant and too myopic. The change was one of the major intellectual developments, for the Indian landscape began to witness a new pattern of modernist thinking, and a new way of looking at history and Indian politics which identified itself with hinduism without becoming fundamentalist. "Times have changed," declared one of them, "the committed progressive of yesterday is the unthinking conservative of today."[492]

The third important factor was geo-political. Islamic fundamentalism had surged all over India's north-western neighbourhood—in Pakistan, Afghanistan, the Gulf area, and among the newly independent Muslim Central Asian states. Compounded to this new geopolitical reality was a disquieting perception, fixated among many Hindus, that large segments of the Muslim minority in India too were being exposed to fundamentalism through education in *Madrasas* (Muslim schools), through the proliferating construction of Mosques financed from outside, particularly Saudi Arabia, and through the increasing determination of many Muslims to keep themselves away from any real integration with the Indian mainstream.

The fourth dimension was Vajpayee himself. His image underwent a major mutation—a mutation that projected him as someone with a benign personality, with moderate views and a high level of tolerance for his political adversaries with whom he maintained an affable relations; in sum as someone who was very much a part of the Indian pluralist system, and who was not out to destablise the Indian pattern of governance. This was indeed a weighty factor, since the existing political system would have disallowed the emergence, at its helm, of a political leader who had not established an aura of moderation and abstemiousness around his personality. Extremists within the BJP and other political groups, of course, will continue to thrive, but is unlikely that they can make it to the top political decisional level. The ethos of the country does not permit such impregnation. This is where India's greatness lay. The image of political moderation was a fundamental pre-condition for any political personality that wished to govern India.

PERCEPTIONS

Vajpayee was one of the first major figures in the opposition who was interested in foreign affairs, and who had acquired experience in the sector as foreign minister of the Janata Government, and as the Indian delegate to myriad international conferences to which he was sent by different Indian governments.

But, his vision of India's foreign policy was different from his predecessors. While accepting the broad framework of a non-aligned policy, he consistently lamented the fact that India was not firm enough in its attitude to the outside world, that it did not behave as a major power, that it did not have tenacious policies towards its adversial neighbours, Pakistan and China, that it was indifferent to the plight of overseas Indians, that it was not looking after its security interests, and so on. But, by far the most important dimension on which he was fixated was the nuclearisation of India. While most mainstream political leaders had hidden their indecisiveness about the subject by proclaiming an ambiguous policy of not taking any position—for or against—he came out clearly and decisively in favour of India going nuclear—which is what he did when he became the Prime Minister.

In sum, the real epicentre of his conceptualised thinking on foreign policy was nationalism: firmness towards its adversial neighbours, obtainment of a great power status through nuclear weapons, continuous identification and pursuit of India's national interest in a changing multi-polar world, and a steadfast protection of India's economy in an increasingly globalised world.

FOREIGN POLICY

The first important foreign policy act was Vajpayee's dramatic decision to detonate a series of five nuclear explosions between 11-13 May 1998. The explosions were conducted in utmost secrecy, so much so that no country had been able to detect the preparations preceding the operation, not even the US, which had set up a permanent sophisticated system of spy satellites to monitor such an eventuality.

This was a flamboyant manifestation of what Vajpayee always wanted to do. He had welcomed the nuclear detonation that Indira Gandhi had conducted in 1974, and had personally given the green light to the scientists to conduct such an operation during his brief first prime ministership. He had summoned the chief of the Department of Atomic Energy, R.Chidambran, to his office to this effect, but as his mandate lasted for only 13 days this was hardly possible.

Porous as India has always been, with foreign agents operating all over the strategic areas, it has hardly ever been able to keep a secret. All of them invariably filter out. But, this time the telltale activity was successfully kept out of sight.

While, there were differences between the Indian and foreign experts regarding the technical perfectibility of the detonations, the fact of the matter is that India had put the world on notice that it was now unambiguously a nuclear power.

The tests were consensually approved within the country. The Indians were indeed proud of it with opinion polls as high as eighty per cent endorsing the tests. Lal Krishna Advani, Vajpayee's Deputy, reflected the Indian endorsement in an article he wrote for the *Motherland*. "Only twice," he said "in recent years has one witnessed such a mood of national elation. First when the Indian Army entered Dhaka to liberate Bangladesh, and now when India has entered the nuclear club." [493]

But in the West it was different. While there were indeed people in Europe and the US who admired the fact that India had developed the capacity of conducting such tests, they were denounced by most outside powers—including China, which, hypocritically attacked India while it was itself determinedly becoming a nuclear power, and Pakistan which was moving in the same direction by conducting its own nuclear tests.

While the three neighbouring countries were in different stages of nuclear development—China most advanced, India in the middle, Pakistan as the third—the fact of the matter was that nuclearisation had invaded the region. The so-called nuclear game was now on among the three countries.

So far as India was concerned, it had to reckon with two nuclear adversaries, China and Pakistan. And, with both of them it found itself in an uncomfortable and exposed position. The Chinese, more developed, had the credible capacity of striking India without being deterred. And, India had to embroil itself in the nuclear game of competition with the Chinese by producing more nuclear war heads, and more missiles to effectively target Chinese territories; whereas with Pakistan the situation was worse; for before the onset of nuclearism India was far more superior in conventional weapons, and possessed a credible capacity of militarily defeating Pakistan. In any full-scale ground assault it could dismember Pakistan within two weeks, as had happened in 1971. But, in the post-nuclear stage, India lost its capacity of effectively defeating Pakistan due to the important fact that the latter could neutralise India's conventional superiority by deterring it with its own nuclear capacity.

So what has India really gained in the event of any confrontation? Hardly anything. While, on the one hand, it had to increasingly involve itself in the ongoing nuclear race with China to establish a minimum credible deterrence; whereas with Pakistan it lost its conventional superiority, but could not use its nuclear superiority since Pakistan could deter India by using its minimal nuclear capacity.

It is true that, with the passage of time, India could neutralise Chinese nuclear superiority by having in its nuclear arsenal the capacity of striking China; but what about Pakistan? It will always have—in the face of any future dismemberment— the nuclear capacity of deterring India.

Relations with the US

The other major adverse ramification was the deterioration of Indo-US relations. Clinton had expressed his personal anger at a meeting in the White House. "We are going to," he said to his staff, "come down on those guys like a ton of bricks."[494] And he did; the first manifestation of which was the imposition of a array of sanctions. The US Congress too denounced India. Senator Jesse Helms, Chairman of the Foreign Relations Committee, thundering against India, made an unusual statement to the effect that the Indian action now "clearly constitute(d) an emerging threat to the territory of the US."[495]

The Indians were expecting American retaliation, and had prepared themselves for it. But, this was not that adversely impactful to make India cringe. Besides, all this was really provisional. The US business groups, feeling the pinch, and the US Congress, realising its ineffectiveness, did not see any point in continuing the sanctions. Finally, Clinton, too, gave in. For the first time in diplomatic experience, India effectively stood up to the Americans, pushing Vajpayee to launch an offensive which translated itself into a personal letter sent out to 177 heads of state. The one to Clinton, pointed out that the tests were conducted because China had installed nuclear weapons "on our borders," and because Pakistan had become "covert nuclear weapon state."

The Indians then came up with their nuclear doctrine that was truculent of the US. It called for the development and deployment of a "triad of aircraft, mobile land-based missiles, and sea-based assets," a replica of American strategic deterrent—clearly a worst possible answer to Washington of how India intended to define its "minimum credible deterrence."[496]

Indians furthermore disagreed with Washington's evaluation that the Indian subcontinent had become the most dangerous place in the world, and were annoyed at Clinton for having had the temerity of proposing that China should mediate between India and Pakistan—hardly a diplomatic proposition given India's inimicality against its two neighbours. They also expressed defiantly their firm opposition to adhere to CTBT. When pressed by Washington to sign the treaty, in exchange for a world bank loan of $210 million for the construction of several power plants in Andhra Pradesh, the Indians, rightly, says Strobe Talbot, "turned up their nose and asked for more relief on a faster timetable with fewer strings attached...They seemed to think that rather than making any concessions of their own they could simply wait for further erosion of support for sanctions in the US Congress and in the G-7".[497]

Indeed, there were two major ramifications of the defiant Indian nuclearisation on US policies. The first was the erosion of support for US sanctions. On 13 July 1998 the US Assistant Secretary of State for South Asian Affairs formally requested a waiver authority from the US Congress for all sanctions imposed on India and Pakistan. "We fully recognise," he declared, "that New Delhi and Islamabad will have to assess them (US stipulations in the light of their own national security arrangements."[498]The second was US accord to discuss informally and discreetly all matters related to security. While Clinton and Gujral had agreed in their meeting of 22 September 1997 to launch "a comprehensive and sustained dialogue" between India and the US on issues pertaining to disarmament and non-proliferation; it was Vajpayee who picked up the whole issue of security.[499] It is, of course, not clear if Gujral had discussed the issue with Vajpayee—as he often did—and that Vajpayee in effect was following what had been agreed in September 1997, or if it was Vajpayee's own idea.

In any event " the comprehensive and sustained dialogue," now called "security dislogue", began between Jaswant Singh and Strobe Talbott. The 14 meetings that resulted between them—of which both Brajesh Mishra and L.K. Advani were apparently against—had no real effect in ameliorating Indo-US relations. They may have cleared the positions of the two countries on a host of nuclear issues, but they really led nowhere. Notwithstanding all the friendly promises Jaswant Singh made on the CTBT to Talbot, he knew well that he could hardly convince the Indians to accept the CTBT. Towards the end of the dialogue, he declared that, while he was willing to give a last try to what had become a personal obligation, he did make it clear that "an obligation to deliver does not mean an ability to deliver—it means a determination to try."[500] He never delivered. He could'nt. And, what is more he knew it.

Clinton's visit to India in March 2000, and Vajpayee's reciprocal visit to the US in September 2000 certainly improved the atmosphere between the two nations, but they hardly had any beneficial effect on the substance of Indo-US relations.

Relations with Russia

With the onset of the new Russian Federation, the new leadership, under Boris Yeltsin was less interested in India. Directing its diplomatic focus at the US and Western Europe, India had lost its importance.

By the time Vajpayee became the Prime Minister, Indo-Russian relations were becoming increasingly constricted to the buying of Russian arms and of maintaining minimal economic relations. Having become severly dependent on Moscow for the arms it needed and on the limited Russian economic market it had developed through the years, Indian dependence was evident; but so was the Russian reliance on the Indian market.

Vajpayee and Yeltsin, therefore, maintained the façade of develping commendable ties in the two sectors.

But in the political sector the convergence were tapering off. If anything, it was going downhill with Yeltsin taking a critical position on a host of political issues that concerned India directly. The Russian leader no more supported India on Kashmir, criticised New Delhi for not adhering to the CTBT, cancelled most of the ballistic missile development deals, condemned India for conducting nuclear tests, supported Pakistani-sponsored UN resolution for the establishment of the South Asian nuclear free-zone, and even began to reconsider Russian plans of selling two Russian-made VVER-1000 nuclear power reactors to India.[501]

What made things even worse was the Indian suspicion that Yeltsin was taking a critical stand on a number of issues under pressure from Clinton. It was apparently the US President who pushed the Russian President to back out on the Indo-Russian ballistic missile deal and to attack India on conducting nuclear tests. Yeltsin also accepted the Clinton proposal that the two countries, along with China, should cooperate to work out a "joint approach towards the problem of India and Pakistan."[502] The goal would be to persuade the two South Asian countries to sign up the CTBT and "reinvigorate the peace process on Kashmir."[503]

With the disappearance of Yeltsin, and the emergence of Vladmir Putin as the new President, Russian policy rapidly began to change in favour of India. In December 2002, during Putin's official visit to India, a series of agreements were concluded, including the Delhi Declaration on further consolidation of strategic partnership, the joint declaration on stengthening and enhancing economic, scientific and technological cooperation, and combating terrorism. This new ongoing process was continued during Vajpayee's visit to Russia in 2003.[504]

Indo-Russian relations were once again back on track, though not on the same level as during the Soviet period.

Relations with China

Vajpayee's perception of China was invariably adversial. In his mind, Beijing's occupation of Tibet, combined with the strategic partnership it had forged with Pakistan, generated a detrimental security environment, the most dramatic manifestaion of which was India's humiliating defeat in the 1962 military conflict.

His landmark visit to Beijing in 1979, as Morarji Desai's foreign minister, was not so much an expression of his avidity to go there, as it was an articulation of the Prime Minister's fixed determination to open up to the big northern neighbour.

Desai would have gone himself, had he been invited, but the Chinese, prudent as they are in such matters, did not consider that it was the right time to organize a summit meeting.

Vajpayee's first visit was organised in a peculiar fashion. From the debate in the Parliament it would seem that there had not been any preliminary official exchanges regarding the matter. The whole matter, it would seem, was evoked, casually and informally, by a correspndent who asked Vajpayee, after his visit to Pakistan whether he would be willing to go to China, to which he had replied in the affirmative. "Let the invitation come, I will consider the matter."[505] The invitation was finally conveyed by the leaders of the Chinese goodwill mission visiting India, undoubtedly an unusual procedure. Finally, when the dates were fixed, Vajpayee postponed the visit for medical reasons, though there were strong rumours that the postponement was due to political reasons—presumably pressures from erstwile Soviet Union and the powerful pro-Soviet lobby in the Ministry of External Affairs.

In the end, the Foreign Minister did go to China, but cut short his visit because of Chinese "massive attack on Vietnam."[506]

With Prime Minister Vajpayee's decision to conduct nuclear tests, relations deteriorated conspicuously. In his communication with Clinton on the subject, he explicitly attributed this decision to security threats emanating from China and Pakistan. And the myriad remarks made by the Defence Minister, George Fernandes, to the effect that China was India's principal threat, did not help Sino-Indian relations.

But, the two countries attempted to get over their period of tensions. Both of them came around to the idea that the process of normanlisation, inaugurated by Indira Gandhi, should be continued.

As an initial process in this direction, the Chinese presented a map regarding the line of actual control of the middle sector of the border—an initiative that Beijing had avoided so far. Economic interaction was also accelerated with the Sino-Indian trade going up to $4 billion, and with the sending out of signals to India of the Chinese hope that it will reach $10 billion in the not too distant a future.

But the process of normalisation was really accelerated by mutual visits of dignatories.

The first was that of the Indian President K.R. Narayanan, in May 2000. This was indeed, symbolically, an important visit, since the Chinese considered him as a "friend of China," a designation they gave to those to whom they were close. The Chinese had, in fact, given him this designation from the days when he came to China as Indira Gandhi's Ambassador. The two Chinese premiers, Li. Peng and Zhu Rongji visited India in January 2001 and January 2002 respectively. Both of them were conspicuously outgoing during the visits. Indian Defence Minister, Georges Fernandes', week long visit in April 2003, at the invitation of his Chinese counterpart, General Cao Gangchuan, was an important signal from the Chinese side, that Beijing was eager to inaugurate a new turning point in the process of normalisation.

But, by far the most important visit was that of Vajpayee between 22—27 June 2003. While many declarations, emanating from both the sides, were a reiteration of their past friendly relations, a number of agreements were concluded during Indian Prime Minister's visit: an agreement to set up a Joint Study Group (JSG), composed of officials and economists, to examine the potential complementaries in their bilateral trade and economic cooperation, an accord to coordinate their activities within the framework of WTO, a covenant to establish cultural centres in each other's capital, an arrangement to appoint special representatives to explore, from political perspective, a framework for boundary settlement, and finally an agreement that the two countries would designate Chengdu in Sikkim and Renquinggang in Tibet as the Indian and Chinese venues for expanding border trade.[507]

It is indeed remarkable that, notwithstanding myriad differences, relations had indeed become quite close as a result of all these visits.

SOUTH ASIA

India's bilateral relations with South Asian neighbours (Pakistan excluded) was a continuation of policies already constructed by previous governments. The only difference was that Vajpayee was more open in his declarations and more blunt in his attitude regarding South Asian developments. He defended Bhutan against infiltration by militants from India's north-east, made it clear to Bangladesh that his government will not tolerate Bangladeshi infiltrations into India, and frankly told the Sri Lankans that India will not intervene even if Jaffna falls.

But, as with preceding governments, Pakistan was the focal point of Vajpayee's diplomatc behaviour in South Asia. In fact, even more so than with his predecssors. For one thing, Pakistan was perceptually fearful of the new government; dominated as it was by the BJP,which, in its estimation, had never recognised the partition of India and the consequent establishment of the Pakistan state. There was thus the emergence of a perception of a security threat. For another, the circumstances had changed in South Asia with the two neighbours having effectively gone nuclear, thus creating, in the eyes of many, an explosive situation, particularly among the US leadership which had convinced itself that South Asia had become the most dangerous place on earth. Still another reason, in Vajpayee's estimation, was the ongoing expansion of Islamic fundamentalism whose imperitive containment was only possible through cooperation with the secular forces, one of which was embodied by Nawaz Sharif, the then existing Prime Minister.

So the Indian Prime Minister made it a point, at the very beginning of his mandate, to assure the Pakistan leadership that he favoured the "renewal of the dialogue process, and interaction at the high political levels between the two countries"—a process, he asserted, represented the Indian consensus to which he was committed "on a constructive and sustained basis."[508]

The dialogue process, therefore continued at different levels, the most dramatic initiative of which was his visit to Lahore on 20-21 February 1999 on the inaugural run of the Delhi-Lahore-Delhi bus service. The visit, as the Pakistani newspaper, *The News,* commented, turned out to be an event whose symbolic nature can be compared to the fall of the Berlin wall. Besides, it had been ten years since an Indian Prime Minister had visited Pakistan.

Of all the declarations and accords the ones concluded in Lahore on 21 February 1999 were historic since it was the first time that an agreement was reached after the two countries had gone nuclear.

Much of the contents of the three agreements (The Lahore Declaration, The Joint Statement, and the Memorandum of Uniderstanding) were a reiteration of what had already been agreed upon by I.K.Gujral and his counterpart Nawaz Sharif. What was new were a host of nuclear agreements the most important of which were (a) to "engage in bilateral consultations on security concepts and nuclear doctrines," (b) to notify each other in advance of the ballistic missile flight tests, (c) to mutually take measures to reduce " the risks of accidental and unauthorised use of nuclear weapons," and (d) to mutually abide "by their respective unilateral moratorium on conducting nuclear tests."

Hardly had the agreements been signed, the relations got impassed. As it has always been the case, it was the litigious issue of Kashmir on which no agreement could be reached, given the fact that the fixed positions of the two countries has never changed.

But the relations got further deteriorated after several assailants launched a suicide attack on the Indian Parliament on 13 December 2001—an attack that led to 90 minute gun battle in which 7 policemen were killed and many (policemen and civilians) were seriously injured. The attackers drove through one of the compound gates in a white Indian-made car with official Parliament and Home Stickers and a flashing siren on the roof. The objective was somehow to get into the Parliament while it was in session.

Tensions now mounted resulting in the recall of the top Indian diplomat from Pakistan, and the withdrawal of the two countries from South Asian Summit meeting scheduled to meet on 4 January.

Relations were back to where they had always been: tensions and distrust, etc.

Finally the relations were resumed and the Indo-Pakistan dialogue was once again reopened follwing a meeting in Islamabad between Pakistan President Pervez Musharraf and Prime Minister Vajpayee.

For how long remains an open question.

DECISION MAKING

The decision making process furthermore has become more diffused. In addition to what existed already, Vajpayee made foreign policy making even more institutionalised by appointing a Foreign Minister, by attributing greater decisional authority to the PMO; even more important was the establishment of a three tier National Security Council (NSC) composed of a powerful Council, headed by the Prime Minister, a Secretariat led by experienced bureaucrat and a large Advisory Board.

The sources providing the inputs for foreign policy making thus had been enlarged. While the Prime Minister was the decision maker, the decision making process became more institutionalised, more sophisticated, and more input-oriented than was the case before.

However, notwithstanding a developed institutionalized decisional process, Vajpayee had to reckon with a host of political forces and individual personalities who surrounded him. Closely linked as he was with his political party (BJP) and extreme right wing RSS a good part of his political life, he could hardly ignore them when he became the Prime Minister. How could he when he was dependent on them, and when his mandate as Prime Minister would not have lasted were they to withdraw their support, particularly then when they had become a major part of the Indian political system. Besides, there was a great deal of compatibilty and understanding between them, particularly they were all desirous to make India strong through the nuclearisation of the country. On this they all agreed.

But, on the other hand, Vajpayee was well aware of the fact that he had to project himself as a moderate in politics if he wished to survive as Prime Minister. For the mainstream Indian political system, as it had been architected, through the years, did not lend itself to any form of extremism.

So how did he construct his decision making—a decision making that was firm but moderate. The firmness came with the institutions, while moderation emanated through benign personalities he had surrounded himself.

There was, first of all, Brajesh Mishra, his Principal Secretary and National Security Adviser. He had long experience as a diplomat, the most dramatic manifestation of which was his famous Chinese-inspired public encounter with Mao Zedong. Soon after retirement, he joined the BJP where he became the principal spokesman of the party on foreign affairs. By the functions he was holding he was closest to Vajpayee since all diplomatic matters went through his office before they arrived at the table of the Prime Minister.

The second was Jaswant Singh, Vajpayee's Foreign Minister. While he was close to the Prime Minister, since the contours of their argumentation were analogous, it is not clear if his proximity was comparable to Mishra's. One of his main functions, for which he became known was his 14 meetings with Steve Talbott, the purpose of which was to clarify Indian and American positions in the aftermath of Indian option to go nuclear. This was an important diplomatic dialogue, but nothing substantial came out of it.

The third person in the decisional process was the Foreign Secretary, Lalit Mansingh who regularly interacted with the Prime Minister, but not at levels of Mishra and Singh. There were naturally a host of technical matters that needed to be resolved, for which Mansingh was the man.

Vajpayee established another procedure in decision making— of seeking clearance from some of his cabinet ministers. Whenever the Prime Minister had to reckon with delicate matters on which he did not wish to take a decision on his own, he referred the matter to the Cabinet Subcommittee on Security; apparently he initiated this procedure more often than not. Consider the US pressures on Vajpayee to collaborate in Iraq—undoubtedly a delicate situation. Vajpayee referred the whole matter to the Cabinet Subcommittee, whose response was in the negative. Vajpayee obviously wanted such a decision, but did not wish to take the decision on his own. If one were to consider the three aspects of India's foreign policy—routine, visible and macro—it would seem that if Vajpayee had the central decisional authority on all the three aspects, the inputs that now go into foreign policy making became much more diverse, and, at the same time, much less traceable and identifiable. In sum, at least so far as the decision making process in foreign policy was concerned, India began to resemble the countries of the west

EVALUATION

Vajpayee's operational policies as Prime Minister are basically the same as that of his predecessors. With the exception of course of his decision to go nuclear, continuity rather than change are Vajpayee's pattern of governance. If he was remarkable in his consistency of beliefs, he is, like the others, unremarkable in his actions. Rhetoric is easy in the opposition; it can be a big vote-catcher; but governance is difficult. It needs a different frame of mind—a mind that is more benign and more universally acceptable. Compounded with this was another constraint—the constraint of coalition politics which had slowed down or paralysed the decision making process.

Vajpayee displayed considerable interest in foreign affairs during his entire political life. When Nehru was at the height of his political power, he was generally considered as one who was the leading light in global affairs. He was one of the very few parliamentarians who openly questioned Nehru's views.

Of all the luminaries of his party (BJP) he was the one who was known for his interest in global affairs.

Based on the perception he acquired through the years, Vajpayee considered that there were some priorities in international affairs that India should focus on.

He had consistently and firmly believed that India must become a major power—a power that would exercise a primordial impact on the working of the international system. While economic potency was perceived as a weighty component in the system of power, conventional and nuclear power remained the most critical dimensions in his thinking. When Indira Gandhi exploded a nuclear device in 1974, he was the first opposition leader who welcomed this development. And when he became the Prime Minister this was one of his very first acts—to conduct a series of five nuclear explosions. While the catalytic decision to go nuclear may be partly attributed to the nuclearity of China and Pakistan, Vajpayee, fascinated as he was with the phenomenon of power, would have chosen to take the nuclear path even if the others were not nuclear oriented. For him it embodied power, and dimensional India merited such a status.

For Vajpayee, taking the nuclear path was the most important objective of his foreign policy for which he shall be remembered by history. It is not at all clear if Vajpayee had seriously evaluated the benefits and the drawbacks of such a step.

The benefit was obvious: India acquired the status of a power. And with an expeditious on-going economic development, combined with a stable democratic system, plus the new acquisition of nuclear power, it was more than likely that India would have acquired a global status—not of the same dimension as USA and Russia, but a global power nonetheless. Even if the permanent members of the UN Security Council refused to accept India's new status—which was the case—it was a matter of time that the international community would have to reckon with this growing phenomenon. The other beneficial ramification was the US attitude. It changed—from one of anger, irritation and sanction-imposed policy—to one of seeking an understanding with India, the most important manifestation of which were Indo-US talks to arrive at some mutual understanding, and President Clinton's official visit to India.

On the other hand there are negative aspects of nuclearisation. India is in close proximity (neighbours) with adversial nuclear China and Pakistan.

The adoption of a militant nuclear strategy meant that India was now embroiled in a nuclear competition with China; and since the latter was much more advanced in the sector, India would have to invest considerable technology and capital to keep up with the Jones—particularly in the missile technology in which India was less advanced, and which it needed in order to effectively target China.

With nuclear Pakistan it was different. India, by going nuclear, had lost its pre-nuclear conventional superiority, and had to now reckon with Pakistan with its nuclear deterrence since it had now credibly developed a minimal nuclear capacity to strike at India.

In any event, it is not clear if Vajpayee had gone through all this reasoning.

The second major diplomatic move was towards Pakistan. He introduced bus diplomacy and went to Pakistan in a bus, and received Musharaf in India, not to speak of the continuous interaction at the foreign secrataries' level. But nothing came out it. The impasse on Kashmir continued, for neither the views of Pakistan nor that of India underwent any change whatsoever.

In any event the most important foreign policy event for which Vajpayee will be remembered is that the ramifications of nuclearised India are going to be multi-faceted and are certainly going to effect the future of Indian diplomacy.

MANMOHAN SINGH

Chapter XV

Manmohan Singh
22 May 2004—

Manmohan Singh became Prime Minister in unusual circumstances. Having won the 2004 general elections, Sonia Gandhi should have been the legitimate candidate to head the government. But, this was not to be. The controversy surrounding her foreignness (being of Italian origin) became so rampant within the party as well as outside, that she wisely decided not to project herself for the post of Prime Minister. It was undoubtedly a big decision for, it would seem, that she, and her family were looking forward to the acquisition of this powerful position. Now that she had won the national elections, her ambitions had loomed up. What a contrast from the days of her husband, Rajiv Gandhi, when he was being prepared for prime ministership, and she was trying to persuade him not to go into politics. It was in these untypical circumstances that she turned to Manmohan Singh for the high post, while continuing as the Congress President. This was probably the first time in the history of post-independent India that the one who embodied power did not become the Prime Minister. It is true that in the past there were indeed political situations where the one who had the real power did not or could not become the head of the government. But, Sonia Gandhi had the power but the circumstances did not allow her to aspire for the high office. It was not so much because she did not relish the idea of prime ministership as the fact that she was fearful of the possible aggravation of the controversy surrounding her origins.

Manmohan Singh thus became Prime Minister by default. There were, of course, other aspirants in the corridors of power, but for Sonia Gandhi, Singh was the most comfortable and credible candidate. For he appeared to be consensually popular, both inside and outside the country for his turnaround of the Indian economy when he was the Finance Minister during the time of Rao.

Formation and Perception

Mamohan Singh is a typical embodiment of a westernised intellectual, who had his initial university education in India before he went for higher studies to Cambridge and Oxford universities. Amongst all the Prime Ministers, he is the only one whose formal university education was most diverse and most advanced.

None of the Prime Ministers devoted so much of their time exposing themselves to universities. Though it is by no means a meritorious criteria for high political office, a good education in known universities is nonetheless helpful in embarking on a high political career.

Singh's public service career is also wide-ranging, holding powerful and visible national and international posts. It would be too long to extensively trace his career. Suffice it to say that almost all the positions he held were essentially connected with the economic sector—including the one he held in Geneva as the General Secretary of the South Commion, originally launched by Julius Nyerere in 1987.

His visible political career began with his nomination as Finance Minister in Narasimha Rao's government and Congress party's leader in the Rajya Sabha. He did not hold any elective position. The one for which he tried in 1999 proved abortive.

Perceptually Singh, like many Indian intellectuals, believes in socialism of the Nehruvian variety; but given his vast educational experience, at some stage of life, he came to the conclusion that for India to survive, develop and prosper in the future, it was important for the country (a) to deregulate the Indian economy, (b) to introduce optimal marketisation, (c) to adapt the economy to the rapidly expanding process of globalisation, and (d) to torridly grow Indian economy. This is what he inaugurated when he was Finance Minister; and this is what has become the ongoing process with India.

FOREIGN POLICY

Though the broad framework of India's foreign policy, as originally constructed by Nehru, was consensually followed by all Prime Ministers, it has been continuously adapted to the changing circumstances of the international system. So much so that, by the time Singh came to office, little remained of India's foreign policy compared to what it used to be in Nehru's time. While all Prime Ministers have formally gone on record that they were following in the steps of Jawaharlal Nehru, it is evident that it has, slowly and steadily, changed radically through the years.

The privileged relationship that India constructed with the erstwhile Soviet Union had disappeared, the interaction with the US had continuously expanded, while the nexus with China had become more and more normal. Furthermore non-alignment and international solidarity with other southern countries had become less relevant, and nationalism and sovereignty, the very basis of India's foreign policy, had been jettisoned in the face of growing globalisation.

While all these mutations, and many more, were already emerging under preceding Prime Ministers, they became more palpable under Manmohan Singh. With the possible exception of privileged relations that he had constructed with Washington in the nuclear sector, practically everything else was a continuation of the constructions already designed before.

What had really changed was the methodology of diplomacy. It had become more benign, more friendly and more outgoing. This was not only the signs of the time, but an emulation of Manmohan's own personality and character.

Relations with Russia

Relations with Russia had conspicuously ameliorated with the emergence of Vladimir Putin as the President of the Russian Federation. He had realised the vital importance of India, and attempted to maintain an even keel relations with the country."I hope," declared the Russian President on Singh's visit to Russia in November 2007, "that inspite of the chilly winter in Moscow, you will be able to feel, the warmth of our hearts, noble and very friendly attitude towards your country."[509]

In fact the two countries had agreed to establish a strategic partnership.[510] A number of agreements were concluded in the military sector, the most important of which were to develop a supersonic cruise missiles BrahMos, a state-of the art fifth generation combat aircraft, laser-guided anti-tank missiles, Kornet with a maximum range of about 5000—5500 metres, and extending the 10 year agreement on military cooperation that would go beyond 2010.

Putin also ackowledged India's nuclear weapon capabilities, and agreed to build four more civilian nuclear reactors in Kudankulam in Tamil Nadu. It is expected to come into force after the international community changes the nuclear rules in favour of India.[511]

There were also signs that some broad Indo-Russian agreements were also agreed upon on a host of international policical issues including Iran on which the two countries demanded that Iran abandons any plans of nuclear proliferation.[512]

The two countries also agreed that India, Russia and China should build relations on a wide network of issues.

Equally important was the expansion of economic interaction which would no more operate within the framework of the traditional rupee-rouble arrangement, but will become, in the words of Manmohan Singh " a fully market determined phenomenon."[513]

Manmohan Singh and Vladimir Putin have really upgraded Indo-Russian relations. Singh has indeed been more successful in reaching a range of strategic understandings than any other Prime Minister since the Russian change-over.

Relations with the US

The great leap forward, however, was really in Indo-US bilateral relations. While a secular trend, in this direction, was already visible under previous Indian administrations, it was under Manmohan Singh that they took a dramatic and almost unprecedented upbeat turn generating a widespread clamour of discontent everywhere in the country, particularly within the coalition government and the opposition led by the Communist parties and the BJP. This was the first time that there was such a loud outcry against a Prime Minister whose real hold on the country was indeed weak.

Actually, the initiative for such a step emanated from the US President, Bush, who, after long deliberations, had decided to focus on India—more than any other U.S. president.

A number of factors had collectively contributed to the initiative. There was, of course, the disengagement of India from its privileged relationship with erstwhile USSR after the disappearance of the communist system. There was the emergence of a powerful, internationally outgoing, China, which, in Republican US perception, needed to be counterpoised. There was the broad prevalence of a general US feeling that Indian decision makers were increasingly ready to forge close ties with Washington. The growing deregulated Indian economy was also a source of great attraction to US international economic expansion. And, then there was the fearful expansion of the terrorist-oriented Islamic fundamentalism in north-western regions beyond India, of which India was perceived as a major target.[514]

All this finally resulted in the US decision to conclude a nuclear deal with India—a deal that resulted in the separation of civil and military nuclear facilities, and a deal to place civilian facilities under IAEA. [515]

As a result of these political understandings and commitments, made during Singh's visit to Washington in July 2005, and Bush's visit to India in March 2006, a round of five secret negotiations took place between June 2006 and July 2007 that resulted in the incorporation of all this into a legal document.

This has indeed created a clamourous discontent within the coalition government, in the parliamentary opposition and within the country. Notwithstanding all the assurances given by the Prime Minister that India is pursuing a independent foreign policy, and that it could conduct nuclear tests if necessary, the opposition to the agreement is threatening the very existence of the government.

In the face of all this, Manmohan Singh, has indicated that he may have to renounce the agreement. In any event, never before in the history of independent India has a Prime Minister faced such an opposition—and that even a Prime Minister who does not wield considerable power in politics.

While India's relations continue to expand with Washington in a host of sectors, including trade, investments , etc., it is no more certain that the crucial nuclear deal will ever go though in India.

It is interesting to note that while practically all the Prime Ministers agreed with the politics of upbeating relations with the US, the level of anti-Americanism remains considerable.

Manmohan Singh's Chinese Dimension

Sino-Indian, relations, on the other hand, were showing signs of developing even faster than under any other previous administrations. It was indeed becoming an ongoing phenonmenon, under Manmohan Singh, with both India and China apparently determined to go forward.

The original Deng Xiaoping axiom, that both the countries should place litigious border issues on the backburner and, focus on interacting at the economic level , paid off. For they are developing at faster rate than ever before.

Consider Sino-Indian trade. From the year 2000 when trade was $ 2.9 billion, it has made a quantum jump to $ 20 billion going in all directions. The leap has been almost ten times.

This upgraded step has been initiated by leaders like Hu Jitao (President), Wen Jiabao (Prime Minister) and Manmohan Singh for all of whom, and many others, the dark side of the Sino-Indian relations belongs to the past, and to which they do not wish to revert.

Undoubtedly there appears to exist even a greater future to which they would like to focus on. Though China now is seen as the factory and India as the laboratory of the world, the distinction is expected to blurt in years to come as India strengthens its manufacturing abilities and as China improves its service sector; besides there exists consensus in China as well as India "that it is unlikely that both countries will be producing the same things."[516]

But the current wave of cooperation is more about China coming to India than India going to China. The rise of India's software, which now extends to biotech, pharma and industrial research and development are the factors that made China sit up. That the Chinese Prime Minister, Wen Jiabao chose to go to Bangalore before Delhi is the reflection of the shift. But, this is not only in goods, for China, as it engages more and more with India, is also realising that the Indian private sector is remarkably modern and sophisticated than the Chinese private sector. So the scope of learning from each other is considerable,

Another opportunity of cooperation is in the steel sector. Riding on the back of the boom, India's steel exports to China have risen from $157 million in 2000, to 1.4 billion in 2003-04. The boom has sown some seeds of joint partnership under which India would send semi-finished steel to China and receive finished steel from China.

The other economic dimension that is growing is partnership. More than 1000 Indians and Chinese companies have reached formal partnerships or are operating in each other's country. And this type of interaction is going to grow by leaps and bounds as the years go by,

The Indian and Chinese mind-set is also changing. It seems to be integrating the idea that the future of one is linked to the other. This is what came out, when Wen Jiabao stressed that India and China "are partners, not rivals," and declared that "strong and prosperous India serves China's interests." Consider his address to the students of the New Delhi's Indian Institute of Technology (IIT) where he declared that the 21st century would belong to China and India if the two countries were to establish close relations, and if they were to work together. He quoted from the writings of Indian leaders and thinkers such as Mahatma Gandhi, Rabindranath Tagore, Jawaharlal Nehru and Amartya Sen. He ended his speech with the slogan of the 1950s, "Hindi-China, Bhai-Bhai.[517]

Mohmohan Singh, too was using the same type of tuneful language. After signing an agreement with the Chinese, on "strategic peace and prosperity" he declared that the two countries could "reshape the world order."[518] And during his trip to Beijing in January 2008 he urged the Indian business community in Indian and China to "think big." The rise of India and China, he declared, should be viewed as an" international public good" by the global community since it offers new opportunities to sustain global growth. At a time when there are concerns about a global economic slowdown, China and India can sustain global growth through their own development, and this represents a "historical necessity"...for our two nations to work together."[519]

The intensification of close economic relations, compounded with some feeling of commonality, has had a benefical effect on their political situation; for one thing it is witnessing, slowly and steadily, a subtle upgradation of bilateral political interaction, including an exchange of maps regarding the border, the conclusion of a series of confidence building measures to prevent any conflict, and the expression of some degree of commonality on a variety of international issues.

PROLIFERATION OF DIPLOMACY

Asia

Indian diplomacy took a proliferating turn during Manmohan Singh's mandate. It is ubiquitous, spreading out in different directions. While the previous administrations had already forged ties with Southeast nations—ties inaugurated by Narasimha Rao were ties essentially focussed on economic issues.

Manmohan Singh was different, it certainly had an economic dimension; but it was also politically and internationally oriented—like Nehru's, though they were more functional and more limited.

The ones that already existed, like ASEAN, were further activated with growing Indian participation.

But there were many others which coincided with his emergence as Prime Minister. Consider India's association with Russia, China and India Troika—an association that is expected to change the contours of geopolitical strategy in Asia Pacific countries. The importance of the troika would be considerable in international politics, since all the three countries are indeed dimensional demographically, and since all of them are well-equipped in national resources. Besides, all of them know each other well since each of them have had adverse and beneficial results with the others. And also consider the important fact that an identity of views existed on most important issues.

And consider the so-called Shanghai group composed of the four Central Asian states, plus China and Russia, and plus four observers—Mongolia, India, Pakistan and Iran. This is an area of considerable national resources to which all countries have shown an interest.

Consider the establishment of 16 nation East Asia Summit in 2004. It has indeed a vast plan of international cooperation among themselves, but also to work collectively on issues facing the world.

Also take the establishment of India, Brazil and South Africa Forum. At it last meeting, held on 17 July 2007,[520] it "reaffirmed that the IBSA is an important mechanism for political consultation and coordination on important regional and global developments.

THE EUROPEAN UNION

Parallel to Asia there also emerged the European Union (EU) as a weighty dimension in Manmohan Singh's ongoing diplomacy. Though some interaction had already developed during previous governments it acquired a pivotal position under his administration. For one thing, the EU was becoming globally important showing greater political interest in India than ever before. For another, economic relations were growing at a rapid pace with EU becoming India's largest trade partner, and a leading investor in a wide array of Indian industries.[521]

Even more significant is India's own outward investment in the EU which is expected to reach more than Euros 25 billion mark by 2008. This is by far the most significant development in India's relations with the outside world, particularly with the EU. While it was investing in the EU even in earlier stages, the recent considerable growth in outward investments is a sign that (a) India is acquiring large foreign reserves, and (b) they are being increasingly used by Indian multinationals to buy European companies, the most recent example being that of Tata's acqistion of UK based Corus for about $8 billion, and Suzlon Energy Limited takeover of German firm Repower Systems AG for almost $1.7 billion.

With the rapid ongoing economic growth, it is more than possible that Indian investments in the EU will become even more important. Gone indeed are the days when foreign investments were one-sided with investment flows originating from the developed countries to the developing world. India and China today, for example, have become major investors outside the borders of their countries.

In a bid to give further impetus to Indian overseas investments, the Reserve Bank has further liberalised overseas investments for both direct and portfolio investments hiking the overseas investment limit from 300 per cent to 400 per cent, and by allowing, among other things, to make an aggregate investment to the tune of $ 5 billion in overseas avenues from an earlier cap

Political

But, Indo-EU relations are no more limited to the economic sector. Having increasingly become an international actor, the EU took the initiative of reaching out to India politically. On the occasion of the second EU-India summit that took place in Delhi in November 2001, Michel Caillouet, head of the EU delegation in India, underlined the importance of political interaction.[522] "The challenge," he declared, "is to give effect to our intentions stressed in Lisbon and reaffirmed in New Delhi to build a strong partnership and to create at all appropriate levels of our institutions and or our civil societies the framework and the mechanism which will sustain the necessary political will and give joint endeavours their fullest realisations."[523]

Consider all that has been done in the political sector. A strong institutional architecture has been established. While annual ministerial meetings and the summits are the most visible institutional features of the ongoing political dialogue between the EU and India, regular meetings at the senior official and expertise levels are equally important where a host of issues of mutual concern are also discussed, including acts of terrorism. The launching of an EU-India round table of eminent personalities, and the creation of an EU-India network of think-tanks are significant steps in this direction. In the same spirit, the development of academic and cultural exchanges are also playing an important role in EU-India relations.

All efforts are thus being made to strengthen the relations, by the regular exchange of visits between EU and Indian Parliamentarians. Increasing number of EU Commissioners are also visiting India. For instance, in 2001,

External Affairs Commissioner, Chris Patten, Agricultural Commissioner Franz Fischler, and Trade Commissioner Pascal Lamy visited India. These regular visits at the high level have continued since then, including on the occasion of 8th EU-India summit on 30 November 2007.

Strategic Partnership

"Strategic partnership" is the other development that has brought India-EU closer. It was officially launched on 8 November 2004 at the fifth EU-India Summit at the Hague thus taking the relations even to a higher level.

In its extensive response to the EU Communication on "EU-India Strategic partnership" of 16 June 2004, the Indian Government has accepted the strategic partnership of 27 August 2004. While welcoming "The EU's desire to develop a 'strategic relationship" between the two sides," India nonetheless expressed its unhappiness at the poor image it still has among the EU countries. Notwithstanding all the changes that India has gone through, "the country's image in the Western mind has undergone little change." "It is, therefore, imperative," argues the Indian note, "that a coordinated exercise be undertaken to enhance India's visibility in the EU and also to change the way in which India is percieved in these countries."[524]

Joint Action Plan

The "Joint Action Plan" for strategic partnership was agreed by India and the EU, at the EU-India Summit in Delhi on 7 September 2005. It is taking the two signatories even further in their ongoing political interaction. The objective of the plan is to strengthen even more dialogue and consultation mechanisms, deepen political dialogue and cooperation, etc., between EU and India.

The new action plan has made it possible for the two of them to palpably discuss and cooperate on political issues including problems of terrorism, and a host of security issues that the two parties are confronted with. In sum, the new action plan has opened perspectives for discussing and cooperating on practically everything under the sun.

The Joint India-EU Statement of 30 November 2007 in effect indicates the dimension of all the discusions that have taken place between the two signatories, and the broad framework of what they plan to do in a wide sector of areas. The strategic partnership, the statement declared, "flows from a shared conviction in the values of democracy, fundamental freedoms (including religious), pluralism, rule of law, respect for human rights and multilateralism in the international political architecture as the means to tackle global challenges effectively."[525]

In this connection, it is important to note that the European Union has established a large presence in India—probably bigger than any of its members. All its work is shared between 9 large sections—sections as varied as political affairs, trade and economic affairs and humanitarian aid office. Each of these sections has a head of the section with a large staff of its own. In addition to all the interactions it has with all the Indian Government departments, the European delegation participates with the missions of all the 27 State members in India in all matters falling under the ambit of the Common Foreign and Security Policy. Also it participates in all "Troika* and other EU diplomatic initiatives and contacts with India. Furthermore, it also informs and assists the European Parliament and other European Institutions (e.g. Economic and Social Committee, Committee of Regions) in their relations with India.

Differences

However, notwithstanding all the ongoing progress that is now visible, it must be admitted that there are a host of dissenting elements that have generated some degree of uneasiness in their relationship—uneasiness that is in growing contrast with the new emergence of greater Indian affability and understanding with the US.

While India also has problematic relations with the US that do tend to get exacerbated by its traditionally ingrained anti-Americanism, it has nonetheless less problems with the US than with the European Union.

EU's known bias, for example, for China is still very robust, even though most European leaders continue to insist that it is no more the case, China has generally been perceived as a major diplomatic object to be cultivated with both economically and politically. In any event the Indians perceive it this way. The US administration, on the other hand, while maintaining an even keel relations with Beijing, has diplomatically opted for India on the ground that it is more important to long-term US strategic interests than China. Though the Indians themselves are striving to develop friendly relations with China, the new US orientations in favour of India is naturally perceived positively. In this respect, the EU thus remains a minus for India.

Another negative dimension for India is the EU squabbleness over Indian human rights, over policies towards Kashmir, and over a large-scale presence of child labour in Indian economic activities. How often the EU has questioned India's human rights record, and how often has it shown signs of some understanding with the Pakistani position over its dispute with India over Kashmir. Whereas, the US, contrastingly, has avoided criticising India over its human rights record, and is now, under the Bush Administration, showing even signs of neutrality over Kashmir. If anything, the Washington Administration is going out of its way in cultivating with India.

India, also, has difficulties with the EU regarding multilateral negotiations within the WTO framework. It is not only on trade in agriculture and textiles that they disagree, but also on a number of other issues that are being discussed within the organization. While the EU defends its Common Agricultural Policy, that makes European markets inaccessible, other differences include core labour standards, multilateral agreements on investments and competition, on environments, etc. Here again the US attitude is not as firm as that of the EU—at least that is the Indian perception.

But consider another important issue: EU policy concerning Indians and professionals studying and working in Europe. Brussels is becoming increasingly difficult of letting Indians into Europe, but what is even more striking is that students studying in Europe are required by EU regulations to return to India once they have finished their studies. Labour and immigration standards are indeed very strict. In contrast consider the US. Students studying there, and professionals working in US industries appear to have an easier possibility of prolonging their residence in the country; besides they are far greater in numbers than in EU, not to speak of the fact that over a million and a half persons of Indian origin are US citizens holding responsible positions in the administration, in politics and in academia. This can partly be explained by the fact that US laws on immigration—at least so far as the Indians are concerned—are liberal and partly because of Indian attraction to the English language.

India-EU relations thus still have a long way to go. Potentially, of course, there are a large number of issues that should bring them closer: combating terrorism, maintaining a balanced environment, and seeking alternative sources of energy to meet the growing energetic needs of the Indians and the Europeans But, then even on these issues, the Indian position is probably closer to that of the US than the European Union, with the possible exception of energy.

SOUTH ASIA

However, notwithstanding contemplative globalisation of Indian diplomacy, its pivotal dimension nonetheless remains South Asia. How could it be otherwise since most of the unsettling external problems are nonetheless concentrated in the region—problems no preceding Prime Minister has been able to disentangle.

The level of distrust of India, among the South Asian countries, is elevated, and the depth of insecurity among decision makers is agonising. While this may partly be attributed to the gigantic size of India, it also emanates from the fact that the preceding Indian decision makers have not come out with reassuring solutions.

With Manmohan Singh in office the problems, of course, are similar at the bilateral and multilateral levels.

While bilaterally he has no choice but to continue with the broad policies constructed by the preceding Prime Mministers, he has, nonetheless, generated a well-disposed bilateral atmosphere that is more outgoing, more friendly and more reassuring vis-à-vis neighbouring South Asian countries. Diplomacy is not only declaration of policies, or transnational interactions; it is also amiable or unfriendly behaviour that a state may have constructed vis-à-vis its diplomatic counterparts; for they too could have ramifications on the effectiveness of a nation's actions.

Consider Indo-Pakistani interaction during Manmohan Singh's mandate. The whole gamut of these relations are interspersed by a series of brutal terrorist attacks on India (October 2005 in Delhi, December 2005 in Bangalore, July 2006 in Mumbai and February 2007 on Indo-Pakistan train), by diplomatic negotiations at all levels (summit, foreign ministers, bureaucratic, etc.), by mutual visits, and by such effusive track two actions, including Indian material help to Kashmiri victims (in Pakistan-Kashmir) of earthquake in October 2005, the exchange in September 2005 of 500 civilian Indian-Pakistani prisoners in Wagah, etc.

SAARC

Another significant South Asian development is in the sector of multilateralism. Manmohan Singh directed his diplomatic strategy towards regional integration in the hope that SAARC will eventually grow into a viable South Asian Community, modelled after the EU in Europe and ASEAN in Southeast Asia.

The process of South Asian integration, in Manmohan Singh's way of thinking, is an instrument of economic growth which should assist in optimising trade, in removing poverty, and in helping the development of "convergence of economic levels between members" as in Europe where it has and is contributing in narrowing the economic gap between the rich and poor countries.[526]

Such a regional arrangement should also make it possible for "efficiency seeking restructuring of industry on a pan-regional basis." "The experience, of European Union," declared Singh "suggests that the formation of the single European market led to a substantial restructuring of industry on a pan-European basis and hence enabled it to exploit economies of scale, scope and specialization."[527]

At the back of all this thinking, there is an implicit argumentation that successful regional cooperation, and the ultimate establishment of a real union, should diminish political tensions, and help in the minimization of political differences between member states, as it has done and is still doing in Europe.

In order to help in the continuation of this ongoing process, the 14th Summit of SAARC agreed, for the first time in its history, to make tangible progress, within six months, on four issues that effect the daily lives of the people of South Asia. These are water, (including flood control) energy, food and environment. It was also decided to make SAARC Development Fund operational earlier than planned since India offered to provide $100 million for poverty alleviation and other projects.[528] Mammohan Singh also informed the SAARC Summit, India's unilateral decision of liberalizing the Indian visa regime for South Asian students, teachers, journalists and patients.

DECISION MAKING

There are three broad dimensions in decision making in Manmohan Singh's foreign policy. The first is political, the second is institutional while the third is manpower.

The political dimension pertains to power in decision making. Manmohan Singh became Prime Minister in 2004 without wielding any real decisional power. It was elsewhere, in the hands of Sonia Gandhi, who had, almost singlehandedly won the general elections, and who had become the Congress President and the Chairperson of the coalition parties that composed the government. The Indian power system, asymmetrically constituted, was, therefore, unevenly divided between the Prime Minister and the Congress President with major decisional authority in the hands of Sonia Gandhi.

But, since more than four years have gone by when the dualistic authority was established, it is difficult to imagine that the power structure has not evolved during all these years. While Sonia Gandhi still wields predominant decisional authority, the Prime Minister, after having visibly administered the government for so many years, has undoubtedly widened his own authority. It can hardly be otherwise since he has been very much in the forefront of Indian politics with a towering image of trust-worthiness, incorruptability and good governance.

Since Sonia Gandhi has apparently no more any ambition to head the government, and has apparently cast her longing eyes—presumably in accord with Singh—on the future of her own son, Rahul Gandhi; they seem to have implicity concluded a non-conflictual bilateral arrangement of succession. The decisional power has thus been split with an understanding that mutual consultations will take place when deemed desirable and necessary. In an answer to a question by *Time* regarding his power relations with Gandhi he declared " I carry out all the responsibilities that a Prime Minister should. I meet with her, interact with her quite often. I have been in Congress for nearly 30 years and worked very closely with Mrs. Gandhi for the last six years. But that is not to say there is interference. This is a misconception."[529]

In the sector of foreign affairs the power tilt is even greater with Manmohan Singh having acquired a large autonomy, except in very critical situations where the two appear to interact. Both of them have learnt through osmosis that they do not have any other choice.

This may partly be due to the fact that their broad foreign policy vision is not incompatible, as it has emerged in the case of Indo-US nuclear deal. In the backdrop of the Left onslaught Sonia Gandhi has come out in full support of the Prime Minister saying that the agreement fulfils all the assurances he had given repeatedly in the Parliament. "Our Government," she declared to the Congress Parliementary Party, with Singh by her side, "has entered into this agreement after tough negotiations. The agreement fulfils all the assurances that the Prime Minister has given repeatedly in Parliament."[530]

The other political dimension that the Prime Minister is confronted with is with Left wing parties, which, while supporting the coalition government, have declared their firm opposition to a whole series of international issues, with the most dramatic opposition to the Indo-US nuclear deal, It will, they have declared, "suck" India into "imperialist designs" of the US.[531]

Notwithstanding the important fact that the Communist parties are marginal in Indian politics, they have successfully managed to acquire immoderate authority in NDA alliance; so much so—in addition to a host of other issues—the ratification of the Indo-US Nuclear deal has been blocked in the Parliament in close cooperation with BJP forcing the Prime Minister to place the whole issue on the backburner.

The institutional dimension has become considerably important—even more so under Manmohan Singh than ever before. There is indeed a proliferation of institutions dealing with foreign policy. Gone indeed are the days when the MEA, under the control of the Prime Minister, was the principal authority dealing with diplomacy. There is the Prime Minister's Office(PMO) originally concieved by Lal Bahadur Shastri, which has become a powerful institution. There is the RAW, established by Indira Gandhi which is concerned with external intelligence matters. There is the National Security Council (NSC), launched during Vajpayee's prime ministership, that has become the powerful apex agency looking into the political, energetic and strategic security concerns of India. As if all this was not enough, the Prime Minister, during the early stages of his mandate, revived two high-powered sub-committees of the Cabinet—the Committee on Security and another on Political Affairs to initiate and oversee crucial decision making, both of which are headed by the Prime Minister himself.

While the complexity of foreign affairs has contributed to the process of institutional proliferation, there is nonetheless a secular tendency among all governments to create more than what is really necessary and what is required. And, as it is often the case, they generate institutional jealousies and rivalries often resulting in the destruction of each other, and, more often than not, in the issuance of contradictory recommendations that may have an adverse effect on foreign policy making.

The third dimension is the personnel that acts as advisers to the decision makers. They are probably the most important since they are ones, who, in unison with the Prime Minister, take a number of foreign policy decisions. It is difficult to list all or even most of them, for there are indeed personalities, known and unknown, who discreetly function in the corridors of power, and towards whom the Prime Minister may turn for advice and action on specific issues of foreign policy. But there are nonetheless institutionalised personalities who advise the Prime Minister and who act on his behalf.

The first clearly is the Congree President, Sonia Gandhi. Having the power and the authority in Indian politics, the Prime Minister finds himself under an obligation to discuss foreign policy matters with her—at least the ones that are critical. It is not so much a discussion on the details as on the broad issues on which he may need her approval. Consider the Indo-US nuclear deal. It is more than likely that Manmohan Singh discussed the broad framework of his foreign policy towards the US surrounding the nuclear agreement. While there are certainly a number of other international issues on which Mrs. Gandhi was privy to, the most recent one is regarding the nomination of a Foreign Minister. After the Foreign Minister, K. Natwar Singh, was excluded from the Cabinet, after his alleged financial involvement, according to the Paul Volcker report, on the Iraqi Oil for Food Programme scandal, the Prime Minister took over the portfolio himself for quite sometime before Sonia Gandhi pressed him to appoint a new Foreign Minister, which he did by appointing Pranab Mookerjee.

The second personality was J.N. Dixit, who, until he died in early January 2005, was the National Security Adviser to the Prime Minister. He had served in many diplomatic posts, including one as Foreign Secretary. He had the ear of the Prime Minister, and was in constant contact with him. Dixit had one advantage over the others, that of a scholar who had written several books.on India's foreign policy. Besides, he was one of those rare diplomats who had a great capacity of looking at the larger picture of Indian diplomacy— a characteristic of building broad visions of India's foreign policy. It is generally known that his disappearance was percieved as a great loss to India's foreign policy, and to Manmohan Singh personally. Now that Dixit is no more he has been succeeded by M.K. Narayanan, who is an expert on security matters, but does not appear to have the same intellectual dimension as Dixit.

The third personality is the Foreign Minister. Natwar Singh, was the first Foreign Minister until he was excluded from the Cabinet after his alleged financial involvement in the Iraqi Oil for Programme scandal, Manmohan Singh subsequently appointed Pranab Mukherjee as the Foreign Minister. While it is not known the level of Mukerjee's interaction with the Prime Minister, it is most unlikey to consider the decisional process in foreign policy without the Foreign Minister.

The other personality is the Foreign Secretary, Shiv Shankar Menon, who is a very sharp diplomat with considerably experience, including one important stint in China. It is more than likely that he does have important and continuous interaction with the Prime minister.

EVALUATION

When this author quizzed Manmohan Singh in Geneva regarding his future plans at the end of his Geneva stint as the head of the South Commission, he expressed the hope of teaching in the Indian capital. Little did he know that he was going to end up as the Prime Minister of India.

While his prime ministership was an accident, his academic and professional background, compounded with the political experience as Congress leader has stood him in good stead for the high position he is currently holding. Besides, the high image he has earned as one who is trustworthy, incorruptable and modest have greatly facilitated his political responsibilities.

At the beginning of his mandate. he hardly had any real power, for it was elsewhere—in the hands of Sonia Gandhi whe had handedly won the general elections. But, through the years of good governance he had acquired autonomous power of his own. Obviously, this was inevitable, for you cannot remain at the political summit for so many years surrounded by a power vacuum.

Manmohan Singh's foreign policy has more substance than that of many of his predecessors. To risk a generalisation, it could be suggested that there are four dimensions of his substantive foreign policy—the dimensions of seeking out great powers, of constructing an architecture of interaction with developing countries, of joining hands with a very limited group of countries for economic and political interaction, and of coming up with a new vision regarding India's neighbours.

In all of them Manmohan Singh has been successful. And in all of them he has made significant inroads.

He has forged meaningful and non-conflictual ties with four planetary powers—US, Russia, China and the European Union.

To suggest that India's foreign policy has changed in the American direction does not correspond with the facts. It is indeed an exaggeration, even though there has been a concentrated Indo-US interaction since the conclusion of the nuclear deal with Washington—a deal that has opened considerable prospects of growth between the two countries.

Manmohan Singh has concluded a series of strategic relations with all the four powers

The second dimension is the architecture of relations with South-East and East Asia, including his particpation in the latest East Asian Summit.

The third dimension pertains to the new form of trilateral institutionalised interactions between India, Brazil and South Africa,and between India, China and Russia both of which are on the road to becoming a new pattern Indian diplomatic behaviour.

And the fourth dimension pertains to South Asia where India is becoming bilaterally more outgoing, and multilaterally more insistent on transforming SAARC into a South Asian Community modelled after the EU and ASEAN.

India, thus is coming a long way in widening its international relations in which Manmohan Singh's role is not insignificant.

Chapter XVI
THE SUMMING UP

The importance of inputs in foreign policy making are contingent on two factors: personal and political.

It is impossible to visualise an Indian Prime Minister playing a crucial role in the determination of India's Foreign Policy if he has no knowledge and no interest in what is happening in the world. The intellectual interest in the panorama of global events, on the part of the Prime Minister, is indeed vital, and is a major precondition for any viable investigation of the personality factor in India's foreign policy making. The possibility of another powerful personality intervening—from the the government or the opposition—in foreign policy cannot, of course, be excluded. This has happened in other countries. But, it has so far not been the case in India since hardly any Foreign Minister or Foreign Secretary has been politically powerful enough to replace the Prime Minister, with the possible exception of I.K.Gujral who did play a crucial role under Prime Ministers V.P.Singh and Deva Gowda since neither of them were really interested in foreign affairs.

While the phenomenon of mainstream non-governmental political personalities playing a determinative role in foreign affairs is still infrequent, it cannot be excluded in the future. With the increasing emergence of coalition politics, and with the increasing national emanation of dissension on foreign policy issues, it may indeed become significant factor in Indian politics. Rajiv Gandhi was perhaps the first example who openly challenged Prime Minister Chandra Shekhar on his pro-American policy during the Gulf crisis—a policy that finally resulted in his downfall. The opposition generated by Manmohan Singh's nuclear deal with the US is another important example; for it resulted in pushing the Prime Minister to intially abandon the obtainment of ratification of the agreement in the Parliament. But, finally he did and succeeded. While this was probably the first time that

Singh was challenged in foreign policy, it did not project onto the forefront a mainstream political figure of the same dimension as Rajiv Gandhi.

The second factor is political. It is difficult to imagine a Prime Minister playing a determining role if he is faced with difficult domestic situation where he has to depend on other parties to continue in office.

Thus the role of the Prime Minister is greatly contingent on his own personal proclivities, and the difficult political situation he may have to reckon with.

There is, however, an exception to this rule: irrespective of the personal interest or the political situation, no Prime Minister can politically afford to ignore India's visible policies towards other countries of South Asia. For, at least so far as the region is concerned, the line that separates such foreign policies from internal affairs is indeed very thin, to a point that it has almost vanished.

To evaluate the role of the personality factor in international affairs, it is important to distinguish between the routine, the visible and the macro issues—the three components that have been advanced in this study. The role can be varied in routine and macro affairs, but not in visible regional developments, since no Prime Minister can afford to ignore them, given their linkage with domestic issues.

If one were to make a typology of the personality factor in the making of India's foreign policy, it could be argued that Jawarharlal Nehru, Lal Bahadur Shastri, Indira Gandhi, Rajiv Gandhi and Manmohan Singh were interested and controlled varyingly all the three aspects of foreign policy; whereas Morarji Desai, V.P.Singh ,Chandra Shekhar, Charan Singh and Deve Gowda had a minimal interest in routine and global matters, but took, albeit varyingly, an interest in visible affairs.

Narasimha Rao, I.K.Gujral and Atal Behari Vajpayee fall between the two categories. Their interest and capacity to contribute to foreign policy making was as great as that of Nehru and the two Gandhis. While, they were all pushed to take an interest on all the three levels, their political position, on the other hand, being as uncertain and as weak as that of Desai, Singh, Chandra Shekhar and Deve Gowda restrained them from becoming too dominant in the foreign policy sector.

In any event, it must be argued that the increasing globalisation and marketisation of the international system, compounded with the nuclearisation of South Asia, has generally upgraded the role of foreign policy in Indian politcal behaviour. Besides, the ramifications of global developments on the domestic scene have become so overwhelmingly important , it is hardly possible for any Prime Minister to sideline them.

Modernisation

Consider the foreign components of modernisation. They have become increasingly vital in India's economic development, Though they were always important, they have, through the years, become so crucial that the pattern of Indian economic development no longer resembles the model of the Nehru years. The break with the past is becoming decisive and almost irreversible.

During Nehru's time, India had designed a strict import substitute strategy, the basic objective of which was to establish an indigenous industrial, agricultural and infrastructural base. That India was successful in this endeavour is evident from the significant growth of the economy, and from the wide array of industries that dot the land, the agriculture that feeds the country, the infrastructure that services the economy, and the rapidly growing middle class that has become the backbone of entrepreneurial economy. All these achievements had been made without generating any serious disequilibrium in the economy. The growth rate was high, inflation low, and the balance of payments deficit economically acceptable.

Though much of the effort in building up this base was essentially Indian, it would not have acquired the solidity it did without external assistance. It is indeed to the credit of India's original politics of non-alignment that, during the fifties and sixties, it was able to use this political stance to gain the support of the two competing blocs for its economic development, which no other third world country was able to achieve.

But all this did not last long. Problems grew in the seventies; difficult problems for that matter. The economy began to sputter. The industrial sector became less self-sustaining. Agricultural growth was increasingly nullified by a galloping demographic increase, and the rapidly growing technical manpower, thrown into the market, was no longer absorbable by the economy.

Externally, the situation was even worse. It had an horrendous effect on the economy. Significant price hikes in the oil sector, compounded with the constriction of concessionary aid, and the growing Indian demand for sophisticated arms from abroad set in motion an irreversible process of mounting deficits in the balance of payments.

What aggravated the situation was India's decision to raise capital in the international market to compensate for declining concessionary aid, and to import capital goods to modernise industries to make them more competitive internally as well as externally.

All these problems led the Indian Prime Ministers in the seventies and the eighties to adopt a string of pragmatic measures to rectify the situation.

But all these reforms and initiatives, though undoubtedly meritorious, were no more adequate for a rapidly spreading disease in the nineties. What India really needed was a radical treatment. Paradoxically, this was provided by the weak relatively unstable Narasimha Rao government in 1991, when, in the aftermath of another major hike in oil prices, and in the face of a serious foreign exchange crisis, it introduced a real deregulation of the economy through a series of initiatives: the encouragement of private foreign investment, the formulation of a courageous export-oriented policy, and the introduction of some degree of rupee convertibility— in sum a policy that would render Indian economy less insular. This was a landmark decision comparable in importance to what Nehru did when he introduced an insular socialistically-oriented economy.

But, has this globalisation of the economy helped India to tackle the economic problems it is currently faced with? Will all these new ongoing internationalisation of the economy finally open possibilities for it to grow rapidly, to obtain the necessary transfer of resources, and to become more export-oriented?

It is, of course, impossible, to make any forecasts regarding the successful outcome of these new endeavours. Much will, of course, depend on India's political determination to continue on this path, and the administrative doggedness to overcome myriad bureaucratic hurdles.

In any event one thing is certain: internal and external ramifications of such a policy were far-reaching. Internally, this process of macro-adjustments and structural reforms, leading to the marketisation of the economy, has resulted in the remarkable increase in the rate of growth; so much so that India has become the second fastest growing economy in the world, reaching the growth rate of almost ten per cent.

Consider the result of all this on the Indian economy: the expansion of the Indian middle class, a considerable rise in the export of goods and capital, a remarkable augmentation of foreign reserves, and a conspicuous application of scientific and technological capacity to lift the Indian production.

But, on the other hand, this economic opening has resulted in the emergence of mounting external pressures by multinationals, by other States, by the World Bank, by the International Monetary Fund, etc., to accelerate this process, and to open even larger economic windows to the outside world. The question that one can validly ask is whether the Indian system will have the capacity to withstand these unavoidable pressures which are going to become more and more tenacious as India moves more and more in the direction of a market economy;

Externally the ramifications of the economic reforms on India's foreign policy are also growing. Whatever resistance India was able to offer in the past to international pressures was partly due to the protection it had received from the erstwhile Soviet Union, and partly due to the insular character of the Indian economy. Now that the Soviet Union is no more, and the politics of economic insularity has been abandoned, the independent character of India's foreign policy may well be jeopardised. For this is clearly what happens to most third world nations that opt for the globalisation of their economies. The "ground-break shift" in India's foreign policy, in fact, became increasingly evident with the establishment of diplomatic relations with Israel, with the support extended to the repealing of the 1975 UN resolution equating Zionism with racism, with growing relations with the EU, with the increasing Indo-US entente leading to the conclusion of the nuclear deal, with the inauguration of a new pattern of relations with China and Russia, with the emergence of some disinterestedness in north-south relations, with nuclearisation of India, and with a new urge to economically cooperate with distant and nearby neighbours, etc. These are perhaps some signs of the shape of things to come.

Hegemonic ambitions

The other foreign policy dimension that is closely linked to domestic affairs is India's objective of attaining a hegemonic position in South Asia.

India, of course, has always been a predominant power in South Asia. This was unavoidable given the fact that it was bigger–much bigger–more densely populated, more democratic, more stable, more endowed with national resources, more economically developed and more technically equipped than all the South Asian nations combined together. Besides, all the ethnic groups that inhabit the neighbouring countries are present in India—only in larger numbers—and all the nations of the subcontinent are either contiguous to India, or are separated by narrow waters. "Giantism" does have an influence on the nation's foreign policy. It cannot be otherwise.

Therefore, whatever happens in India effects these countries. Whether, they are ethnic or religious conflicts, natural or political upheavals, or economic difficulties, they all impact on South Asia.

The Indian goal to play a major role in South Asia is therefore congruous with what it represents—giantism. What has, however, changed is the nature of the role. After the upgradation of India's military clout, this role has been expanded to exercise a predominant, hegemonic control over the entire region to the exclusion of other powers who were perceived as unfriendly or adversaries. Since Indira Gandhi's mandate, and particularly after the liberation of Bangladesh, this has become an important feature of India's foreign policy. It became even more accentuated under Rajiv Gandhi who had the ambition of making India a major power even beyond the frontiers of South Asia, not to speak of Vajpayee's decision to go nuclear. Some of the successive Prime Ministers have denied any intention of wanting to acquire the necessary clout in South Asia, but the fact is that they have always reverted to such a policy. The giantism of India was there, and it could hardly be set aside. In fact, if there is any region in the third world to which the dichotomy of a dominant versus subordinate system applies most appropriately, it is South Asia.

But has India really been successful in achieving this role? Has it reached a generally recognised hegemonic position in the region. It has not. Its achievements have fallen short of its ambitions ; even more so now that India and Pakistan have become nuclear powers through which the latter has neutralised India's conventional superiority.

The United State has always refused any hegemonial status to India. During the cold war, it had maintained significant presence in Pakistan. Though US attitude towards India has become more friendly in recent years it can hardly ever accept India's predominance in the region. The Chinese too have declined to accept Indian ambitions in South Asia. They are very much present in the region—and not only in Pakistan.

Indian military intervention in Sri Lanka proved abortive. The cost was heavy, and now with the recrudescence of the civil war, the government has turned to Norway for mediation. India has been left out of the whole process. Pakistan continues to remain as defiant as ever, and the explosion of violent conflict in Kargil (Kashmir) testifies to the refusal of Pakistan to accept any subordination. The new democratic process and the recent agreement on the sharing of the water has not brought Bangladesh any closer to India. And, if Nepal, after considerable pressure, has fallen in line with India, it is not at all certain that this will continue indefinitely.

While, it is understandable that India—because of its 'giantism'—would like to exercise some degree of control over South Asia, this should be possible if it were to design an alternative pattern of intra-South Asian relations–a pattern that would be based on gaining the confidence of smaller nations, assisting them economically, helping them to solidify pluralistic political structures, settling intractable bilateral problems with each of them by making concessions, interacting jointly to resolve regional issues regionally.

The South Asian Association For Regional Co-operation (SAARC) of seven South Asian nations, established in 1985, (now eight with Afghanistan as the additional member) could become a catalyst to generate and accelerate regional co-operation in which India has to prudently give the lead without using its powerful position to dominate other members. Though concrete intra-SAARC steps have been taken for the expansion of tourism, exemption of visa for certain category of persons, free movement of published material, of artists, films and so on; they should help in confidence building, but what is really needed is something more dramatic in which India—the biggest of them all—would have to take the initiative. Recent unilateral gestures by India to open its market for the free movement of various goods from neighbouring countries, without demanding any reciprocity from other members (with the exception of Pakistan), should help to accelerate regional co-operation, and to break down barriers among the member states. The utilisation of its powerful and dimensional economy to seek a new partnership with its small neighbours is the new road India is taking. Though mistrust of India is enormous, this should help. Manmohan Singh's remarkable suggestions to eventually expand SAARC into a South Asian Community, on the lines of ASEAN and EU, is a major development in South Asia.

International role playing

Playing a role in the international system—another Indian foreign policy objective – has also evolved. During Nehru's time, with the upright international image that India had acquired, he was able to design a generally acceptable role—one that was concerned with global politics.

But, this pattern of role playing too has changed with the evolution of the Indian and global situations. For one thing, most of Nehru's successors had no real interest in global affairs. They lacked his sensitivity and intellectuality regarding international developments; and what is more, they lacked the international prestige he had established for himself through the years; for another, the different military actions in which India was involved against the Portuguese in Goa (1961), against the Chinese in the north (1962), against Pakistan in the West (1965) and in the East (1971) and against the Tamil Tigers in Sri Lanka across the sea (1987) seriously affected its global image. Furthermore, the international system, having evolved radically, did not need any more the mediatory skills India had acquired at the global level during Nehru's time. Besides, India's public stand on Hungary (1956), Czechoslovakia(1968) Afghanistan (1980) and Kampuchea (1980) did not help matters as it gave the impression as if it was against nationalism.

In sum, India's broad interest after Nehru thus had moved away from macro internationalism to down-to-earth regional issues; and it is difficult to imagine that the growing domestic uncertainties, compounded with South Asian destablisation is ever going to permit India to extricate itself from domestic and regional preoccupations to once again acquire the original global role. Besides, and this is important for role-playing, well-equipped, well-informed, and internationally well-motivated charismatic leaders have disappeared from the Indian political scene, with no hope of their re-appearing in the foreseeable future.

The signs of change are becoming more and more evident with palpable Indian signs of avoiding to play any frontal role in international conferences where India, once upon a time, was the centre of attraction The interest has clearly declined. But, on the other hand, the increasing Indian focalisation on domestic development has resulted in the vast construction of a significant international economic interaction, replacing the Nehruvian diplomatic dimension that was essentially political. It was inaugurated by V. P.Singh, Chandra Shehkar, I.K.Gujral, Deve Gowda, conspicuously expanded by Narasimha Rao, has taken the great leap forward under Manmohan Singh—a leap that has made economic relations the central dimension of India's foreign policy.

DECISION-MAKING PROCESS:

What about the decision making process? Does India really possess well-institutionalised system where different inputs contribute to the elaboration of foreign policy making; or is it faced with a phenomena where all the three decisional components (decisions, decision making process and the decision maker) are in the hands of one recognisable authority centred around the Prime Minister.

The main thrust of this study is that the decisional process is contingent on two factors: the dimension of the Prime Minister's intellectual interest in foreign affairs, and the nature of his real power within the political system. Prime Ministers, who have personal interest and fascination for international affairs, and who have not been sapped by coalition politics, have invariably arrogated to themselves the whole process, ably supported by their advisers centred in and around the Prime Minister's Secretariat. The process is centralised, and all the three components that constitute the decisional process—decision, decision making and the decision maker—are visible and traceable. On the other hand, in the case of Prime Ministers, who have no intellectual interest in foreign affairs, and who are politically debilitated by coalition politics, the whole decisional process results in decentralisation and in the diffusion of the whole process, with different institutions having a greater role to play. In such situations the whole process becomes opaque, and is less traceable, at least so far as all the inputs that have gone into the process are concerned.

The whole process of foreign policy making, thus, has continuously fluctuated since 1947. Like a pendulum it has swung from one position to the other, changing with Prime Ministers, and swinging with different governments.

Thus, given the oscillating nature of Indian foreign policy making, it is almost impossible to congeal the whole process in a set pattern, or design a broad theoretical framework that would be valid for all situations and for all eventualities. Only, a systematic, detailed and objective investigation of major events in which India was heavily involved would permit us to draw firm and valid general conclusions about the real functioning of the Indian decisional system.

Where is India going? Looking at the whole panorama of six decades of Indian independence, can we discern a real direction, from the determinants we have examined, the goals we have conceptualised, and the decisional process we have traced. Or is India like a rudderless ship lost in an endless sea with no captain aboard, with no radar to give it a direction completely bogged down with problems of its own?

India really was never rudderless, but then it was also never direction-oriented after the Nehru era. Having abandoned the vocation of a globally-oriented nation it has, through the years, been pushed in the dual direction of politically focussing on the region, and of opening up a wide window to the outside world to interact with it economically in order to accelerate its process of modernisation.

Will India succeed in this new dual endeavour it has now chosen. It is of course difficult to predict, since the whole of South Asia, and indeed the whole world, is living in uncertain times. However, since India's future is indelibly linked with the region politically, and the planet economically, there is no reason to believe that it will not succeed in the twenty first century.

NOTES

1. Joseph Frankel, *The Making of Foreign Policy: An Analysis of Decision Making*, Oxford University Press, 1963, p.15.
2. Michael Clarke & Brian White. *Understanding Foreign Policy: The Foreign Policy Systems Approach*, Aldershot: Edward Elger, 1989, p. 136 & p. 141.
3. Ibid.
4. Joseph Frankel, op. cit. p.15.
5. Personal notes.
6. Vir Sanghvi, 'Chandra Shekhar: End of an Era, Counterpoint,' *Sunday Hindustan Times*, 15 July 2007.
7. Harish Chander & Padmani (ed.), *P.V. Narasimha Rao: Biographical Glimpses*, Delhi: Noida News Pvt Ltd, 1995.
8. Surjit Mansingh, *Nehru's Foreign Policy: Fifty Years On*, New Delhi: Mosaic Books 1988. p. 64.
9. Nirad C. Chaudhuri, *Thy Hand Great Anarch: India 1921-1952*, London: Chatto & Windus, 1987, p. 32.
10. Kamaladevi Chattopadhyay, *Inner Recesses Outer Spaces: Memoirs*, New Delhi: Navrang, 1986, p.119.
11. Cited in B.R. Nanda, *The Nehrus: Motilal and Jawaharlal*, London: George Allen and Unwin Ltd, 1962, p.77.
12. Cited in Nayantara Sahgal (ed.), *Nehru's Letters to his Sister: Before Freedom 1909-1941*, New Delhi: Roli Books, 2004, p.8.
13. Sonia Gandhi (ed.), *Two Alone, Two Together: Letters between Indira Gandhi & Jawaharlal Nehru, 1922-1964*, New Delhi: Penguin Book, 2004.
14. Ibid., p.101.
15. Jawaharlal Nehru, *Glimpses of World History*, New Delhi: Oxford University Press, 1989, p. vii.
16. Ibid. p.viii.
17. Jawaharlal Nehru, *A Bunch of Old Letters*, Bombay: Asia Publishing House, 1958.
18. Jawaharlal Nehru, *An Autobiography*, (Sixth impression), London: Oxford University Press, 1988, p. 153.
19. Ibid.,p.361.
20. Ibid., 364.
21. M.O.Mathai, *Reminiscences Of The Nehru Age*, New Delhi: Vikas Publishing House Pvt.Ltd , p.170.
22. Jad Adams and Phillip Whitehead, *The Dynasty: The Nehru-Gandhi Story*, London: Penguin and BBC Books, 1997, p.178.
23. V.K.R.V. Rao, *The Nehru Legacy*, Bombay: Popular Prakashan, 1971, p.23.

24. D.G.Tendulkar, *Mahatma Gandhi,* Bombay: Vithal Bhai Javeri, 1953, Vol VII, p. 90.
25. Jawaharlal Nehru, *Selected Speeches,* September 1946-April 1961, New Delhi: Government of India, Publications Division, 1961, p.13.
26. Ibid.
27. Extracts from different speeches, see A.B. Shah (ed.), *Jawaharlal Nehru: A Critical Tribute,* Bombay:Mankatalas, 1965,p. 98.
28. A.P. Rana, 'The Nehruvian tradition in World affairs. Its evolution and relevance in the Post-Cold war international relations', in Surjit Mansingh (ed.), *Nehru's Foreign Policy, Fifty Years On,* Mosaic Books 1998, p.46.
29. M.W.Childs, *Witness to Power,* New York: McGraw Hill, 1975, p. 133.
30. Chaman Lal, *India: Cradle of Cultures,* New Delhi: Modern School, n.d. p. 7.
31. Ibid., p. 35.
32. Robert Trumball, *As I see India,* London: Cassell and Co, 1957, p. 249.
33. K.J.Holsti, *International Politics: A Framework for Analysis,* Englewood Cliffs, N.J. Prentice Hall, 1967, p. 193.
34. Sumit Ganguly, 'The Prime Minister and Foreign and Defence policies,' in James Manor (ed.) *Nehru to the Nineties: The Changing Office of Prime Minister of India,* New Delhi: Viking 1994, p. 142.
35. Nayantara Sahgal, op.cit., p. 399.
36. V.P. Bhatia, 'Cabbages and Kings', *Organiser,* 29 October 2000.
37. Badr-ud-din Tyabji, *Memoir of an Egoist,* Volume 1 1897-1956, Roli Books, 1988, p. 257.
38. Girja Shankar Bajpai, 'India and the Balance of Power', *The Indian Yearbook of International Affairs,* 1952, Madras: University of Madras, 1953, p. 20.
39. Prabhu Chopra (ed.), *Diary of Maniben Patel,* New Delhi: Vision Books 2001, p.70.
40. Personal notes.
41. Cited in Judith M. Brown, *Nehru: A Political Biography,* New Delhi: Oxford University Press, 2004, p.264.
42. Ibid. p.250.
43. Durga Das (ed.), *Sardar Patel's Correspondence, 1945-50,* Volume 10, Ahmedabad: Navjivan Publishing House, 1974, p.336.
44. 'Tibet, China, Nehru and Panikkar', http://www.tibet.ca/wtnarchive/2000/3/23_2 html, p. 6.
45. *Foreign Relations of the US, 1951,* Vol VI, part 2, Washington DC: Government Printing Press,1952, p.2188.
46. Cited in Christopher Andrew and Vasili Mitrokhin, *The World was going our Way: The KGB and the Battle for the Third World,* New York: Basic Books, 2005, p. 314.
47. Ibid.
48. M.O.Mathai, op.cit., p.166.
49. Ibid.
50. 'Oral History Interview with Elbert G. Mathews', *Truman Presidential and Museum Library,* p.1.
51. Personal notes.
52. Govind Talwalkar, 'India knew that it was too weak for War', *The Asian Age,* 4 July 2007.

53. M.O.Mathai, op. cit.
54. UN Security Council, *Official Documents*, Supplement No 16, Annex 41, New York: 1948, p. 50.
55. UN General Assemby, *Offical Records 1949, Vol 1*, New York: 1950, p.50.
56. *India Record*, 29 January 1949.
57. Mandela's speech in India on 26 January 1995 on the occasion of the unveiling of the statute of Pandit Jawaharlal Nehru, full text in http://www.anc.org ze/an sp 9501268.html.
58. Gamal Abdel Nasser, 'Where two worlds meet', in Rafiq Zakaria (ed.) *A Study of Nehru*, Bombay: Jaico, 1959, p. 80.
59. A.W. Singham & Shirley Hune, *Non-alignment in an Age of Alignment*, London: Zed Books 1986, p. 62.
60. T.J.S. George, *Krishna Menon: A Biography*, Bombay: Jaico Publishing House, 1966.
61. Kenneth T. Young, *Negotiating with the Chinese Communists: 1953-1967, The US Experience*, New York: McGraw-Hill Book Company, 1968, p. 47.
62. The Presidential Papers of Dwight David Eisenhower, Letter to Jawaharlal Nehru, 7 July 1955, http://www.eisenhowermemorial.org/ presidential- papers/ first term/ documents/1497.cfm.
63. Ibid.
64. Ibid.
65. Ibid.
66. *Le Monde*, 21 September 1962.
67. Erika Leuchtag, *With the King in the Clouds*, London: Hutchinson, 1958, p. 63.
68. This disagreement within the Cabinet was reported by K.P.S. Menon, Foreign Secretary in the MEA, cited by B. Krishna, *Sardar Vallabhbhai Patel, India's Iron Man*, New Delhi: Harper Collins, 1996, p.
69. Tin Thin Aung & Soe Myint, "Indo-Burma Relation," http://www.ideas.int/asia-pacific/Burma/upload.
70. Aung San Suu Kyi, *Freedom from Fear*, New Delhi: Penguin Books 1995, p. 104.
71. S. Gopal (ed.) *Selected Works of Jawaharlal Nehru*, Vol. 8, op. cit., p.235.
72. Statement in the Lok Sabha, 25 August 1960, *Lok Sabha Debates*, 1960, Vol. XLV, Col. 4747.
73. Ibid.
74. Durga Das (ed.), *Sardar Patel's Correspondence 1945-1950, Volume 8*, Ahmedabad: Navjivan Press, 1973, p. 388.
75. Ibid, p.350.
76. K.T. Rajasingham, 'Sri Lanka: The Untold Story', Chapter 19, *Anguish and Pain, Asia Times*, 15 December 2001.
77. *Frontline*, 9 April 1999, p. 66.
78. Ibid.,p.66.
79. Ibid., 23 April 1999.
80. Remark made to M.O.Mathai, op. cit., p.107.
81. Cited in Jad Adams and Phillip Whitehead, *The Dynasty: The Nehru-Gandhi Story*, London: Penguin & BBC Books, 1997, p. 168.
82. *Foreign Relations of the US 1949*, Volume VI, Washington DC: Government Printing Press, 1977.

83. Secret letter from Loy Hendersen to US Secretary of State of August 15, 1949. *Foreign Relations of the US 1949*, Volume VI, Washington DC: Government Printing Office 1977, pp. 1732-33.
84. Truman Library, Loy Henderson "Oral History Interview," http://www.trumanlibrary.org/oralhist/henderson,htm.p.1.
85. Cited in Michael J. Lacey, *The Truman Presidency*, Cambridge: Cambridge University Press, p. 357.
86. Ibid, 9 April 1999, p.66.
87. V.P.Bhatia, 'Nehru's Utopian globalism,' *The Organiser*, August 24, 2003.
88. Siddharth Varadarajan," A Forced one-on-one," *Times of India*, 15 March 2000.
89. Escott Reid, *Envoy to Nehru*, Delhi: Oxford University Press, 1981, p. 4.
90. *Selected works of Jawaharlal Nehru*, Second Series, Vol 14, Part II, p. 380.
91. *The Presidential Papers of Dwight D. Eisenhower*, Document 1360, op.cit. p.1.
92. Ibid.
93. *Foreign Relations of the US*, 1958-1960, volume X1X, Washington DC: Government Printing Press, 1962, p.5.
94. 'India sheltered Dalai Lama for nuclear technology', *Indian Express*, 11 August 1999.
95. While Krishna Menon, leader of the Indian delegation to the UN declared that the decision to support the Russian resolution was taken on his own since he did not have any instructions from New Delhi, this has been challenged by Nehru's secretary, who wrote that he had, on Nehru's orders, cabled instructions to Menon to abstain from voting on the 5-nation resolution. For details, see M.O.Mathai, op. cit.
96. Ibid., p. 173.
97. 'More Documents from the Russian Archives', *Cold War International History Project: Virtual archives*, Woodrow Wilson International Center for Scholars, Washington DC.
98. Minutes of the Meeting between the Hungarian and Chinese Delegations in Budapest, January 16, 1957, Document 10, Published by the Woodrow Wilson Center for International Scholars.
99. Ibid.
100. Top secret note from Pillai to Nehru, 2 November 1956, cited in Judith M. Brown, *Nehru: A Political Life*, Delhi: Oxford University Press 2003, p.164.
101. Ibid, p.164.
102. Ibid, p. 165.
103. Ibid.
104. Cold war International History Project, Document 10, op. cit.
105. Durga Das (ed.), *Sardar Patel's Correspondence, 1945-50, Volume 10*, Ahmedabad: Navajivan Publishing House, 1974, p. 340.
106. Ibid., p. 236.
107. Ibid, p. 399.
108. Cited in B.Krishna, *Sardar Vallabhai Patel: India's Iron Man*, op.cit., p. 523.
109. Ibid., 523.
110. Personal notes.
111. B. Krishna, op. cit., p.523.
112. Kuldip Nayar, *India: The Critical Years*, New Delhi: Vikas Publishing House, 1971, p.153.

113. Ibid., p.173.
114. M.J. Akbar, *Nehru: The Making of India,* London: Penguin 1988, p.561.
115. J. Bandopadhyaya, *The Making of India's Foreign Policy, Determinants, Institutions, Processes and Personalities,* Bombay: Allied Publishers, 1979.
116. Govind Talwalkar, 'India knew it was too weak for war', *Asian Analysis,* 4 July 2007, also see A.G.Noorani, 'The CIA Papers', *Frontline,* 7 September 2007.
117. Cited in 'India's Nuclear Weapons Program: The beginning: 1944-1960', *India's Nuclear Weapons Programme,* Internet.
118. "Bhabha's Quest for the Bomb," *Bulletin of the Atomic Scientists,* 23 November 2005.
119. See 'US intelligence and the Indian Bomb', *National Security Archive,* Internet, 6 May 2006.
120. Ibid.
121. 'India's Nuclear Weapons program: The Beginning', op. cit.
122. Personal notes.
123. K.J.Holsti, op.cit., p. 192.
124. Cited in Narendra Singh Sarila, *The Shadow of the Great Game: The Untold Story of Partition,* Harpers Collins, p.408.
125. Cited in V.P.Bhatia, 'Nehru's utopian Globalisation', *Organiser,* 24 August 2003.
126. Jad Adams, and Phillip Whitehead, op.cit., p.189.
127. Ibid.
128. An Indian website *samachar.com,* conducted a poll in 2003 that asked "which Prime Minister has contributed the most to India's development." Atal Bihari Vajpayee held a huge lead with 596 votes and Nehru came third with seventy five votes.
129. Janardan Thakur, *Prime Ministers, Nehru to Vajpayee,* Mumbai: Eeshwar, 1999, p.77.
130. C.P.Srivastava, *Lal Bahadur Shastri: Prime Minister of India 1964-1966, A Life Of Truth in Politics,* Delhi:Oxford University Press, 1995.
131. Ibid.
132. Janardan Thakur, op.cit., p. 78.
133. Ibid., p. 16.
134. John D. Barrow, *Theories of Everything: The Quest for Ultimate Explanation,* London: Vintage 1991, p.1X.
135. L.P. Singh, *Portrait of Lal Bahadur Shastri: A Quintessential Gandhian,* Delhi: Ravi Dayal Publisher,1996, p.7.
136. Under Presidential order, cited in D.R. Mankekar, *Lal Bahadur Shastri: A Political Biography,* Bombay: Popular Prakashan, 1966, p.110.
137. Government of India, *Speeches of Prime Minister Lal Bahadur Shastri June 1964-May 1965.* New Delhi:Publications Division, 1965, p.5.
138. C.P. Srivastva, op. cit., p. 415.
139. M.O. Mathai, op.cit., p. 239.
140. Janardan Thakur, op. cit, p. 72.
141. Ved Mehta, *Portrait of India,* Delhi:Vikas Publications, 1987.
142. Personal notes.
143. Michael Brecher, *Nehru's Mantle:The Politics of Succession in India,* Westport, Connecticut: Greenwood Press, 1966, p. 117.

144. Kuldip Nayar, *The Judgement: Inside Story of the Emergency in India,* New Delhi: Vikas Publishing House, 1977,p. 23.
145. L.P. Singh, *India's Foreign policy: The Shastri Period,* New Delhi: Uppal Publishing House, 1980, p.41.
146. C.P. Srivastava, op. cit., p.107.
147. Ministry of External Affairs, *Report of the Committee on the Indian Foreign Service,* New Delhi: Publications Division, 1966, pp. 25-26.
148. T.V.Kunhi Krishnan, *Chavan and the Troubled Decade,* Bombay: Somaiya Publications Pvt Ltd, 1971.
149. Chester Bowles'papers at Yale University.
150. Ibid., p.11.
151. Text in ibid.
152. Ibid., in one of the papers accessible at Yale, Bowles jotted down "the talking points for discussions" with the Prime Minister.
153. *The Economic Times,* 19 September 2007.
154. Government of India, *Speeches,* op.cit, p. 5.
155. Ibid.
156. L.P.Singh, *Portrait of Lal Bahadur Shastri,* op.cit., p. 121.
157. Ibid., p.120.
158. Conversation of L.K.Jha with John Freeman, the British High Commissioner to India; text in Roedad Khan (compiled and selected), *The British Papers, Secret and Confidential, India-Pakistan-Bangladesh Documents 1958-1969,* Oxford University Press, 1989.
159. Ibid.
160. Cited in V.P. Bhatia, 'Cabbages and Kings', *Organiser,* 29 October 2000.
161. L.P.Singh, op.cit., p. 50.
162. Ibid., p. 50.
163. *Janata,* 25 January 1965.
164. For the text of the agreement see Indo-Nepalese Agreement in the Ministry of External Affair's publication, *Foreign Affairs Record,* 1965.
165. *The US in World Affairs,* op.cit.
166. Envirolink network, *India's Nuclear Weapons Program. On To Weapons Development: 1960-1967, http/nuketesting. Environweb.org /hew India/IndiaWDevelopment.htm 29 June 2002.*
167. *Shastri's Speeches,* op cit., p. 5.
168. Ashok Kapur "India's Nuclear Politics and Policy. Janata Party's evolving Stance" in T.T.Poulose (ed.) *Perspectives of India's Nuclear Policy,* New Delhi: Young Asia Publications 1978, 1978, p. 172.
169. Sri Ram Sharma, *Lal Bahadur Shastri: An Era of Transition in Indian Foreign Policy,* New Delhi; Kanishka Publishers, Distributors, 2001, p.116.
170. For details, see George Perkovich, 'Bhabha's Quest for a Bomb', *Bulletin of Atomic Scientists,* May-June 2000. pp. 54-63.
171. Envorolink Network, op. cit.
172. George Perkovitch, *India's Nuclear Bomb: The Impact on Global Proliferation,* Berkeley: University of California Press, 1999, p. 97.
173. Letter from John G. Palfrey on 23 November 1964 to Llewellyn E. Thompson, US Under Secretary of State, p.22, text in *National Security Archive Electronic Briefing Book No 6,* published by Joyce Battle, *India and Pakistan—On the Nuclear Threshold.* Internet.

174. *India's Nuclear Weapons Programme, op. cit.*
175. Ibid.
176. *Bulletin of the Atomic Scientists,* op.cit., pp.54-63.
177. US Department of State, *Memorandum of Conversation,* 22 February 1965 in Foran's *US Nuclear Non-Proliferation Policy, 1945-1991.*
178. Ibid.
179. *Speeches of Shastri,* op. cit., p. 101.
180. Cited in L.P.Singh, op. cit. p.51.
181. General (Retd.) H.J. Mohammad Musa, *My Version: India-Pakistan War 1965,* Lahore: Wajidalis Limited 1983, p. 6.
182. C.P.Srivastava, op. cit.
183. Ibid.
184. S. Mallon and Louis J. Smith (ed.), *Foreign Relations of the US, 1964-1968.* Washington: US Government Printing Press.
185. According to a senior Pakistani journalist, Abdul Aziz, this was certainly a factor that led Ayub to accept the "operation Gibraltar" against India, for details, see Shabir Choudry, Director of the Institute of Kashmir Affairs, 'Kashmir and the 1965 War,' Internet, *Sawaal Channel http://news.sawaal.com/expertssays/guest/index39.htm p.2.*
186. A.G. Noorani, 'Lyndon Johnson and India', *Frontline,* 12-25 May 2001.
187. K.Sarwar Hassan (ed.), *Documents on the Foreign policy of Pakistan,* Karachi: Pakistan Institute of International Affairs, 1966.
188. A.G. Noorani, op. cit.
189. J.N.Chaudhury, *Aims, Arms and Aspects,* Bombay: Manaktales Publishers, 1966, p.265.
190. Kuldip Nayar, *India—The Critical Years,* New Delhi; Vikas Publications, 1971, p.209.
191. Cited in *Hindu,* 2 May 1965.
192. Noorani, op. cit.
193. Tashkent Delaration, text in L.P.Singh, op.cit., p. 119.
194. J. Bandopadhyaya, op.cit., p.135.
195. A.P. Rana, "The Nehruvian Tradition in World Affairs: Its Evolution and Relevance to Post-Cold War International Relations," in Surjit Mansingh (ed.), op.cit., p. 46.
196. Werner Levi, 'Foreign Policy: The Shastri Era', in K.P. Mishra (ed.), *Foreign Policy of India: A Book of Readings,* New Delhi: Thompson Press, 1977, p. 144.
197. Cited in Katherine Frank, *Indira: The Life of Indira Nehru Gandhi,* London: Harper Collins, 2001., p.119.
198. Sonia Gandhi (ed.), *Two Alone, Two Together, Letters Between Indira Gandhi and Jawaharlal Nehru, 1922-1964,* New Delhi: Viking 2004, p. xvii.
199. Raj Thapar, *All These Years: A Memoir,* New Delhi: Penguin Books, p. 1991, p. 52.
200. Pupul Jayakar, op.cit.
201. Cited in Katherine Frank, op.cit.
202. *The Hindustan Times,* 28 June 1980.
203. Raj Thapar, op.cit. p. 267.
204. Ibid.
205. M.O.Mathai, op.cit., p. 251.
206. Satish Gujral, *A Brush with Life, An Autobiography,* New Delhi: Viking 1997, p. 178, (edited by Khushwant Singh).

207. Janardan Thakur, *All the Prime Minister's Men*, New Delhi: Vikas Publishing House, 1981.
208. Ibid., p. 155.
209. Ibid., p. 288.
210. Ibid., p. 131.
211. Satish Gujral, op. cit., p. 243.
212. Katherine Frank, op. cit., p. 297.
213. Rowland Evans & Robert Novak, *Lyndon B. Johnson: The Exercise of Power, A Political Biography*, London: George Allen and Unwin Ltd, 1967, p. 324.
214. Ibid. p. 324.
215. V.P. Dutt, "India and the Superpowers" in A.K. Damodaran and U.S.Bajpai(edited), *Indian Foreign policy: The Indira Gandhi Years*, London: Sangam Books Limited, 1990, p.29.
216. Pupul Jayakar, *Indira Gandhi: A Biography*, New Delhi:Viking 1992, p. 188.
217. Chester Bowles, *Promises to Keep: My Years in Public Life 1941-1969*, New York: Harper & Row, 1971, p.526.
218. Katherine Frank, op. cit., p. 318.
219. G. Parthsarathy, 'A Former Foreign Secretary Looks Back', *Financial Express*, 18 April 2004.
220. Henry Kissinger, *White House Years*, Boston: Little Brown and Company, 1979, p. 874.
221. A.P. Jain (ed.), *Shadow of the Bear: Indo-Soviet Treaty*, New Delhi: 1971, p. 170.
222. Christopher Andrew and Vassili Mitrokhin, op.cit., p. 321.
223. Ibid.
224. Ibid.
225. Ibid., p. 322.
226. *BBC News*, 24, 29 June 2005.
227. Pupal Jayakar, op. cit., p. 185.
228. Christopher Andrew and Vasili Mitrokhin, op. cit., p.327.
229. Personal notes.
230. Ibid.
231. Katherine Frank, op. cit., p. 238.
232. Satish Gujral, op. cit., p. 243.
233. Mathai, M.O., op.cit., p. 200.
234. Janardan Thakur, op. cit., p.123.
235. Xuecheng Liu, *The Sino-Indian Border Dispute*, Lanham(Maryland), University Press of America, 1970, p.126.
236. R.K.Jain (ed.), *China-South Asia Relations 1947-1980*, Vol.1, New Delhi: Radiant Publishers, 1981, p. 473.
237. Ibid.
238. Ibid., p. 467.
239. ibid., p.466.
240. Arun Gandhi, *The Morarji Desai Papers: Fall of the Janata Government*, New Delhi: Vision Books, 1983, p.28.
241. R.K.Jain, op.cit.,p 477.

242. Personal notes.
243. Ibid.
244. Interview with Robert Goheen in *Rediff on the Net,* 1997.
245. For the text, see *Public Papers of the Presidents, American Presidency.org.*
246. Text of the Joint Communique, *http://www.Presdency.ucsb.edu/ws/index.php?.*
247. Arun Gandhi, op. cit., p. 31.
248. Ibid.
249. *Associated Press,* 24 March 1977.
250. Arun Gandhi, op. cit., p.33.
251. Ibid., pp. 33-34.
252. Ibid. p. 34.
253. Ibid., p. 29.
254. Ibid., p. 40.
255. Ibid., p. 42.
256. Ibid., p. 30.
257. Ibid., p.39.
258. Personal notes.
259. Personal notes.
260. N.M.Gatate (ed.), *Atal Behari Vajpayee. Four Decades in Parliament,* Delhi: Shipra Publications, 1008, p.100.
261. *Dawn,* 25 December 2004.
262. Ibid.
263. Shyam Bhatia, 'The rediff special', rediff. Com, 21 July 2001, Internet, p. 1.
264. Ibid., p. 1.
265. Ibld.
266. Ibid., p.1.
267. *Dawn Wire Service ,* 13 April 1995.
268. 'NTI: Country Overviews:India Nuclear Chronology', *http://www.nti.org//e_research/profiles/India/Nuclear/2296 6291.*
269. Ibid.
270. Ibid.
271. Ibid.
272. 'Quest For Peace,' Prime Minister Morarji Desai's Statement at the Special Session of the UNGA, New York, 9 June 1978.
273. B.Raman, *The Kaoboys of R&AW, Down Memory Lane,* New Delhi: Lancer Publishers, 2007, p. 66.
274. Ibid.
275. Thakur, op.cit., p. 146.
276. Ibid., p. 153.
277. Ibid., p. 153.
278. For details see the *Cold War International History Project.* op.cit.
279. David N. Gibbs, "Reassessing Soviet Motives For Invading Afghanistan," *Crtical Asian Studies,* 38:2, 2006.

280. When Kosygin, who was passing through India, was informed of Afghan communist activity by Gujral, who had gone to receive him at the airport, was very annoyed. Personal notes.
281. 'India online Link. A random harvest of political stories', Part one, Political News, October-November, http://www.indialink.Online.com/index.php?id=147 & PHPSESSID, 28 October 2008.
282. Ibid.
283. T.P. Sreenivasan, 'From Stalin to Putin: a man of all seasons', http://inhome.rediff.com 1 January 2008.
284. Narasimha Rao, *The Insider*, New Delhi: Viking, 1998, p. 220.
285. Ibid.
286. Pupul Jayakar, op. cit.
287. Inder Malhotra, op. cit., p. 217.
288. Pupul Jayakar, op.cit., p. 399.
289. Inder Malhotra, op. cit., p. 225.
290. Pupul Jayakar, op.cit., p. 409.
291. Ibid., p. 419.
292. Ibid.
293. Thakur, op. cit., p.189.
294. Words of D.P. Mishra, her close adviser who knew Indira Gandhi well.
295. Pupul Jayakar, op. cit.
296. Asoke Mitra, *The Telegraph*, 31 August 1982.
297. Remarks by Vir Sanghvi, cited in Jad Adams and Phillip Whitehead, *The Dynasty: Nehru-Gandhi Story*, London: Penguin Group and BBC Worldwide Ltd, 1997, p. 300.
298. Pupul Jayakar, op. cit., p. 203.
299. V.P.Dutt, *India's Foreign Policy*, New Delhi: Vikas, 1987, p. 289.
300. Cited in A.K. Damodaran & U.S.Bajpai (ed.), *Indian Foreign Policy, The Indira Gandhi Years*, London: Sangam Books Limited, 1990, p. 109-110.
301. Personal notes.
302. *Summary of World Broadcasts*, Part III, 19 May 1980.
303. Inder Malhotra, op. cit., p. 266.
304. Ibid.
305. *India Today*, 15 January 1989, p. 28.
306. Personal notes.
307. This is the explanation given by P.C. Alexander, Indira Gandhi's Secretary; for details, see P.C. Alexander, *My Years with Indira Gandhi*, New Delhi: Vision Books, 1991, p. 65.
308. Inder Malhotra, op.cit., p. 269.
309. Pupul Jayakar, op.cit., p. 448.
310. Inder Malhotra, op.cit., p. 269.
311. Lok Sabha debates, Vol. 39, No. 10, 5 August 1983, column 518.
312. Pupul Jayakar, op. cit.
313. B. Raman, 'We should leave Pakistan to stew in her own juice', *rediff.com*, 18 January 2003.

314. Ibid., p. 401.
315. P.C. Alexander, op. cit., p. 65.
316. Sreeram Chaulia, 'Wanted a New Indira Doctrine' 4 June 2006, *Yahoo News*, Internet.
317. Harish Chander & Padmini, *Rajiv Gandhi: Many Facets,* Delhi: Noida News PVT, 1192, p. 24.
318. Bhabani Sen Gupta, 'At ease with the World', *Seminar,* June 1989, p. 25.
319. For details, see Maharajakrishna Rasgotra (ed.), *Rajiv Gandhi's World View,* New Delhi: Vikas Publishing House Pvt Ltd, 1991.
320. Text in Ibid., p. 231.
321. Ibid., p. 260.
322. For details see, India's Nuclear Weapons Program, The Long Pause: 1974-1989, http://nuclearweaponarchive.org/India/India Pause.html.
323. 'From the Archive' , *The New Yorker,* 7 April 2005.
324. Ibid.
325. Ibid.
326. This analysis is based on discussions with some who were close to Rajiv Gandhi.
327. Maharajakrishna Rasgotra, op. cit., p. 231.
328. Ibid., p. 237.
329. Ibid.,p. XIV.
330. 'The Malta Meeting', *Internet.*
331. John T. Woolley & Gerhard Peters, *The American Presdency Project,* 1987: University of California at Santa Barbara, 1987. p. 1.
332. Personal notes.
333. Ibid.
334. Ibid.
335. Ibid.
336. Ibid.
337. N. Ram, 'Defining Moments', *Frontline,* September 12-25, 1998, pp.1-2.
338. From the Sino-Indian Joint Press Communiqué, 23 December 1988, Text in the Internet.
339. Mararajakrishna Rasgotra, op. cit., pp. 172-173.
340. Address to the UN Special Committee on Apartheid in New York on 22 October 1985. Text in Rasgotra, op. cit., p. 221.
341. *Mission to South Africa. The Commonwealth Report,* London: Penguin Special, 1986.
342. *The Hindustan Times,* 5 August 1986.
343. Ibid., 6 August 1986.
344. Rasgotra, op. cit., p. 223.
345. Iqbal Akhund, *Trial and Error : The Advent and Eclipse of Benazir Bhutto,* Oxford: Oxford University Press, 2000, p.91.
346. Iqbal Akhund, op. cit, p. 95.
347. Romesh Bhandari, in Harish Chander & Padmini, op.cit.
348. Ibid., p. 204.
349. Janardan Thakur, *Prime Ministers,* op. cit, p. 263.

350. Anees Syed and Shri Prakash, *Twenty Tumultous Years: Insights into Indian Polity* 1973-1994, 2 Volumes, New Delhi: Gyan Publishing House, 2003, p. 603.
351. *The Times of India*, 26 September 1990.
352. Hamish McDonald, 'Mauled but Unbeaten', *Far Eastern Economic Review* 12 September 1991.
353. Ibid., 12 September 1991.
354. Iqbal Akhund, op. cit., p. 207.
355. Iqbal Akhund, op.cit., p. 208.
356. Cited in ibid, p. 205.
357. Ibid. p. 232.
358. Ibid.
359. Personal notes.
360. Personal notes.
361. Iqbal Akhund, op.cit., p. 229.
362. Iqbal Akhund, op.cit., pp. 230-231.
363. *The Times of India,* 9 June 1960.
364. Ibid., 11 June 1990.
365. Personal notes.
366. Ibid.
367. *Foreign Affairs Record.* 38 (10), October 1992, p. 30.
368. V.P.Singh, *Selected Speeches and Writings,* 1989-90, New Delhi: Ministry of Information and Broadcasting, 1993, p. 263.
369. Sumit Chakravarty, 'New direction anticipated in Indo-Bangladesh relations', *New Age*, 18 March 1990.
370. Ibid.
371. Ibid.
372. *The Cei News,* January 1990 (Journal of Confederation of Engineering Industry).
373. Charles Haviland, « Despair of Nepal's Unwanted Exiles, » *BBC News*, 30 August 2005.
374. V.P.Singh, op.cit., p. 269.
375. Dileep Padgaonkar, 'Post-Gulf War agenda: Neither Rhetoric Nor Acquiescence,' *Times of India*, 4 March 1991.
376. Ibid.
377. Personal notes.
378. Ibid.
379. *National Herald,* 28 July 1990.
380. L.P. Singh, op.cit., p. 283.
381. Ibid., p. 285.
382. I.K.Gujral, *Continuity and Change: India's Foreign Policy,* New Delhi: Macmillan 2003, p. 65.
383. Personal notes.
384. *Patriot,* 1 June 1990.
385. Quote in *The Hindustan Times*, 3 June 1990.
386. Manoj Joshi, 'The Sino-Indian Border Problem', *Strategic Analysis,* October 1992, p. 686.

387. Cited in Dileep Padgaonkar, 'Post-Gulf War Agenda: Neither Rhetoric Nor Acquiescence', *The Times of India*, 3 March 1991.
388. B.G.Deshmukh, *From Poona to the Prime Minister's Office: A Cabinet Secretary looks Back*, New Delhi: Harper Collins Publishers, 2004, p. 264.
389. Expression used by Gujral. For details see I.K.Gujral, *Continuity and Change : India's Foreign Policy*, New Delhi: Macmillan India Ltd, 2003, p. 250.
390. Personal notes.
391. Ibid.
392. B.G. Deshmukh, op.cit., p. 241.
393. Ibid.
394. Ibid., p. 240.
395. Janardan Thakur, op.cit., p. 250.
396. Ibid., p. 265.
397. Ibid. p. 256.
398. Ramesh Thakur, 'India after non-alignment', *Foreign Affairs*, Spring 1992.
399. Praful Bidwai, 'Why V.P.Singh remains relevant', *Transnational Institute, rediff.com*, 3 July 2006.
400. Personal notes.
401. *Indian Express*, 19 June 1990.
402. B.G. Deshmukh, op.cit., p. 310.
403. Janardan Thakur, op.cit., p. 303.
404. Ibid., p. 297.
405. Venkitesh Ramakrishnan, 'A rebel's journey', *Frontline*, 27 July 2007.
406. See two volumes of his editorials, Chandra Shekhar, *The Quest the Hurdles: A Socialist Testament*, New Delhi: Konark Publishers Pvt Ltd., 2004.
407. Ibid., p. xxx.
408. Ibid., p.xxxiv.
409. Ibid., p.xxxv.
410. Attar Chand, *The Long March : Profile of the Prime Minister Chandra Shekhar*, New Delhi: Mittal Publications, 1991, p. 329.
411. Chandra Shekhar, *Selected Speeches*, 1990-91, New Delhi: Ministry of Information and Broadcasting, 1993, p. 14.
412. Ibid., p. 15.
413. Ibid., p. 17.
414. Attar Chand, op.cit., p. 329.
415. Interview by V.C. Shukla, text in *Indian Express*, 9 January 1991.
416. Ibid.
417. Yogendra Bali, *Chandra Shekhar: A Political Biography*, New Delhi: Vikas Publishing House Pvt Ltd, 1991, p. 194.
418. For this debate, see 'Special relations or equidistance concept', *The Telegraph*, 6 March 2002.
419. *Indian Express*, 9 January 1991, op.cit.
420. Chandra Shekhar, *Selected Speeches*, op.cit., p. 56.

421. *Indian Express*, 9 January 1991, op. cit.
422. Ibid.
423. Nihal Singh, 'Foreign Policy :Need for another look', *The Hindustan Times*, 1 June 1991.
424. Arun Shourie, *The State As Charade : V.P.Singh, Chandra Shekhar and the Rest*, New Delhi: Roli Books, 1991, p. 260.
425. Personal notes.
426. Dilip Rath & Amerendra Sahoo, 'India's exports of capital goods', *Economic and Political Weekly*, 25 August 1994.
427. Group Captain Ranjit Singh, *P.V. Narasimha Rao: The Man, The Politician: Some Problems and Issues*, New Delhi: Patriot Publishers, 1992, pp. 21-22.
428. Amit Bahaduri and Deepak Nayyar, *The Intelligent Person's guide to Liberalisation*, New Delhi: Penguin Books, 1996, p. 30.
429. *Times of India*, 8 May 1994.
430. *Indian Express*, 21 May 1994.
431. Personal notes.
432. See the text of Rao's speech in the Parliament; full text in *National Herald* 21 December 1991.
433. Ibid.
434. Prime Minister Narasimha Rao at Beijing University, 9 September 1993, full text in http://ignca.nic.in/ks_41006.htm, 21 August 2007.
435. The author was carried with this impression in the long off-the-record meeting he had with Rao.
436. *Times of India*, 18 November 1993.
437. Text in *Official Journal of the Commission*, No 1 223/225, 27 August 1994.
438. Kamal Ghose, 'India and Europe, 1992: Possible effects on imports.' *Fortune India*, 16 December 1990.
439. *The Hindustan Times*, 15 August 1990.
440. Ibid.
441. Ibid.
442. I. Gopalkrishnan, 'Easing Indian ventures abroad', *India Today*, 29 May 1992.
443. See *EU-India Partnerariat 1999*, Brussels: 1999.
444. Statement by Prime Minister on 13 September 1991. Parliament of India.*nicin/is/Isdeb/Is10/ses1/04130991.htm* 28.08.2007.
445. Tony Allison, 'Myanmar shows India the road to Southeast Asia', *Asia Times*, 21 February 2001.
446. A.N.Ram, 'Historical Perspectives', in *http://www.india-seminar-com/2000/487/487%/20ram.htm*, 4 September 2007.
447. *International Herald Tribune*, 29 January 1994.
448. *Daily Times*, 1 September 2007.
449. Ibid.
450. 'Indo-Israel : A Strategic Relationship', *http://www.indian cricket fans.com/showthread.php?t=24884*, 9 September 2007.
451. *Times of India*, 14 November 1991.
452. Ibid., 12 November 1991.

453. Ibid.
454. Bansidhar Pradhan, 'Indo-UAE Ties: an epitome of good neighbourliness,' *Link*, 17 May 1992.
455. http://www.hinduonet. Com/fline/fline/fl1907/19070560.htm. 13 September 2007.
456. Harsh V. Pant, 'India and Iran: An axis in the making?' *Asian Survey*, May/June 2004.
457. P.V. Narasimha Rao, *Selected Speeches*, July 11 1992-June 1993, Volume 11, New Delhi: Publications Division, Ministry of Information and Broadcasting, 1994, p. 460.
458. Ibid.
459. Sunanda K. Datta Ray, 'Love of Obscurity—The Prime Minister of Consensus', *The Telegraph*, 25 December 2004.
460. Personal notes.
461. Janardan Thakur, op. cit., p. 341.
462. Ibid., p. 344.
463. *Prime Minister H.D. Deve Gowda: The Gain and the Pain. A Biographical Sketch*, New Delhi: Gyan Publishing House, 1997, p. 251.
464. Attar Chand, op.cit., p. 252.
465. Ibid., p. 284.
466. Personal notes.
467. Attar Chand, op.cit, p. 224.
468. 'The Historic Treaty' in http://www.rediff.com/news/1996/301chin.ht, 20 February 2008.
469. Personal notes.
470. Ibid.
471. Attar Chand, op. cit., p. 280.
472. Ibid.
473. Ibid.
474. Ibid., p. 257.
475. Personal notes.
476. Ibid.
477. Ibid.
478. Ibid.
479. I.K.Gujral, *A Foreign Policy of India*, New Delhi: Ministry of External Affairs, 1998, p. 139.
480. Ibid.
481. Ibid.
482. I.K.Gujral, *Continuity and Change : India's Foreign Policy*, New Delhi: Macmillan, 2003, p. xviii.
483. U.S.Congress, *congress.org*.
484. Gujral's speech to the Council on Foreign Relations in New York, for full text see http://www.indianembassy.org/policyl Foreign Policy global (Gujral) htm.
485. I.K.Gujral, *Foreign Policy of India*, op.cit., p. 195.
486. Ibid.
487. Ibid., p. 201.

488. Janardan Thakur, op.cit., p. 387.
489. Ibid.
490. Girilal Jain, *The Hindu Phenomenon*, UBS Publishers' Distributors Ltd, New Delhi: 1994, p. V.
491. Cited by Harish Kapur, 'From Marginality to Centrality: Vajpayee's Political Journey', *World Affairs*, No 4, Vol 1, January-March 2000, p. 99.
492. Arun Shourie, *Eminent Historians, Their Technology, their Line, Their Fraud*, New Delhi: Harper Collins Publishers India, 1998, p. xii.
493. Janadan Thakur, op.cit, p. 420.
494. Strobe Talbot, *Engaging India: Diplomacy, Democracy and the Bomb*, New Delhi: Viking 2004, p.52.
495. Ibid., p. 54.
496. Ibid. p. 171.
497. Ibid. p. 149.
498. Dr. C.P. Thakur & Devandra P. Sharma, *India Under Atal Behari Vajpayee: The BJP Era*, New Delhi: UBS Publishers' Distributors Ltd: 1999, pp.139-140.
499. Strobe Talbott, op. cit., p. 43.
500. Ibid., p. 203.
501. 'Russian Reaction to the Indian Nuclear Tests', http//cns.miis.edu/research/India/Russia.htm, 4 March 2008.
502. Strobe Talbott, op. cit., pp.67-68.
503. Ibid.
504. 'Russian Indian Relations', *The Embassy of the Russian Federation in the Republic of India*, 4 March 2008.
505. N.M.Gatate (ed.), *Atal Bihari Vajpayee, Four Decades in Parliament*, Delhi: Shipra, 1998, p.134.
506. Ibid.,p.135.
507. For texts, see http://bjp.org/today/July_02, 4 March 2008.
508. M.L.Sondhi & Prakash Nanda, *Vajpayee's Foreign Policy, Daring the Irreversible*, New Delhi: Har-Anand Publications Pvt Ltd, 1999, p.113.
509. 'Putin accords warm welcome to Manmohan Singh', *Express India*, 8.02.2008.
510. Ibid.
511. C. Raja Mohan, 'India, Russia join hands on N-deal, and put down on Iran', *Indian Express*, 26 January 2007.
512. Ibid.
513. *rediff.com*, 20.02.2008.
514. See Bush's interview with Indian journalists of 6th March 2006, text in *Rediff News*, 9 March 2008.
515. See ibid., 27 July 2007.
516. *Frontline*, 18 April 2005.
517. Ibid.
518. Ibid.
519. Chris Devonshire-Ellis, 'India Prime Minister Dr. Manmohan Singh: "Think big",' *rediff news,"* 8 February 2008.

520. South African Government Information, *Ministerial Communiqué 2007 of India- Brazil-South Africa Forum*, 12 March 2008.
521. EU-India Political Dialogue, *http://www.delind.eec.euint/en/political_dialogue/introduction.htm*
522. Ibid.
523. Ibid.
524. *EC Communication Titled, 'An EU-India Strategic Partnership: India's Response*, 27 August 2004.
525. *India-EU Joint Statement*, New Delhi, 30 November 2007.
526. 'Prime Minister Dr. Manmohan Singh's speech at the Haksar memorial conference', on 9th November 2005, *http://www.indian embassy org/press_release/2005/Nov/11 htm*.
527. Ibid.,p. 2.
528. 'SAARC : Optimistic Plans for South Asian Progress', *http://english.ohmynews.com/article view/article_view.asp?menu*, 13 March 2008.
529. *Time*, 20 September 2004.
530. *Financial Express*, 20 February 2008.
531. 'Atlantean Thoughts', *http://atlantean.word press.com/category/manmohan-singh*, 18 March 2008.

SELECT BIBLIOGRAPHY

STUDIES AND PRIMARY SOURCES

Adams, Jad & Phillip Whitehead, *The Dynasty: The Nehru Gandhi Story,* London: Penguin Books/ BBC Books, 1997.

Akhund, Iqbal, *Trial & Error:The Advent and Eclipse of Benazir Bhutto,* Karachi:Oxford University Press, 2000.

Alexander, P.C., *My Years with Indira Gandhi,* New Delhi:Vision Books, 1991.

Ambekar, G.V. & V.D.Divekar, *Documents on China's Relations with South and South-East Asia (1949-1962),* New Delhi: Allied Publishers Private Ltd, 1964.

Andrew, Christopher and Vasili Mitrokhin, *The World was going our Way: The KGB and the Battle for the Third World,* New York: Basic Books, 2005.

Ansari, Yusuf, *Triumph of Will: Sonia Gandhi,* New Delhi: Tara-India Research Press, 2006.

Bakshi, S.R., & Sita Ramvashist, *I.K.Gujral: The Progressive Prime Minister,* New Delhi: Kanishka Publishers, 1997.

Bali, Yogendra, *Chandra Shekhar: A Political Biography,* New Delhi: Vikas Publishing House Pvt Ltd, 1991.

Bhutto, Benazir, *Daughter of the East: An Autobiography,* London: Mandarin, 1988.

Bowles, Chester, *Ambassador's Report: Asia's Problems Seen by a Friend,* London: Collins 1954.

——, *Promises to keep: My Years in Public Life 1941—1969,* New York: Harper & Row, 1971.

Brecher, Michael, *Nehru: A Political Biography,* Boston: Beacon Press, 1962.

———, *India and the World Politics: Krishna Menon's View of the World*, London: Oxford University Press, 1968.

Brown, Judith M., *Nehru: A Political Life*, New Delhi: Oxford University Press, 2003.

Carras, Mary C., *Indira Gandhi in the Crucible of Leadership*, Boston: Beacon Press, 1979.

Chakravarty, Suhash, *Crusader Extraordinary: Krishna Menon and the India League 1932-1936*, New Delhi:Indian Research Press, 2006.

Chand, Attar, *Prime Minister H.D. Deve Gowda*, New Delhi: Gyan Publishing House, 1997.

———, *The Long March: Profile of the Prime Minister Chandra Shekhar*, New Delhi: Mittal Publications, 1991.

Chander, Harish, & Padmini, *Rajiv Gandhi: Many Facets*, Delhi: Noida News Pvt.Ltd, 1992.

Chaudhuri, Nirad C., *Thy Hand Great Anarch: India 1921-1952*, London: Chatto and Windus, 1988.

Clarke, Michael, & Brian White, *Understanding Foreign Policy: The Foreign policy Systems Approach*, Aldershot: Edward Elger, 1989.

Clément, Catherine, *Pour l'amour de l'Inde: Roman*, Paris : Flammarion, 1993.

Das, Durga (edited), *Sardar Patel's Correspondence, 1945-50*, 10 volumes, Ahmedabad : Navjivan Publishing House, 1974.

Deshmukh, B.G., *From Poona to the Prime Minister's Office: A Cabinet Secretary Looks Back*, New Delhi: HarperCollins Publishers India, 2004.

Frank, Katherine, *Indira Gandhi: The Life of Indira Nehru Gandhi*, London: HarperCollins Publishers, 2002.

Frankel, Joseph, *The Making of Foreign Policy: An Analysis of Decision Making*, London: Oxford University Press, 1963.

Gandhi, Arun, *The Morarji Desai Papers: Fall of the Janata Government*, New Delhi: Vision Books, 1984.

Gandhi, Sonia (edited), *Two Alone, Two Together: Letters between Indira Gandhi and Jawaharlal Nehru 1922-1964*, New Delhi: Penguin Books, 2004.

Ghatate, N.M. (edited), *Atal Bihari Vajpayee: Four Decades in Parliament*,

3 volumes, Delhi: Shipra, 1998.

Government of India, *Speeches of Prime Minister Lal Bahadur Shastri, June 1964—May 1965,* New Delhi: Ministry of Information and Broadcasting, 1965.

Gupta, M.G., *Rajiv Gandhi's Foreign Policy: A Study in Continuity and Change,* Agra: M. G. Publishers, 1997.

Gujral, I.K., *Foreign Policy of India,* New Delhi: External Publicity Division, 1998.

——, *Continuity and Change: India's Forein Policy,* New Delhi: Macmillan, 2003.

Gujral, Satish, *A Brush with Life: An Autobiography: Satish Gujral, (edited by Khuswant Singh),* New Delhi:Viking: 1997.

Gujral, Shiela, *My Years in the USSR: Recollections and Revelations,* Delhi: Macmillan India, 2002.

Jayakar, Pupil, *Indira Gandhi,* New Delhi: Viking, 1992.

Jayewardene, J.R., *Men and Memories: Autobiographical Recollections and Reflections,* New Delhi: Vikas Publishing House Private Ltd., 1992.

Kaul, T.N., *A Diplomat's Diary(1947-1999): China, India and USA,* New Delhi: Macmillan, 2000.

Khan, Roedad (Compiled and selected), *The British Papers: Secret and Confidential: India-Pakistan- Bangladesh: Documents 1965—1969,* Karachi: Oxford University Press, 2002.

Kissinger, Henry, *White House Years,* Boston: Little Brown and Company, 1979.

Lala, R.M., *A Touch of Greatness: Encounters with the Eminent,* New Delhi: Penguin, 2003.

Mathai, M.O., *Reminiscences of the Nehru Age,* New Delhi: Vikas Publishing House Pvt Ltd, 1978.

Mende, Tibor, *Conversations avec Nehru,* Paris: Editions du Seuil, 1956.

Mankekar, D. R., *A Political Biography,* Bombay: Popular Prakashan, 1966.

Mullick, B.N., *My Years with Nehru,* Bombay:Allied Publishers, 1971.

Nayyar, Kuldip, *The Judgement: Inside Story of the Emergency in India*, New Delhi: Vikas Publishing House Pvt Ltd, 1977.

—— *Between the Lines*, Allied Publishers, 1969.

—— *Scoop: Inside Stories from the Partition to the Present*, New Delhi: HarperCollins, 2006.

Nehru, Jawaharlal, *Glimpses of World History*, New Delhi: Oxford University Press, 1989.

—— *An Autobiography*, New Delhi: Oxford University Press, 1988.

—— *The Discovery of India*, New Delhi: Oxford University Press, 1988.

—— *A Bunch of Old Letters, Written Mostly to Jawaharlal Nehru and some Written by Him*, Bombay: Asia Publishing House, 1958.

—— *Speeches, 8 volumes*, New Delhi: Publications Division, 1954-1958

Pouchadass, Emmanuel, *Indira Gandhi: My Truth*, New Delhi: Vision Books, 2004.

Raman, B., *The Kaoboys of R&aw: Down Memory Lane*, New Delhi: Lancer Publishers, 2007.

Rao, K.N., *Chandra Shekhar: The Survivor*, Delhi: Manek Publications, 1991.

Rao, Narashima, P.V., *Selected Speeches, July 11 1992—June 1993*, New Delhi: Publication Division 2 volumes, 1994.

—— *The Insider*, New Delhi: Viking 1998.

Rasgotra, MaharajaKrishna (edited and introduced), *Rajiv Gandhi's World View*, New Delhi: Vikas Publishing House Pvt Ltd, 1991.

Sahgal Nayantara (edited and compiled), *Nehru's Letters to his Sister, Before Freedom 1909-1947*, New Delhi: Roli Books, 2000.

Sarvepalli Gopal, *Jawaharlal Nehru: A Biography*, Delhi: Oxford University Press, 1993.

Sen, Mohit, *A Traveller and the Road: The Journey of an Indian Communist*, New Delhi: Rupa.Co, 2003.

Sharma, Shri Ram, *Lal Bahadur Shastri: An Era of Transition in Indian Foreign Policy*, New Delhi: Kanishka Publishers, 2001.

Shastri, Lal Bahadur, *Speeches of Prime Minister, June 1964-May 1965*, New Delhi: Publication Division, 1965.

Shekhar, Chandra, *Selected Speeches 1990-91*, New Delhi:Publications Division, 1993.

———, *The Quest, the Hurdles: A Socialist Testament:* New Delhi: Konark Publishers Pvt Ltd, 2004.

Singh, Davinder, *Deve Gowda The Unfinished Agenda: A Political Retrospective*, Noida: Sahara India Mass Communication, 1998.

Singh, L.P. *India's Foreign Policy: The Shastri Period*, New Delhi: Uppal Publishing House, 1980.

———, *Portrait of Lal Bahadur Shastri: A Quintessential Gandhian*, New Delhi: Ravi Dayal Publisher, 1990.

Singh, V.K., *India's External Intelligence:Secrets of Research and Analysis Wing (RAW)*, New Delhi: Manas Publications, 2007.

Singh, V.P., *Selected Speeches And Writings, 1989-90*, New Delhi: Publications Division, 1993.

Sondhi, M.L. & Prakash Nanda, *Vajpayee's Foreign Policy: Daring the Irreversible*, New Delhi: Har-Anand Publications, 1999.

Srivastava, C.P., *Lal Bahadur Shastri: Prime Minister of India 1964-1966: A Life of Truth in Politics,* Delhi: Oxford University Press, 1995.

Subramanian, T.S.R.,*Journeys through Babudom and Netaland: Governance in India,* Rupa Co, 2004

Talbott, Strobe, *Engaging India: Diplomacy, Democracy and theBomb*, New Delhi: Penguin Books, 2004.

Thakur, C.P., & Devendra P. Sharma, *India Under Vajpayee: The BJP Era*, New Delhi: UBS Publishers, 1999.

Thakur, Janardan, *Prime Ministers Nehru to Vajpayee*, Mumbai:Eeshhwar, 1999.

———, *All the Prime Minister's Men,* New Delhi: Vikas Publishing House Pvt. Ltd, 1977.

Vandana, S., *I.K.Gujral: New Hope of India*, New Delhi: Aph Publication Corporation, 1997.

Venkataraman, R., *My President Years*, New Delhi: Indus Publications.

II ARTICLES AND INTERVIEWS

Bajpai. Girija Shankar, "India and the Balance of Power," *Indian Year Book of International Affairs,* 1952.

Gujral, I.K., "India's Journey: Fifty Years of Independence," *World Affairs,* January 1998.

Hersh, Seymour M., "From the Archive," *New Yorker* 29 March 1993.

Joshi, Manoj, "The Sino-Indian Border Problem, " *Strategic Analysis,* October 1992.

Kalyanaraman, S., "Travails of Intelligence Assessment: From Failed to Fertile Imagination," *Strategic Analysis,* Jan-Mar, 2005.

Kapur, Harish, " From Marginality to Centrality: Vajpayee's Political Journey," *World Affairs,* January-March 2OOO.

Mishra, Rajesh Kumar, " India-Pakistan Nuclear Stability and Diplomacy," *Strategic Analysis,* Jan-Mar 2005.

Perkovich, George, "Bhabha's quest for a Bomb," *Bulletin for Atomic Scientists,* May-June 2000.

Pant, Harsh V., "India and Iran: An axis in the making,"*Asian Survey,* May-June 2004.

Rose, Charlie, "Charlie Rose Interviews Indian PM Manmohan Singh," on 27 February 2006, Council on Foreign Relations, *http://www.cfr. org/publications/9986/*

Singh, ManMohan, "Where is India Heading," (interview)" *World Affairs* January-March 1997.

Thakur. Ramesh, " India After Non-alignment," *Foreign Affairs,* Spring 1992.

Index

A

Afghanistan, 90, 94, 167, 178, 179, 191, 195, 196, 201, 202, 204, 208, 210, 221, 340, 367, 411, 412
Africa, 40, 41, 230
Algeria, 102, 103
Allahabad, 121, 129
Amritsar, 107, 208
APEC, 357
A. P. J. Abdul Kalam, 219
ASEAN, 265, 309, 311, 336, 337, 343, 357, 391, 397, 403, 411
ASEM, 357
Asia, 41, 62, 195
Assam, 189, 236, 248
Atal Behari Vajpayee, 153, 154, 156, 158, 159, 165, 313, 322, 327-328, 331, 365-381, 406
   decision maiking, 377-379
   evaluation, 379-381
   foreign policy, 369-375
   relations with China, 373-375
   relations with Russia, 372-373
   relations with US, 370-372
   formative years, 365-368
   perceptions, 368-369
   South Asia, 375-377
Atomic Energy Commission (AEC), 71, 72
Australia, 40, 56
Ayub Khan, 90, 107, 108, 110, 111, 112, 113, 114

B

Bangladesh (East Pakistan), 135, 136, 138, 139, 141, 143, 144, 166, 167, 195, 204, 205-206, 208, 236-237, 238, 249, 258, 259-261, 280, 281, 285, 318, 339, 341, 343, 353, 354, 355, 356, 375, 410
Beijing, 34, 53, 59, 91, 92, 94, 103, 137, 140, 142, 143, 154, 156, 157, 196, 197, 198, 208, 210, 226, 241, 262, 266, 267, 302, 304, 333, 373, 374, 375, 391
Benazir Bhutto, 220, 221, 233, 234, 255, 339, 354
Bengal, 185
Bhutan, 138, 166, 206-207, 233, 237-238, 261-263, 285, 339, 355, 356, 375
Bill Clinton, 301, 313, 337, 351, 370 373, 380
BJP, 270, 277, 327, 365, 367, 368, 376, 378, 379, 388, 400
Boris Yeltsin, 297, 298, 300, 332, 372, 373
B. K. Nehru, 58, 129, 189, 190
B. Raman, 171, 172
Britain, 27, 63, 87, 96, 229, 230

C

Canada, 56, 115
Ceylon, 94
Chandra Shekhar, 247, 277-292, 295, 405, 406, 412
   decision making, 288-290
   evaluation, 290-292
   foreign affairs, 279-282
   gulf war, 287288
   neighbours, 282-285
   World beyond, 285-287
Charan Singh, 166, 171, 173, 177-181, 278, 289, 406
   evaluation, 181
Chester Bowles, 88, 100, 133, 141
China, 27, 32, 33, 34, 35, 38, 39, 40, 41, 44, 45, 49, 50, 51, 53, 54, 55, 56, 59, 60, 61, 62, 63, 66, 68, 69, 70, 71, 74, 87, 89, 90, 91, 92, 93, 94, 95, 96, 100, 101, 102, 103, 104, 105, 107, 108, 111, 112, 115, 117, 135, 136, 138, 139, 141, 142, 145, 152, 154, 155, 156, 157, 158, 159, 163, 169, 172, 192, 193, 196, 197, 198, 199, 204, 206, 222, 223, 224-228, 235, 236, 237, 238, 240, 241, 256, 257, 258, 259, 261,

262, 264, 266, 283, 298, 301, 302, 303, 304, 308, 310, 311, 312, 313, 323, 334, 336, 337, 349, 351, 352, 357, 360, 368, 370, 371, 373, 374, 375, 380, 387, 388, 389, 390, 391, 392, 393, 395, 402, 409, 412
CIA, 59, 70, 72, 108, 141, 159, 220
CTBT, 249, 312, 332, 334, 337-338, 341, 343, 352, 358, 371, 372, 373
Czechoslovakia, 26, 27, 145, 412

D

Dalai Lama, 61, 67, 69, 72
Deng Xiaoping, 157, 158, 196, 197, 224, 227, 266, 389
Devi Lal, 250
DRDO, 170
Dutch, 40

E

Egypt, 41, 65, 115
England, 24, 25, 121, 122, 321
Europe, 25, 26, 121, 122, 123, 254, 297, 304-308, 337, 369, 392-396, 402, 403, 409

F

Farooq Abdullah, 189
Fascism, 26, 121
Feroze Gandhi, 122, 125
France, 27, 71, 122

G

General Aslam Beg, 255
George Bush, 222
George. W. Bush, 388, 389
George Fernandes, 166, 374, 375
George F. Kennan, 178
Germany, 136
Girija Shankar Bajpai, 32, 57
Goa, 67
Golden Temple, 208
G. Parthsarathy, 136, 144, 198, 199, 209

H

Harayana, 178, 271
H. D. Deva Gowda, 331-344, 347, 349, 350, 352, 353, 359, 360, 405, 406, 412
    decision making, 340-342
    evaluation, 342-344
    post-cold war configurations, 332-338
    attempts at reaching out to US, 333-334
    CTBT, 337-338

increasing involvement in South-East Asia, 336-337
Sino-Indian relations, 334-336
SAARC, 340
South Asia, 338-339
Henery Kissinger, 139, 140, 141
Hillary Clinton, 334
Hindus, 48, 49, 78, 79, 186, 189, 205, 236, 254, 260, 366, 367
Hiroshima, 72
Homi Bhabha, 71, 72, 73, 87, 92, 97, 98, 99, 170, 219
Hong Kong, 38
Hungary, 46, 63-65

I

IAEA, 98, 389
I. K. Gujral, 154, 162, 163, 164, 165, 250, 252, 255, 259, 263, 265, 267, 268, 269, 271, 272, 274, 285, 322, 332, 336, 339, 340, 341, 343, 347-361, 376, 405, 406, 412
    construction of foreign policy, 350-353
    configuration of international forces, 350-352
    nuclearisation of India, 352-353
    decision making, 358-359
    evaluation, 359-361
    formative years, 348-349
    perceptions, 349-350
    South Asia, 353-358
    bilateral economic cooperation, 356-357
    bilateral relations, 353-355
    Gujral doctrine, 355-356
    relations with other Asian countries, 357-358
India, 24, 25, 26, 27, 28, 29, 30, 31, 32, 33, 36, 37, 39, 40, 41, 43, 44, 45, 46, 47, 48, 49, 50, 51, 52, 53, 55, 56, 57, 58, 59, 60, 61, 62, 63, 64, 67, 68, 71, 72, 73, 74, 77, 82, 86, 87, 89, 90, 91, 92, 93, 95, 96, 98, 99, 100, 101, 102, 103, 104, 105, 106, 107, 109, 110, 111, 112, 113, 114, 115, 116, 117, 118, 122, 124, 131, 132, 133, 135, 136, 137, 138, 139, 140 141, 142, 150, 152, 154, 155, 156, 157, 158, 159, 160, 161, 166, 167, 168, 169, 173, 180, 185, 186, 188, 189, 190, 191, 192, 197, 200, 201, 202, 204, 205, 211, 216, 217, 218, 222, 223, 224, 227, 230, 232, 233, 235, 236, 238, 241, 242, 248, 249, 250, 251, 253, 255, 256, 257, 258, 260, 263, 266, 270, 271, 272, 278, 279, 283, 286, 288, 291, 297, 298, 299, 300, 301, 303, 304,

308, 310, 311, 312, 313, 315, 323, 332,
333, 334, 335, 337, 338, 339, 340, 342,
348, 349, 350, 351, 352, 353, 354, 355,
356, 358, 359, 360, 366, 368, 369, 370,
371, 375, 379, 380, 381, 386, 387, 388,
389, 390, 391, 392, 393, 394, 395, 400,
402, 403, 405, 407, 408, 412, 413, 414
(*passim* throughout text)
Indian National Congress, 410, 412
Indira Gandhi, 34, 37, 38, 73, 83, 121-146,
149, 150, 151, 152, 153, 154, 155, 156,
159, 170, 171, 172, 178, 180, 185-211,
215, 222, 223, 234, 238, 240, 241, 253,
270, 271, 273, 285, 295, 296, 321, 348,
349, 369, 374, 380, 406, 410
activation of channels of foreign policy,
207-209
changing international environment, 191-
192
character and personality, 124-127
configuration of great powers, 131-144
Chinese dimension, 141-143
Indira Gandhi style of diplomacy, 143-144
intervention in Bangladesh, 135-136
ramifications of Bangladesh, 136-138
Soviet dimension, 138-141
US dimension, 131-135
decision making, 127-130
dense record of diplomatic activity, 192-
193
diplomacy towards superpowers, 194-199
evaluation, 145-146, 210-211
foreign policy, 130-131
formation, 121-123
growing national disenchantment, 189-
190
new strategy of power, 188-189
participation in multilateral conferences,
193-194
perception, 123-124
public relations diplomacy, 199-200
South Asia Neighbours, 200-207
Indonesia, 38, 40, 93, 101
IPLF, 252
Iraq, 171, 267, 287
Italy, 27
Jagat. S. Mehta, 153, 154, 165
Jagjivan Ram, 70, 278
Jana Sangh Party, 92
Japan, 89, 101, 209
Jawaharlal Nehru, 23-74, 77, 80, 81, 82, 83,
85, 88, 89, 91, 93, 95, 96, 98, 100, 101,
106, 115, 117, 121, 122, 123, 124, 125,
134, 135, 145, 146, 150, 151, 155, 156,

159, 162, 163, 172, 178, 189, 199, 200,
203, 216, 217, 296, 322, 348, 349, 355,
356, 366, 379, 386, 387, 391, 406, 407,
408, 41, 412
decision making process, 31-39
evaluation, 73-74
foreign policy nehruvian model, 39-55
emulative role, 42-43
global component, 39-40
hostile global environment, 55
mediatory role, 43-45
Myanmar (Burma), 51-53
Nepal, 49-51
normative role, 45-46
Pakistan, 48-49
regional component, 46-48
rhetorical diplomacy, 40-42
Sri Lanka, 53-55
formation, 23-25
Nehru and nucleaurisation, 71-73
Nehru turns to west, 55-63
coincidental mutation in international
system, 62-63
US changes attitude under Eisenhower, 60-
62
perceptions, 25-29
public opinion and foreign policy, 63-71
Hungary, 63-65
Sino-Indian war, 69-71
Tibet, 66-69
what is role playing?, 29-30

J

Jayaprakash Narayan, 149, 185, 278
Jimmy Carter, 159, 160, 161, 168, 202, 209
John Kennedy, 73, 88, 107, 132

K

Kabul, 179
Karachi, 90, 135
Kashmir, 32, 33, 48, 49, 58, 67, 74, 82, 90,
105, 106, 107, 108, 110, 113, 114, 136,
167, 189, 191, 201, 203, 233, 248, 254,
255, 256, 257, 271, 282, 292, 297, 339,
343, 351, 354, 355, 373, 377, 395, 396,
411
Kathmandu, 51, 81, 91
K.M. Panikkar, 34, 35, 66, 69
Korea, 43, 44, 64
K. R. Narayanan, 142, 143, 154, 158, 217,
375
K. Subrahmanyam, 219

L

Ladakh, 71, 91
Lal Bahadur Shastri, 51, 77-118, 121, 128, 131, 132, 145, 151, 170, 200, 203, 219, 241, 255, 400, 406
   configuration of international forces, 86-89
   decision making, 82-86
   evaluation, 115-118
   focus on neighbours, 89-115
   adverse perception of China, 91-94
   diplomatic initiatives, 94-97
   growing alienation with Pakistan, 104-106
   Indo-Pakistan conflict, 109-111
   multilateral initiative against Chinese, 100-104
   Pakistan acts, 106-109
   road to Tashkent, 111-115
   what could Shastri do?, 97-100
   foreign affairs, 81-82
   formation, 77-79
   perception, 79-81
L.K.Advani, 322, 369
L. K. Jha, 80, 83, 84, 85, 116, 128, 129, 133
London, 24, 37, 38, 61, 65, 103, 111, 123, 229
LTTE, 234
Lyndon Johnson, 88, 97, 100, 107, 112, 131, 132, 133, 139, 145

M

Mahabharata, 151
Maharashtra, 33
Mahatma Gandhi, 27, 28, 31, 32, 78, 79, 81, 117, 150, 178, 216, 365, 391
Maldives, 237, 238, 250, 259, 263-264, 280, 285, 290, 291, 355, 356
Mandal Commission, 248
Maneka Gandhi, 188
Manmohan Singh, 298, 321, 385-403, 405, 406, 411, 412
   decision making, 398-402
   European Union, 392-396
   differences, 395-396
   joint action plan, 394-395
   political, 393-394
   strategic partnership, 394
   evaluation, 402-403
   foreign policy, 386-391
   Chinese dimension, 389-391
   relations with Russia, 387-388
   relations with US, 388-389
   formation and perception, 386
   proliferation on diplomacy, 391-392
   SAARC, 397-398
   South Asia, 397
Mao Zedong, 35, 57, 143, 378
Marxism, 26, 80
McMahon Line, 68, 266
Mikhail Gorbachev, 221, 222, 227, 241, 256, 264, 265, 297, 298
M. O. Mathai, 26, 64, 150,126, 150, 287
Moscow, 36, 37, 63, 94, 102, 111, 112, 134, 135, 138, 141, 145, 154, 158, 161, 162, 163, 164, 165, 166, 178, 179, 180, 181, 191, 193, 195, 196, 197, 198, 201, 210, 219, 221, 222, 250, 265, 268, 271, 286, 287, 297, 300, 311, 333, 348, 349, 350, 372, 387
Morarji Desai, 70, 89, 149-173, 177, 181, 189, 196, 200, 201, 203, 219, 222, 241, 248, 270, 278, 286, 352, 374, 406
   decision making, 151-154
   evaluation, 172-173
   foreign policy, 154-172
   attitude towards nuclear developments, 168-171
   intelligence service, 171-172
   problems with Soviet Union, 161-166
   reaching out to Washington, 159-161
   signals to China, 156-159
   South Asia, 166-168
   formation and perception, 150-151
Motilal Nehru, 23, 24
Mujibur Rehman, 135, 236, 261
Muslims, 48, 49, 78, 79, 186, 189, 254, 292, 367, 368
Myanmar (Burma), 51-53, 55, 56, 90, 91, 94, 95, 115, 124, 192, 303, 340

N

Nagasaki, 72
Nambia, 229, 232, 233
Nani Ardeshir Palikhavala, 154, 159
Nazism, 26, 121
Nelson Mandela, 41, 230
Nepal, 32, 49-51, 55, 81, 82, 90, 91, 94, 95, 96, 115, 124, 137, 138, 143, 166, 206, 233, 235-236, 238, 249, 257-259, 260, 262, 274, 282-283, 290, 291, 339, 354, 355, 356, 411
Nawaz Sharif, 280, 282, 292, 317, 339, 354, 355, 376
New Delhi, 36, 57, 61, 107, 133, 138, 167, 181, 192, 194, 204, 259, 264, 267, 284, 333, 339, 393

New York, 58, 180, 349, 361

P

Pakistan, 41, 48-49, 55, 60, 68, 74, 82, 87, 90, 93, 94, 101, 104, 105, 106, 107, 108, 109, 110, 111, 112, 113, 114, 115, 124, 136, 138, 139, 140, 143, 144, 145, 166, 167, 168, 170, 172, 191, 195, 197, 201-203, 204, 210, 220, 221, 223, 227, 233-234, 236, 237, 238, 249, 252, 254-257, 266, 274, 280, 282, 292, 301, 302, 304, 311, 312, 317, 323, 334, 335, 339, 341, 351, 355, 367, 368, 370, 371, 373, 374, 374, 375, 376, 380, 381, 392, 410, 411
Panachtantra, 151
P. N. Haskar, 122, 128, 129, 136, 144, 207, 225, 240, 144, 207, 225, 240
Prevez Musharraf, 377, 381
Punjab, 178, 189, 201, 202, 203, 233, 248, 271
P. V. Narasimha Rao, 226, 285, 295-324, 327, 336, 339, 386, 391, 412
   decision making, 319-322
   evaluation, 322-324
   foreign policy innovations, 298-304
   economic sector, 298-300
   extrication from great power configurations, 300-304
   new directions, 304-316
   Europe, 304-308
   Gulf and Middle East, 315-316
   Israel, 313-315
   nuclearisation, 311-313
   South-East Asia, 308-311
   South Asia, 317-419
   uneasy environment, 297-298

R

Rabindranath Tagore, 391
Raja Ramanna, 219
Rajasthan, 178
Rajiv Gandhi, 125, 129, 137, 189, 215-242, 247, 252, 253, 257, 264, 265, 266, 270, 271, 273, 277, 286, 287, 289, 290, 291, 295, 296, 302, 317, 321, 322, 323, 339, 354, 385, 405, 406, 410
   decision making process, 238-240
   engagement in Southern Africa, 229-233
   independence of Namibia, 232-233
   South Africa, 229-231
   Southern Africa, 231-232
   evaluation, 240-242
   foreign policy framework, 217-228

   great powers: balanced approach, 221
   projection of India, 218-221
   China, 224-228
   USA, 222-224
   USSR, 221-222
   formation and perception, 216-217
   South Asia, 233-238
   Bangladesh, 236-237
   Bhutan, 237-238
   Maldives, 237
   Nepal, 235-236
   Pakistan, 233-234
   Sri Lanka, 234-235
Ramayana, 151
Rangoon, 52, 53
Rann of Kutch, 109
RAW, 130, 135, 153, 155, 171, 172, 198, 208, 226, 237, 400
R. Chidambaram, 219, 369
Richard Nixon, 139, 140, 141, 143, 144, 145, 155, 159, 169, 202, 210
R. N. Kao, 171, 198, 205, 208, 226
Ronald Reagan, 191, 193, 195, 202, 220, 221, 223, 227, 237, 241

S

SAARC, 233, 236, 255, 280, 281, 285, 290, 291, 292, 319, 340, 343, 353, 356, 357, 397, 398, 403, 411
Saddam Hussein, 171, 268, 287, 315
San Francisco, 37
Sanjay Gandhi, 125, 130, 135, 149, 171, 186, 187, 188, 189, 216, 240, 273
Sardar Vallabhbai Patel, 31, 32, 33, 34, 50, 52, 58, 66, 67, 74, 95, 150
Sikkim, 137, 143
Sino-India War, 27, 53, 69-71, 72
Sonia Gandhi, 236, 295, 385, 398, 399, 401, 402
South Africa, 40, 41, 229-231, 232, 233, 251
South Asia, 39, 47, 49, 74, 112, 137, 143, 145, 146, 157, 159, 166, 193, 196, 211, 218, 233-238, 242, 251-264, 285, 301, 302, 312, 338-339, 353, 375-377, 406, 410
Soviet Union (USSR), 36, 45, 49, 55, 57, 63, 64, 65, 70, 86, 87, 92, 93, 98, 102, 104, 111, 112, 115, 123, 132, 133, 135, 138, 139, 145, 146, 151, 154, 155, 157, 161, 162, 163, 164, 173, 177, 178, 180, 181, 191, 194, 197, 201, 216, 218, 219, 221, 241, 251, 264, 265, 269, 286, 287, 297, 298, 300, 310, 349, 360, 387 388, 409
Sri Lanka, 53-55, 90, 95, 124, 137, 138, 143,

166, 203-205, 230, 233, 234-235, 238, 249, 250, 251-253, 274, 280, 281, 283-284, 317, 339, 354, 355, 356, 375, 410, 412

T

Taliban, 202, 341
Tamil Nadu, 185, 204, 234, 250, 387
Tashkent, 88, 113
Tibet, 32, 33, 34, 55, 61, 63, 66-69, 70, 89, 96, 137, 228, 303, 373

U

United Kingdom (UK), 24, 55, 56, 58, 65, 87, 96, 111, 115, 163, 199, 204, 321, 392
United Nations (UN), 32, 33, 35, 37, 40, 41, 43, 45, 53, 64, 65, 66, 67, 98, 104, 111, 113, 139, 168, 180, 192, 218, 229, 232, 241, 262, 268, 269, 272, 291, 300, 311, 361, 380, 409
United States (US) (USA), 33, 37, 38, 43, 44, 45, 49, 53, 55, 56, 57, 58, 59, 60, 61, 62, 63, 65, 67, 72, 73, 87, 88, 89, 92, 93, 96, 97, 98, 99, 100, 103, 107, 108, 111, 112, 116, 131, 132, 133, 134, 135, 136, 139, 141, 145, 152, 154, 155, 159, 160, 161, 163, 164, 165, 168, 169, 172, 178, 191, 193, 195, 201, 202, 204, 208, 218, 221, 222, 223, 224, 237, 241, 252, 254, 255, 256, 257, 259, 264, 265, 268, 269, 271, 280, 286, 287, 288, 291, 292, 297, 298, 300, 301, 303, 310, 311, 312, 313, 327, 332, 333, 334, 337, 341, 349, 351, 352, 353, 357, 360, 369, 370, 371, 372, 373, 376, 379, 380, 387, 388, 389, 395, 396, 400, 401, 402 405, 410(*passim* throughout text)
Uttar Pradesh, 178, 248, 271

V

V.K. Krishna Menon, 34, 35, 36, 37, 44, 45, 52, 64, 69, 70, 71, 402

Vietnam, 44, 103, 112, 116, 132, 133, 134, 195, 252
Vijaya Lakshmi Pandit, 24, 34, 37, 60, 91, 124
Vishwanath Pratap Singh, 247-274, 277, 285, 289, 295, 331, 342, 348, 349, 352, 359, 360, 405, 406, 412
  decision making, 269-272
  evaluation, 272-274
  foreign affairs, 249-251
  South Asia, 251-264
  World beyond, 264-269
  configuration of international forces, 264-267
  Gulf crisis, 267-269

W

Washington, 32, 33, 37, 57, 58, 59, 60, 61, 62, 87, 97, 100, 107, 111, 112, 131, 132, 133, 138 139, 140, 154, 156, 159, 160, 161, 163, 178, 191, 195, 197, 202, 219, 220, 222, 223, 237, 241, 249, 256, 264, 267, 268, 271, 286, 287, 291, 298, 301, 337, 351, 371, 387, 388, 389, 402
World War I, 136, 232
World War II, 27, 67, 72, 146, 200

Y

Yaqub Khan, 255
Y.B. Chavan, 87, 89
Yugoslavia, 115, 199, 232

Z

Zhou Enlai, 39, 44, 45, 51, 64, 101, 108, 142, 143, 158, 196, 199, 224, 266
Zia ul-haq, 167, 168, 172, 172, 201, 202, 203, 233, 234
Zulfikar Ali Bhutto, 101, 105, 106, 107, 108, 136, 143, 201